DECISION SUPPORT SYSTEMS

Edited by **Chiang Jao**

Decision Support Systems

http://dx.doi.org/10.5772/3371
Edited by Chiang Jao

Contributors

Thomas M Hemmerling, Kaya Kuru, Yusuf Tunca, Ramdane Hedjar, Victor E Cabrera, Po-Hsun Cheng, Heng-Shuen Chen, Hsin-Ciang Chang, Wen-Chen Chiang, Gabriela Prelipcean, Mircea Boscoianu, María Teresa Lamelas, Oswald Marinoni, Juan de la Riva, Andreas Hoppe, Edward Lusk, Monica Adya, Luciene Delazari, Leo Van Raamsdonk, Christine Chan

Published by InTech

Janeza Trdine 9, 51000 Rijeka, Croatia

Copyright © 2012 InTech

Notice

Publishing Process Manager Sandra Bakic
Typesetting InTech DTP Team
Cover InTech Design Team

Additional hard copies can be obtained from orders@intechopen.com

Decision Support Systems, Edited by Chiang Jao
p. cm.
ISBN 978-953-51-0799-6

For EU product safety concerns:
IN TECH d.o.o., Prolaz Marije Krucifikse Kozulić 3, 51000 Rijeka, Croatia,
info@intechopen.com or visit our website at intechopen.com.

Meet the editor

Chiang S. Jao, Ph.D., is a chief biomedical informaticist at Tranformation Inc., based in Maryland. He has been involved in medical informatics since he joined the University of Illinois at Chicago in 1992 to work on clinical decision support systems. His research was awarded with a grant from National Patient Safety Foundation in investigating the matching of prescribing medications and clinical problems in electronic heath records. He acted as the visiting scholar in the Lister Hill National Center for Biomedical Communications, National Library of Medicine and built a standard drug-problem database based on authoritative information from approved drug package sources. He has extensive experience as a software consultant for healthcare institutions. He has edited two series of books in decision support systems. He is a senior member of the Institute of Electrical and Electronic Engineers (IEEE) and the American Medical Informatics Association (AMIA).

Contents

Preface

Pacing through second decade of the 21th century, more computer users are widely adopting technology-based tools and information-enriched databases to focus on supporting managerial decision making, reducing preventable faults and improving outcome forecasting. The goal of decision support systems (DSS) is to develop and deploy information technology-based systems in supporting efficient practice in multidiscipline domains. This book aims to portray a pragmatic perspective of applying DSS in the 21th century. It covers diverse applications of DSS, primarily focusing on the resource management and outcome forecast. Our goal was to provide the broad understanding of DSS and illustrate their practical applications in a variety of fields related to real life.

Chiang Jao
Chief Biomedical Informaticist,
Tranformation Inc, USA

Section 1

Biomedical Applications

Chapter 1

Whether Moving Suicide Prevention Toward Social Networking: A Decision Support Process with XREAP Tool

Po-Hsun Cheng, Heng-Shuen Chen,
Wen-Chen Chiang and Hsin-Ciang Chang

Additional information is available at the end of the chapter

http://dx.doi.org/10. 5772/51985

1. Introduction

Although social workers provide diverse assistance, the incidence of suicide is still high in Taiwan [20]. However, due to cultural characteristics, people who own suicidal ideation often reluctant to seek help as well as passively wait for help. The social networking (SN) becomes one of the social tools. Some users utilize it to interact with their friends and express their mood or feelings in the SN.

Several real suicide cases are rescued by notifying from the messages of the SN [1] [2] , however, the evidence is not enough for endorsing amount of the budgets to emerge the suicide prevention (SP) process to the SN. Therefore, it is a problem for decision-makers to decide which user groups are the targets for the SP in the SN, what kind of the messages are keys for the SP and have to be extracted from the SN [10] , when is the best time to emerge the SP process to the SN, which region is the best place for trial, and which SN is the best adopting platform? The decision-making is not only medical-oriented, but also technology-oriented.

This chapter illustrates an explicit decision support process for management of software requirements elicitation and analysis. As Shi, *et al.* [15] illustrates their research outcomes by utilizing the Unified Modeling Language (UML) as the basis of their decision support system to help decision-makers to distinguish regional environmental risk zones. Similarly, Sutcliffe, *et al.* [19] tries to visualize the requirements by user-centred design (UCD) methods in their visual decision support tools to support public health professionals in their analysis activities. Our proposed process, Extensible Requirements Elicitation and Analysis Process

(XREAP) [5] , is revised from part of the use case driven approach [7] [9]. Therefore, it is necessary for an analyst to understand the UML [8] visualization knowledge.

On the other hand, Perini and Susi extend their decision support system research to the environmental modelling and software field [11]. Their research approach is to hold interviews of producers, technicians anddomain experts as well as acquisition of domain documentation. Meanwhile, they also try to analyse actor roles and strategic dependencies among actors, goal-analysis and plan-analysis. Furthermore, Schlobinski, *et al.* [13] illustrates the user requirements that are derived from a UCD process to engage diverse user representatives for four cities in Europe.

Based on the knowledge sharing concept, Shafiei [14] and his team members develop a multi-enterprise collaborative decision support system for supply-chain management and show their idea is feasible. This evidence shows that the collaborative knowledge sharing is a possible route to promote the quality of the decision-making. Further, Cercone and his partners predict that their e-Health decision support system can find and verify evidence from multiple sources, lead to cost-effective use of drugs, improve patients' quality of life, and optimize drug-related health outcomes [3]. That is, a series of the knowledge and evidence can be collected, shared and reused further for related fields as well as promote our health life to next higher e-Health generation.

Our proposed process includes functions to elicit the diverse requirements from users by utilizing the XREAP tool, analyses all requirements on-line, transforms the final requirements into use case diagram, and provides on-demand complexity metric. Essentially, the process can elicit sufficient sources for user requirements and provide enough complexity information for decision makers. In conclusion, we can straightforwardly understand the complexity between the diverse user requirements and even make an appropriate decision, whether it is the right time to move one of the specific SP activities toward one of the SN's with our proposed process.

2. Background

A definition of suicide from [12] is death from injury, poisoning, or suffocation in which there is evidence that the injury was self-inflicted and that the deceased intended to kill him/her-self. The generation of suicidal behaviour is from suicidal ideation, which means any self-reported thoughts of engaging in suicide-related behaviour. Therefore, everyone who commits suicide will have suicidal ideation before s/he commits suicide;so suicidal ideation can be regarded as the motivation for suicide.

As the official report from the World Health Organization (WHO) [18] said that the world almost one million people die from suicide every year. That is, one death every 40 seconds in 2011. Surprisingly, a global map of suicide rates is drawn by the most recent year available as of 2011, which is also provided by the WHO, discloses that the suicide rate is beyond 16 per 100, 000 people in some countries. That is, one suicides oneself every 40 seconds.

These countries, for example, at least include Lithuania (31. 5), South Korea (31. 0), Japan (24. 4), Russia (23. 5), Finland (18. 3), Belgium (17. 6), France (17. 0), Sweden (15. 8), South Africa (15. 4), and Hong Kong (15. 2) [20]. Therefore, the suicide behaviour is one of the implicit social problems for many countries.

Based on the above, it is necessary to reduce the suicidal ideation in order to decrease the occurrence of suicide. Shneidman, *et al.* [16] proposed a three-level prevention model to do exactly that. The model is divided into three program response categories: prevention, intervention and postvention. Within this three-level prevention model, prevention is to increase the protection factor and decrease the risk factor. The research team tries to focus on the second level of the three-level prevention model and analyses, whether moving SP to SN can elicit the high-risk group so that early detection can lead to early treatment.

3. Decision support process

The mission of the Taiwan Suicide Prevention Centre (TSPC) is tried to decrease the suicide rate. However, it was found that adolescents and young adults, for example, aged 15 to 24, are difficult for the TSPC to intervene to help them from the viewpoint of the TSPC managers. Therefore, the TSPC's chairman called for a brainstorm meeting to invite a group of enthusiastic scholars and participants to find some feasible solutions to reduce the suicide rate of Taiwanese adolescents and young adults in 2010 [6]. Although there are several alternative solutions for the TSPC to promote the suicide prevention capacity, it is hard for the TSPC to decide which solution is the best one and worthwhile to invest substantial resources. Note that these alternatives are belonging to the preliminary decision, not final decision, in the TSPC meeting.

It is worth mentioning that the social networking, such as the Facebook, is one of the alternatives in the TSPC meeting. Anyhow, the social-networking service includes diverse online social platforms such as the Facebook, the Twitter, and the Google+. Hence it is necessary for us to be carefully considerate whether moving suicide prevention toward social networking, to propose our analysis outcomes, and to assist the TSPC chairman to make a final decision.

This study utilizes a requirements elicitation and analysis process, the XREAP [5] , to explore whether moving the SP to the SN is feasible. Because the XREAP is an exhausted approach to elicit the requirements from the execution domain, the outcomes of the XREAP tool will illustrate the overview of the required requirements. Therefore, the implicit needs will be extracted from the XREAP process, and the decision-makers will own most options and situations for further decision-making.

Furthermore, the XREAP tool is a requirements engineering utility that is based on the XREAP concept and is designed by Java programming language [5]. It is suitable for software-development process and acts as a role for eliciting and analysing the software requirements from users as well as generates a series of use case diagrams for further design

[17]. Here our research team tries to adopt the XREAP tool in the decision support process, to generate a complex use case diagram, and to assist the TSPC managers to decide.

In Summary, the research team utilizes the XREAP tool to assist us to elicit, collect, and analyse the all possible requirements from the TSPC managers, users of social networking, information technologies, health promotion concepts, and social environment. That is, the XREAP tool is acted as a decision support process tool.

3.1. Execution procedures

This step utilizes at least two approaches. The first method enhances the requirements analysis integrity by plus-minus-interesting (PMI) and alternative-possibilities-choice (APC) thinking styles. The second one bases on both UML and Extensible Markup Language (XML) standards to cope with all activities. To understand the execution procedures of the XREAP tool, Figure 1 utilizes the UML state diagram to illustrate the execution procedures of the XREAP tool.

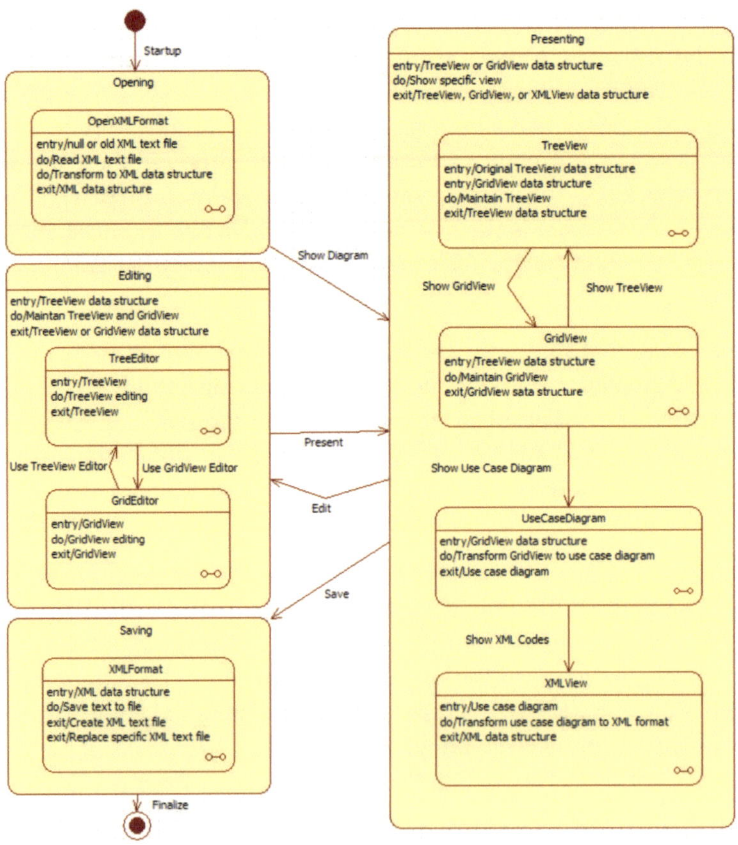

Figure 1. Execution procedures of the XREAP tool

Explicitly, The XREAP tool owns four states and the presenting state, including another four sub-states such as TreeView, GridView, UseCaseDiagram, and XMLView. Meanwhile, the editing state includes two sub-states: TreeEditor and GridEditor. That is, the analyst can maintain the requirements between TreeView and GridView states and then transform to a use case diagram as well as save as the XML text format. The XML text format can also be read as the input file of the XREAP tool for further revising. The following sections illustrate these approaches, respectively.

3.2. Input requirements

Firstly, the PMI thinking style is shown in Figure 2 and categories the requirements by three views of points, including plus, minus, and interesting. This method will not only collect the stakeholder's requirements, but also elicit the implicit requirements that do not mention by users. The first step of the PMI thinking is concentrated on the plus view of points. That is, the analyst must focus on the positive facet of the user requirements and record all requirements from users, and all possible derived needs. Similarly, the analyst has to utilize the same thinking process to achieve the minus and interesting facets, respectively.

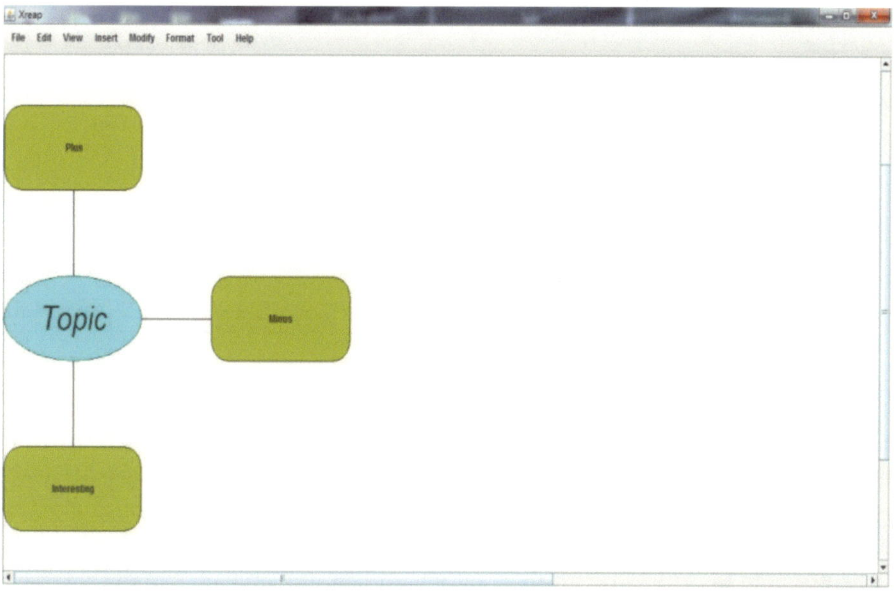

Figure 2. Graphical user interface for user requirements by categories

On the other hand, the APC thinking includes three parts: alternatives, possibilities, and choice. That is, the analyst has to focus on the requirements, actors, and use cases to consider the specific requirement for alternatives, feasibility, and decision-making. To facilitate the alternative generation, the APC thinking suggests at least ten progressive questions for further analyze and is shown in Figure 3. The illustration of detail processing is also listed as below.

Explanation (E): it asks for an analyst to describe the specific requirement again in order to confirm that the analyst understands the user illustration.

Assumption (A): the analyst has to confirm the specific requirement's executive constraint.

Viewpoint (V): the analyst has to consider the specific requirement by different view of points.

Problem (P): the analyst might propose any questions for specific requirement.

Review (R): the analyst bases on the E, A, V, and P illustrations to consider again for specific requirement.

Design (D): the analyst summaries the R illustration and proposes a solution to handle the specific requirement.

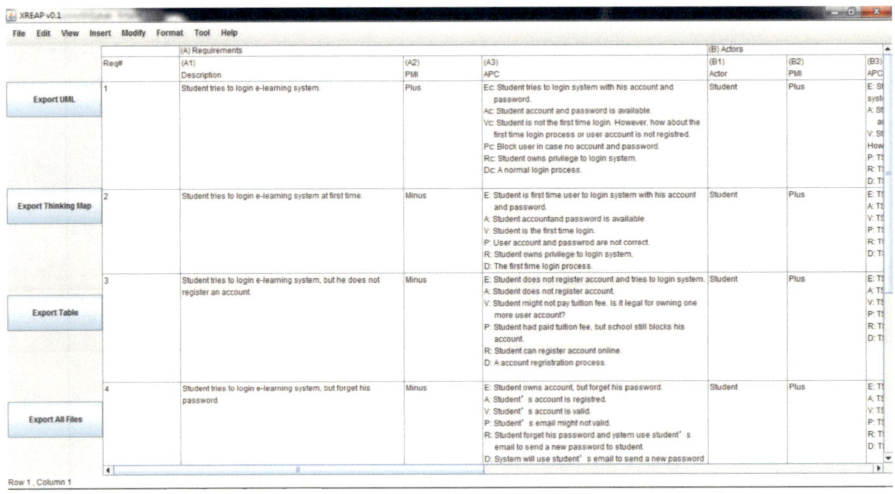

Figure 3. Sample collection of use requirements by grid

Note that the APC processing focuses on the specific requirement that is categorized by the PMI method. If an analyst finds any new requirement during the APC's first five steps, the analyst should insert a fresh requirement to the requirements list. Then the analyst can elicit the actor from the specific requirement. Every actor also needs PMI and APC processing as well as it is possible to find some implicit actors. At last, the analyst can derive the use case from the specific requirements by treating the PMI and APC thinking. Similarly, it is also possible for an analyst to discover some implicit use cases during the whole processing.

This kind of the analysis means prevents an analyst only to elicit the favorable requirements from users and ignores the implicit requirements inadvertently. Ordinarily, most of the exceptions might be disregarded by the analyst during the system analysis phase and be inserted during the programming phase, even maintenance phase. Such a conventional analysis processing might waste a lot of time revising the system architecture and let the system weaker than original version. Accordingly, the PMI and APC processing can compensate the aforementioned drawback, try to elicit all possible requirements from users, and maintain the requirements' integrity during system analysis phase.

In order to minimize the problem-solving scale, the decision-makers can utilize the divide-and-conquer methodology to decomposite the original problem to several independent sub-problems. That is, decision-makers can integrate all sub-problems' solutions into one solution and make their final decision. For example, the social networking is a large field and includes several famous social websites such as the Facebook, the Twitter, the Google+, etc. Therefore, we can divide our original problem from "whether moving suicide prevention toward social networking" into "whether moving suicide prevention toward the Facebook social networking", "whether moving suicide prevention toward the Twitter social networking", and "whether moving suicide prevention toward the Google + social networking. "

3.3. Export use case diagram

As shown in Figure 4, a use case diagram is transformed from the XREAP grid collection format. In order to simplify the decision scope, we utilize the divide-and-conquer method to decompose our original problem and only consider the Facebook social networking part in this chapter. Therefore, Figure 4 shows the use case diagram of "whether moving suicide prevention toward the Facebook social networking. "Note that the human icon represents an actor, the oval icon means use case, and the line represents the association between actors and use cases. Normally, the use case diagram is one-to-one mapping to the XREAP grid collection phase. Note that the use case diagram also reflects the original requirements listed in the XREAP tree collection phase.

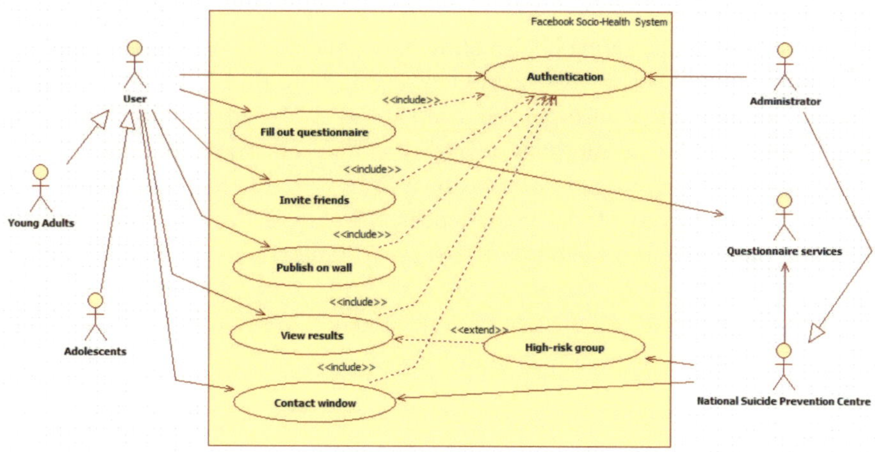

Figure 4. Use case diagram of whether moving suicide prevention toward the Facebook social networking

The analyst can modify the use case diagram. However, the reverse flow is not allowed by the XREAP tool. That is, the analyst has to roll back to the grid collection phase to revise the specific sources of the requirements' illustration and then further transform a new use case diagram to replace the original diagram. Although such a modification procedure of the XREAP tool is not so convenience, anyhow, it urges the analysts to reconsider and confirm their requirements carefully, not unceremoniously.

4. Results

This research utilizes the grounded theory to prove the correction rate of the XREAP tool. The success of the XREAP approach can be indirectly proven by the comparison results of traditional method and the XREAP tool. The XREAP tool is a method for requirements elicitation and analysis. Alternatively, it can be adopted to list the problem variables, extract the implicit problems, and analyze the at-hand solutions.

The more association lines among actors and use cases, the more complex relationship with the requirements of the specific problem-solving. For example, a use case diagram with twenty association lines among its actors and use cases is absolutely complex than the other use case diagram with only five association lines.

As the use case diagram shown in Figure 4, the decision-makers can count on the numbers of the association lines among actors and use cases. That is, there are seven use cases and six actors that are associated with eleven directed association lines and five <<include>> dependency lines, one <<extend>> association line, and three generalization relationship linesfor implementing a virtual suicide prevention gatekeeper, Socio-Health, in the Facebook environment. Note that this case study only covers the adolescents and young adults in Taiwan.

The statistical table of shape items is also shown in Table 1 and the final score of the complexity calculation of the Socio-Health problem is 58. Note that the shape item of the use case is categorized as three levels: generic use case(s), included use case(s), and extended use case(s). A generic use case can include and/or extend one more use case. Therefore, the generic use case might own higher complexity weight than the included and extended use case(s). Based on our implementation experiences, the complexity of most included use cases is higher than the one of most extended use cases. Similarly, the shape item of the actor is also categorized into six levels: related to one use case, related to 2~4 use cases, related to 5~8 use cases, related to at least nine use cases, and generalized. The corresponding weights are assigned by their implementation complexities.

Table 2 shows the problem complexity assessment range for the analyst to estimate the final calculation of the XREAP tool. Based on the Table 2, the complexity score is below 100 is categorized as tiny problem and correspondingly easy to handle.

Based on complexity assessment for such a use case diagram, we can decide to execute these implementation tasks. Correspondingly, the generic decision-making by intuition for the same task might be also similar to the result for utilizing the XREAP tool and consider this task is a small task. However, our proposed process provides a visual and standard diagram for decision-makers to make their decision through understanding of their problems.

Shape Items		Weight	Number	Calculation
Use case	Generic use case(s)	5	1	5
	Included use case(s)	3	5	15
	extended use case(s)	2	1	2
Actor	Related to one use case	1	2	2
	Related to 2~4 use cases	2	1	2
	Related to 5~8 use cases	3	1	3
	Related to 9+ use cases	5	0	0
	Generalized	1	3	3
Association lines		1	11	11
<<include>> dependency line		2	5	10
<<extend>> association line		2	1	2
Generalization relationship line		1	3	3
Calculation of complexity weight				58

Table 1. Statistical table of shape items for utilizing XREAP tool

Problem Complexity Score	Possible Assessment
Less than 100	Tiny problem
101~200	Small problem
201~300	Medium problem
300~400	Large problem
Greater than 400	Huge problem

Table 2. Problem complexity assessment range

5. Discussion

Based on our empirical outcomes, the following arguments will focus on five significant concerns: limitation of the XREAP tool, the ratio of requirements elicitation, divide-and-conquer, complexity assessment, and decision-making guidelines.

5.1. Limitation of the XREAP tool

As the utilization of the XREAP tool to make some decisions for several projects, we found some pros and cons. They are listed in Table 3 for the analyst further reference. Furthermore, the XREAP tool owns some limitations. For example, the mind brainstorm function supports graphical user interface for user requirements by categories. That is, every PMI item can provide a number of the entries. However, the arrangement of the requirements' map is not so concise that some of the requirements might be overlapped each other, and the screen will be too small to browse while every PMI item is more than 15 entries.

Pros	Cons
Is cross-platform	Is a bit slow during execution
Is visualization	Is not beautiful on graphic user interface
Supports mind brainstorm function	Is not easy for utilization
Can transfer from requirements to a use case diagram	Cannot reverse transfer from a use case diagram to requirements
Can exchange use case diagram with the XML metadata interchange standard	Can only exchange with the Star UML tool
Can be utilized as a decision support tool	Does not yet include the calculation function of the complexity assessment

Table 3. Pros and cons of the XREAP tool

5.2. The ratio of requirements elicitation

Fundamentally, the requirements elicitation is the first phase in our decision-making process. As most of the decision-makers known, the higher ratio of requirements elicitation is obtained, the better quality of decision-making will be executed. If decision-makers are eager for the highest quality of their decision-making, it is necessary for them to try to focus on the requirements elicitation phase. Fortunately, our proposed methodology can elicit required information from users by utilizing the XREAP tool. Meanwhile, the implicit information for persons, actions, tenancies, environment and equipment can be elicited by the XREAP tool as possible as it could extract from user requirements by both PMI and APC methods. Furthermore, all requirements are listed within a tabular frame in the XREAP tool, and it is convenient for the decision-makers to browse and review. As compared with other decision-making tools, we believe the XREAP tool can supply the exhaustive capability to elicit user requirements.

5.3. Divide-and-conquer

If the problem is too large to solve, it is feasible for problem-solvers to utilize the divide-and-conquer approach to decompose the problem into several smaller problems. If the smaller problem is still too large to handle, problem-solverscan divide such a problem again until they can cope with the scope of the problem. The divide-and-conquer methodology is widely used in several fields such as computer science. Similarly, the decision-makers are problem-solvers. Therefore, decision-makers can try to analyze the small problems one by one and integrate all solutions into a total solution for original problem.

5.4. Complexity assessment

Generally speaking, the complexity assessment is not an easy task. As our proposed methodology illustration, the complexity can be counted for the numbers of the actors and use cases in the final use case diagram. The more actors and use cases, the more complex interwoven network for requirements will be presented. Although the roughly count of the use cases and actors might be too simple to convey the complexity of the requirements, such a computation method is easy for decision-makers to confirm the existing input requirements quickly and repeatedly. However, it is possible for researchers to propose better complexity assessment for the XREAP tool in the future. Based on the complexity assessment results, decision-makers can conveniently make their decision.

5.5. Decision-making guidelines

Although the XREAP tool is one of the simple software for eliciting requirements, it can become a supplement to improve the decision-making quality for decision-makers. Normally, it is necessary for decision-makers to refer the decision-making guidelines that are gathered by other decision-makers. As the popularity of the Internet, it is possible for decision-makers to share and revise their decision-making guidelines in the cloud. Based on the knowledge management experiences from the healthcare field in 2008 [4] , it is feasible to share, revise and manage the specific knowledge through the network. That is, if the decision-making guidelines are utilized and revised by most decision-makers, then the optimal decision-making process will be generated.

6. Conclusion

It is a smart behaviour for decision-makers to spend more time to realize the whole views of the problems and solutions before they make wise decisions. However, an effective decision analysis tool is hard to obtain. The XREAP software is an optional choice for assisting decision-makers. As the tool results said, the SP service can be spread through SN, and it explores and assists the potential subjects who present the trend of suicide ideation.

Acknowledgements

The authors would like to thank all research colleagues in the National Suicide Prevention Centre, Taipei, Taiwan. The authorsalso express thanks for partial financial support from the National Science Council, Taiwan, under grant number NSC101-2220-E017-001.

Author details

Po-Hsun Cheng[1*], Heng-Shuen Chen[2,3,4,5], Wen-Chen Chiang[1] and Hsin-Ciang Chang[1]

1 Department of Software Engineering, National Kaohsiung Normal University, Taiwan

2 Family Medicine Department, Medicine College, National Taiwan University, Taiwan

3 Institute of Health Policy and Management, National Taiwan University, Taiwan

4 Family Medicine Department, National Taiwan University Hospital, Taiwan

5 National Suicide Prevention Centre, Taiwan

References

[1] Alao AO. , Soderberg M. , Pohl EL. and Alao AL. Cybersuicide: Review of the Role of the Internet on Suicide. Cyberpsychology and Behavior 2006; 9(4) 489-493.

[2] Biddle L. , Donovan J. , Hawton K. , Kapur N. and Gunnell D. Suicide and the Internet. British Medical Journal 2008; 336(7648) 800-802.

[3] Cercone N. , An X. , Li, J. , Gu Z. and An A. Finding Best Evidence for Evidence-based Best Practice Recommendations in Health Care: The Initial Decision Support System Design. Knowledge and Information Systems 2011; 29(1)159-201.

[4] Cheng PH. , Chen SJ. , LaiJS. and Lai F. A Collaborative Knowledge Management Process for Implementing Healthcare Enterprise Information Systems. IEICE Transactions on Information and Systems 2008; E91-D(6) 1664-1672.

[5] Cheng PH. , Chang HC. and Chang FH. Another extensible requirements elicitation and analysis method. In: AI-Dabass D. , Tandayya P. , Yonus J. , Heednacram A. and Ibrahim Z. (eds.) IEEE CICSyN2012: proceedings of the 4th International Conference on Computational Intelligence, Communication Systems and Networks, IEEE CICSyN2012, 24-26 July, 2012, Phuket, Thailand. Los Alamitos: IEEE Computer Society's Conference Publishing Services; 2012.

[6] Chiang WC. , Cheng PH. , Su MJ. , Chen HS. , Wu SW. and Lin JK. Socio-Health with personal mental health records: suicidal-tendency observation system on Facebook for Taiwanese adolescents and young adults. Shyu CR. (eds.) IEEE HEALTHCOM2011: proceedings of the IEEE 13th International Conference on e-Health Networking, Applications and Services, IEEE HEALTHCOM2011, 13-15 June, 2011, Columbia, Missouri, USA. Leonia: EDAS Conference Services; 2011.

[7] Fox CJ. Introduction to Software Engineering Design: Processes, Principles and Patterns with UML2. New York: Addison-Wesley;2006.

[8] Fowler M. UML Distilled: A Brief Guide to the Standard Object Modeling Language, 3rd Edition. New York: Addison-Wesley Professional; 2004.

[9] Ivar J. Object-oriented Software Engineering: A Use Case Driven Approach. New York: ACM Press; 1997.

[10] Manning CD. , Raghavan P. and Schutze H. An Introduction to Information Retrieval. New York: Cambridge University Press; 2008.

[11] Perini A. and Susi A. Understanding the Requirements of a Decision Support System for Agriculture: An Agent-Oriented Approach. Environmental Modelling and Software Journal 2004; 19(9)821-829.

[12] Rudd MD. , Joiner T. and Rajab MH. Treating Suicidal Behavior: An Effective, Time-limited Approach. New York: Guilford Press; 2004.

[13] Schlobinski S. , Denzer R. , Frysinger S. , Güttler R. and Hell T. Vision and Requirements of Scenario-Driven Environmental Decision Support Systems Supporting Automation for End Users. In: Qian Z. , Cao L. , Su W. , Wang T. , and Yang H. (ed.) Environmental Software Systems, Frameworks of Environment, IFIP Advances in Information and Communication Technology, Vol. 359. New York: Springer;2011. p. 51-63.

[14] Shafiei F. , Sundaram D. and Piramuthu S. Multi-enterprise Collaborative Decision Support System. Expert Systems with Applications 2012; 39(9)7637-7651.

[15] Shi W. and Zeng W. Analysis and Design on Environmental Risk Zoning Decision Support System Based on UML. In: Qian Z. , Cao L. , Su W. , Wang T. , and Yang H. (ed.) Recent Advances in Computer Science and Information Engineering Vol. 2, Lecture Notes in Electrical Engineering, Vol. 125. New York: Springer; 2012. p. 799-804.

[16] Shneidman ES. , Farberow NL. and Litman RE. The Psychology of Suicide: A Clician's Guide to Evaluation and Treatment. New York: Jason Aronson Inc. Publishers; 1977.

[17] Sommerville I. Software Engineering, 9th Edition. London: Addison Wesley; 2010.

[18] World Health Organizatoin. WHO: Suicide Prevention: SUPRE. http://www. who. int/mental_health/prevention/suicide/suicideprevent/en/ (accessed 17 December 2011).

[19] Sutcliffe A. , Bruijn de O. , Thew S. , Buchan I. , Jarvis P. , McNaugh J. and Procter R. Developing Visualization-based Decision Support Tools for Epidemiology. Information Visualization 2012, DOI: 10. 1177/1473871612445832. (accessed 15 June 2012).

[20] Taiwan Suicide Prevention Center. TSPC. http://www. tspc. doh. gov. tw (accessed 7 Janruary 2012).

Chapter 2

Decision Support Systems in Medicine - Anesthesia, Critical Care and Intensive Care Medicine

Thomas M. Hemmerling, Fabrizio Cirillo and Shantale Cyr

Additional information is available at the end of the chapter

http://dx.doi.org/10.5772/51756

1. Introduction

A decision support system (DSS) in medicine is a software designed to assist the medical team in the decision making process; it deals with organizational, diagnostic and therapeutic problems, using data (e.g. variables of the patient) as inputs to combine with models and algorithms giving advice in form of monitor alerts, color codes, or visual messages; it does not replace the human operator, but can improve the quality of care. Modern society more and more asks the medical community for 'infallibility' in clinical practice, but errors is part of human intervention: emotions, behavioral and psychological patterns, or difficult contexts can influence human performances. For humans, it is simply impossible to recall all diagnostic and therapeutic options at any time for any given patient [1]. The use of DSSs in the clinical management could solve this problem helping specialists with diagnostic or therapeutic suggestions, making it easier to follow validated guidelines, reducing the incidence of faulty diagnoses and therapies [2], and changing incorrect behaviors.

Early computerized medical systems date back to the early 60ies [3]. First prototypes were used to train medical students in establishing a diagnosis [4]. The evolution of these systems has followed the general innovation in technology and their capacities constantly increase over time, from only educational tools to intelligent systems for patient management.

Basically, a DSS can be designed using knowledge representation, in the form of clinical algorithms, mathematical pathophysiological models, Bayesian statistical systems and diagrams, neural networks, fuzzy logic theories, and symbolic reasoning or "expert" systems [5]. A DSS has to be conceived suitable and user-friendly; the 'rules structure' should be easily understood, the rules process should be intuitive and open for collaboration, all decisions should be reproducible and the user interface easy to use (Figure 1) [6].

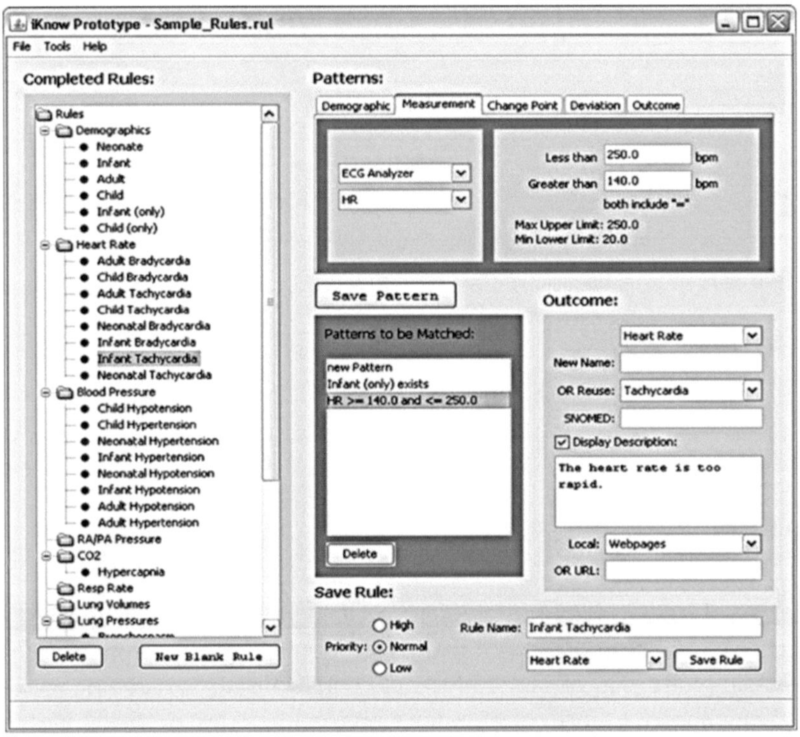

Figure 1. Graphical user interface [6].

DSSs in medicine could play a role in every field: a modern DSS is conceived to predict rehabilitation protocol for patients with knee osteoarthritis [7]. Another example of a modern DSS is a system that uses anthropometric information and questionnaire data to predict obstructive sleep apnea [8]. The use of DSSs has been proposed to treat major depression [9]; a DSS has been validated recently to diagnose the common flu [10]; a DSS has been developed to support the treatment of epilepsy [11]. Another DSS has been presented in the field of gynecology [12].

At present, it is not clear if an improvement of medical performance can always be transferred into an improvement of patient outcomes [13, 14] [15], and although better adherence to guidelines is proven, this cannot always be translated into abandoning habits of wrong-doing [16]. Furthermore, there are some considerable barriers to the widespread diffusion of these systems, like costs, cultural issues and lack of standards [2] [17] [18].

These systems are usually produced with limited private funds; mass production is limited by economic pressures. Lack of standardization often represents a "political" problem. There are always emotional barriers for physicians and other health care providers to 'rely' on the help of devices in order to make proper decision.

Anesthesiologists and critical care specialists are very involved in patient safety; excellence in their fields needs a collection of nontechnical, nonclinical skills that may be classified as "task management", "team working", "situation awareness", and "decision-making"[19]. Developing information and decision technology support systems for these skills also means to significantly improve the quality, flow, and efficiency of medical performance [20].

This chapter will focus on DSSs for anesthesiologists and critical care specialists in different areas: perioperative management, the emergency and intensive care medicine.

2. Decision support systems for anesthesia in the operating room

Anesthesiologists in the operating room have to provide direct patient care. Anesthesiologists are considered the "pilots of human biosphere" [21], and terms like "takeoff" and "landing" for the process of inducing anesthesia and reversing it, are very common; since these are the two dominant and critical moments of anesthesia, often, maintenance of anesthesia receives less attention [22]. To assure safe and good patient care during the surgical procedure, an anesthesiologist interacts with several devices: he becomes "the mediator between patient and machine while the machine is mediating between patient and anesthesiologist; all are hybrids in action and each is unable to act independently" [22]. It is impossible to consider the anesthetic work without machines just as it is impossible to imagine a pilot without his joysticks, buttons and computers.

Decision support systems for anesthesia in the milieu of the operating room are software shaped to assist the anesthesiologist in his difficult work during the surgical procedure. Let's divide DSSs for anesthesia in the operating room into three classes: DSSs designed for perioperative use, DSSs for one single intraoperative problem (*simple DSSs*) and DSSs for multiple problems (*complex DSSs*).

2.1. Organizational DSSs and implementation in AIMS in the perioperative context

In his everyday activity, the anesthesiologist deals not only with patient-related issues, but also with many kinds of organizational problems, like strictly hierarchical command structures or deficits in providing important drugs or devices that can cause serious accidents. Reason [23] has proposed a scheme of the development of an organizational accident (Figure 2).

It is not possible to consider the anesthesiologist's responsibility only during the surgical intervention; as a pilot has to control his systems before the flight, anesthesiologists must continuously assess the patient status, from pre-operative assessment till post-operative care. As a 'commander-in-chief', he has to make the final check of everything 'anesthetic' in the operating room, despite the presence of nurses or respiratory technicians. One type of DSS can deal with organizational problems in order to prevent accidents.

The first example of how DSSs may improve safety in the operating environment is a DSS whhi generates dynamically configured checklists for intraoperative problems [24]. It is interesting that the database built with 600 entries of two anesthesia textbooks and organized in problems and corresponding abnormalities, considers also technical hitches, like e.g. inefficiency in anesthesia machines or incorrect position of an endotracheal tube. For each abnormality detected by monitors and confirmed by the practitioner, the software formulates a list of questions, starting with a recognized "high-impact abnormality" (every abnormality uniquely associated with a problem); questions about the "high-impact abnormality" are presented to users as closed-type questions, i.e. they can be answered as "yes" or "no", to facilitate a quick response.

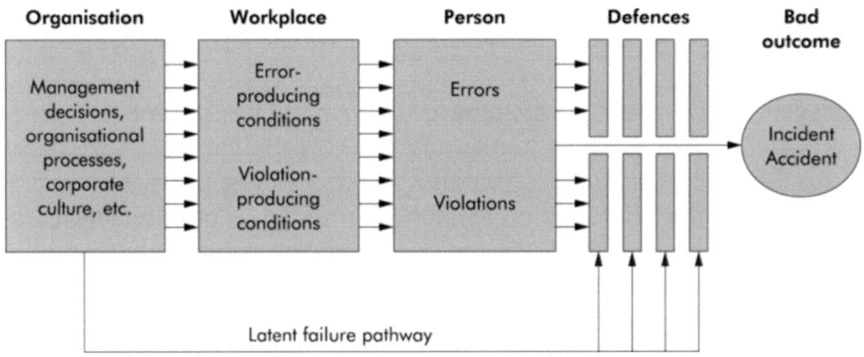

Figure 2. The development of an organizational accident [23].

Preoperative tests are crucial for the stratification of the anesthetic risk, for the choice of the anesthesia technique but also to define the anesthesiologist's behavior. A Canadian group [25] found that the mean cost of investigations was reduced from $124 to $73 if data for patients were assessed by staff anesthesiologists. Another study [26] demonstrated that, following definite preoperative diagnostic guidelines, possible savings per 1000 patients would be €26287 and €1076 if duplicated tests were avoided.

A DSS for this purpose, the System for Pre-Operative Test Selection (SPOTS), has been developed to assist physicians in selecting the right preoperative, individualized and clinically relevant tests [27]. The software uses a database comprising of patient data, clinical history, a list of surgical procedures, standard guidelines for preoperative investigations, type and cost of investigations, and investigation results: the DSS then suggests the tests and performs a cost comparison.

Airway management represents one of the most important challenges for the anesthesiologist. The main causes of anesthesia-related mortality are respiratory and cardiocirculatory events [28, 29]. One of the most important aims of preoperative assessment is predicting a difficult intubation; it means to timely prepare airway devices to facilitate a possibly difficult procedure. Currently, the gold standard for the evaluation of the difficulty of intubation is the Cormack and Lahane classification, but it's feasible only through direct laryngoscopy. A DSS for estimating the Cormack classification was presented in 2009 [30]; it was based on data of 264 medical records from patients suffering from a variety of diseases. It used 13 basic anthropometrical features (Figure 3) to predict easy (Cormack I and II) or difficult intubation (Cormack III and IV). The system showed an average classification accuracy of 90%.

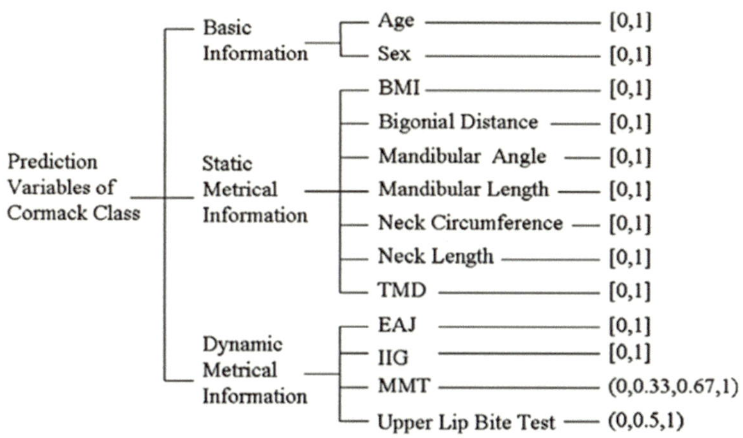

Figure 3. The 13 variables for Cormack classification and their encoding schemes. BMI, for body mass index; TMD, tyro-mental distance; EAJ, atlanto-axial joint; IIG, interincisor gap; MMT, modified Mallampati test. Binary values (0, 1) were used for variables with only two attributes. Values as 0, 0.5 and 1 were used for variables with three attributes. Values as 0, 0.33, 0.67, 1, were used for variables with four attributes [30].

Anesthesia information management systems (AIMS) can reduce the anesthesiologist's workload. Implementation of DSSs in AIMS represents a natural evolution of information technology: DSSs can use data stored in AIMS to give diagnostic or therapeutic messages. This development increases the usefulness of both systems [31, 32].

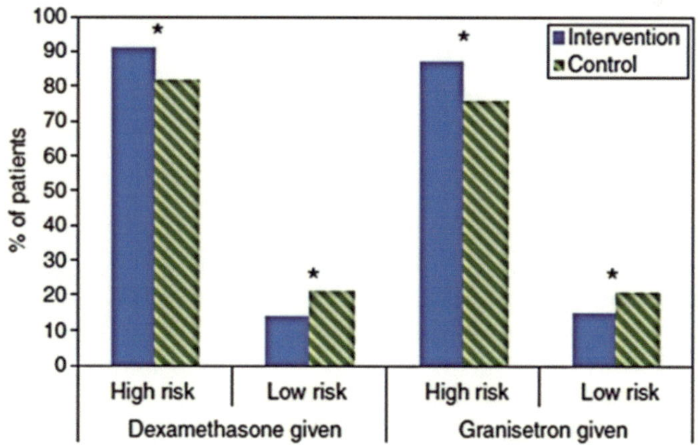

Figure 4. Percentage of patients involved in prophylaxis. *Statistically significant difference [33].

A recent example of how a DSS combined with an AIMS can improve performance and outcomes is shown in a study about automated reminders for prophylaxis of postoperative nausea and vomiting (PONV) [33]. A database was implemented with PONV prophylaxis guidelines. The comparison of two groups (one with only AIMS and the other with AIMS and also DSS), found that automated reminders were more effective for adherence to PONV prophylaxis (Figure 4).

It also showed a reduction of inappropriate administration of PONV prophylaxis medication to low-risk patients: automated reminders not only are effective in promoting correct actions, but may also prevent unnecessary prescription of medication, hence reducing drug costs. Although the DSS significantly improved adherence to the PONV guidelines, guidelines adherence decreased to the level before use of the DSS after its withdrawal from clinical routine (Figure 5).

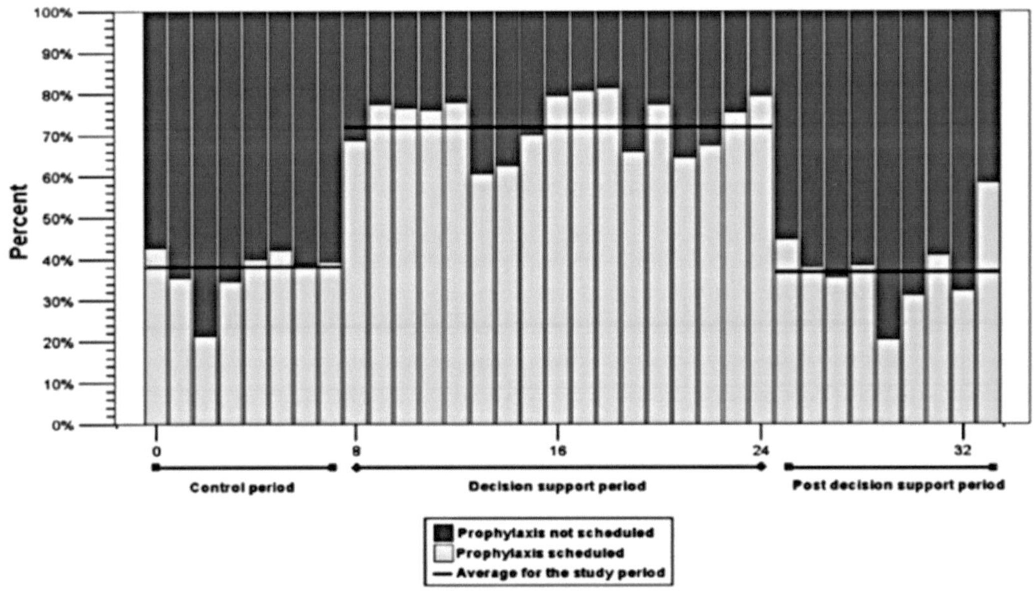

Figure 5. Guidelines adherence for high risk patients by week [16].

Surgical wound infections are relatively common, as they are considered the second most common complications occurring in a hospitalized patient [34, 35], and the second most common nosocomial infections, occurring in 2%–5% of surgeries and in up to 20% of abdominal surgeries [36]. They have a significant economical impact, because patients affected spend more time in the hospital and are more in danger to be admitted to an intensive care unit, to be readmitted to the hospital after discharge, or to die [37]. Antimicrobial prophylaxis is most effective when administered before surgical incision, with an optimal time to be within 30 minutes before incision or within 2 hours if vancomycin is administered [38, 39].

In order to facilitate timely administration, DSSs were implemented in AIMS to obtain better adherence with those guidelines. One of these is an automated computer-based documentation that generates automatic reminders to the anesthesia team and the surgeon[40]. In this study, authors found that 70% of all surgical patients received their antibiotics within 60 min of incision (Figure 6); after one year, the adherence increased to about 92%.

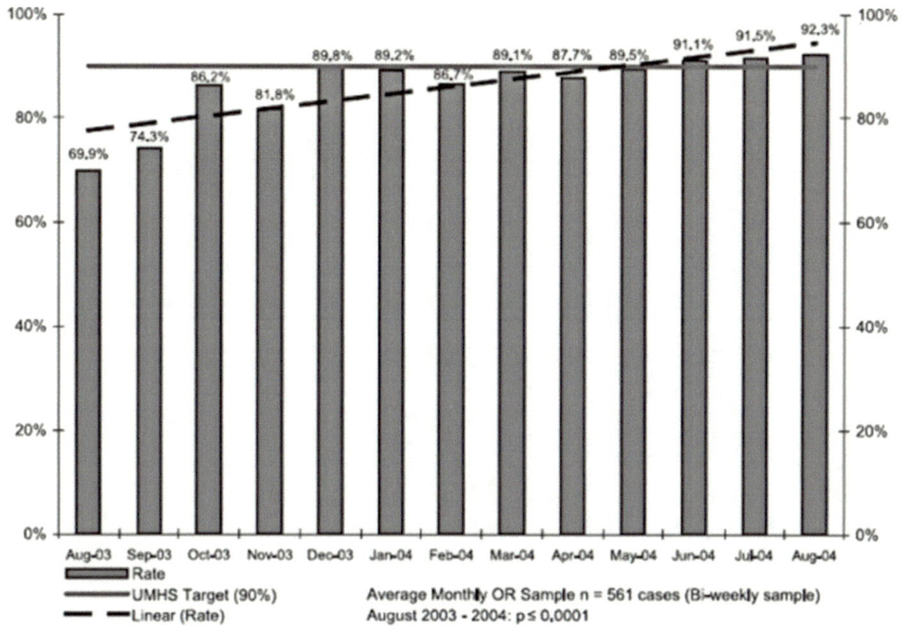

Figure 6. Administration of antibiotic: gradually increasing to about 92% [40].

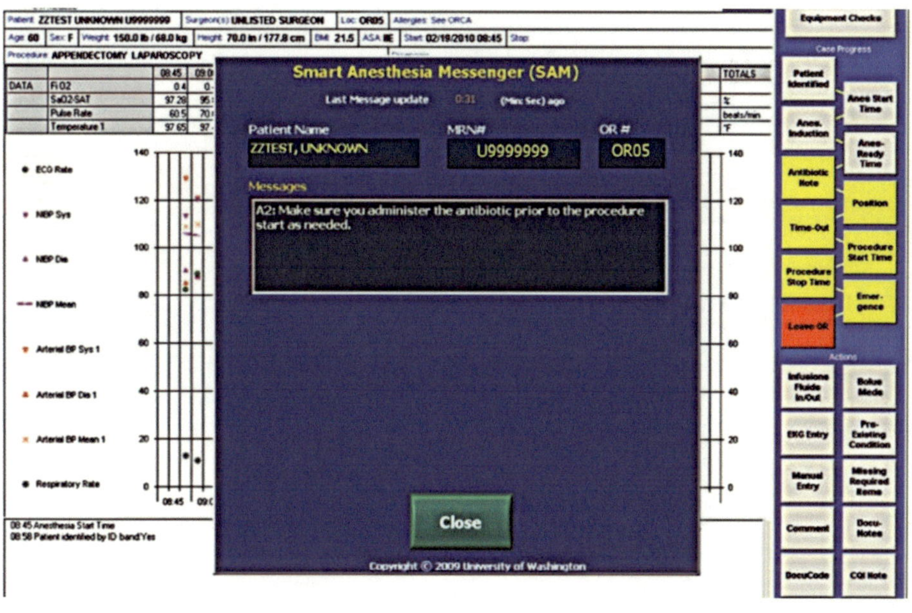

Figure 7. Anesthesia information management system screen overlaid by SAM screen [41].

Another DSS for antibiotic prophylaxis, the so-called Smart Anesthesia Messenger (SAM) [41], analyzes AIMS documentation data in real-time. Conceived as the final stage of intervention, after implementation in an AIMS, SAM transmits reminder messages to the AIMS screen to improve compliance of antibiotic administration before surgical incision (Figure 7). The addition of real-time reminders and feedback via SAM achieved near 100% compliance.

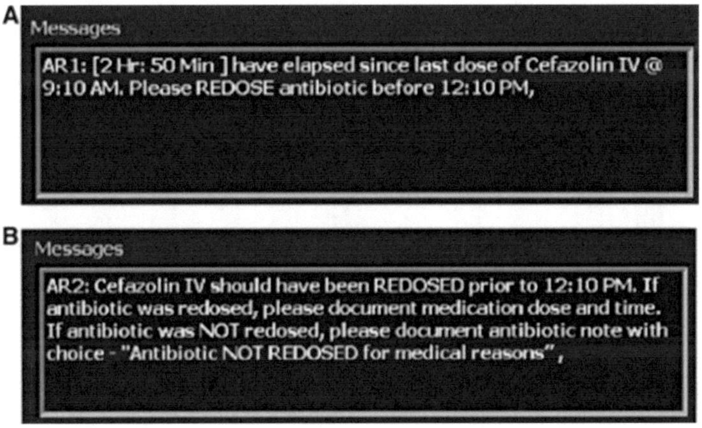

Figure 8. Messages for antibiotic re-dose. (A) Message reminding anesthesia team about need for re-dose. (B) Message about documenting re-dose [42].

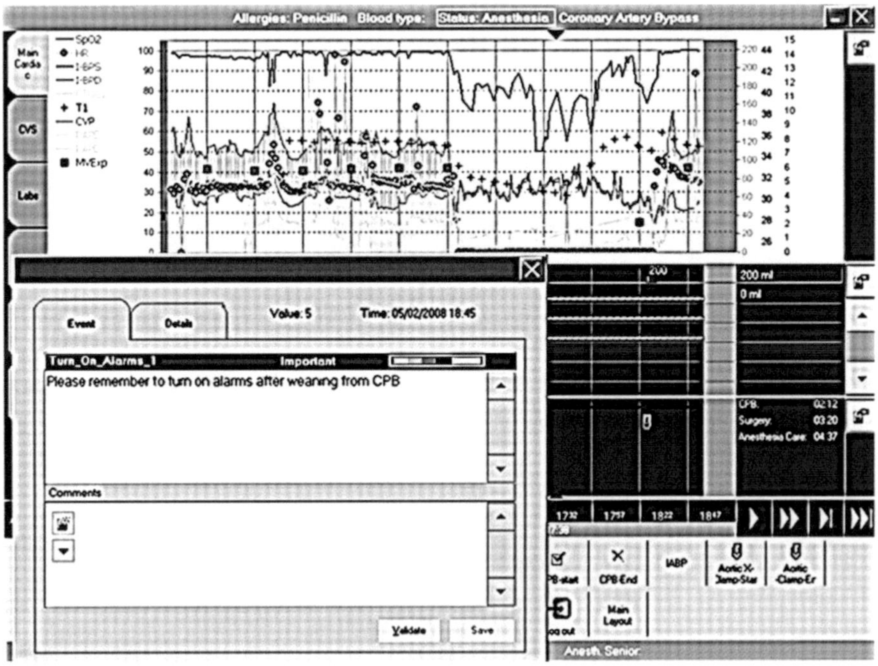

Figure 9. Main window of anesthesia information management system with the electronic reminder [45].

A follow-up study investigated the impact of the same DSS on the re-dosing of antibiotic therapy [42] in comparison with the use of only AIMS. Re-dosing could be important to maintain the necessary serum concentration of drug, to reduce the risk of postoperative wound infections in procedures that exceed of two half-lives of an antibiotic drug [43, 44]. In this study, a reminder message of re-dosing was effectuated every 3 hours (the shortest re-dose interval in guidelines of University of Washington Medical Center). The SAM detected the eventual administration of the prophylactic antibiotic drug, if necessary, it triggers an internal timer specific to that antibiotic and generates reminder icons 15 min prior to the time of re-dosing; these messages are repeated every 6 minutes until the dose is administered and documented (Figure 8). The employment of real-time decision support improved the success rate to 83.9%.

A further example of advantageous use of DSS integrated in AIMS is an electronic reminder to switch on the ventilator alarms after separation from cardiopulmonary bypass (CPB) [45]. In cardiac surgery, during the CPB period, monitor alarms are often disabled; the alarms are frequently not reactivated. The software detects the separation from CPB by return of aortic and pulmonary blood flow, the resumption of mechanical ventilation and the reappearance of end-tidal CO_2. If alarms have not been reactivated after the separation from CPB, an electronic reminder appears on the AIMS screen (Figure 9). The alarm reactivation increased from 22% to 83%.

2.2. Simple DSSs for a single intraoperative problem

A simple DSS combines a small amount of data to deal with one particular problem; it is like an electronic textbook about a specific issue, with the capability of giving the important information at the right time. Usually, problems for which these DSSs are created are very common or insidious. A simple DSS could represent the first step for the progressive development of a more complex DSS.

An example of a simple DSS is a system that detects 'light' anesthesia using as input the changes of mean arterial pressure (MAP) [46]. Krol and Reich considered a 12% change in median MAP in comparison with the median value of MAP over the previous 10 min period a parameter to trigger warnings for recognition of light anesthesia.

Another DSS involved in the detection of light anesthesia is an algorithm that relates different MAC values of volatile anesthetics to different intravenous sedative or hypnotics agents administered at the same time [47].

The introduction of fuzzy logic for setting up DSSs is founded on the ability of fuzzy-logic in dealing with the incompleteness and vagueness that often characterize medical data and knowledge [3]; in 1997, a fuzzy-logic based DSS to control the supply of oxygen in a patient during low-flow/closed-loop anesthesia was presented (Figure 10) [48].

A more recent Fuzzy-Logic Monitoring System (FLMS) has been developed [49]; this is a DSS conceived to detect critical events during anesthesia; it is able to detect only hypovolemia, using as inputs heart rate (HR), blood pressure (BP) and pulse volume (PV). Hypovolemia is classified as mild, moderate or severe. The FLMS was evaluated in 15 patients using off-line data and was found to be in good agreement with the anesthetist's diagnosis. An upgrading of this system, FLMS-2 [50], tested in 20 off-line patients, has demonstrated a sensitivity of 94%, specificity of 90% and predictability of 72%. The user interface of FLMS-2 is shown in Figure 11.

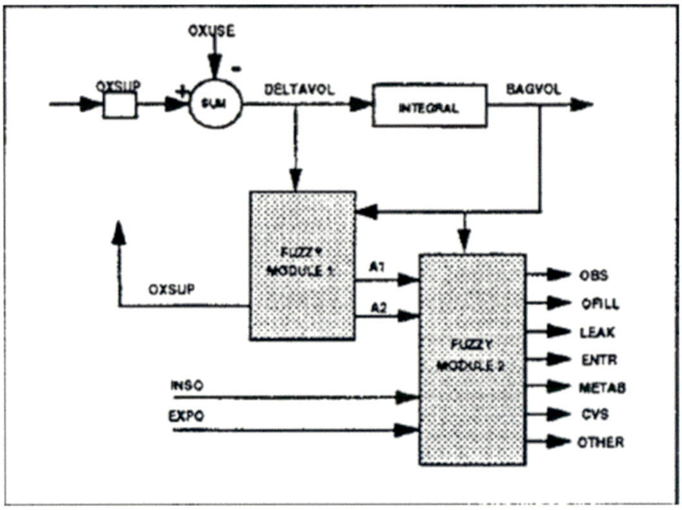

Figure 10. Scheme of fuzzy logic control system. Volume of the reservoir bag (BAGVOL) and his rate of change (DELTAVOL) are the inputs data for the first module (FZ module 1) to calculate the supply of oxygen (OXSUP); this value is sent as output data together with generated alarms (AL 1 and AL 2) to the second module (FZ module 2), that correlates them with oxygen concentration values in inspired (INSO) and expired air (EXPO) to generate simple diagnostic messages including obstructions (OBS), overfilling (OFILL), leakage (LEAK), and entrapment ((ENTR) in the system and metabolism (METAB), cardiovascular (CVS) and other (OTHER) problems with patient [48].

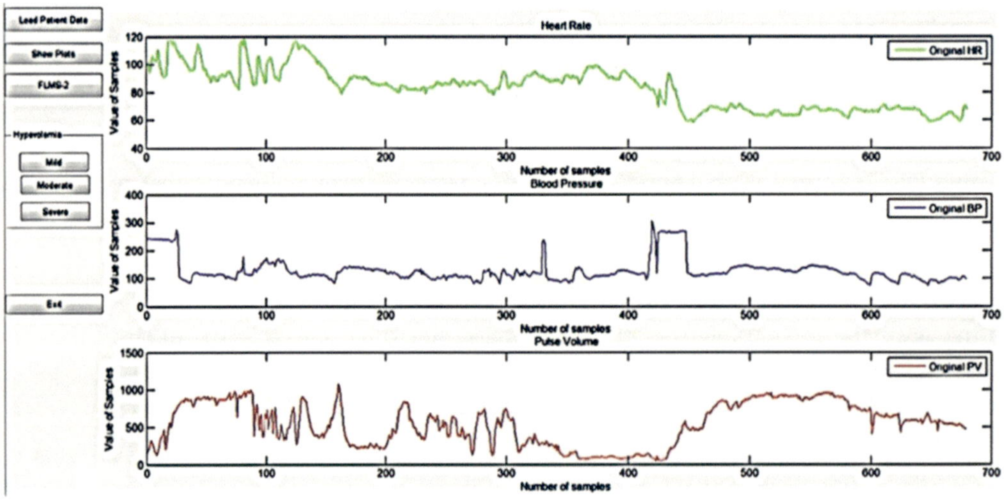

Figure 11. Graphic user interface [50].

http://dx.doi.org/10.5772/51756

2.3. Complex DSSs for intraoperative use

A complex DSS is software dealing with multiple problems. According with the complexity of the issue, it usually requires the collection of a certain number of information to combine with mathematical algorithm. It does not respond only to one problem, but can recognize different questions, sometimes inherent in a same category. These systems have to be considered as "intelligent textbooks".

One of the first complex DSSs for critical events in anesthesia was SENTINEL [51]. Based on fuzzy logic templates, this system used signals to establish a diagnosis despite missing information: it calculated the impact of lack of one or more signals for a certain condition via the estimation of the *completeness factor* [52]; the combination of some signals was judged as more important than others. The likelihood of a given diagnosis is measured considering two parameters of evidence: the *belief* (total of data supporting the evidence of a diagnosis) and the *plausibility* (the amount of data that do not contradict the diagnosis). At the beginning, this system was designed to detect only one problem, malignant hyperpyrexia (MH, between 1:5000 and 1:100000 episodes [53]). Lowe and Harrison [54] set up rules based on characteristic patterns of changes in heart rate, end-tidal carbon dioxide and temperature found in the literature and tested their software in a human simulator (Human Patient Simulator, version 1.3, University of Florida). During open surgery, the algorithm detected MH 10 minutes before the anesthetist; during laparoscopic surgery, in a condition with some similarities to MH (high end tidal CO_2, cardiovascular changes), the diagnosis was only transient. Afterwards, SENTINEL was implemented with other rules to deal with other six conditions (Table 1). The interface of the system is depicted in Figure 12. SENTINEL was only tried in off-line tests, and its diagnostic alarms were compared with the annotations of anesthetists, showing a sensitivity of 95% and a specificity of 90% (during the period between induction and recovery phases).

Problem	Description
Inadequate analgesia (IA)	Significant increases in heart rate and systolic blood pressure over about half a minute; fall in pulse volume over the same period
Malignant hyperpyrexia (MH)	Significant rises in heart rate and end-tidal CO_2 concentration over a number of minutes, followed by low peripheral saturation and a high core body temperature
Increased intracranial pressure (IICP)	Short term decrease in heart rate and simultaneous rise in systolic blood pressure
Pulmonary shunt (PS)	Low peripheral saturation
Cardiac output failure (COF)	Sudden drop in end-tidal CO_2 concentration and systolic blood pressure; followed by desaturation
Absolute hypovolaemia (AHV)	Fall in systolic blood pressure, and pulse volume; corresponding increase in heart rate
Relative hypovolaemia (RHV)	Fall in systolic blood pressure; increase in pulse volume and heart rate

Table 1. Diagnoses and their descriptions for the fuzzy trend templates [52].

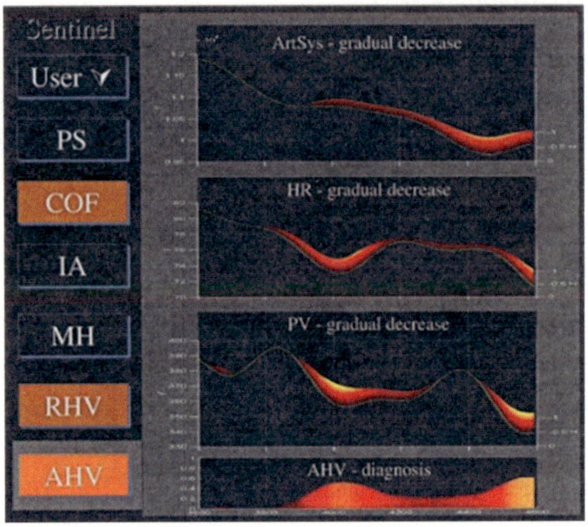

Figure 12. Prototype of SENTINEL user interface. Weak diagnosis of absolute hypovolemia (AHV) [55].

In the wake of SENTINEL, another DSS for critical events in anesthesia was presented in 2007, called Real Time-Smart Alarms for Anesthesia Monitoring (RT-SAAM) [56]. Initially, it was proposed to recognize and suggest treatment options of hypovolemia and decreasing cardiac output. Based on the evidence that hypovolemia can be detected by monitoring systolic pressure variations (SPV) in patients artificially ventilated [57], the DSS filtered the blood pressure (BP), pulse volume (PV), end-tidal carbon-dioxide ($ETCO_2$) waveforms and calculated the SPV and the absolute PV values, providing diagnostic information on the monitor in real-time (Figure 13). Tested in 18 patients in retrospective tests and in 8 patients during real-time tests, a moderate level of agreement between the DSS and the anesthesiologist was determined.

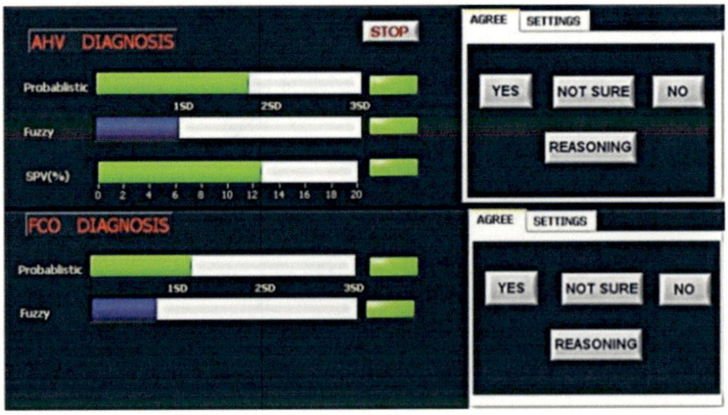

Figure 13. RT-SAAM screen with windows diagnoses. AHW (acute hypovolemia), hypovolemia; fall in cardiac output (FCO) [56].

http://dx.doi.org/10.5772/51756

With the implementation of a Multi-Modal Alarms System (MMAS) [58], RT-SAAM was able to diagnose also sympathetic activity, relative hypovolemia and inadequate anesthesia; diagnostic messages and alerts were sent every 10 seconds to MMAS. Every outcome alarm was connected to a specific sound that was directly transmitted to the anesthetist through a bluetooth headset. The MMAS display had two different modalities of presentation, depending on the presence or not of the symptoms (Figure 14).

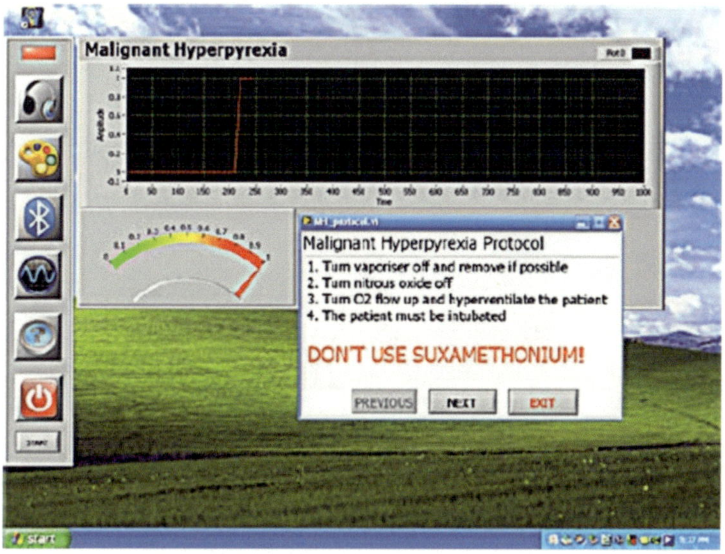

Figure 14. Alert modality of presentation [59].

In 2008, Perkin and Leaning presented Navigator, a DSS involved in the therapeutic control of the circulation and the oxygen delivery optimization and management [60]. They developed a mathematical model to create an algorithm for the control of circulation based on the values of the effective circulating volume (Pms), systemic vascular resistance (SVR) and heart performance (Eh). Using mathematical techniques, the values were derived from measured circulatory variables, the mean arterial pressure (MAP), the right atrial pressure (RAP) and the cardiac output (CO): corrected with a factor, *c*, that correlates with height, weight and age of the subject.

Through the combination of these values, Navigator supports the decision process with continuous therapeutic informations about the hemodynamic status and the oxygen delivery index related to the cardiac output, based on the entered hemoglobin and the arterial oxygen saturation (Spo2). The system display (Figure 15) is organized as such: on the right side, there is the current status of the patient, with his current values acquired from the monitors, target values and other data; on the left side, there is the patient's position (the red dot in the yellow arrow) on an orthogonal graph, in which: x-axis is the resistance axis (SVR values); y-axis is the volumetric axis (Pms values); MAP and CO are shown as lines corresponding to their upper and lower target ranges; the equivalent delivery oxygen indices are shown on the CO lines; the heart performance (Eh values) is displayed like a vertical axis parallel to the Pms axis.

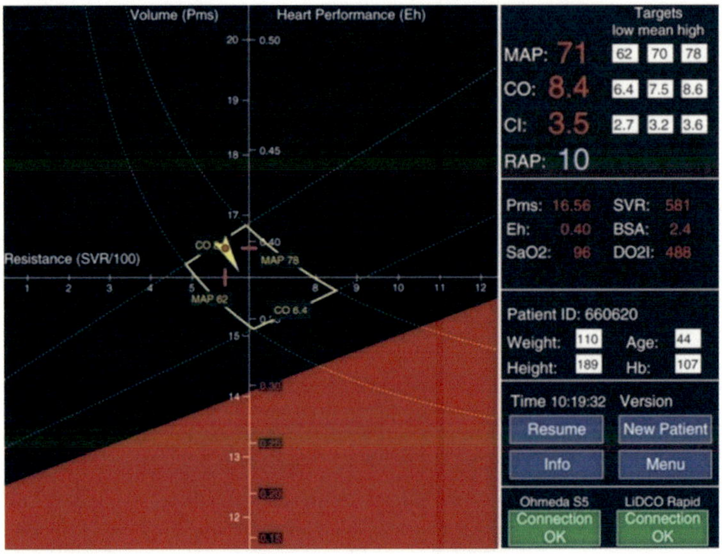

Figure 15. Navigator display [61].

	Guidance (n=57)	Control (n=48)	*P* value
ASD (mean standard distance from the central point of the target values)			
Entire period the patient was connected to Navigator	1.71 (SD 0.65)	1.92 (SD 0.98)	0.202
1-3 hours (SD)	1.77 (0.87)	1.88 (0.90)	0.541
3-6 hours (SD)	1.62 (0.83)	1.96 (1.38)	0.123
6-9 hours (SD)	1.65 (0.81)	1.79 (0.94)	0.434
9-12 hours (SD)	1.57 (0.73)	1.84 (0.96)	0.124
12-15 hours (SD)	1.58 (0.78)	1.80 (1.01)	0.216
15-18 hours (SD)	1.76 (0.80)	1.93 (0.94)	0.388
18-21 hours (SD)	1.67 (0.78)	1.88 (0.94)	0.318
21-24 hours (SD)	1.92 (0.96)	1.73 (0.97)	0.563
Average deviation in MAP to the central point of the target MAP range, mmHg	7.3 (SD 2.68)	7.4 (SD 2.14)	0.976
Average deviation in CO to the central point of the target CO range, l/min	0.99 (SD 0.47)	1.05 (SD 0.69)	0.566
Mean percentage of time in the target cardiovascular range	38.38 (SD 17.59)	32.40 (SD 21.04)	0.098
Percentage of patients with clinically significant AF during connection	5.08	5.77	1.00
Percentage of patients with clinically significant AF during and after connection	37.29	42.31	0.590
Mean day 1 SOFA score	5.89 (SD 2.88)	6.50 (SD 3.36)	0.335
Mean day 2 SOFA score	5.89 (SD 2.88)	6.75 (SD 2.67)	0.240
Mean day 3 SOFA score	6.00 (SD 1.63)	9.20 (SD 1.92)	0.011

Table 2. ASD=average standardized distance, MAP=mean arterial pressure, CO=cardiac output, AF=atrial fibrillation, SOFA=Sequential Organ Failure Assessment [62].

http://dx.doi.org/10.5772/51756

Pellegrino et al [62] assessed Navigator in postoperative cardiac surgical patients. Fifty-seven patients received DSS-guided care and were compared with 48 patients who received conventional care. The performance of the system, considered as "average standardized distance" (ASD) between actual and target values of MAP and CO, was statistically not inferior to the control, and there were no significantly differences in the hospital length of stay (Table 2).

Sondergaard et al. [61] tested the Navigator's hemodynamic control and oxygen delivery during elective major abdominal surgery. They compared two groups of patients, one treated using DSS and the other one treated by expert anesthetists. They found a high concordance between the advices of the system and the intervention of the anesthetists.

Another complex DSS conceived to assist the anesthetist during surgery is Diagnesia [63]. It uses the input from the anesthesia panel to estimate the likelihood or unlikelihood of a diagnosis; it then gives the five most probable diagnoses in descending order (from the most to the least likely) with respective information that support or are against the evidence (Figure 16). Tested in 12 realistic situations from simulated anesthesia monitoring displays, its diagnoses were compared with those of a group of anesthesiologists, and in 11 test cases (92%), the most probable diagnosis was the same; however, the system couldn't distinguish between two or more specific problems from the same category and couldn't deal with diagnosis in which the indicators were only observable but not measurable.

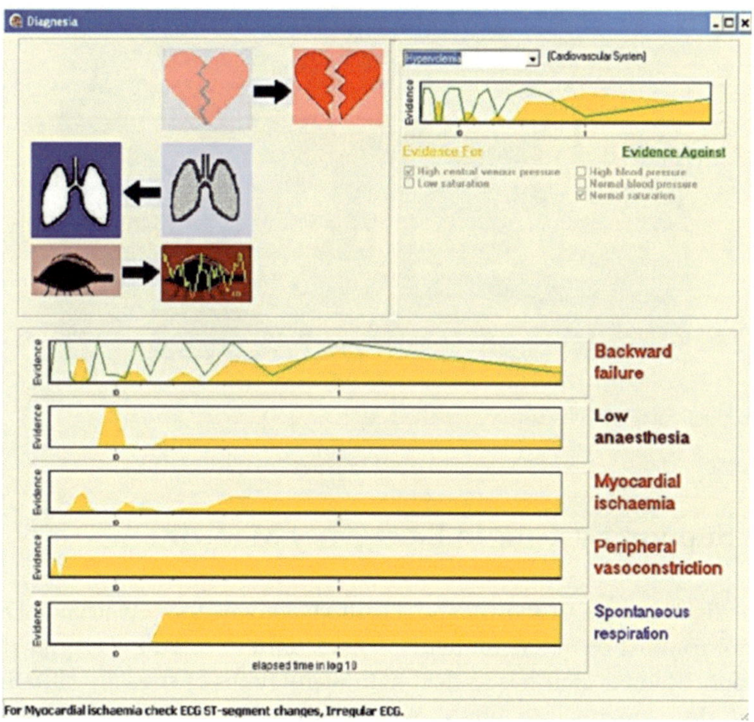

Figure 16. Graphical user interface [64].

Lastly, a hybrid system for conscious sedation (HSS) with DSS, was presented [65]. This system integrates closed loop sedation with a DSS, offering pop-up menus as smart alarms with several treatment advices for hemodynamic or respiratory adverse events, which need to be confirmed by the anesthetic team by clicking respective touch buttons on a touch screen (Figure 17).

Tested on two groups of 50 patients, the detection of critical events was significantly improved by the DSS, as shown in Table 3.

	Protocol Group (N=50)	Control Group (N=50)	P
Events not detected (%)	0	25	***<0.0001**
			#<0.000
AVG Delay (s)	7.4±4.0	32.6±21.7	**1**
Critical events/h	5.6±4.1	7.4±5.1	#0.05
MAP /h	3.2±3.1	3.7±3.6	N.S.
RR/h	4.3±3.6	3.8±4.1	N.S.
HR/h	0.9±0.5	0.7±0.3	N.S.
Sat/h	1.6±1.1	2.2±2.4	N.S.

Table 3 Comparison of detecting critical events by the time [65].

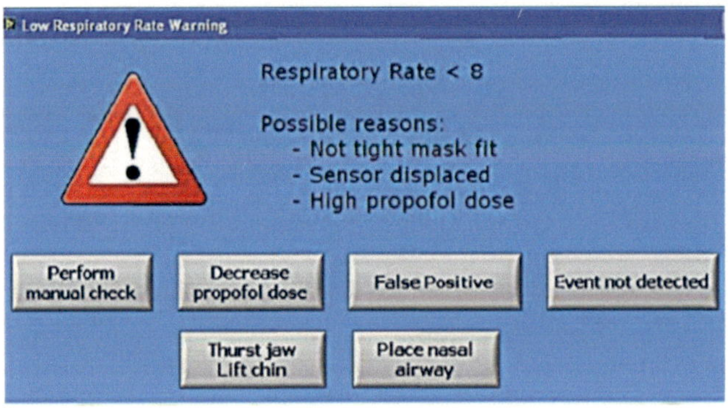

Figure 17. Pop-up menu for respiratory critical event [65].

3. Decision Support Systems in Emergency Medicine

Emergency medicine is one of the most difficult challenges for physicians. Diagnostic and therapeutic choices must be quick, immediate, even if there could be a significant inadequacy of information. Medical staff has to deal with many types of stressful situations: in-hospital emergency departments are often overcrowded [66-68], out-of-hospital emergency situations sometimes carry possible environmental risks. It is not possible to refuse care to anyone and there is also a high legal risk. All these elements can yield a huge stress load for the whole health care team [69-72]. These considerations lead to a request for decision support. There are several difficulties for designing systems for this environment and testing them. In a study of 2003, the diagnostic performance of two DSSs planned for an emergency department [73] were compared with expert decision making. Only in one third of the cases, the experts' diagnosis was within the top five diagnosis generated by the software.

We discuss further DSSs for in-hospital emergency medicine and DSSs for pre-hospital and out-of-hospital emergency medicine.

3.1. Decision support systems for in-hospital emergency medicine

Chest pain and abdominal pain represent principal causes of admission to the emergency room [74]. An example of a DSS for in-hospital emergencies is an artificial neural network designed to diagnose acute myocardial infarction [75]. It was tested in 118 patients, with a sensitivity of 92% and specificity of 96%; without the input of the electrocardiogram, the sensitivity decreased to 86%, while the specificity was 92%. In a later study, the same DSS was tested in 331 patients with anterior chest pain in emergency department [76]. Whereas sensitivity and specificity of physicians in diagnosing myocardial infarction was 77.7% and 84.7%, the DSS values were higher at 97.2% and 96.2%, respectively. This suggests that the system performed better than physicians.

A simple DSS that could be useful in emergency medicine is an artificial neural network designed to detect microembolic Doppler signals [77]; it resulted in a specificity of 56.7% and sensitivity of 73.4%, increasing to 75.9% in patients with mechanical prosthetic cardiac valves. However, this study did not test this system in emergency situations. Results about a favorable use of DSS to diagnose pulmonary embolism in emergency medicine in fact are not uniform. For example, the study of Roy et al. tried to evaluate the importance of the introduction of a computer-handled DSS in diagnosing pulmonary embolism compared with the use of paper guidelines [78]. The software yields a list of tests, specifying which of them is appropriate or inappropriate considering the pre-test probability, entered before by the physician according to the revised Geneva score; the DSS recommends as first choice the least invasive investigation among the appropriate tests. The system was compared with paper guidelines in two groups of patients, one with DSS and one without it. In the intervention group (the DSS group), there was an increase of appropriate diagnostic testing by 30.2% while in the other group it only increased by 10.9%. The DSS was used in 80% of cases during real time intervention, suggesting a good performance in the emergency environment and good acceptance by physicians. A study by Drescher evaluated the impact of the integration of a computerized DSS in a computerized physician order entry on the frequency of positive CT angiography results for pulmonary embolism and the staff's acceptability of such a DSS[79]. The DSS was designed based on a modified Wells score to give diagnostic options to physicians when ordering a CT angiography or D-dimer testing (Figure 18). Although the study showed a superior performance of the DSS rather than physicians in ordering diagnostic investigations, adherence and acceptability of the DSS were quite low. Probably, the principle reasons were the time needed to enter data and mistrust in the effectiveness of the software.

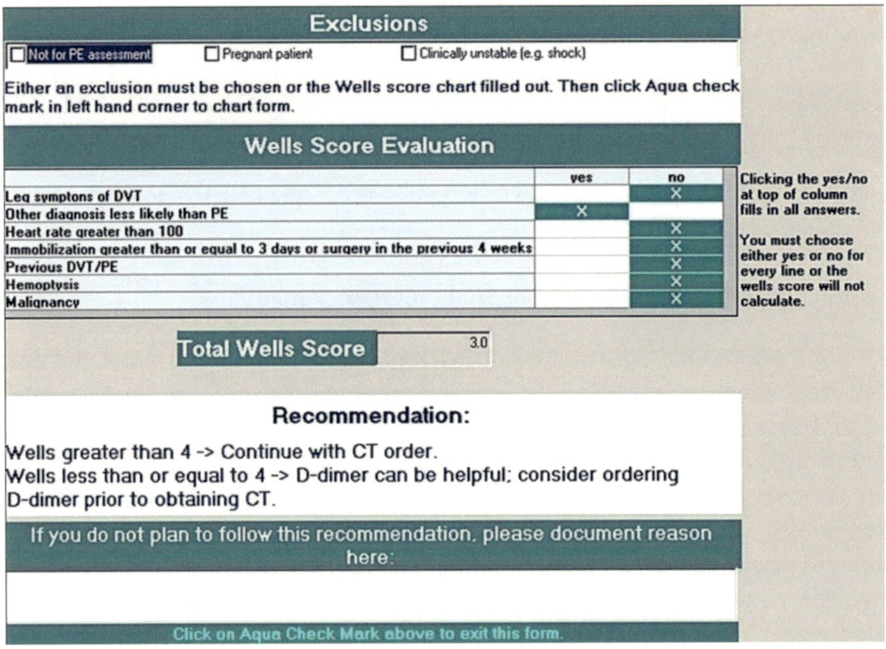

Figure 18. User interface for entering Wells criteria [79].

3.2. Decision support systems for out-of-hospital and pre-hospital emergency medicine

Decision support systems conceived for out-of hospital and pre-hospital interventions are complex systems designed for receiving and sending a multitude of inputs through a variety of platforms and different situations. These systems can interface with different signals, managing a great number of data also at distance. In his review [80], Nangalia describes five basic components of a telemedicine system: the acquisition of data through appropriate sensors; transmission of data from patient to clinician; ability to combine all data of different sources; decision support for appropriate action and response; storage of data.

One DSS used for pre-hospital emergency care is a system installed in ambulances that provides data communication, documentation, triaging and presentation of a checklist [81].

A similar pre-hospital DSS is iRevive, a system which permits rapid acquisition of data in an electronic format [82] through several components: vital sign sensors, wireless patient location and a central command center for discussing and collection of data, all linked by a network of wireless and hand-held computers. There is a combination of real-time sensor data, procedural data, and geographic data giving real-time decision support at three different hierarchical levels: at the local site, at the local command center and at the central command center, which is responsible for general coordination (Figure 19).

Another DSS for pre-hospital emergency care delivers real-time decision support during transport of trauma casualties [83]. It consists of a monitor that acquires data from patients in real-time, and a computer, that is implemented with three different types of software: the Controller software which records the data from monitor; the Shell software, which protects data by possible corruption and passes to the other software, and the Analysis software, which enables decision support. One important aim of this DSS is avoiding the loss or damage of information during the transport; this is possible by a special way of transmission of data that allows the system to know which data are not valid or missed.

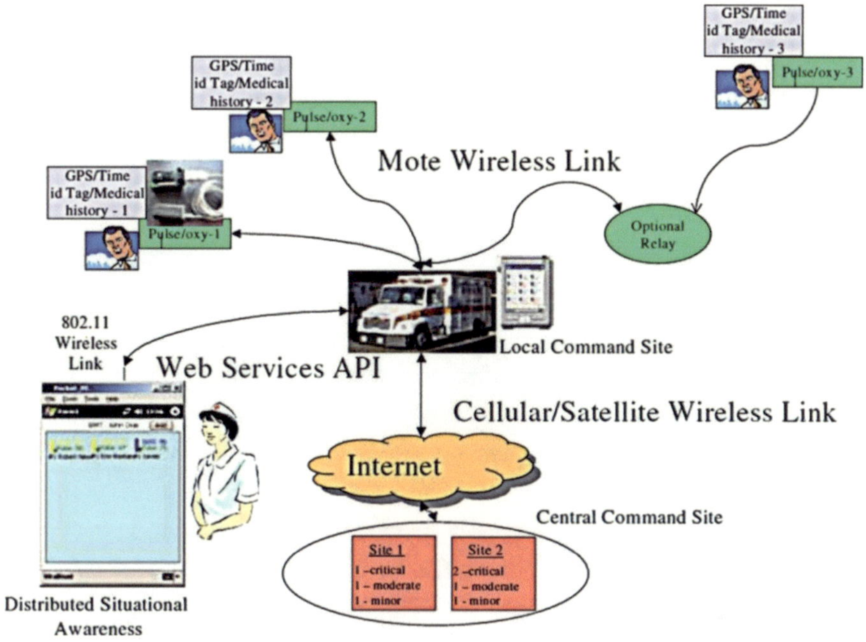

Figure 19. Basic architecture of iRevive [82].

Evaluated during a simulation of possible fault scenarios, the performance of each component was good and sufficient to prevent data corruption; decision support was considered useful.

4. Decision Support Systems for Intensive Care Unit

Intensive care medicine represents an equally challenging field for physicians. Patients are usually affected by multiple disease and need to be constantly supervised; often in a state of unconsciousness, patients cannot directly communicate with the practitioner and have to be monitored using a multitude of parameters, producing a significant amount of data. There are significant costs involved.

We will focus on general DSSs, DSSs for artificial ventilation and DSSs for infections.

4.1. General DSSs for ICU

One DSS designed to deal with general issues of intensive care medicine is ACUDES (Architecture for Intensive Care Unit Decision Support), which takes into account the evolution of the patient following her/his diseases over time and gives information about illness and concomitant signs [84]. Another general DSS for intensive care unit is RHEA [85]; like ACUDES, it collects data from patients and gets information about adverse events and nosocomial infection risk for each patient. Data are entered manually; the system launches useful messages or alerts about the therapy by prediction models.

A general DSS designed for neuro-intensive care unit is iSyNCC (intelligent System for Neuro-Critical-Care) [86]. This system collects data from patients in a continuous way and uses them to provide decision support in terms of alerts or therapeutic messages, predicting also the patients' recovery. This is possible by the integration of four modules: data acquisition module, data storage module, data transmission module and user interface (Figure 20).

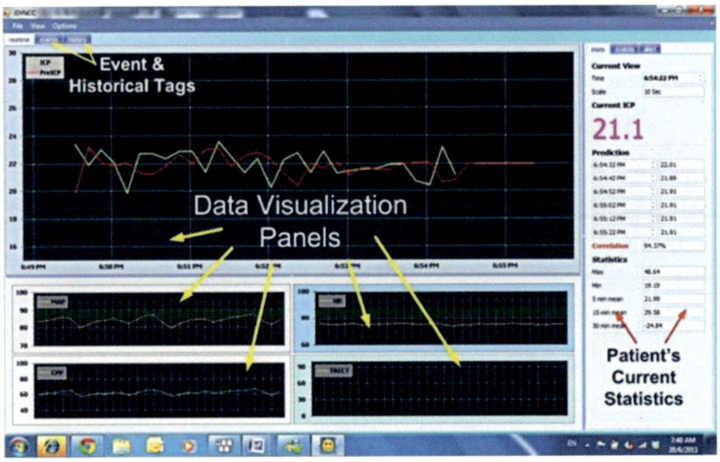

Figure 20. Graphical user interface [86].

4.2. Decision support systems for artificial ventilation

Systems for artificial ventilation have to be effective, safe and easy to use at the patient bedside. To be useful, its software must remove all noise and artifacts, processing only validate data. Ventilation requires constant monitoring, in order to ensure a timely weaning. Tehrani [87] suggests four possible barriers:

1. lack of accessibility,
2. no immunity to noise and erroneous data,
3. inadequate training for use of the systems, and
4. lack of implementation in commercial ventilators.

The acceptability of DSSs by medical staff in the ICU is quite good; in his review [88], East found that DSSs were well accepted by ICU physicians and provided good performance improving outcome.

A DSS for artificial ventilation and weaning is the knowledge-based closed-loop system SmartCare™ [89]. Based on respiratory rate, tidal volume and end-tidal CO_2, it takes a picture of the patient's present state, and using this picture, it continuously adapts the level of pressure support to maintain the patient in a respiratory comfort zone. The system contains a weaning protocol that gradually decreases the level of pressure support when patient's respiratory status improves (Figure 21). The use of the DSS resulted in more efficient weaning, with a decrease of the total duration of artificial ventilation from 12 to 7.5 days [90].

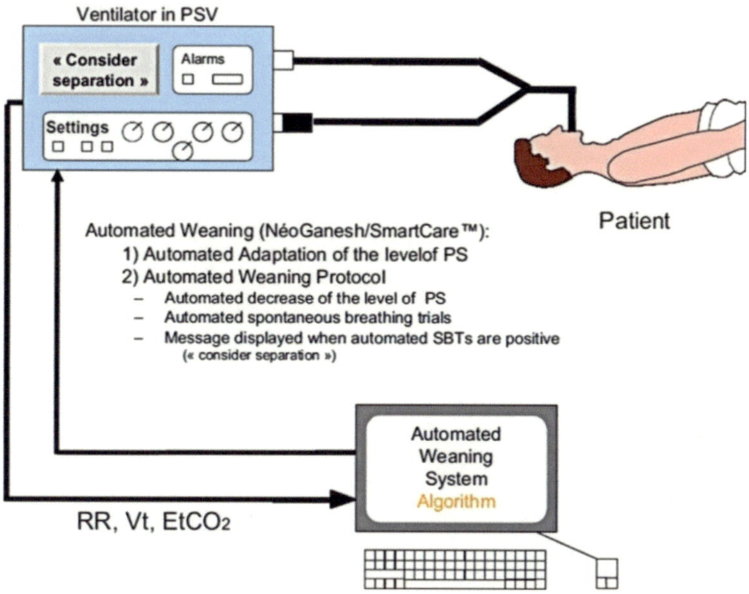

Figure 21. Working principles of NeoGanesh/SmartCare. PS, pressure support; SBT, spontaneous breathing trial [91].

Another closed-loop ventilation system is IntelliVent-ASV. The system provides automatic setting of ventilator parameters and closed-loop regulation based on the inputs of ET-CO_2, SpO_2 and FiO_2 after individualization of correct target ranges. Initial results appear interesting [92].

A hybrid knowledge-based and physiological model-based DSS is the Sheffield Intelligent Ventilator Advisor (SIVA). It gives advices and adaptive patient-specific decision support using FiO_2, PEEP, inspiratory pressure and ventilatory rate. When compared with expert decision making, appropriated decision making was obtained with the system and the control of blood gases was similar in both groups [93].

Another DSS for artificial ventilation is the INVENT project, based on physiological modelling. This system uses two software modules to process patient data to suggest specific ventilator settings. These modules are the Automatic Lung Parameters Estimator (ALPE system), that is based on a model of pulmonary gas exchange with particular attention to the oxygen transport, and the system for the arterializations of venous blood (ARTY system), integrating arterial values from venous blood. All data produced are used to send suggestions of ventilator settings based on the prediction of outcome (Figure 22).

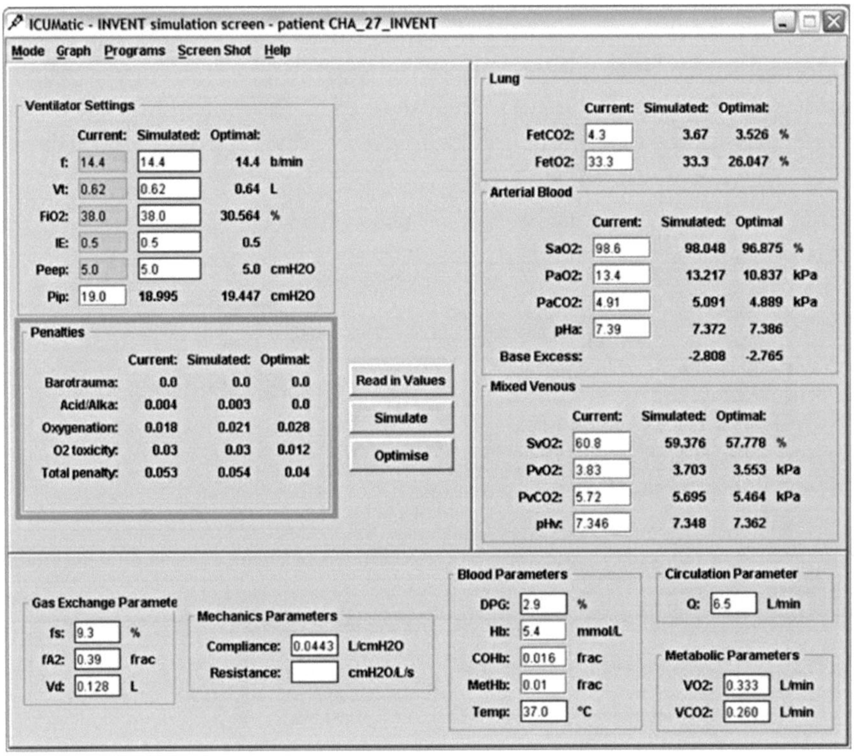

Figure 22. Graphical user interface with its 3 sections. The left side shows the ventilator settings and penalties, displayed as current, simulated and optimal. The right side displays variables of lungs, arterial and venous blood described as current, simulated and optimal value. On the bottom, patient specific parameters and related organ systems. In this illustration, data of a single post-operative cardiac patient are showed [94].

4.3. Decision support systems for infections in ICU

Infections in ICU represent 26% of nosocomial infections [95] and usually are accompanied by a high rate of serious problems like sepsis and mortality. Bacteria in the ICU are more resistant to antibiotic therapy. Patients in ICU are monitored by a variety of invasive devices; these devices can transmit germs directly. The most frequent nosocomial infections are catheter-associated urinary infections, and occur in about 35% of the cases, characterized by low mortality and costs, while bloodstream infections and respiratory ventilator-associated infections occur at about 15% of the cases, but are associated with high mortality and costs [34, 95]. For all these reasons, antimicrobial infection surveillance in ICU has to be very strict, usually more than in other hospital wards [95].

After observation of infection management in a 21-bed mixed medical/surgical adult ICU, an Australian group [96] designed a software, ADVISE, that allowed the digitalization of patient data to create appropriate antibiotic recommendations in real-time. Messages are not only strictly about therapy, but also about the general theory of the specific pathogens or other patient-related information (Figure 23). Comparison between 6 months before and 6 months after the use of this DSS revealed a better rationalization of the antibiotic use, with a reduction of 10.5% in the overall prescription of antiobiotics, mostly cephalosporin and vancomycin [97].

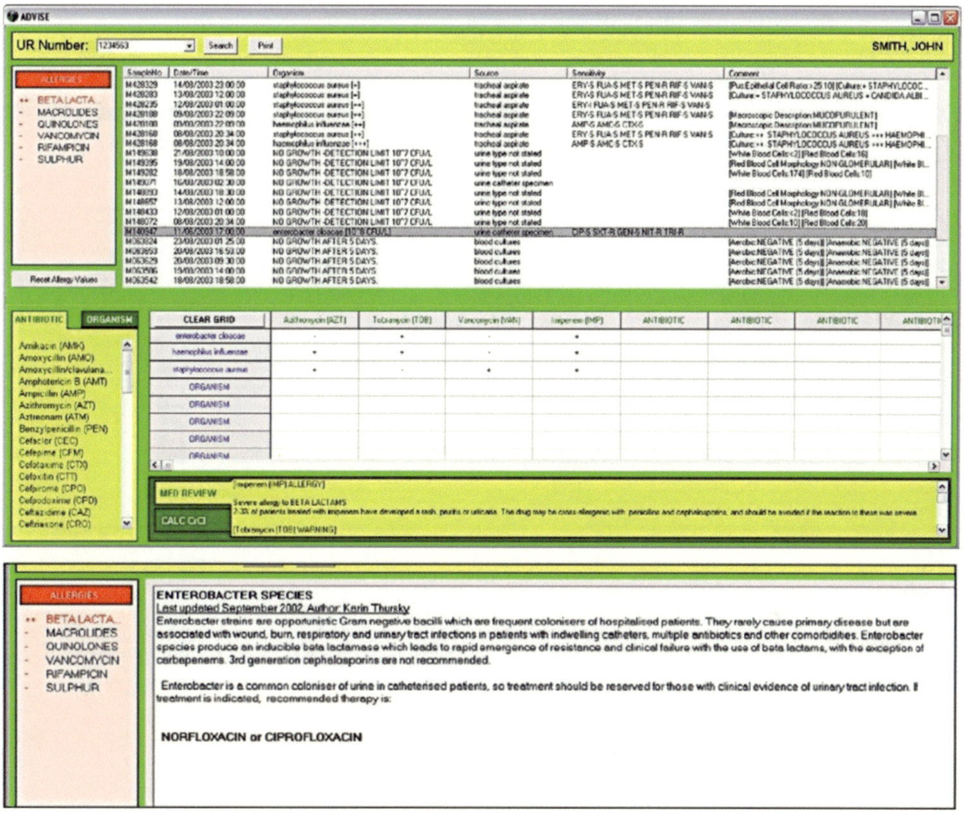

Figure 23. Screenshot of ADVISE showing with microbiology results, allergy profile, and antimicrobial/isolate matrix. It is displayed the medical review panel, alerting the user to potential allergy risks or overlapping antibiotic coverage, and the rule-based recommendation generated by clicking on the isolate in the tabular view [96].

A sepsis computer protocol was implemented in a 27-bed surgical ICU to manage sepsis [98]. International validated scores were used to make a daily assessment of outcome together with all patient data. All this material was placed in a computer protocol, with nine logical diagrams displayed individually to be used at bedside. Computer instructions had to be confirmed by the clinician before the execution of interventions. The system's performance was evaluated via the comparison with paper guidelines: the DSS improved the administration of antibiotics, supported therapeutic decision making and reduced mortality.

The COSARA research project (Computer-based Surveillance and Alerting of nosocomial infections, Antimicrobial Resistance and Antibiotic consumption in ICU) is a complex system that automatically acquires patient data and records all information about the patient's clinical history, therapy and antibiotic resistance, providing decision support through visual presentation of graphs, icons, visual bars, pop-ups and audible alerts [99]. The DSS consists of different modules, having each one the ability to manage some functions, as e.g. X-ray photos. For each antibiotic prescription, there is a pop-up menu prompting the physician to register the motivation for starting therapy (Figure 24). Clinical decision support is delivered through mail or messages based on guidelines. After 3 months of implementation, clinical outcome was improved.

Figure 24. Screenshot with infections and antibiotics history; there also graphs that represent common used values [99].

5. Discussion

Decision support systems have been successfully developed in the areas of intensive care, emergency medicine and anesthesia. These are areas with an overload of information and necessity to react quickly and adjust the reactions throughout a short time interval. More and more, DSSs are integrated in AIMS in the perioperative period. These have been successfully used to configure checklists to reduce the incidence of intraoperative problems, thus even reducing costs significantly. Decision support systems in that context can reduce the amount of laboratory investigations performed. More anesthetic specific DSSs are also being developed, allowing risk stratification for difficult intubations, better PONV prophylaxis, appropriate timing of antibiotic prophylaxis and thus reducing the incidence of wound infections. In the arena of emergency medicine, both in- and out-of-hospital DSSs have been created and successfully tested. They range from systems to help identify microemboli or pulmonary embolism, to systems to help coordinating the pre-hospital logistics. Some of these systems are met with skepticism by physicians because they fear of handing over decision making to these systems. In ICU units, DSSs can help with the setup of artificial ventilation and significantly reduce infections: this is specifically important in the complex decision making and establishment of appropriate treatment options in patients suffering from sepsis.

6. Conclusion

Decision support systems are useful tools in modern medicine. They can improve clinical practice, adherence to best evidence based medicine and, in some cases, clinical and health education and patients outcomes.

In the operating room, DSSs can be effective to deal with a variety of problems. In emergency medicine, they have shown good performance, but their acceptability by clinicians has not been sufficient. Decision support systems in intensive care medicine allow the possibility to manage a large number of data whilst allowing the clinician to follow them in a more efficient way. However, a widespread use of these systems is obstructed by economical and cultural barriers; a greater involvement of the medical users in the design of the systems, including better user interfaces, could improve their clinical acceptance. DSSs are software designed to assist the physician but are not a substitutes of this figure.

Key messages

1. Decision support systems improve quality of practice and patient safety.
2. There is an increased development of DSSs in any medical field, specifically in the area of critical care medicine.
3. Despite the increasing request, cultural and economical barriers obstruct the diffusion of these systems.

Author details

Thomas M. Hemmerling[1*], Fabrizio Cirillo[3] and Shantale Cyr[2]

*Address all correspondence to: thomas.hemmerling@mcgill.ca

1 Dept. of Anesthesia, McGill University & Institute of Biomedical Engineering, University of Montreal, Montreal, Canada

2 Dept. of Anesthesia, McGill University

3 Dept. of Anesthesia, University of Naples, Italy

References

[1] Hemmerling, T. M. (2011). *Decision Support Systems in Anesthesia, Emergency Medicine and Intensive Care Medicine, in Practice and Challenges in Biomedical Related Domain, J.S. C., Editor*, InTech, 239-260.

[2] Bates, D. W., & Gawande, A. A. (2003). Improving Safety with Information Technology. *New England Journal of Medicine*, 348(25), 2526-2534.

[3] Miller, R. A. (1994). Medical diagnostic decision support systems--past, present, and future: a threaded bibliography and brief commentary. *J Am Med Inform Assoc*, 1(1), 8-27.

[4] de Dombal, F. T., Hartley, J. R., & Sleeman, D. H. (1969). A computer-assisted system for learning clinical diagnosis. *Lancet*, 145-148.

[5] Peleg, M., & Tu, S. (2006). Decision support, knowledge representation and management in medicine. *Yearb Med Inform*, 72-80.

[6] Dunsmuir, D., et al. (2008). A knowledge authoring tool for clinical decision support. *J Clin Monit Comput*, 22(3), 189-198.

[7] Hawamdeh, Z. M., et al. (2012). Development of a decision support system to predict physicians' rehabilitation protocols for patients with knee osteoarthritis. *Int J Rehabil Res*.

[8] Su, C. T., et al. (2012). Prediagnosis of Obstructive Sleep Apnea via Multiclass MTS. *Comput Math Methods Med*, 212498.

[9] Shelton, R. C., & Trivedi, M. H. (2011). Using algorithms and computerized decision support systems to treat major depression. *J Clin Psychiatry*, 72(12), e36.

[10] Ebell, M. H., et al. (2012). Development and validation of a clinical decision rule for the diagnosis of influenza. *J Am Board Fam Med*, 25(1), 55-62.

[11] Legros, B., et al. (2012). Development of an electronic decision tool to support appropriate treatment choice in adult patients with epilepsy--Epi-Scope((R)). *Seizure*, 21(1), 32-39.

[12] Van Belle, V. M., et al. (2012). A mathematical model for interpretable clinical decision support with applications in gynecology. *PLoS One*, 7(3), e34312.

[13] Garg, A. X., et al. (2005). Effects of computerized clinical decision support systems on practitioner performance and patient outcomes: a systematic review. *JAMA*, 293(10), 1223-1238.

[14] Kawamoto, K., et al. (2005). Improving clinical practice using clinical decision support systems: a systematic review of trials to identify features critical to success. *BMJ*, 330(7494), 765.

[15] Pearson, S. A., et al. (2009). Do computerised clinical decision support systems for prescribing change practice? A systematic review of the literature (1990-2007). *BMC Health Serv Res*, 9, 154.

[16] Kooij, F. O., et al. (2008). Decision support increases guideline adherence for prescribing postoperative nausea and vomiting prophylaxis. *Anesth Analg*, 106(3), 893-898, table of contents.

[17] Hunt, D. L., et al. (1998). Effects of computer-based clinical decision support systems on physician performance and patient outcomes: a systematic review. *JAMA*, 280(15), 1339-1346.

[18] Bates, D. W., et al. (2001). Reducing the frequency of errors in medicine using information technology. *J Am Med Inform Assoc*, 8(4), 299-308.

[19] Glavin, R. J. (2009). Excellence in anesthesiology: the role of nontechnical skills. *Anesthesiology*, 110(2), 201-203.

[20] Seim, A. R., & Sandberg, W. S. (2010). Shaping the operating room and perioperative systems of the future: innovating for improved competitiveness. *Curr Opin Anaesthesiol*, 23(6), 765-771.

[21] Hemmerling, T. M. (2009). Automated anesthesia. *Curr Opin Anaesthesiol*, 22(6), 757-763.

[22] Mort, M, et al. (2005). Safe asleep? Human-machine relations in medical practice. *Soc Sci Med*, 61(9), 2027-2037.

[23] Reason, J. (2005). Safety in the operating theatre- Part 2: human error and organisational failure. *Qual Saf Health Care*, 14(1), 56-60.

[24] Sawa, T., & Ohno-Machado, L. (2001). Generation of dynamically configured check lists for intra-operative problems using a set of covering algorithms. *Proceedings / AMIA... Annual Symposium*, 593-597.

[25] Finegan, B., et al. (2005). Selective ordering of preoperative investigations by anesthesiologists reduces the number and cost of tests. *Canadian Journal of Anesthesia / Journal canadien d'anesthésie*, 52(6), 575-580.

[26] Flamm, M., et al. (2011). Non-adherence to guidelines for preoperative testing in a secondary care hospital in Austria: the economic impact of unnecessary and double testing. *Eur J Anaesthesiol*, 28(12), 867-873.

[27] Tisavipat, S., & Suesaowaluk, P. (2011). Development of an automated decision system for selection of preoperative investigations based on cartesian product and gaussian distribution, in Information Reuse and Integration (IRI). *IEEE International Conference on*, 502-503.

[28] Gannon, K. (1991). Mortality associated with anaesthesia. A case review study. *Anaesthesia*, 46(11), 962-966.

[29] Braz, L. G., et al. (2009). Mortality in anesthesia: a systematic review. *Clinics (Sao Paulo*, 64(10), 999-1006.

[30] Yan, Q., et al. (2009). SVM-based decision support system for clinic aided tracheal intubation predication with multiple features. *Expert Systems with Applications*, 6588-6592.

[31] Chau, A., & Ehrenfeld, J. M. (2011). Using real-time clinical decision support to improve performance on perioperative quality and process measures. *Anesthesiol Clin*, 29(1), 57-69.

[32] Wanderer, J. P., Sandberg, W. S., & Ehrenfeld, J. M. (2011). Real-time alerts and reminders using information systems. *Anesthesiol Clin*, 29(3), 389-396.

[33] Kooij, F. O., et al. (2012). Automated reminders decrease postoperative nausea and vomiting incidence in a general surgical population. *Br J Anaesth*.

[34] Burke, J. P. (2003). Infection control- a problem for patient safety. *N Engl J Med*, 348(7), 651-656.

[35] Leape, L. L., et al. (1991). The nature of adverse events in hospitalized patients Results of the Harvard Medical Practice Study II. *N Engl J Med*, 324(6), 377-384.

[36] Auerbach, A. D. (2001). Prevention of surgical site infections. *Making Health Care Safer: A Critical Analysis of Patient Safety Practices*, 221.

[37] Kirkland, K. B., et al. (1999). The impact of surgical-site infections in the 1990s: attributable mortality, excess length of hospitalization, and extra costs. *Infect Control Hosp Epidemiol*, 20(11), 725-730.

[38] Gyssens, I. C. (1999). Preventing postoperative infections: current treatment recommendations. *Drugs*, 57(2), 175-185.

[39] Dellinger, E. P. (2007). Prophylactic antibiotics: administration and timing before operation are more important than administration after operation. *Clin Infect Dis*, 44(7), 928-930.

[40] O'Reilly, M., et al. (2006). An anesthesia information system designed to provide physician-specific feedback improves timely administration of prophylactic antibiotics. *Anesth Analg*, 103(4), 908-912.

[41] Nair, B. G., et al. (2010). Feedback mechanisms including real-time electronic alerts to achieve near 100% timely prophylactic antibiotic administration in surgical cases. *Anesth Analg*, 111(5), 1293-1300.

[42] Nair, B. G., et al. (2011). Automated electronic reminders to improve redosing of antibiotics during surgical cases: comparison of two approaches. *Surg Infect (Larchmt)*, 12(1), 57-63.

[43] Gordon, S. M. (2006). Antibiotic prophylaxis against postoperative wound infections. *Cleve Clin J Med*, 73(1), S42-S45.

[44] Steinberg, J. P., et al. (2009). Timing of antimicrobial prophylaxis and the risk of surgical site infections: results from the Trial to Reduce Antimicrobial Prophylaxis Errors. *Ann Surg*, 250(1), 10-16.

[45] Eden, A., et al. (2009). The impact of an electronic reminder on the use of alarms after separation from cardiopulmonary bypass. *Anesth Analg*, 108(4), 1203-1208.

[46] Krol, M., & Reich, D. L. (2000). Development of a decision support system to assist anesthesiologists in operating room. *J Med Syst*, 24(3), 141-146.

[47] Mashour, G. A., et al. (2009). A novel electronic algorithm for detecting potentially insufficient anesthesia: implications for the prevention of intraoperative awareness. *J Clin Monit Comput*, 23(5), 273-277.

[48] Hooper, B., et al. (1997). A fuzzy logic based decision support system for low-flow closed-loop anaesthesia, in Fuzzy Systems. *Proceedings of the Sixth IEEE International Conference on*, 1615-1620, 3.

[49] Mirza, M., Gholamhosseini, H., & Harrison, M. J. (2010). A fuzzy logic-based system for anaesthesia monitoring. *Conf Proc IEEE Eng Med Biol Soc*, 3974-3977.

[50] Baig, M. M., et al. (2011). Detection and classification of hypovolaemia during anaesthesia, in Engineering in Medicine and Biology Society, EMBC. *Annual International Conference of the IEEE*, 357-360, 1557-170X.

[51] Lowe, A. (1999). *Evidential Inference for Fault Diagnosis, in Mechanical Engineering*, University of Auckland, Auckland.

[52] Lowe, A., Harrison, M. J., & Jones, R. W. (1999). Diagnostic monitoring in anaesthesia using fuzzy trend templates for matching temporal patterns. *Artif Intell Med*, 16(2), 183-199.

[53] Rosenberg, H., et al. (2007). Malignant hyperthermia. *Orphanet J Rare Dis*, 2, 21.

[54] Lowe, A., & Harrison, M. J. (1999). Computer-enhanced diagnosis of malignant hyperpyrexia. *Anaesth Intensive Care*, 27(1), 41-44.

[55] Lowe, A., Jones, R. W., & Harrison, M. J. (2001). The graphical presentation of decision support information in an intelligent anaesthesia monitor. *Artif Intell Med*, 22(2), 173-191.

[56] Gohil, B., et al. (2007). Intelligent monitoring of critical pathological events during anesthesia. *Conf Proc IEEE Eng Med Biol Soc*, 4343-4346.

[57] Lai, H. Y., et al. (2004). Effect of esmolol on positive-pressure ventilation-induced variations of arterial pressure in anaesthetized humans. *Clin Sci (Lond)*, 107(3), 303-308.

[58] Ken, Lee. K. J. T. Y., Plimmer, B., & Harrison, M. (2008). Real-time Anaesthesia Diagnosis Display System with Multi-Modal Alarms.

[59] Lee, K., et al. (2008). Real-time anaesthesia diagnosis display system with multi-modal alarms. *ACM*.

[60] Parkin, W. G., & Leaning, M. S. (2008). Therapeutic control of the circulation. *J Clin Monit Comput*, 22(6), 391-400.

[61] Sondergaard, S., et al. (2012). High concordance between expert anaesthetists' actions and advice of decision support system in achieving oxygen delivery targets in high-risk surgery patients. *Br J Anaesth*.

[62] Pellegrino, V. A., et al. (2011). Computer based haemodynamic guidance system is effective and safe in management of postoperative cardiac surgery patients. *Anaesth Intensive Care*, 39(2), 191-201.

[63] Kizito, J. (2008). Diagnesia: A Prototype of a Decision Support System for Anesthetists, in Broadband Communications, Information Technology & Biomedical Applications. *Third International Conference on*, 12-19.

[64] Kizito, J. (2009). *Decision Support in the Operating Theatre- Usability Aspects, in Strenghtening the Role of ICT in Development, J.M.L. Kizza, K., Nath, R., Aisbett, J., Vir, P., Editor,* Fountain Publishers, Kampala, 109-117.

[65] Hemmerling, T. M., Arbeid, E., & Tang, L. (2011). HSS'- A Novel Hybrid System for Conscious Sedation. *in Annual Conference of Society of Technology in Anesthesia: Las Vegas*, 34.

[66] Mc Cabe, J. B. (2001). Emergency department overcrowding: a national crisis. *Acad Med*, 76(7), 672-674.

[67] Derlet, R. W., & Richards, J. R. (2000). Overcrowding in the nation's emergency departments: Complex causes and disturbing effects. *Ann Emerg Med*, 35(1), 63-68.

[68] Olshaker, J. S., & Rathlev, N. K. (2006). Emergency Department overcrowding and ambulance diversion: the impact and potential solutions of extended boarding of admitted patients in the Emergency Department. *J Emerg Med*, 30(3), 351-356.

[69] Kuhn, G., Goldberg, R., & Compton, S. (2009). Tolerance for uncertainty, burnout, and satisfaction with the career of emergency medicine. *Ann Emerg Med*, 54(1), 106-113 e6.

[70] Popa, F., et al. (2010). Occupational burnout levels in emergency medicine--a nationwide study and analysis. *J Med Life*, 3(3), 207-215.

[71] Healy, S., & Tyrrell, M. (2011). Stress in emergency departments: experiences of nurses and doctors. *Emerg Nurse*, 19(4), 31-37.

[72] Schmitz, G. R., et al. (2012). Strategies for coping with stress in emergency medicine: Early education is vital. *J Emerg Trauma Shock*, 5(1), 64-69.

[73] Graber, M. A., & Van Scoy, D. (2003). How well does decision support software perform in the emergency department? *Emerg Med J*, 20(5), 426-428.

[74] Niska, R., Bhuiya, F., & Xu, J. (2007). National Hospital Ambulatory Medical Care Survey: emergency department summary. *Natl Health Stat Report*, 2010(26), 1-31.

[75] Baxt, W. G. (1990). Use of an Artificial Neural Network for Data Analysis in Clinical Decision-Making: The Diagnosis of Acute Coronary Occlusion. *Neural Computation*, 2(4), 480-489.

[76] Baxt, W. G. (1991). Use of an Artificial Neural Network for the Diagnosis of Myocardial Infarction. *Ann Intern Med*, 115(11), 843-848.

[77] Kemeny, V., et al. (1999). Automatic embolus detection by a neural network. *Stroke*, 30(4), 807-810.

[78] Roy, P. M., et al. (2009). A computerized handheld decision-support system to improve pulmonary embolism diagnosis: a randomized trial. *Ann Intern Med*, 151(10), 677-686.

[79] Drescher, F. S., et al. (2011). Effectiveness and acceptability of a computerized decision support system using modified Wells criteria for evaluation of suspected pulmonary embolism. *Ann Emerg Med*, 57(6), 613-621.

[80] Nangalia, V., Prytherch, D. R., & Smith, G. B. (2010). Health technology assessment review: remote monitoring of vital signs--current status and future challenges. *Crit Care*, 14(5), 233.

[81] Karlsten, R., & Sjoqvist, B. A. (2000). Telemedicine and decision support in emergency ambulances in Uppsala. *J Telemed Telecare*, 6(1), 1-7.

[82] Gaynor, M., et al. (2005). A dynamic, data-driven, decision support system for emergency medical services. *Computational Science-ICCS*, 61-100.

[83] Khitrov, M. Y., et al. (2009). A platform for testing and comparing of real-time decision-support algorithms in mobile environments. Conference Proceedings. *Annual International Conference of the IEEE Engineering in Medicine & Biology Society*, 3417-3420.

[84] Palma, J., et al. (2002). ACUDES: architecture for intensive care units decision support. in Engineering in Medicine and Biology. *24th Annual Conference and the Annual Fall Meeting of the Biomedical Engineering Society EMBS/BMES Conference, Proceedings of the Second Joint.*

[85] Metais, E., Nakache, D., & Timsit, J. F. (2006). Rhea: A Decision Support System for Intensive Care Units. *4th International Multiconference on Computer Science and Information Technology CSIT*, 5-7.

[86] Feng, M., et al. (2011). iSyNCC: an intelligent system for patient monitoring & clinical decision support in Neuro-Critical-Care. *Conf Proc IEEE Eng Med Biol Soc*, 6426-6429.

[87] Tehrani, F. T., & Roum, J. H. (2008). Intelligent decision support systems for mechanical ventilation. *Artif Intell Med*, 44(3), 171-182.

[88] East, T. D., et al. (1999). Efficacy of computerized decision support for mechanical ventilation: results of a prospective multi-center randomized trial. *Proc AMIA Symp*, 251-255.

[89] Dojat, M., et al. (1992). A knowledge-based system for assisted ventilation of patients in intensive care units. *Int J Clin Monit Comput*, 9(4), 239-250.

[90] Lellouche, F., et al. (2006). A multicenter randomized trial of computer-driven protocolized weaning from mechanical ventilation. *Am J Respir Crit Care Med*, 174(8), 894-900.

[91] Lellouche, F., & Brochard, L. (2009). Advanced closed loops during mechanical ventilation (PAV, NAVA, ASV, SmartCare). *Best Practice & Research Clinical Anaesthesiology*, 23(1), 81-93.

[92] Arnal, J. M., et al. (2012). Safety and efficacy of a fully closed-loop control ventilation (IntelliVent-ASV((R))) in sedated ICU patients with acute respiratory failure: a prospective randomized crossover study. *Intensive Care Med*, 38(5), 781-787.

[93] Kwok, H. F., et al. (2004). SIVA: a hybrid knowledge-and-model-based advisory system for intensive care ventilators. *IEEE Trans Inf Technol Biomed*, 8(2), 161-172.

[94] Rees, S. E., et al. (2006). Using physiological models and decision theory for selecting appropriate ventilator settings. *J Clin Monit Comput*, 20(6), 421-429.

[95] Wenzel, R. P., et al. (1983). Hospital-acquired infections in intensive care unit patients: an overview with emphasis on epidemics. *Infect Control*, 4(5), 371-375.

[96] Thursky, K. A., & Mahemoff, M. (2007). User-centered design techniques for a computerised antibiotic decision support system in an intensive care unit. *Int J Med Inform*, 76(10), 760-768.

[97] Thursky, K. A., et al. (2006). Reduction of broad-spectrum antibiotic use with computerized decision support in an intensive care unit. *Int J Qual Health Care,* 18(3), 224-231.

[98] Mc Kinley, B. A., et al. (2011). Computer protocol facilitates evidence-based care of sepsis in the surgical intensive care unit. *J Trauma,* 70(5), 1153-1166, discussion 1166-7.

[99] Steurbaut, K., et al. (2012). COSARA: Integrated Service Platform for Infection Surveillance and Antibiotic Management in the ICU. *J Med Syst.*

Chapter 3

Reliability and Evaluation of Identification Models Exemplified by a Histological Diagnosis Model

L.W.D. van Raamsdonk, S. van der Vange,
M. Uiterwijk and M. J. Groot

Additional information is available at the end of the chapter

http://dx.doi.org/10.5772/51362

1. Introduction

Expert systems, or more precise decision support systems, are valuable tools for structuring the results of scientific research and to translate this to knowledge. The decision support system Determinator is now used for several years as a platform for models to identify subjects [1, 2]. The system is based on the two main different procedures for identification [3, 4]; a single access key (tree) and a free access key (matrix). The latter option provides the possibility to calculate the match between the subject as chosen by the user and the objects as included in the data model, based on a range of characteristics. In addition, a matrix allows to make selections, to filter the set of available objects and to compare two objects for their variability.

Datamodels for Determinator can be constructed using a Developer, which is part of the entire Determinator platform. Besides defining the objects (descriptions, illustrations and labels), the characteristics, and the connection between them (the matrix), the Developer also allows to evaluate the structure of the data model. Several parameters and metadata for the evaluation of a data model are part of the Developer.

This chapter provides the logic basis for the Determinator platform and introduces the background and calculation of four different parameters for the evaluation of data models: the coverage of variability space of the total data model or of a single object, the redundancy in a data model, and the capability to distinguish between different objects. The way in which these parameters are developed and applied will be demonstrated using a real case concerning the diagnosis of illegal hormone treatment of veal calves [5, 6]. The applicability of the parameters will be discussed and the development of a specific case (histological diagnosis) in a general platform (Determinator) will be evaluated.

2. Material and methods

Conventions

A datamodel developed in the framework of the DSS Determinator includes the following tables:

- List of features, with image file names and descriptions,
- Groups of features, with names and descriptions,
- List of targets, with image file names, descriptions and labels,
- Match table, with the feature on the rows and the targets on the columns,
- Tree information per node, with descriptions and image file names.

A data model consists of n features (denoted by i, j) to describe m objects (targets in the terminology of Determinator, denoted by p, q, r, s). Every feature consists of two or more feature states (k, l, and K for composite features). The basic principles are defined using first order logic [4, 7].

2.1. Logic basis

Free access key

Every cell in the matrix *Target x Features* contains a decision rule. These decision rules describe the logical relationship between the feature states and the targets, by specifying valid feature states for each target. A feature state can apply to one or more targets which imply that there might be no unique relation:

$$F_{i,k} \Rightarrow \{T_p \vee \cdots \vee T_s\} \tag{1}$$

with $F_{i,k}$ as feature state k of the ith feature, and T_p ... T_s as a series of targets which can be assigned individually. Otherwise, applying more specific feature states can limit the choice of targets:

$$F_{i,k} \wedge F_{j,l} \Rightarrow T_p \tag{2}$$

with $F_{i,k}$ as feature state k of the ith feature, $F_{j,l}$ as feature state l of the jth feature, and T_p as target.

The use of different states of a feature can add to the separation capability of that feature. Assuming three feature states:

$$\{(F_{i,1} \vee F_{i,2} \Rightarrow p) \wedge (F_{i,2} \vee F_{i,3} \Rightarrow q)\} \Rightarrow (F_{i,2} \Rightarrow p \vee q) \tag{3}$$

In this logic distribution, feature state $F_{i,1}$ identifies exclusively target *p*, and feature state $F_{i,3}$ identifies exclusively target *q*, but feature state $F_{i,2}$ can either identify target *p* or target *q*. This dual relationship can be indicated as *overlap* in a Venn diagram.

The DSS Determinator allows the user to choose a subject for identification and to answer a range of questions denoting the *n* features available in the model. Every possible answer represents a certain feature state *k*. The match between the chosen subject (represented by the answers given) and a target *p* is calculated by summing up all the true relationships between the chosen feature states $F_{i,k}$ and the defined target *p*:

$$\sum_{i=1}^{n} ([F_{i,k} \Rightarrow T_p]^* W_i) \tag{4}$$

with W_i as weighting factor for feature *i*. The sums for all targets are represented as *Match percentages* in the output of the system and listed in descending order.

Single access key

A typical dichotomous tree consists of nodes (lemmas), which can point to either two targets (leaves), two nodes (branches) or combination of the two. Basically, every lemma in a tree is based on the decision rule:

$$F_{i,\mathrm{K}} \Rightarrow P(x), \quad \neg F_{i,\mathrm{K}} \Rightarrow \neg P(x) \tag{5}$$

The functions *P(x)* and *¬P(x)* can describe a target or a further node. The structure of a dichotomous key can be defined as:

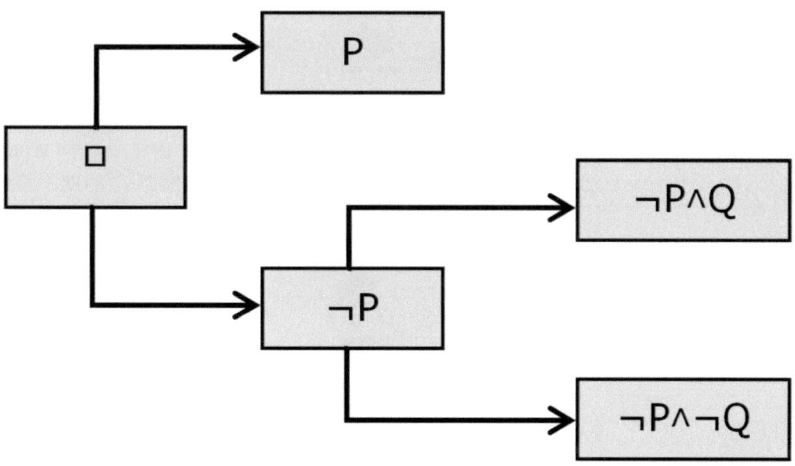

Figure 1. A hypothetical tree with two features indicated by the functions P and Q and three targets.

The combined feature state $F_{i,K}$ can combine more than one simple state, e.g. k and l. Determinator allows to construct a tree in which a node can point to a node in another part of the tree, and more than one node can point to a defined target T_p .

2.2. Quality parameters

The following parameters for validation of data models are being developed and evaluated in the framework of this paper.

Redundancy

Overlap between the areas of two targets exists when a variability range for target p overlap with the variability range for target q for the same feature (see figure 2, targets B and C; equation (3)). The overlap between the area of target p and of target q is the sum of the overlap regions for all features. Assuming the set of feature states that apply to target p as $\{F_{i,pmin}, F_{i,pmax}\}$ and the set of feature states that apply to target q as $\{F_{i,qmin}, F_{i,qmax}\}$, then:

$F_{i,a}$ = smallest $\{F_{i,pmax}, F_{i,qmax}\}$ (upper limit of the overlap region)

$F_{i,b}$ = largest $\{F_{i,pmin}, F_{i,qmin}\}$ (lower limit of the overlap region)

min_i = smallest $\{F_{i,pmin}, F_{i,qmin}\}$ (lower limit of the feature state range of both targets)

max_i = largest $\{F_{i,pmax}, F_{i,qmax}\}$ (upper limit of the feature state range of both targets)

Overlap per feature:

$$r_{i,p,q} = \frac{F_{i,p} - F_{i,q} + 1}{max_i - min_i + 1}; r_{i,p,q} \geq 0 \tag{6}$$

Average overlap for all feature differences between two targets p and q:

$$R_{p,q} = \left(\sum_{i=1}^{n} \frac{F_{i,p} - F_{i,q} + 1}{max_i - min_i + 1} \right) \Big/ n \tag{7}$$

The average redundancy of the total data model is the averaged overlap of every combination between two targets p and q. There are $(m * (m - 1)) / 2$ different combinations of targets.

Average redundancy:

$$R_{tot} = \left(\sum_{p=1}^{m} \left(\sum_{q=1}^{p-1} R_{p,q} \right) \right) \Big/ \frac{m*(m-1)}{2} * 100 \tag{8}$$

The smaller the average redundancy, the smaller the chance that a certain range of feature states of a chosen subject will result in two or more match percentages of 100 % (according to (4); see object 3 in Figure 2). Redundancy is related to the correlation coefficients among features.

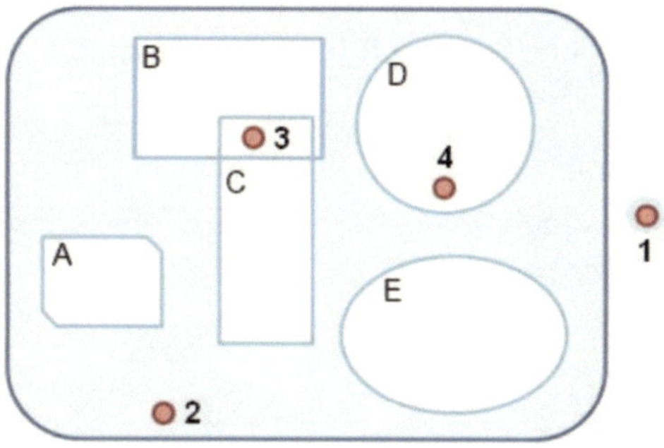

Figure 2. A hypothetical variation space with five targets A-E and four user chosen subjects. 1: subject outside the total variation space of the data model, a 100% match is impossible; 2: subject inside the total variation space of the data model, but without fit with one of the targets, a 100% match will not occur; 3: subject in the overlap of the variation of two or more targets, two or more 100% matches will result; 4: subject in one and only one variation space of a target, one 100% match will be found.

Uniqueness

The capability to distinguish between two targets p and q depends on the presence of at least one feature with unique variability ranges for each of the two targets. If overlapping regions exist for all features, there is at least a possibility to have a set of features states, describing a chosen subject, which shows a full match with more than one target. So, two targets p and q can uniquely be differentiated if and only if a feature i exists for which no state identifies target p as well target q:

$$U_{p,q} \Leftrightarrow \exists\, i : P(\forall\, k : Q(F_{i,k} \Rightarrow T_p \wedge F_{i,k} \nRightarrow T_q)) \tag{9}$$

This can be rewritten as:

$$U_{p,q} \Leftrightarrow \exists\, i : P(r_{i,p,q} = 0) \tag{9b}$$

with: $U_{p,q}$= TRUE: the two targets p and q have at least for one feature i non-overlapping feature ranges; there is at least one value $r_{i,p,q}$ equalling zero (equation (6)), and there is at least one feature indicated red in the menu option Compare of Determinator.

$U_{p,q}$= FALSE: the two targets p and q have overlapping ranges for all features; there is no value $r_{i,p,q}$ equalling zero (equation (6)), and there is no feature indicated red in the menu option Compare of Determinator.

If the distinction between two targets is based on only one feature i with a value $r_{i,p,q}$ equaling zero (no overlap), then the distinction could be considered as weak. Targets A, C and E in Figure 2 can be distinguished along the X-axis, targets A and B, and targets D and E can be distinguished along the Y-axis, whereas targets B and C can neither be distinguished along the X-axis nor the Y-axis. If the group with the distinctive feature is disabled, Determinator could give for more than one target a full match in a query.

Separation capability

A data model can identify uniquely every target if and only if every combination between two targets p and q can be described with $U_{p,q}$ = TRUE:

$$D_{tot} = \left(\sum_{p=1}^{m} \left(\sum_{q=1}^{p-1} U_{p,q} = TRUE \right) \right) \Big/ \frac{m*(m-1)}{2} * 100 \qquad (10)$$

A datamodel can be indicated as suboptimal or not valid when the differentiation coefficient D_{tot} is less than 100%. Whether or not a data model could be validated with a value for D_{tot} lower than 100 % depends on the intention to have non-distinguishable targets (synonyms) present in the model or not.

Coverage of variability space

Every target possesses a part of the n-dimensional space defined by the data model. The share of a target in the total space is calculated as:

Coverage of space of a single target p:

$$o_p = \left(\prod_{i=1}^{n} (s_{i,p} / t_i) \right) * 100 \qquad (11)$$

with:

$s_{i,p} = F_{i,pmax} - F_{i,pmax} + 1$

$t_i = F_{i,max} - F_{i,min} + 1$

In the situation of D_{tot} equalling 100 %, the sum of all individual target coverages is an indication of the total coverage of the variability space:

$$O_{tot} = \sum_{p=1}^{m} o_p \; ; \; D_{tot} = 100\% \qquad (12)$$

The larger the coverage of the total variability space, the smaller the chance that a certain range of values of a subject will result in no match percentage of 100 % (according to (4)). In the situation that D_{tot} is smaller than 100% an overestimation occurs.

The diagnosis for illegal growth hormone use in veal calves will be used as illustration of model development and performance testing.

3. Model development and application

The use of illegal growth promoters is, although prohibited in the European Union, still part of current practice in animal farming. Reasonable monitoring of the hormones is hampered by the fact that the hormone or hormone cocktail is metabolised or excreted within a period of a few weeks. The effects of the use of hormones, however, can be seen in histological stained sections of either the prostate (male calves) or gland of Bartholin (female calves) with different staining techniques. The monitoring by means of histological examinations appears to be an important instrument in maintaining legislation for food safety and animal health [5, 6]. The interpretation of histological disorders needs a high level of expertise. An expert model has been developed in the framework of the DSS Determinator, in order to support the user to identify the extent of hormone treatment of veal calves. The different quality parameters will be illustrated after a further presentation of the model.

The data model consists of 13 features to identify a treatment level indicated as "normal", "suspect" or "positive". The features are presented in Table 1, and some of them are illustrated in Figure 3.

Group	Number	Feature	States
I	1	Presence of metaplasia (male)	[none,mild,severe]
II	2	Ratio between ducts and glandular tissue	[normal,more_ducts,mainly_ducts]
II	3	Presence of metaplasia (female)	[none,mild,severe]
II	4	Combined presence of metaplasia and an elevated duct ratio	[no,yes]
III	5	Presence of hyperplasia	[none,mild,severe]
III	6	Presence of cysts	[none,mild,severe]
III	7	Presence of hypersecretion	[none,mild,severe]
III	8	Presence of vacuolisation	[none,mild,severe]
III	9	Presence of muceus cells	[none,moderate,severe]
III	10	Presence of inflammation	[none,moderate,severe]
III	11	Presence of folding in the urethra	[none,moderate,severe]
III	12	Presence of thickening in the urethra	[none,moderate,severe]
IV	13	Number of deviating features	[0,....,9]

Table 1. Overview of histological features for identifying the level of hormone treatment. The number of deviating features (group IV) is the sum of features in group III and either group I (male) or group II (female) that have a state differing from "none". Feature 2 is excluded from this sum since it only applies to female animals.

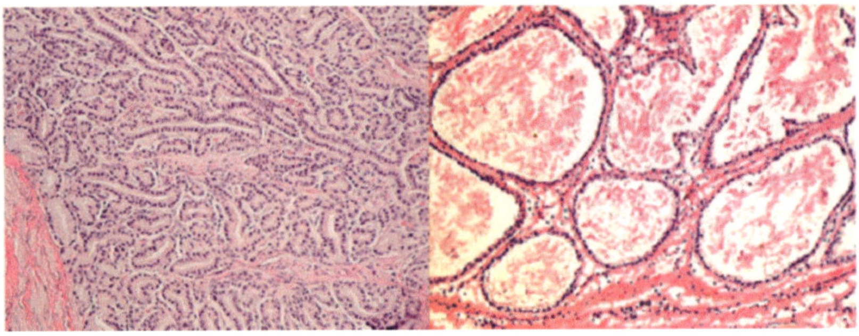

Figure 3. Normal appearance of prostate (left) and intensive presence of hypersecretion and cysts (right).

There are two strategies to reach a diagnosis:

A. A quick, general diagnosis. Depending on the sex of the calf, selecting either feature groups I and IV (male) or groups II and IV (female) is sufficient.

B. An extended diagnosis. In addition to the feature groups as indicated in strategy A group III is necessary.

The kernel of the data model consists of the groups I, II and IV to give a diagnosis of the treatment level. The diagnosis for possible hormone treatment in female calves is more complicated than for male calves. This is caused by the natural production of oestrogen hormones, which is lacking in male calves. The simple diagnosis <IF metaplasia=present THEN target positive> needs further support in female calves. A second diagnostic feature is used based on a larger share of ducts in the glandular tissue. The basic rule is then expanded to <IF metaplasia=present AND duct_ratio=elevated THEN target positive>. For both male and female calves the diagnosis "suspect" is supported by the number of deviating features. The duct ratio is excluded from this feature since it applies only to female calves. The logic tables to diagnose the level of treatment are presented in Table 2.

female	Metaplasia	
Duct ratio	[mild,severe]	[none]
[more,mainly]	"positive"	#=[0,1,2] → "normal" #=[3,...,8] → "suspect"
[normal]	#=[1,2] → "normal" #=[3,...,9] → "suspect"	

male	Metaplasia	
	[mild,severe]	[none]
	"positive"	#=[0,1,2] → "normal" #=[3,...,8] → "suspect"

Table 2. Logic tables for the diagnosis of hormone treatment in veal calves. #: total number of deviating features including the presence of metaplasia, excluding an elevated duct ratio.

http://dx.doi.org/10.5772/51362

The diagnoses as illustrated in Table 2 can be extended further by including the individual features of group III (Table 1). The number of deviating features (feature 13) needs to be adjusted accordingly. The basic rules are translated in a formal decision tree, as shown in Figure 4.

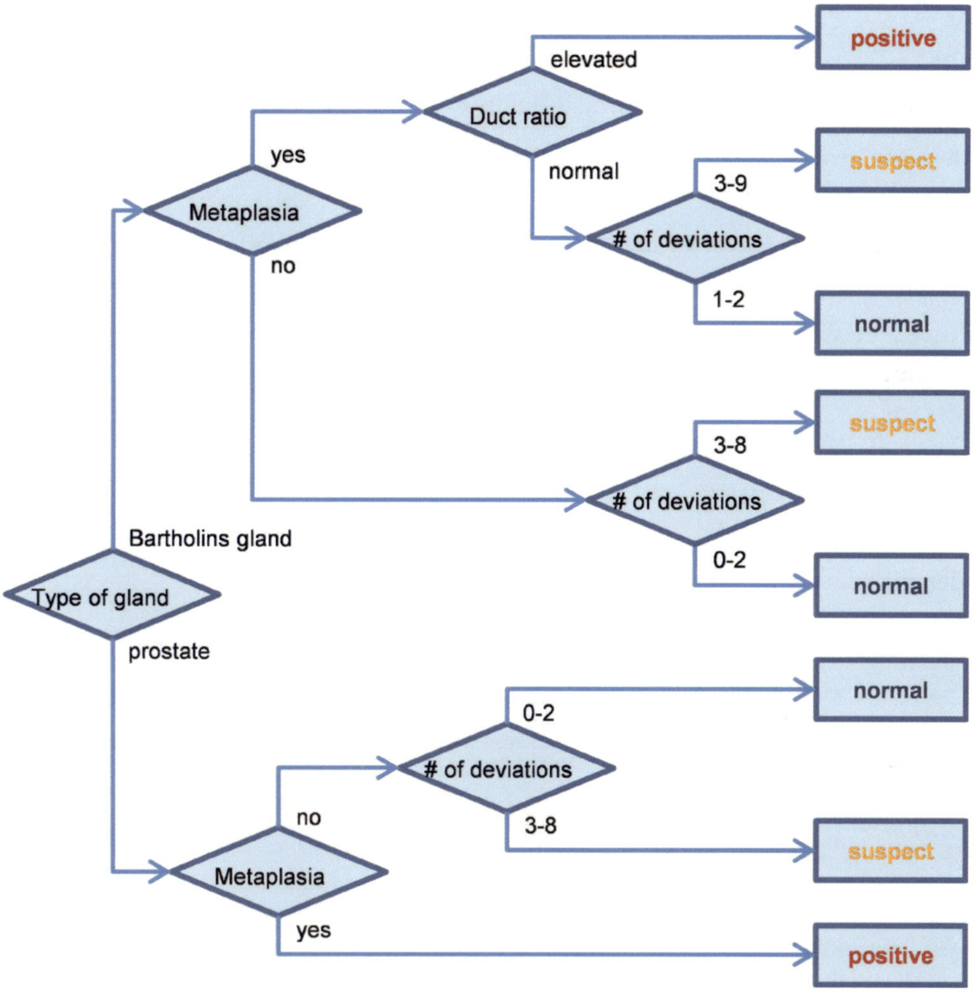

Figure 4. Decision tree for the diagnosis of hormone treatment in veal calves.

Finally, the decision tree is used as basis for a free access key. The importance and position of the feature indicating the presence of metaplasia is different for male and female diagnosis. For the latter only the combination of metaplasia and elevated duct ratio is decisive for the diagnosis "positive". As a consequence, the presence of metaplasia is included twice in the free access key as feature 1 (group I for male animals) and feature 3 (group II for female animals). The free access key was optimised by giving all features a suitable weighting factor. All features of group III got the factor one.

The performance of the model is tested in eight runs following the two strategies. The continuous feature 13 is varied between 0 and 9 in every run in combination with the appropriate choices for the other features, as follows:

A1 (male): groups I and IV are used. Choice for feature 1 is [none].

A2 (male): groups I and IV are used. Choice for feature 1 is [mild] unless:

$F_{13,k} = 0 \rightarrow F_{1,k} =$[none].

A3 (female): groups II and IV are used. Choices for features 2 and 3 are [normal] and [none].

A4 (female): groups II and IV are used. Choices for features 2 and 3 are [more_ducts] and [none].

A5 (female): groups II and IV are used. Choices for features 2 and 3 are [more_ducts] and [mild] unless:

$F_{13,k} = 0 \rightarrow F_{3,k} =$[none].

B1 (male): groups I, III and IV are used. Choice for features 1 is [none].

B2 (male): groups I, III and IV are used. Choice for features 1 is [mild] unless:

$F_{13,k} = 0 \rightarrow F_{1,k} =$[none].

$F_{13,k} => 1 \rightarrow$ the appropriate number of features of group B and C get the state [mild] or [moderate].

B3 (female): groups II, III and IV are used. Choice for feature 3 is [mild] unless:

$F_{13,k} = 0 \rightarrow F_{3,k} =$[none].

$F_{13,k} => 1 \rightarrow$ the appropriate number of features of group B and C get the state [mild] or [moderate].

The choice for [severe] instead of [mild] will give identical results except for the presence of hyperplasia (feature 5).

In every run the matches between the simulated subject and all three targets (treatment classes) "normal", "suspect" or "positive" were calculated according to equation (4). The results for the eight runs are shown in Figures 5 and 6.

The model after adjusting the appropriate weighting factors shows the highest match percentage for the same target (class) as indicated by the tree (Figure 4) in all cases. The percentage for a diagnosis "positive" of a male animal (Figure 5) is 0% when no deviating feature is found, in contrast to a diagnosis of a female animal (Figure 6) where an elevated duct ratio can be found in combination with # deviating features = 0. For the same reason is the difference between the diagnoses "normal" and "positive" smaller for male animals (Figure 5d) than for female animals (Figure 6d) in the case that # deviating features = 1. In general, the comparable situations as illustrated in Figures 5a and 6a/b, in Figures 5c and 6c, and in Figures 5d and 6d respectively, shows highly comparable results. The addition of the features of group III (Figures 5b, 5d, 6d) modifies the outcome of the model in the sense that in a lot of cases not 100% score can be reached. This reflects the situation that the finding of metaplasia (male) or the combination of metaplasia and an elevated duct ratio (female) accompanied with only a few or even no other deviations is unlikely or highly unlikely.

Figure	5a; run A1	5b; run B1	5c; run A2	5d; run B2
n features	2 (group I and IV)	10 (group I, III and IV)	2 (group I and IV)	10 (group I, III and IV)
metaplasia	**none**	**none**	**mild**	**mild**
other features	n/a	mild, as far as fitting in *n* deviations	n/a	mild, as far as fitting in *n* deviations

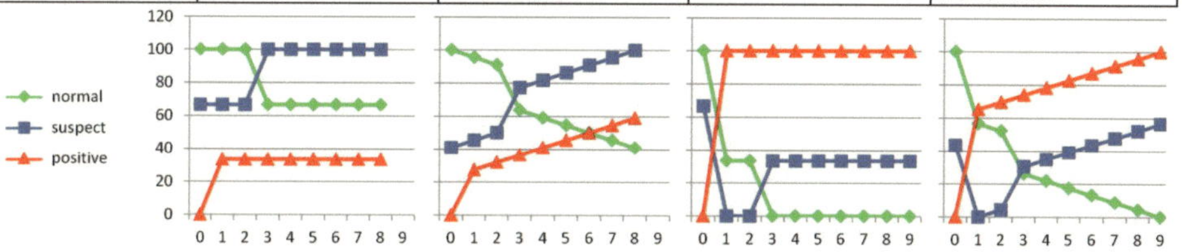

Figure 5. Performance of the free access key (matrix) for the prostate. Four different runs are illustrated. The choices for the main features are indicated in the tables on top of the figures. The choices for feature 13 (number of deviating features) running from zero to nine are given on the x-axis. The match percentage (according to equation 4) is given on the y-axis. The main differentiating feature per animal type is printed bold.

The large coverage of the targets indicated as "positive" (Table 3) is caused by the situation that the model is focusing on the correct diagnosis of possible treatment minimising the possibility of having false negative results. In both cases for male and female calves the final diagnosis is based on one feature (see Table 2 and Figure 4), whereas the states of the other features are overruled.

Figure	6a; run A3	6b; run A4	6c, run A5	6d; run B3
n features	4 (group II and IV)	4 (group II and IV)	4 (group II and IV)	12 (group II, III and IV)
metaplasia	none	none	mild	mild
duct ratio	normal	more_ducts	more_ducts	more_ducts
Combination metaplasia + elevated duct ratio	**no**	**no**	**yes**	**yes**
other features	n/a	n/a	n/a	mild, as far as fitting in *n* deviations

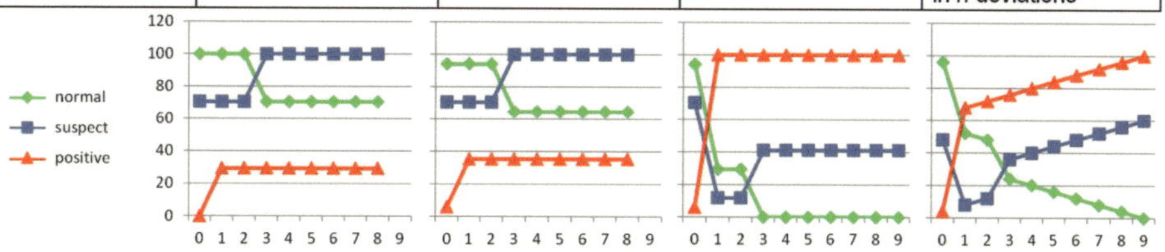

Figure 6. Performance of the free access key (matrix) for the gland of Bartholin. Four different runs are illustrated. The choices for the main features are indicated in the tables on top of the figures. The choices for feature 13 (number of deviating features) running from zero to nine are given on the x-axis. The match percentage (according to equation 4) is given on the y-axis. The main differentiating feature per animal type is printed bold.

Target	coverage	equation
001. Normal (prostate)	0.03	(11)
002. Suspect (prostate)	2.89	(11)
003. Positive (prostate)	34.68	(11)
004. Normal (Bartholins gland)	0.01	(11)
005. Suspect (Bartholins gland)	13.49	(11)
006. Positive (Bartholins gland)	34.68	(11)
Total coverage	85.79	(12)

Table 3. Coverage of the variability space by the individual targets and the total dataset.

The correlation between the features is shown in Table 4. Only a full correlation is found between the two features indicating the presence of metaplasia. This feature is included twice since different weighting factors appeared to be needed for the different animal types. Another reasonable high correlation factor was found between the duct ratio and the combined presence of metaplasia and elevated duct ratio. The presented level of correlation coefficients is in line with the calculated average redundancy: 0.405 (equation (8)).

Feature	001. Metaplasia (male)	002. Duct ratio	003. Metaplasia (female)	004. Combinatio	005. # of features
001. Metaplasia (male)	1.000	0.537	1.000	0.572	0.509
002. Duct ratio	0.537	1.000	0.537	0.840	0.518
003. Metaplasia (female)	1.000	0.537	1.000	0.572	0.509
004. Combination	0.572	0.840	0.572	1.000	0.222
005. # of features	0.509	0.518	0.509	0.222	1.000

Table 4. Matrix with Pearson's correlations between the features of the kernel model for diagnosis of illegal hormone use in veal calves. The colour of every cell (running from red to green) represents the value of the correlation coefficient.

The match table (Table 5) shows the relative resemblance between the targets based on equation (7). Except for the diagonal, the green colour, based on the calculations using equation (9), indicates that every target can be diagnosed uniquely compared to any other target. Hence, the separation capability is 100% (equation (10)).

Target	001. Normal (prostate	002. Suspect (prostate	003. Positive (prostate	004. Normal (Bartholir gland)	005. Suspect (Bartholir gland)	006. Positive (Bartholir gland)
001. Normal (prostate)	1.000	0.733	0.373	0.667	0.333	0.173
002. Suspect (prostate)	0.733	1.000	0.533	0.400	0.438	0.333
003. Positive (prostate)	0.373	0.533	1.000	0.040	0.356	0.800
004. Normal (Bartholins gland)	0.667	0.400	0.040	1.000	0.500	0.040
005. Suspect (Bartholins gland)	0.333	0.438	0.356	0.500	1.000	0.356
006. Positive (Bartholins gland)	0.173	0.333	0.800	0.040	0.356	1.000

Table 5. Matrix with the matches between the targets of the model for diagnosis of illegal hormone use in veal calves. The figure in every cell is calculated according to equation (7), the colour of every cell is based on equation (9).

4. Discussion

The process of identifying the level of treatment with growth hormones of veal calves is a rather specific situation for diagnosing in the broader framework of application of DSS in medicine [8-10]. Only one feature matters, all other features will only modify the probability that a diagnosis belongs to the correct class. Besides that, a constraint dependency rule exist-sbetween feature 13 (number of deviating features; Table 1) and the totalof features from group III plus either from group I or group II which show a state other than normal. The importance of the main features is visible in Table 2 and Figure 4. The two main features (male: presence of metaplasia, female: combined presence of metaplasia and an elevated duct ratio) both got a weighting factor of 9 in order to outnumber the features in group III for reaching a correct diagnosis (number of features in group III plus 1). Since the presence of metaplasia in the diagnosis of a female calf does not form the exclusive indicator for treatment in contrast to the position of that feature in the diagnosis of the male calf, it got a weighting factor of only 1. The weight factors in the current model are fixed instead of being input sensitive [11].

There is no generic method for validation of data models in expert systems [7]. In the current study a top down modelling approach was chosen: logic tables lead to a decision tree, which was the basis for the full matrix of the free access key. This approach does not provide a tool for handling constraint dependency rules [7], which was solved here by optimising the weighting factors. Rass et al. [12] listed a number of requirements for valid expert systems. Of these, the requirements for minimising the redundancy and for avoiding unintended synonyms are now supported bymeasures to calculate the extent of these parameters: redundancy (equation (8)) and separation capability (equation (10)), respectively.

The position of the features of group III (Table 1: indicating the individual deviating characteristics) in an extended diagnosis (Figures 4b, 4d, 5d) can be discussed in terms of fuzzy logic principles. In several experiments with fuzzy logic comparable results have been found [9, 13]. Here, probability or uncertainty is the basic aspect causing patterns in the model outcomes that can be explained as membership functions [13]. As an example, the presence of metaplasia in a prostate is a definite diagnosis for treatment with growth hormones (n = 1 in Figure 5c in concordance with the tree in Figure 4), but it is highly unlikely that with such a diagnosis none of the other features of group III (Table 1) would show a state deviating from normal. The probability that an animal with the sole presence of metaplasia belongs to membership class "positive" is only slightly higher than its membership to the class "suspect" (n=1 in Figure 5d). The kernel model without using the individual features of group III (strategy A) seems sufficient to reach a diagnosis. All the features underlying the depending feature 13 (group IV) are nevertheless included in the model in order to improve the performance of the user by supporting his or her examinations, and to provide the possibility of an iterative process of optimising the diagnosis [14].

Existing results of optimising a datamodel for reaching a diagnosis reveal that lower numbers of features appeared to be optimal [10]. In those cases that a model consists of only a few features, expressing them in terms of space dimensions (e.g. a two-dimensional space in

Figure 2), a major part of the variation space might be covered. Increasing numbers of features (i.e. dimensions) result in an exponentially growing number of theoretically existing feature combinations that are not linked to a target. In the present study a total of approx. 14 % of the variability space was not covered by any target (Table 3). In order to evaluate this non-assigned part of the variability space, let us assume a variable number of features n each consisting of three feature states, a number of targets that can be accommodatedby increasing with a factor of 2 with every additional feature, and one and only one state per feature identifying a target p:

$$(F_{i,k} \Rightarrow T_p) \wedge (F_{i,\neg k} \nRightarrow T_p) \tag{13}$$

Whereas equations (1) and (2) apply.

The resulting multidimensional spaces for a number of features ranging from 2 to 8, the number of targets accommodated and the resulting coverage are shown in Table 6. If more than one state of a feature can identify a target a larger coverage can be expected. This is the case in the here presented datamodel for the diagnosis of hormone treatment, since the probability to correctly classify all situations of hormone treatment was maximised. This is illustrated in Table 3. The high coverage of approx. 85.8% of the current model can be explained by the situation that the model was optimised to find all occasions of illegal use of hormones, i.e. the coverage of the classes "positive" was maximised.

n	Combinations (3^n)	Targets (2^n)	coverage
2	9	4	44%
3	27	8	30%
4	81	16	20%
5	243	32	13%
6	729	64	9%
7	2187	128	6%
8	6561	256	4%

Table 6. Relationship between the number of dimensions of a variability space (n), the possible number of combinations of feature states, and the coverage of the associated number of targets under the assumption of only one state per feature identifying a target (equation (13)).

The development of a specific model for reaching a histological diagnosis in a general platform provides several constraints, such as the lack of automatically calculating the number of deviating features (feature 13) from the number of individually selected features of group III. The advantage of the current procedure is the strict framework which forces to analyse the information structure in detail, and generic tools are available for testing and evaluation.

5. Conclusion

The presented parameters for redundancy, uniqueness, separation capability and coverage of variability space provide useful tools for the validation of a datamodel. The Developer as part of the Determinator system implements these parameters in an ordered manner, as exemplified in Table 5. The development and performance of the datamodel for reaching a diagnosis of the treatment of veal calves with hormones in the framework of Determinator reveals that a specific model can be developed and applied successfully in a generic framework.

Author details

L.W.D. van Raamsdonk[1*], S. van der Vange[1], M. Uiterwijk[2] and M. J. Groot[1]

*Address all correspondence to: Leo.vanraamsdonk@wur.nl

1 RIKILT, Wageningen UR, Wageningen, the Netherlands

2 Alterra, Wageningen UR, Wageningen, the Netherlands

References

[1] Raamsdonk, L. W. D., Mulder, P., & Uiterwijk, M. (2010). Identification tools as part of Feedsafety research: the case of ragwort. *In: P.L. Nimis and R. VignesLebbe, Proceedings of Bioidentify.eu: "Tools for identifying biodiversity: progress and problems", EdizioniUniversità di Trieste*, 213-216.

[2] Uiterwijk, M., van Raamsdonk, L. W. D., & Janssen, S. J. C. (2012). Determinator- a generic DSS for hazard identification of species or other physical subjects. *In: R. Seppelt, A.A. Voinov, S. Lange, D. Bankamp (eds.), Managing resources of a limited planet, sixth international congress of the International Environmental Modelling and Software Society. Leipzig*, July 1-5.

[3] Hagedorn, G., Rambold, G., & Martellos, S. (2010). Types of identification keys. *In: P.L. Nimis and R. VignesLebbe, Proceedings of Bioidentify.eu: "Tools for identifying biodiversity: progress and problems", Edizioni Università di Trieste*, 59-64.

[4] Yost, R., Attanandana, T., Pierce Colfer, C. J., & Itoga, S. (2011). Decision Support Systems in agriculture: some successes and a bright future. *In: C.S. Jao (ed.), Efficient decision support systems: practice and challenges from current to future*, 291-330, Intech, Rijeka, Croatia.

[5] Groot, M. J., Ossenkoppele, J. S., Bakker, R., Pfaffl, M. W., Meyer, H. H., & Nielen, M. W. (2007). Reference histology of veal calf genital and endocrine tissues- an update for screening on hormonal growth promoters. *J. Vet. Med. A Physiol Pathol Clin. Med.*, 54, 238-246.

[6] Groot, M. J., Schilt, R., Ossenkoppele, J. S., Berende, P. L. M., & Haasnoot, W. (1998). Combinations of growth promoters in veal calves: consequences for screening and confirmation methods. *J. Vet. Med. A*, 45, 425-440.

[7] Elfaki, A. O., Muthaiyah, S., Ho, C. K., & Phon-Amnuaisuk, S. (2011). Knowledge representation and validation in a Decision Support System: Introducing a variability modelling technique. *In: C.S. Jao (ed.), Efficient decision support systems: practice and challenges from current to future*, 29-48, Intech, Rijeka, Croatia.

[8] Worachartcheewana, A., Nantasenamata, C., Isarankura-Na-Ayudhyaa, C., Pidetchab, P., & Prachayasittikula, V. (2010). Identification of metabolic syndrome using decision tree analysis. *Diabetes Research and Clinical Practice*, 90, e15-e18.

[9] Das, A., & Bhattacharya, M. (2011). Computerized Decision Support System for Mass Identification in Breast Using Digital Mammogram: A Study on GA-Based Neuro-Fuzzy Approaches. *In: H.R. Arabnia and Q.-N. Tran, Software tools and algorithms for biological systems, Advances in Experimental Medicine and BiologySpringer Science and Business Media.*

[10] Sidiropoulos, K., Glotsos, D., Kostopoulos, S., Ravazoula, P., Kalatzis, I., Cavouros, D., & Stonham, J. (2012). Real time decision support system for diagnosis of rare cancers, trained in parallel, on a graphics processing unit. *Computers in Biology and Medicine*, 42, 376-386.

[11] Kacprzyk, J., & Zadrożny, S. (2009). Supporting decision making via verbalization of data analysis using linguistic data summaries. *In: E.Rakus-Andersson et al., Recent Advances in Decision Making*, 45-66, Springer Verlag, Berlin, Heidelberg.

[12] Rass, S., Machot, F. A., & Kyamakya, K. (2011). Fine-grained diagnosticsof ontologies with assurance. *In: C.S. Jao (ed.), Efficient decision support systems: practice and challenges from current to future*, 79-98, Intech, Rijeka, Croatia.

[13] Chen, G., Yan, P., & Wei, Q. (2009). Discovering associations with uncertainty from large databases. *In: E. Rakus-Andersson et al., Recent Advances in Decision Making*, 45-66, Springer Verlag, Berlin, Heidelberg.

[14] Barthelemy, J. P., Bisdorff, R., & Coppin, G. (2002). Human centered processes and decision support systems. *European Journal of Operational Research*, 136, 233-252.

Chapter 4

Diagnostic Decision Support System in Dysmorphology

Kaya Kuru and Yusuf Tunca

Additional information is available at the end of the chapter

http://dx.doi.org/10.5772/51118

1. Introduction

Dysmorphology is the aspect of clinical genetics concerned with syndrome diagnosis in patients who have a combination of congenital malformations and unusual facial features, often with delayed motor and cognitive development [1]. Making a diagnosis for a dysmorphic patient requires a high degree of experience and expertise [2] since many dysmorphic diseases are very rare. The human brain possesses a remarkable ability to recognize what is familiar or unfamiliar in a face. The general public can recognize the face shape of individuals with Down's syndrome and experienced clinical geneticists develop this innate skill to such a degree that they recognize subtle facial features associated with several hundred dysmorphic syndromes [3]. In some areas of the world, however, genetic diagnosis is generally performed by general practitioners, dermatologists or pediatricians, not particularly trained in dysmorphology, rather than trained geneticists due to the lack in the numbers of geneticists. Dysmorphologic diagnosis is usually performed by referring the images or terms standardized and specified in some limited number of catalogs and databases. However, not being very familiar with the terminology, especially for practitioners in rural areas, is an important handicap to dig into the right diagnosis. This can lead to diagnostic inaccuracy which in turn curtails both the right cure of patients that will best suit their particular needs and the right guiding of their parents who may be at risk of having a new dysmorphic child. The whole process of reaching a genetic diagnosis can be very lengthy and entail struggling with referrals to numerous medical professionals and waiting for appointments. Throughout this process, parents find themselves dragged from one medical professional to another until discovering the accurate diagnosis of their child. These parents often experience high levels of burdensome anxiety and frustration. Moreover, delay in diagnosis may also delay access to critical services such as clinical trials and a patient's referral to supportive services including early intervention, physical or occupational therapy. Syndrome recognition and diagnosis is of clinical importance for several reasons according to Smithson

[1]: first, it influences patient management because awareness of the pattern of anomalies associated with a particular syndrome highlights the investigations that need to be undertaken; second, diagnosis provides information about the long-term prognosis and may help to identify options for treatment: for example, bone marrow transplantation or enzyme replacement therapy can now be offered for some inborn errors of metabolism (e.g. in Fabry disease); third, the diagnosis determines what genetic advice can be given, including an estimation of genetic risks and possible means of prenatal diagnosis. Thus, delays in early treatment can have a miserable impact on the patient's health and can dramatically influence the chances of the child catching up to his/her peers and leading to a normal life. Therefore, reaching a thorough genetic diagnosis at an early stage is crucial. Not only does this affect the choice of cure for the patient, but it also enables the proper guidance, counseling and support for the parents to ensure an overall improvement in the patient's quality of life and care. Most physicians, neurologists or pediatricians are capable of noticing these early signs in a child, but are not equipped to perform a precise genetic diagnosis on their own especially for very rare diseases. Since there are thousands of possible genetic conditions to be taken into account and each condition is in itself very rare, a specialist's evaluation generally seems the best path to ensure a proper genetic diagnosis is reached though it is sometimes very difficult even for geneticists to diagnose these orphan diseases.

The face is widely recognized as an attribute which best distinguishes a person, even at first glance. Facial features give lots of clues about the identity, gender, age and ethnicity. The face develops under the influence of many genes and in many cases a face provides important information to diagnose a syndrome. Thus, facial appearance can be a significant hint in the initial identification of genetic anomalies generally associated with cognitive impairments. There are specific properties, especially for facial dysmorphology caused by genetic syndromes and these properties are used by geneticists to pre-diagnose even before a clinical examination and genotyping are undertaken. Analyzing of properties in faces is sometimes sufficient to diagnose for some cases, however, it is necessary to analyze other specific properties of the body such as the structure of the skeleton and the characteristics of speech produced for some other cases. Diagnosing of genotype-phenotype correlations correctly among many syndromes seems beyond the capability of human especially for very rare diseases. Most of the genetic diagnostic decision support systems (DDSS) have been applied in terms of the anthropometry and more specifically craniofacial anthropometry including stereophotogrammetry[1] so far. It might be possible to diagnose a good number of syndromes correctly by using computer-assisted face analysis DSS as asserted by some scientists such as Farkas [4], Loos [5], Boehringer [2], and Hammond [6, 7]. Farkas [4] pioneered techniques for studying facial morphology using direct anthropometry for nearly 40 years ago [4]. His approach, using a ruler, calipers, tape measure and protractor, has been applied widely in the analysis of facial dysmorphology [7]. Many clinicians undertake such a manual craniofacial assessment and compare a patient's phenotype to the norms of a control

1 Anthropometry is defined as the biological science of measuring the size, weight, and proportions of the human body [4]. Craniofacial anthropometry is performed on the basis of measures taken between landmarks defined on surface features of the head, face, and ears [12]. Stereophotogrammetry refers to combining multiple views of photos to form a 3D image [13].

population of comparable age and sex [7]. A most recent study of Hammond [7] has reviewed the surface-based image capture in 3D in syndrome delineation and discrimination, in the categorization of individual facial dysmorphology and in phenotype–genotype studies which is a very complex implementation of dysmorphological diagnosis process in a clinical environment. For dysmorphic syndromes with known genetic causes, molecular and/or cytogenetic analysis is the appropriate route of investigation in order to confirm a diagnosis. However, applying right analysis method throughout many probable analyses is very much dependent to the accurate diagnosis considered before genotyping is undertaken. The aim of this chapter is to propose a new methodology by observing the characteristic key components of facial dysmorphology associated with genetic disorder to indicate the right diagnostic criteria.

Douglas [8] has stated that classification of faces based on facial patterns in isolation is unlikely to be accepted by dysmorphologists unless the mathematical features extracted and identified by feature selection algorithms to be discriminatory can be related to facial appearance. Principal component analysis (PCA), independent component analysis (ICA), kernel principal component analysis (KPCA), local feature analysis (LFA), probability density estimation (PDA), multi-linear analysis (MLA), elastic graph matching (EGM), kernel discriminant analysis (KDA), support vector machine (SVM), Gabor wavelet and Fischer's linear discriminant analysis (LDA) exist to analyze the features of a face. Among them, the methods of PCA using eigenface, elastic graph matching, Gabor wavelet and Fischer's LDA are popular for face recognition. PCA can be computed as an optimal compression scheme that minimizes the mean squared error between an image and its reconstruction [9] as well as it may achieve good results of up to 96% recognition under ideal conditions [10] which can be provided with either capturing images in ideal environments by having a good illumination and using a good capturing device or preprocessing of images with several image processing techniques before extracting features. PCA using eigenfaces have been identified as computational efficient on even reduced hardware [11]. Additionally it is used for dimension reduction as in our study from 2D to 1D to ease and speed up the calculations. That is to say, the dimensionality of the required space for all images can be reduced to the number of input images instead of the pixel count that all images have in total.

City block distance, Euclidean distance, sub/space method, multiple similarity method, Bayes decision method and Mahalanobis distance are known typical distance functions [9]. Kapoor [9] highlights that the Mahalanobis distance is the most effective of the typical evaluation distance-based approaches that calculate the distance from a point to a particular point in the data set. We have tested the Mahalanobis distance and Euclidean distance in our study to find the genotype-phenotype correlations. The well/known Mahalanobis distance classifier[2] is based on the assumption that the underlying probability distributions are Gaussian [9]. Kapoor [9] indicates the difference such that Mahalanobis distance is a distance measure based on correlations between variables by which different patterns can be identified and analyzed. It is a useful way of determining similarity of an unknown sample

2 Interested reader may found detailed information about Mahalanobis distance from Gul's thesis [14].

set to a known one. It differs from Euclidean distance in that it takes into account the correlations of the data set and is scale-invariant, i.e. not dependent on the scale of measurements. In our study, the well-known Euclidean distance matching process outperformed the process of Mahalanobis distance. Thus, we chose this matching technique in our study.

Hammond [7] pointed out that in terms of future technological support, two (2D) or three-dimensional (3D) models of facial morphology are showing potential in syndrome delineation and discrimination, in analyzing individual dysmorphology, and in contributing to multi-disciplinary and multi-species studies of genotype–phenotype correlations. Our study is an example of substantiating this potential. We have developed a real-time computer system that can locate and track a patient's head, and then recognize the patient by comparing characteristics of the face to those of trained individuals with classified dysmorphic diseases. In this study, in terms of both the feature extraction and helping non experienced practitioners in diagnosis process as well as to support experts in their decisions, we established an application to ease the process and we refer to our method as "Facial Genotype-Phenotype Diagnostic Decision Support System (FaceGP DDSS) in Dysmorphology". Up to date, no complete solution has been proposed that allow the automatic diagnosis of dysmorphic diseases from the raw data (live camera, video or frontal photographs) without human intervention. The FaceGP DDSS aims not only to ease the required on-site expertise, but also to eliminate the time consuming catalog search of practitioners and geneticists to diagnose facial dysmorphic diseases through approximately 4.700 known dysmorphic diseases[3] automatically, no intervention from the user such as preprocessing of images. The FaceGP DDSS methodology can be implemented on any site easily. In the methodology, reference images or reference patients on live subjects having the specific dysmorphic diseases are used as a guide for identifying the facial phenotypes (the outward physical manifestation of the genotypes) to train the system. Digital facial image processing methods are employed to reveal facial features with disorders indicating dysmorphic genotype-phenotype interrelation. A great number of genetic disorders indicating a characteristic pattern of facial anomalies can be classified by analyzing specific features (eigenfaces) with the aid of facial image processing methods such as PCA. Distance algorithms such as Euclidean, Mahalanobis are used to construct the correlation of the input image with the trained images in matching. Some image enhancement methods such as histogram equalization and median filter are implemented on detected images to capture better features and compensate for lighting differences. This study proposes a novel and robust composite computer-assisted and cost-effective method by merging several methods in the characterization of the facial dysmorphic phenotype associated with genotype, in particular a method relying primary on face image capture (acquisition from either camera, video or frontal face images) and manipulation to help medical professionals to diagnose syndromes efficiently.

3 Many new dysmorphic diseases are described each year. London Dysmorphology Database (http://www.lmdatabases.com).

http://dx.doi.org/10.5772/51118

2. Methods

The FaceGP DDSS methodology has been established in C++ programming language. We benefited OpenCV[4] library. The application can function on any present computer, not requiring much CPU and memory while processing thanks to the easy implementation of PCA. The methodology comprises several main modules, namely *face detection and image acquisition, image processing, training and diagnosis/recognition module,* and these main modules are divided into several sub modules as illustrated in Figure1. Functions of these modules are explained in following subsections in detail.

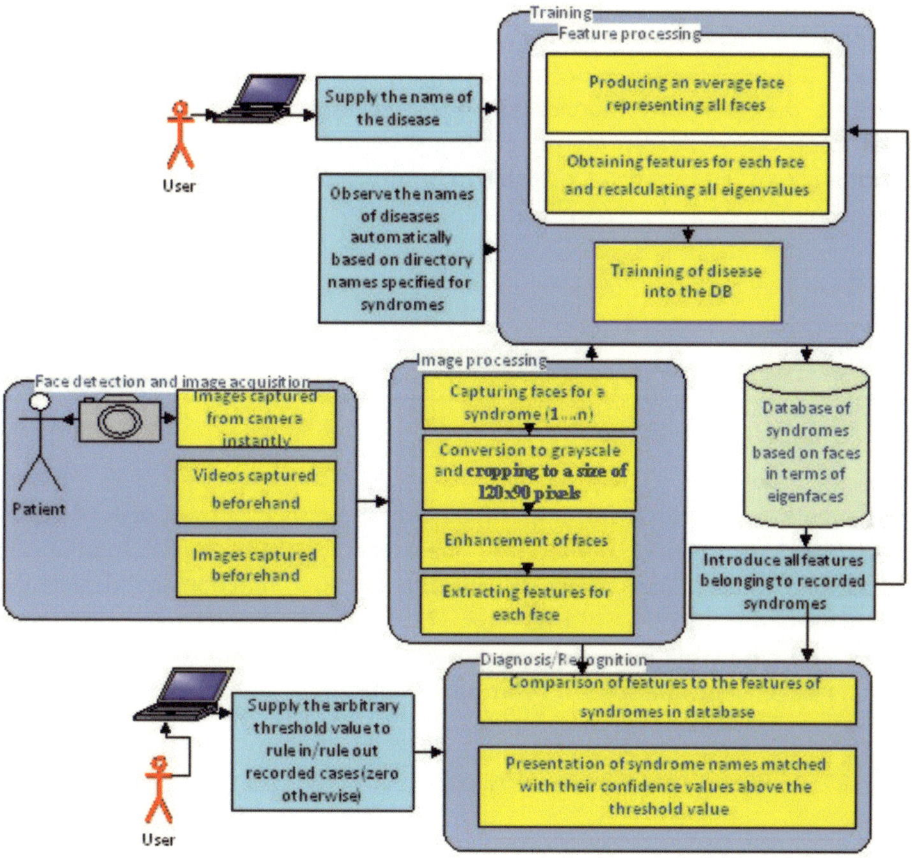

Figure 1. 1. Overall architecture of the methodology: the system consists of four main modules; face detection and image acquisition, image processing, training and diagnosis/recognition module. These modules are divided into several sub modules that are delineated in the specified sections of the modules.

4 OpenCV (Open Source Computer Vision) library can be reached from the site, http://opencv.willowgarage.com/wiki/.

2.1. Face Detection and Image acquisition

The patient images can be captured from several different environments: they can be captured from softcopy images stored in a disk, it can be observed from hardcopy pictures or real-time images which can be detected simultaneously from patients by a camera attached to the computer. The images can be automatically captured on an ordinary high-resolution digital camera (e.g. 8 megapixels) mounted across the patient (no matter what the distance is), provided that a frontal face is detected (to prevent motion artifacts). Natural movements of the body at rest (e.g., breathing), and a person's inability to sit motionless result in no problem as the camera detects and acquire images in a short period of time. Time of capture per image is 0.2s which is triggered by the system automatically excluding time for not acquiring frontal faces. Capturing images is so instantaneous that it may be more suitable for imaging children with mental retardation who are unable to hold a pose for long and potentially uncooperative. Images not including a proper frontal face are not captured and the application is idle during this time, especially when the head turning to sides, up and down. Frontal faces are the essential components of our data preparation and model building. In other words, the process of capturing images is just performed if the application detects an acceptable frontal face. The application is able to capture sufficient number of frontal images in real-time, which is required to train the system for subsequent analyses.

2.2. Image Processing

2.2.1. Capturing faces for a specific case

Images of patients are acquired for a specific syndrome either to train or to diagnose in terms of the function triggered by the user. The functions of the implementation are explained in the next section. The system activates the diagnosis function as it detects the images of patients if this function is triggered. Otherwise, it expects user interference to activate the training function in order to make sure that the procedure of capturing all required frontal face images for a specific syndrome is finished.

2.2.2. Conversion to grayscale and cropping of images

After images of patient are acquired, they are converted to grayscale and cropped to include just faces by relying upon the face outline, forehead, two eyes, cheek, chin and mouth. This stage is finalized by normalizing the image with a size of 120x90 pixels. Processing of this phase as depicted in Figure 2 ensures that all face images are exactly positioned the same regarding a proper rotation. A background removal algorithm is not implemented due to the cropped face in which there is almost no background and the rest of the image is removed before feature extraction.

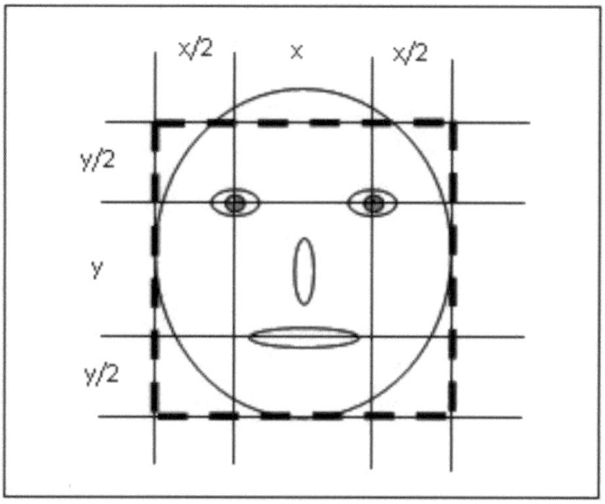

Figure 2. Delineation of cropping a dysmorphic face.

2.2.3. Enhancement of face images

The face images are standardized by employing two essential image enhancement methods, namely histogram equalization and median filtering to remove illumination variations in order to capture better features. Histogram equalization employed on an image is known to provide better extraction of features [14]. Histogram equalization is applied on too dark or too bright face images in order to enhance image quality and to improve diagnostic performance, thus, facial features become more apparent by enhancing the contrast range of the image. Median filtering is very effective to enhance images especially obtained from a camera without losing information [15]. There is no preprocessing of frontal images manually.

2.2.4. Feature extraction

Extraction of facial features is implemented in this sub module. After automatic image preprocessing is employed on raw image data, the feature extraction is implemented on the normalized face image to reveal the key features that are used to classify and recognize dysmorphic diseases. The FaceGP DDSS methodology is designed for modeling and analyzing large sets of face images. Whichever method is used, the most important problem in face recognition is reducing the dimensionality in terms of easing computational complexity. We haven't used craniofacial landmarks or extracting feature graphs[5]. Instead; we performed principal component analysis (PCA) which is a very effective method at classifying face images in the sense of reducing computational complexity. PCA which evaluates entire face is

5 Extracting feature graphs is based on interpolation of the basic parts of a face such as eyes, nose, mouth, and chin. In the method, with the help of deformable templates and extensive mathematics, key information from the basic parts of a face is gathered and then converted into a feature vector. L. Yullie and S. Cohen played a great role in adapting deformable templates to contour extraction of face images[16].

implemented to extract the features of dysmorphic faces in terms of its simplicity, learning capability and speed. PCA may be defined as the eigenvectors of the covariance matrix of the set of face images, meaning an image as a vector in a high dimensional space. It classifies the face images by projecting them to the 2-D space which is composed of eigenvectors obtained by the variance of the face images. These eigenvectors are a set of features that characterize the variation between face images. In other words, the features of the images are obtained by looking for the maximum deviation of each image from the mean image. Each image location contributes more or less to each eigenvector, so that it is possible to display these eigenvectors as a sort of ghostly face image which is called an "eigenface". Eigenfaces can be viewed as a sort of map of the variations between faces. PCA reduces the dimensionality of the dataset. Thus a face of 8-bit intensity values can be represented by an ordered sequences numbers in a vector, one dimensionally with PCA. This is a huge data compaction, as in our case reducing the representation of a face surface from 10800 dimensionality space (120x90 2D points each with x and y coordinates) down to 1 per image. Each face can be regenerated from eigenvalues using a linear weighted sum of the PCA modes in return. The most relevant information contained in a dysmorphic face image is extracted by PCA[6]. Briefly, after capturing sample dysmorphic images and normalizing them following some automatic image processing methods, eigenfaces are generated and saved. An eigenface keep values that make a dysmorphic image unique.

2.3. Training

The eigenfaces, eigenvalues and average image generated by PCA are stored in XML file as Haar-like features[7] together with their labeled diagnosed names. The methodology has the ability to store and read data in XML format. The number of generated eigenfaces (n-1) is almost equal to the number of input images (n) in our study. Classifiers are trained with those features extracted by feature extraction module. As new dysmorphic diseases are trained, the eigenfaces and eigenvalues are recalculated.

Users can easily add new dysmorphic diseases by using their archives in which there are several sample images representing other diseases not defined in the system one by one as well as more than one disease once by the help of the utility provided by the system.

2.4. Diagnosing/Recognition

The trained classifiers are employed for prediction in this sub module. Diagnosing/recognition process is a pattern recognition task. The prediction of the diagnosis of a patient requires the detection of frontal face from a camera or a file, normalizing and processing of face with techniques mentioned in Section 2.2 and extraction of facial features for comparing the trained classifiers. A dysmorphic face image captured and processed is transformed into

6 Details, especially formulas about PCA can be found in Akalin's study [15] and Calvo's article [17].

7 Haar-like features encode the existence of oriented contrasts between regions in the image. A set of these features can be used to encode the contrasts exhibited by a human face and their spacial relationships. Haar-like are computed similar to the coefficients in Haar wavelet transforms. Interested reader can refer to Viola's study for more information about Haar-like features [18].

its eigenface components and then these components are compared to those of predefined labeled classes. There are a number of algorithms in the literature that can compare faces to look for a match. A simple and intuitively appealing way to compare an individual face with two sets of faces is to calculate how close for which a method is a nearest-neighbor classification, how close are they in terms of the Euclidean distance. Once a face has been detected and extracted from an image it is ready to be compared against known/trained syndromes to see if there is a similarity. The captured face image compared to all the syndromes trained in the database one by one for similarities to make sure all similar faces above the threshold value are found in terms of the Euclidean distance[8]. The role of Euclidean distance comparison for image recognition is not much different in that it tries to capture how similar or different a test object is from training objects in terms of the 50 or so mode values, that face surface is to the average face surfaces of each set. Whichever of the average faces is closest determines the classification of the individual. In other words, during the recognition stage, when a new image is input to the system, the mean image is subtracted and the result is projected into the face space. The best match is found for the identity that minimizes the Euclidean distance. For example, for a particular syndrome, the features obtained from the PCA is compared to the trained faces in the database using an Euclidean distance comparison to calculate how close it is to the features of faces in the Database. The similar faces above the threshold value supplied by the user are probable diagnoses displayed to the user. Confidence values can be defined as the resemblance or degree of proximity of eigenface values (how near they are) between two sets of eigenface values obtained from the values of the trained diagnostic images and the identified image to be diagnosed. These values are used for assessing the reliability of the proposed diagnostic inference by the system.

Diagnosis is where the system compares the given patient's face features to all the other trained face features in the database and gives a ranked list of possible matches with respect to the confidence values above the threshold value. In our system, probabilities of similarities in diagnostic process are revealed to the user in a decreasing order rather than either "known" or "unknown" outputs as in face recognition systems, after comparing an undefined dysmorphic face with recorded defined dysmorphic faces that are diagnostically classified. That is to say, our system is not a face recognition system; rather, it is how much a disease is similar to the diseases classified in the database as ruling in or ruling out diseases in terms of the threshold value supplied by the user. This cost effective diagnosis methodology could then help to determine subsequent investigations including more appropriate genetic testing, and possibly even avoiding or delaying the need to undertake some of the more expensive genetic tests.

2.5. Interface and the Functions of the Methodology

A screen shot of the implementation is presented in Figure 3. The main utilities of the implementation are explained in following sub-sections.

8 Interested reader may reach the Calva's article [17] for more information about the Euclidean distance formulations and implementation for the comparison of eigenvalues of a test image to the trained labeled images.

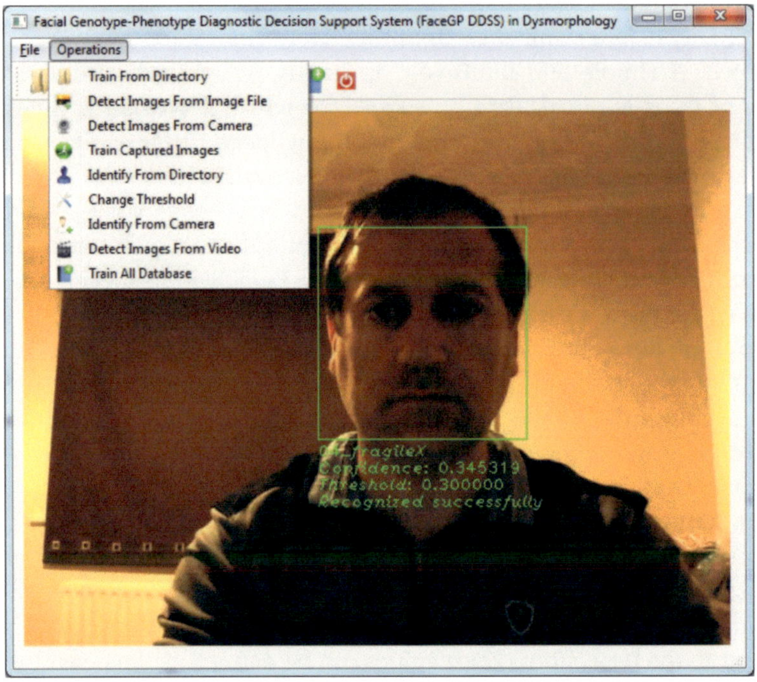

Figure 3. An example for the diagnosing process via camera: Four messages are displayed; the name of the probable diagnosis (e.g. Fragile X), the degree of proximity to that diagnosis (e.g. 0.345319), the threshold value entered by the user (e.g. 0.30), the message about whether a probable disease is found or not as "recognized successfully" or "unknown disease". The messages change if other diseases are found above the threshold value to reveal them on the screen. All the time required to search through 7 trained identified diagnoses that include 34 eigenfaces and find the nearest diagnoses in respect to the threshold value is few seconds.

2.5.1. Detect images from image file:

This utility detects faces from the images displayed on the screen where images are brought from the chosen directory automatically. Detection stops and training process begins when the user clicks the utility "train captured images". The name of the disease is entered by the user.

2.5.2. Detect images from camera:

This utility detects face appearances on live camera from a patient or patients who are diagnosed with same dysmorphic disease. Detection stops and training process begins when the user clicks the utility "train captured images". The name of the syndrome is supplied by the user.

2.5.3. Detect images from video:

Face images of a patient or patients who are diagnosed with same dysmorphic disease are detected from a video or several videos. Detection stops at the end of video and training process begins when the user clicks the utility "train captured images". The name of the syndrome is presented by the user.

2.5.4. Train captured images:

Detected face images from either a directory or a live camera are processed to be classified into the database.

2.5.5. Train from directory:

A directory in which there are several images of a specified disease is chosen and the name of that syndrome is entered by the user. All necessary algorithms are run through training of the diseases automatically. Diseases can be trained one by one by this utility.

2.5.6. Train all database:

All labeled diseases in a directory are processed by "face detection and image acquisition" and "image processing" modules respectively and automatically. Then, processed cropped frontal face images are trained into a database without user intervention by training module. In other words, all modules in Figure 3 are employed automatically. The system accepts the directory names where the dysmorphic images are as the names of the syndromes while training the datasets. The only thing expected from the user is to specify the folder where the datasets are.

2.5.7. Change threshold:

The user can specify the threshold value to rule in or rule out diseases during the identification process. The greater the threshold value is, the less the number of probable diagnoses is proposed, vice versa, the less the threshold value is entered, the greater the number of diagnoses is revealed to the user together with confidence (probability or proximity) values.

2.5.8. Identify from a directory:

Several images in a directory can be chosen at once and these images can be compared to the labeled syndromes stored in the database. A video that has dysmorphic patients can be chosen to diagnose probable diseases as well.

2.5.9. Identify from a camera:

A patient can be captured from a live camera mounted to the computer to diagnose a syndrome stored in the database.

2.6. Evaluation of the Methodology

A case study has been carried out to evaluate the methodology. We have analyzed 2D frontal face pictures of patients, each being affected with one of the syndromes. The scope and the design of the case study are presented in the following subsections. The findings of the study are presented in the next section, results.

2.6.1. Study sample

The study sample was composed of 7 syndromes comprising 35 individual frontal faces (5 for each) of patients that are included from Boehringer's study [2]. These diseases depicted in Figure 4 are microdeletion 22q11.2, Cornelia de Lange, fragile X, Mucopolysaccharidosis III, Smith–Lemli–Opitz, Sotos and Williams–Beuren. The patients for each syndrome are more or less the same age, but, in different genders (10 females and 25 males) for 5 syndromes that are microdeletion 22q11.2 (3 F: Fmales, 2 M: Males), Cornelia de Lange (2F, 3M), Smith–Lemli–Opitz (2F, 3M), Sotos (2F, 3M) and Williams–Beuren (1F, 4M).

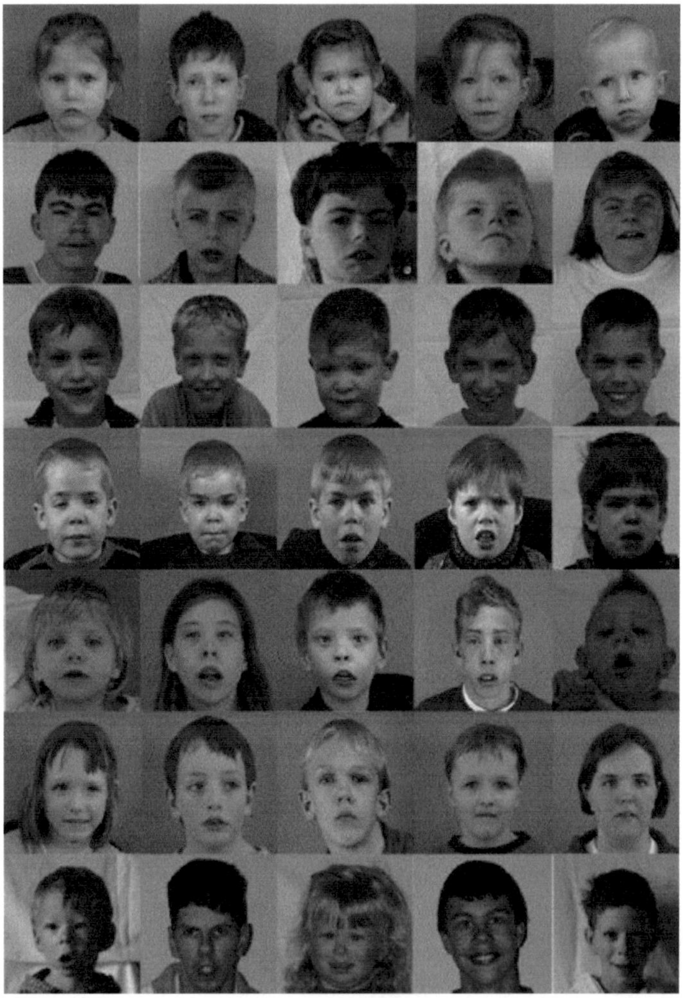

Figure 4. Seven syndromes: each row comprises one syndrome; microdeletion 22q11.2 (3 F: Females, 2 M: Males), Cornelia de Lange (2F, 3M), fragile X (5M), Mucopolysaccharidosis III (5M), Smith–Lemli–Opitz (2F, 3M), Sotos (2F, 3M) and Williams –Beuren (1F, 4M).

http://dx.doi.org/10.5772/51118

2.6.2. Study design

7 syndromes were trained by the utility named "Train all database" mentioned previously. The system could build a training set for 7 syndromes that have 34 eigenfaces for 35 faces less than one minute. The mean face and all 33 eigenfaces are displayed in Figure 5 and Figure 6 respectively. The first four images from the syndromes were used as a testing set to measure the recognition/diagnosis success. All these test images were put in a directory and each test image was compared to other trained 34 images in the database to measure how close it is on the vector space to others by using the utility of "identify from directory". All recognition process lasted about 1 minute in terms of pairwise comparison. This utility produces confidence values in a table and diagnose regarding these values above the threshold value entered by the user. In our case study we have aimed to find the probable diagnoses in the sense of rule-in 1, rule-in 2 and rule-in 3 diagnoses respectively by adjusting the threshold value for each person. Then, the success rates of these n-rule-in observations were obtained.

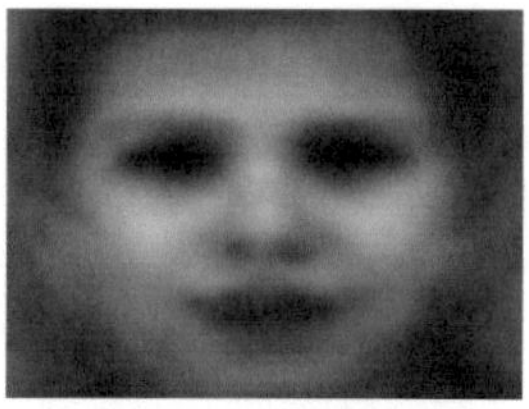

Figure 5. Mean face for 7 dysmorphic diseases generated by the system.

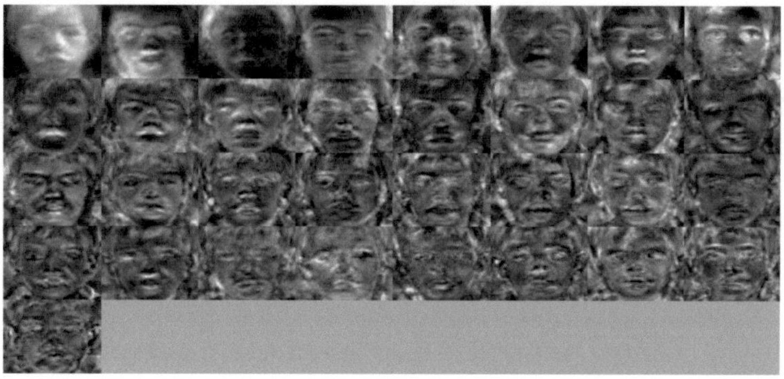

Figure 6. Eigenfaces of 7 dysmorphic diseases that comprise 35 frontal face images.

3. Results

The threshold value entered by the user increases or decreases the possible number of diagnoses, the less the threshold value is entered, the more diagnoses are proposed; vice versa, the less diagnoses are included to be examined by the medical professionals. Pairwise analysis of 28 patients in 7 different syndromes is depicted in Table 1 regarding the confidence values. Each column corresponds to an individual patient's comparison to other patients one-to-one on the vector space of eigenfaces. The greater the value a column, the greater the probable proximity it has corresponding to that row whose syndrome indicates the probable diagnosis. The threshold value for each column is adjusted to rule in one, two and three diagnoses respectively. The results of three diagnoses for each tested patient are presented in Table 2 in which the gray cells correspond to the right diagnoses. Ruling in one, two and three diagnoses yields 21, 26 (extra 5 to rule in one) and 28 (extra 2 to rule in two) correct diagnoses among all 28 tested patients respectively. Ruling in one, two and three diagnoses designates the success rates of 75, 94 and 100 percent respectively as well. The diagnostic success rates are depicted in Figure 7.

		1	1	1	1	2	2	2	2	3	3	3	3	4	4	4	4	5	5	5	5	6	6	6	6	7	7	7	7
		1	2	3	4	1	2	3	4	1	2	3	4	1	2	3	4	1	2	3	4	1	2	3	4	1	2	3	4
1	1	1.00	0.32	0.28	0.46	-0.36	-0.34	-0.25	-0.28	-0.07	-0.13	-0.21	-0.17	0.10	0.21	-0.03	0.16	0.14	0.29	0.31	0.06	0.36	0.22	0.06	0.24	-0.28	-0.09	-0.22	-0.35
1	2	0.32	1.00	0.29	0.29	-0.25	-0.28	-0.13	-0.13	-0.03	-0.22	-0.24	-0.22	0.07	0.07	-0.03	0.18	0.12	0.32	0.32	0.09	0.26	0.27	0.09	0.26	-0.24	-0.02	-0.16	-0.29
1	3	0.28	0.29	1.00	0.27	-0.20	-0.21	-0.11	-0.16	0.13	-0.16	-0.16	-0.09	0.05	0.09	-0.09	0.12	0.09	0.22	0.25	0.04	0.23	0.24	0.08	0.21	-0.16	0.03	-0.06	-0.19
1	4	0.46	0.29	0.27	1.00	-0.43	-0.32	-0.31	-0.29	-0.01	-0.12	-0.23	-0.20	0.20	0.31	-0.05	0.12	0.10	0.31	0.38	0.10	0.33	0.19	0.08	0.24	-0.30	-0.16	-0.30	-0.38
1	5	0.25	0.13	0.08	0.35	-0.52	-0.25	-0.35	-0.20	-0.16	-0.07	-0.27	-0.33	0.29	0.39	0.05	0.09	0.07	0.19	0.23	0.07	0.21	0.06	0.00	0.12	-0.30	-0.23	-0.44	-0.42
2	1	-0.36	-0.25	-0.20	-0.43	1.00	-0.09	0.00	-0.20	-0.06	-0.26	-0.06	0.00	-0.38	-0.45	-0.34	-0.30	-0.26	-0.36	-0.35	-0.31	-0.37	-0.24	-0.27	-0.27	-0.11	-0.01	0.09	0.05
2	2	-0.34	-0.28	-0.21	-0.32	-0.09	1.00	-0.11	0.02	0.03	-0.07	-0.03	-0.12	-0.12	-0.14	-0.08	-0.22	-0.16	-0.27	-0.23	-0.20	-0.29	-0.23	-0.15	-0.21	-0.01	-0.05	-0.20	-0.01
2	3	-0.25	-0.13	-0.11	-0.31	0.00	-0.11	1.00	0.12	0.00	-0.29	-0.12	-0.10	-0.18	-0.26	-0.25	-0.07	-0.09	-0.19	-0.20	-0.25	-0.24	-0.10	0.02	-0.08	0.13	0.02	0.00	0.21
2	4	-0.28	-0.13	-0.16	-0.29	-0.20	0.02	0.12	1.00	-0.12	-0.24	-0.22	-0.28	-0.06	-0.11	-0.09	-0.01	-0.10	-0.16	-0.18	-0.25	-0.20	-0.15	-0.08	-0.10	0.04	-0.08	-0.22	0.05
2	5	-0.05	0.05	-0.02	-0.14	-0.13	-0.27	0.16	-0.02	-0.15	-0.41	-0.29	-0.24	-0.16	-0.18	-0.20	0.07	0.05	-0.01	-0.11	-0.23	-0.10	0.00	0.03	0.00	-0.15	-0.16	-0.07	-0.09
3	1	-0.07	-0.03	0.13	-0.01	-0.06	0.03	0.00	-0.12	1.00	0.02	0.09	0.15	-0.06	-0.10	-0.18	-0.14	-0.06	-0.05	0.04	-0.06	-0.05	0.01	0.01	0.05	-0.03	0.13	0.02	0.05
3	2	-0.13	-0.22	-0.16	-0.12	-0.26	-0.07	-0.29	-0.24	0.02	1.00	0.04	-0.03	-0.03	-0.02	-0.12	-0.18	-0.17	-0.17	-0.10	-0.08	-0.10	-0.19	-0.24	-0.06	-0.18	-0.08	-0.27	-0.18
3	3	-0.21	-0.24	-0.16	-0.23	-0.06	-0.03	-0.12	-0.22	0.09	0.04	1.00	0.16	-0.23	-0.21	-0.14	-0.29	-0.12	-0.32	-0.19	-0.18	-0.28	-0.28	-0.27	-0.22	-0.10	-0.01	-0.01	-0.12
3	4	-0.17	-0.22	-0.09	-0.20	0.00	-0.12	-0.10	-0.28	0.15	-0.03	0.16	1.00	-0.27	-0.27	-0.29	-0.30	-0.21	-0.24	-0.15	-0.17	-0.25	-0.18	-0.24	-0.15	-0.12	0.08	0.10	-0.02
3	5	-0.25	-0.32	-0.20	-0.29	-0.02	-0.14	-0.25	-0.36	0.03	0.13	0.18	0.26	-0.29	-0.28	-0.28	-0.37	-0.28	-0.30	-0.26	-0.17	-0.31	-0.29	-0.33	-0.23	-0.20	-0.04	0.01	-0.09
4	1	0.10	0.07	0.05	0.20	-0.38	-0.12	-0.18	-0.06	-0.06	-0.03	-0.23	-0.27	1.00	0.38	0.12	0.19	0.03	0.12	0.15	-0.07	0.14	0.10	0.12	0.20	-0.10	-0.16	-0.37	-0.18
4	2	0.21	0.07	0.09	0.31	-0.45	-0.14	-0.26	-0.11	-0.10	-0.02	-0.21	-0.27	0.38	1.00	0.09	0.16	0.07	0.17	0.17	0.05	0.17	0.02	0.07	0.17	-0.23	-0.17	-0.39	-0.33
4	3	-0.03	-0.03	-0.09	-0.05	-0.34	-0.08	-0.25	-0.09	-0.18	-0.12	-0.14	-0.29	0.12	0.09	1.00	0.04	-0.02	-0.11	-0.05	-0.13	-0.04	-0.11	-0.15	-0.04	-0.26	-0.29	-0.40	-0.32
4	4	0.16	0.18	0.12	0.12	-0.30	-0.22	-0.07	-0.01	-0.14	-0.18	-0.29	-0.30	0.19	0.16	0.04	1.00	0.17	0.24	0.15	-0.11	0.15	0.10	0.11	0.18	-0.12	-0.17	-0.29	-0.19
4	5	-0.11	-0.02	0.06	-0.12	0.05	-0.01	-0.15	-0.10	0.02	-0.10	-0.11	-0.10	-0.14	-0.14	-0.02	-0.02	-0.04	-0.08	-0.03	-0.07	-0.09	-0.05	-0.16	-0.07	-0.26	-0.13	-0.16	-0.21
5	1	0.14	0.12	0.09	0.10	-0.26	-0.16	-0.09	-0.10	-0.06	-0.17	-0.12	-0.21	0.03	0.07	-0.02	0.17	1.00	0.16	0.15	-0.08	0.06	0.05	0.06	0.13	-0.16	-0.14	-0.21	-0.26
5	2	0.29	0.32	0.22	0.31	-0.36	-0.27	-0.19	-0.16	-0.05	-0.17	-0.32	-0.24	0.12	0.17	-0.11	0.24	0.16	1.00	0.40	0.16	0.25	0.27	0.16	0.21	-0.21	-0.05	-0.18	-0.27
5	3	0.31	0.32	0.25	0.38	-0.35	-0.23	-0.20	-0.18	0.04	-0.10	-0.19	-0.15	0.15	0.17	-0.05	0.15	0.15	0.40	1.00	0.14	0.23	0.26	0.11	0.26	-0.25	-0.08	-0.21	-0.31
5	4	0.06	0.09	0.04	0.10	-0.31	-0.20	-0.25	-0.25	-0.06	-0.08	-0.18	-0.17	-0.07	0.05	-0.13	-0.11	-0.08	0.16	0.14	1.00	-0.01	0.02	-0.03	-0.02	-0.31	-0.11	-0.21	-0.32
5	5	-0.13	-0.20	-0.22	-0.11	-0.35	-0.10	-0.39	-0.26	-0.25	0.09	-0.21	-0.30	-0.07	0.02	-0.10	-0.15	-0.09	-0.08	-0.11	-0.08	-0.11	-0.18	-0.19	-0.14	-0.29	-0.24	-0.39	-0.39
6	1	0.36	0.26	0.23	0.33	-0.37	-0.29	-0.24	-0.20	-0.05	-0.10	-0.28	-0.25	0.14	0.17	-0.04	0.15	0.06	0.25	0.23	-0.01	1.00	0.23	0.07	0.23	-0.26	-0.11	-0.27	-0.31
6	2	0.22	0.27	0.24	0.19	-0.24	-0.23	-0.10	-0.15	0.01	-0.19	-0.28	-0.18	0.10	0.02	-0.11	0.10	0.05	0.27	0.26	0.02	0.23	1.00	0.19	0.35	-0.20	-0.03	-0.15	-0.20
6	3	0.06	0.09	0.08	0.08	-0.27	-0.15	0.02	-0.08	0.01	-0.24	-0.27	-0.24	0.12	0.07	-0.15	0.11	0.06	0.16	0.11	-0.03	0.07	0.19	1.00	0.17	-0.02	-0.06	-0.18	-0.05
6	4	0.24	0.26	0.21	0.24	-0.27	-0.21	-0.08	-0.10	0.05	-0.06	-0.22	-0.15	0.20	0.17	-0.04	0.18	0.13	0.21	0.26	-0.02	0.23	0.35	0.17	1.00	-0.19	-0.04	-0.22	-0.19
6	5	0.13	0.15	0.13	0.16	-0.26	-0.29	-0.06	-0.14	-0.02	-0.18	-0.23	-0.11	0.10	0.10	-0.09	0.10	0.05	0.25	0.21	0.05	0.14	0.18	0.11	0.23	-0.19	-0.09	-0.17	-0.20
7	1	-0.28	-0.24	-0.16	-0.30	-0.11	-0.01	0.13	0.04	-0.03	-0.18	-0.10	-0.12	-0.10	-0.23	-0.26	-0.12	-0.16	-0.21	-0.25	-0.31	-0.26	-0.20	-0.02	-0.19	1.00	0.12	-0.01	0.38
7	2	-0.09	-0.02	0.03	-0.16	-0.01	-0.05	0.02	-0.08	0.13	-0.08	-0.01	0.08	-0.16	-0.17	-0.29	-0.17	-0.14	-0.05	-0.08	-0.11	-0.11	-0.03	-0.06	-0.04	0.12	1.00	0.16	0.13
7	3	-0.22	-0.16	-0.06	-0.30	0.09	-0.20	0.00	-0.22	0.02	-0.27	-0.01	0.10	-0.37	-0.39	-0.40	-0.29	-0.21	-0.18	-0.21	-0.21	-0.27	-0.15	-0.18	-0.22	-0.01	0.16	1.00	0.03
7	4	-0.35	-0.29	-0.19	-0.38	0.05	-0.01	0.21	0.05	0.05	-0.18	-0.12	-0.02	-0.18	-0.33	-0.32	-0.19	-0.26	-0.27	-0.31	-0.32	-0.31	-0.20	-0.05	-0.19	0.38	0.13	0.03	1.00

Table 1. Pairwise comparison: Each column corresponds to an individual patient's comparison to other patients one-to-one on the vector space of eigenfaces in terms of the proximity. The greater the value a column has, the greater the probable proximity it has corresponding to that row whose syndrome indicates the probable diagnosis. First column together with first row corresponds to the syndromes (e.g. 1 corresponds to microdeletion 22q11.2). Second column together with second row indicates the number of the images in the specified syndrome in the first column or first row.

		1	1	1	1	2	2	2	2	3	3	3	3	4	4	4	4	5	5	5	5	6	6	6	6	7	7	7	7
		1	2	3	4	1	2	3	4	1	2	3	4	1	2	3	4	1	2	3	4	1	2	3	4	1	2	3	4
Rule-in	1	0.464	0.323	0.290	0.464	0.085	0.029	0.213	0.124	0.154	0.134	0.184	0.259	0.380	0.387	0.118	0.239	0.166	0.397	0.397	0.164	0.355	0.353	0.189	0.353	0.377	0.160	0.160	0.377
Rule-in	2	0.355	0.321	0.248	0.383	0.046	0.017	0.156	0.047	0.128	0.085	-0.012	0.095	0.288	0.380	0.048	0.186	0.163	0.315	0.383	0.103	0.246	0.266	0.161	0.264	0.129	0.128	0.095	0.213
Rule-in	3	0.307	0.267	0.243	0.331	-0.003	-0.005	0.017	-0.005	0.126	-0.015	-0.026	0.003	0.199	0.172	-0.024	0.183	0.125	0.266	0.258	0.050	0.231	0.265	0.118	0.256	-0.024	0.034	0.085	0.052

Table 2. Ruling in one, two and three diagnoses regarding the greatest values in columns of Table 1: the grey cells correspond to the right diagnosis. Ruling in one, two and three diagnoses yields 21, 26 and 28 correct diagnoses with success rates of 75, 94 and 100 percent among all 28 tested patients respectively. For instance, the value, 0.464, is observed from the cell where the syndrome name is coded as 1 and the frontal face is coded as 4. This indicates that

http://dx.doi.org/10.5772/51118

the frontal face which is coded as 1 in the syndrome list of 1 is the most proximate with a confidence value of 0.464 that is the greatest value in that column.

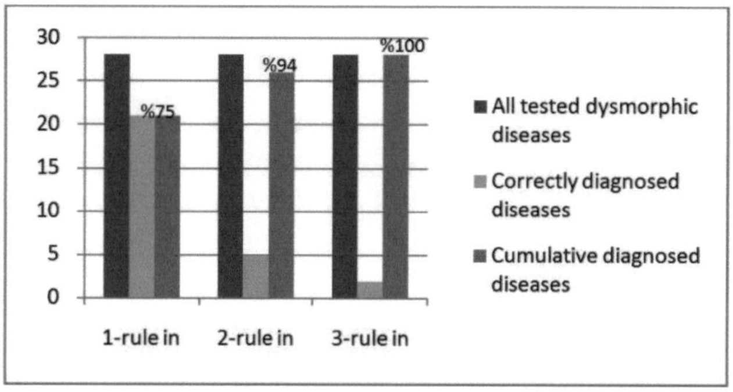

Figure 7. Graphical representation of success rates with respect to ruling in one, two and three diagnoses concerning the values in Table 2. Ruling in one, two and three diagnoses yields 21, 26 (including 5 more) and 28 (including 2 more) correct diagnoses among all 28 tested patients respectively. This designates the success rates of 75, 94 and 100 percent respectively as well.

4. Discussion

4.1. Main findings

FaceGP DDSS methodology has a success rate of 75%, 94% and 100% in terms of ruling in one, two and three diagnoses respectively. The results show that FaceGP DDSS methodology is able to make a biometric identification among syndromes successfully and efficiently based on the features of the patients' frontal faces, even though, the methodology has been tested by a limited number of 7 syndromes. Diagnosing syndromes correctly among many syndromes can be eased by the methodology provided that it is trained with those syndromes. One specific result of the study is that all test frontal faces of three syndromes that are microdeletion 22q11.2, fragile X and Williams–Beuren are correctly diagnosed in ruling in one diagnosis. Ruling in two diagnoses covers the 5 syndromes correctly whereas the ruling three does all seven syndromes. From these results we can conclude that the implemented methodology especially can guide medical professionals to employ correct cyto- and/or molecular genetic analysis that is the appropriate route of investigation in order to confirm a diagnosis with known genetic causes by ruling in probable diseases. Even with adequate knowledge, there remains the problem of reconciling sometimes imprecise descriptions of dysmorphic features in the literature with a personal and potentially subjective examination of an individual patient [7].

Preliminary results indicate that the application can be trained with many syndromes in several minutes and syndrome recognition can be established in few seconds either from an attached camera or from a file. We expect that the performance of the system doesn't degrade as the syndrome number grows owing to the computational efficiency of PCA. Moreover, multiple diagnostic as well as multiple training of syndromes effectively and efficiently can be employed easily with the implementation which will attract medical professionals most. During training process, the larger the training dataset per syndrome, the better the success of syndrome recognition is, thanks to the pair wise comparison in our study, regarding different characteristics even in same syndromes such as Down syndrome that has three subtypes[9] and cri du chat syndrome that has several variations in the feature[10]. Our implementations may be used to assist in diagnosing and defining facial phenotypes associated with syndromes in different ethnic groups and in different age groups provided that these kinds of cases are included into the training process of a specific syndrome.

4.2. Comparison to other published studies

Hammond [7] has pointed out that there are well documented approaches to recording craniofacial dysmorphology in a more objective fashion. Moreover, he [7] has asserted that international experts in dysmorphology are currently developing standardized terminology to address issues of imprecision and inconsistency. Most genome-wide association studies to date have focused on a limited number of specific diseases or traits to test whether a computer can classify syndromes and then recognize them when compared to new cases. There have been successful discrimination studies using images of children with a limited number of dysmorphic syndromes [2, 5, 6, 16]. Some robust composite computer assisted decision support systems are needed to be established not only for practitioners but also geneticists to support their decisions through thousands of dysmorphic diseases. FaceGP DDSS methodology is aimed to serve several needs of medical professionals who work in dysmorphology. This study presenting the FaceGP DDSS methodology contributes to the medical environment in several aspects. One of which is the support of general practitioners or pediatricians in the rural areas rather than trained geneticists as well as making easy of works for geneticists throughout thousands of dysmorphic diseases defined in some catalogs and databases. The other one is that a limitless number of dysmorphic diseases can be trained and tackled with FaceGP DDSS methodology in diagnosing process simultaneously. On the other hand, other similar studies having a fixed number of syndromes up to 10 in number are implemented to reveal the potential rather than to be an application to serve medical professionals for their everyday needs. Right diagnosis and consequently right treatments can influence progression of disease, especially in term of removing the effects of environmental factors[11]. For instance, when you supplement a patient having a syndrome with hormone, the patient may get better. The FaceGP DDSS methodology is designed primarily for investigators who wish to diagnose their patients with dysmorphic diseases quickly, effectively and successfully. Furthermore, it aims to support scientists for their studies who do not have expertise in the particular domain of dysmorphology. A new understanding of rul-

9 Chromosome 21 can be affected in three main ways, leading to the three main sub-types of Down's syndrome. Full trisomy 21 Down's syndrome, Mosaicism Down's syndrome and Translocation Down's syndrome are the three subtypes of Down syndrome.

10 Wilkins's findings delineate the variation in the clinical and karyotypic features of cri du chat syndrome [20].

11 The complex interplay of genetic and environmental factors is a significant confounding factor in various human genetic approaches, including genome-wide and candidate gene association studies as well as linkage analysis [21].

ing in/ruling out diseases in our methodology can be very helpful for geneticists who wish to employ cyto- and/or molecular genetic analysis for their cases to confirm probable diagnoses. Moreover, the application is ready to be used with a user friendly interface when implemented at any site. Our methodology, noticeably different from others, doesn't require any manual intervention or preprocessing of images by users, rather, all necessary algorithms have been embedded into the methodology.

Medical professionals may construct their own databases in terms of their own dysmorphic facial findings, thus facilitating incorporation of their findings into the examination as well as may add their special cases into a formerly constructed database. In addition, these databases, later, can be shared in a web environment, can be easily used as plug-and-play separately and furthermore, valuable databases can be united in a unique database after their evaluation by an expert group to be served to the knowledge of the scientific community. This opens the door to cross-study analyses of not only the primary genotypes-phenotypes dysmorphological diseases (prevalence < 1/25.000) but also secondary genotypes-phenotypes syndromes (prevalence < 1/25.000, maybe 1/100.000). However, probable specified genotype-phenotype diseases should be trained before presenting the application to the use of the medical professionals to gain their support.

Users could benefit the methodology with a user friendly interface without any manual intervention which may cause the users to avoid the use of any system. These findings refute the notion presented in several studies that manual steps cannot be excluded entirely from any dysmorphic facial analysis software that intends to extract as much information as possible.

4.3. Limitations of the study

There are several concerns that we should keep in mind while implementing these kinds of studies. Some genetic dysmorphic diseases could not be brought into scientific literature for especially two reasons. One of which is that many cases are lost before birth and nobody doesn't have any incentive to investigate the reason and eventually no one knows the cause; the other and the most important one is that families facing nonspecific cases don't permit the geneticists to investigate the cases, even though the investigation would help the families greatly for their future decisions[12] and consequently babies or fetus are buried with their genetic secrets in the sense of the ethical rules. On the other hand, in practice, some genetic dysmorphic diseases that are very rare (e.g. prevalence 1/100.000) are not globally defined and they are stored in the local Electronic Medical Records (EMRs) or research databases across different medical institutions without any common data structure or representational format. These data elements are needed to be presented to the knowledge of the genetic communities on behalf of the current and future healthy population. Our ability to fully understand the genetic basis of common diseases is significantly hindered by the inability to precisely specify the phenotypes and in particular, identifying and extracting phenotypes at large varies greatly between different medical specialties and institution, and lacks the sys-

12 Such as having a dysmorphic baby (the recurrence risk: the possibility that the problem would happen again in another pregnancy) and more than that such as early diagnosis, disease prevention, patient management, or even adjunctive therapies to be developed.

tematization and throughput compared to large-scale genotyping efforts [22]. Beyond these clinical aspects, dysmorphology has contributed much to current understanding of the genetic basis of human development [1]. Moreover, imprecise and nonstandardized nomenclature, especially of facial features, places a major difficulty for the communication between clinical geneticists [2]. It has to be noted that neither 2D nor 3D methods have direct applicability in clinical practice yet, as the number of specified syndromes is still very small [2].

As Boehringer [2] emphasize, database support with respect to facial traits is limited at present to apply similar studies as we do to establish better applications. Distinctive dysmorphic frontal faces specific to dysmorphic genotype-phenotype diseases are needed to train the system. Currently, in our study, a very limited number of dysmorphic genetic diseases by using frontal faces have been trained for further recognition process. There are several genetic databases such as eMERGE (Electronic Medical Records and Genomics) and PhenX (Consensus Measures for Phenotypes and Exposures), Dysmorphology Database in Oxford Medical Databases (OMD) and OMIM. One of which named OMD is more appropriate for our study, because it is better prepared to reveal genotype-phenotype associations in terms of images and taxonomy of dysmorphology, although it has very limited number of frontal faces for syndromes. One of the reasons that we work on frontal 2D image analysis is that this prominent database (OMD) that we aim to include into the study contains 2D genetic dysmorphic images rather than 3D videos by which the number of frames are captured and recorded. Moreover, most of the geneticists studying on dysmorphic diseases usually keep 2D images of their patients in their databases. The main drawback of the majority of 3D face recognition approaches is that they need all the elements of the system to be well calibrated and synchronized to acquire accurate 3D data (texture and depth maps) [19]. That will make it easier for investigators to collect and analyze the 2D dysmorphic data associated with genotypes. Whereas capturing of 3D information results in a richer data set and allows for excellent visualization despite the difficulties in possessing the technology and in detecting 3D as mentioned by Kau [13][13], 2D analysis has several advantages in practical use: equipment is cheap and it is easy to handle [2]. Conventional and digital two-dimensional (2D) photography offer rapid and easy capture of facial images. 3D analysis of syndromes would sure give better results as depicted in Hommond's study [6]. However, the lack of available data in 3D invalidates any methodology implemented for the near future.

Of course, recognition of face shape does not imply a diagnosis. A diagnosis is made by an appropriately trained clinician backed up, whenever possible, by genetic testing. For some dysmorphic syndromes there is no definitive genetic test and a clinical diagnosis has to suffice. For others, for example Noonan syndrome, a number of important genes may have been identified, but mutations for those genes may not be found in some children for whom there is a compelling clinical diagnosis [3].

A masking is not applied to remove the background of the cropped faces in our study. By employing a background mask, which simply provides a face shaped region, the effect of

13 Due to inherent faults in technology and the distortion of light, none of the 3D imaging systems is accurate over the full field of view. Furthermore, all systems suffer from a potential for patient movement and alterations of facial expression between the multiple views needed to construct a 3D model of the face.

background change would be minimized and diagnosing success would be better which is going to be an improvement as a further study. Furthermore, we couldn't reach the raw material of 7 syndromes in which the photos we utilized in our study are not in good condition in terms of their appearances. Moreover the patients are not same ages and same sexes for each syndrome. The results would be better if better images were utilized and if the patients were in similar age group and sexes in the study. The more faces bearing the characteristics of any syndrome included in the training, the better the recognition of that syndrome will be.

5. Conclusion

In terms of future technological support, two (2D) or three-dimensional (3D) models of facial morphology are showing potential in syndrome delineation and discrimination, in analyzing individual dysmorphology, and in contributing to multi-disciplinary and multi-species studies of genotype–phenotype correlations [7]. Our study is an example of substantiating this potential. We describe a new approach to syndrome identification by merging several algorithms. The algorithms that we included in our study are not novel. They have been utilized in many studies so far. However we included most essential ones in a robust composite understanding in a way to serve the everyday needs of the medical professionals who work in dysmorphology.

The preliminary results indicate that computer based diagnostic decision support systems such as the one we have established might be very helpful to assist medical professionals in genotype-phenotype dysmorphic diagnosis. The study reveals that the differences between facial regions such as facial landmarks, eyebrows, hair, lips, and chins can give the possibility of predicting the diagnosis of syndromes. It may contribute to the medical professionals in several aspects. Some of these are:

- To support medical professionals who do not have expertise in the particular domain of dysmorphology such as general practitioners or pediatricians in rural areas,
- To support geneticists throughout thousands dysmorphic diseases, most of which are very rare and difficult to memorize,
- Generally to support investigators who wish to diagnose their patients with dysmorphic diseases quickly, effectively and successfully,
- To support investigators who strive to expand their studies by including their cases into the system with the implementation whose database is able to be broadened dynamically and easily, which provides them to keep and deal with their data more efficiently.
- To guide geneticists to employ correct cyto- and/or molecular genetic analysis that is the appropriate route of investigation in order to confirm a diagnosis with - known genetic causes by ruling in probable diseases.
- No preprocessing of data manually that may cause the users to avoid the utilization of any system is required.

- FaceGP DDSS methodology can provide genetic screening which is a preliminary process of applying standard analysis to large populations to pick up underlying symptoms of genetic disorders. Genetic screening is not a diagnosis, but can produce a differential diagnosis which would lead to a definitive diagnosis and hence to early intervention and treatment.

The hope is that the FaceGP DDSS methodology will be widely adopted by the scientific community, fostering a new era of cooperation and collaboration and facilitating cross-study. Based on user feedback, we expect to continue to update the functionality of the methodology. As the data gathering for age groups and ethnic groups becomes more standardized and evolved internationally in the sense of dysmorphology, general implementations valid for everybody will be more possible.

5.1. Future work

Further improvement in diagnosing/recognition seems to be possible by integrating a background cropping mask algorithm that simply provides a face shaped region and minimize the effect of background change [15].

The dysmorphic faces from main databases as well as from individual databases referring to the names of the diseases should be both categorized and trained by the application for further better diagnostic decision support. This is a huge time consuming and challenging process needed to be done in the near future for the easy acceptance of the methodology by the scientific community. We intend to extend this work to a wider environment by including domain experts from academic and government institutions by deploying the methodology at several sites including as possible as many syndromes. Furthermore, 3D image processing and fetus image analysis in dysmorphology is going to be the subject of our future study.

Acknowledgements

The authors are very grateful to TÜBİTAK (The Scientific and Technological Research Council of Turkey) for sponsoring the study.

Author details

Kaya Kuru[1*] and Yusuf Tunca[2]

*Address all correspondence to: kkuru@gata.edu.tr

1 IT Department, Gulhane Military Medical Academy (GATA), Ankara, Turkey

2 Department of Medical Genetics, Gulhane Military Medical Academy (GATA), Ankara, Turkey

References

[1] Smithson, S. F., & Winter, R. M. (2004). Diagnosis in Dysmorphology: Clues from the Skin. *The British Journal of Dermatology*, 151(5), 953-60.

[2] Boehringer, S., Vollmar, T., Tasse, C., & Wurtz, R. (2006). Syndrome identification based on 2D analysis software. *European Journal of Human Genetics*, 14(10), 1082-1089.

[3] Hammond, P. (2011). What's in a face? 31 March 2008 http://www.hospitalmanagement.net/features/feature1767/ (accessed 21 September 2011

[4] Farkas, L. G. (1998). Anthropometry of the head and face. New York, Raven Press.

[5] Loos, H. S., Wieczorek, D., Wurtz, R. P., et al. (2003). Computer-based recognition of dysmorphic faces. *Eur J Hum Genet*, 11(8), 555-60.

[6] Hammond, P., Hutton, T. J., Allanson, J. E., et al. (2005). Discriminating power of localized three-dimensional facial morphology. *Am J Hum Genet*, 77(6), 999-1010.

[7] Hammond, P. (2007). The use of 3D face shape modelling in dysmorphology. *Arch Dis Child*, 92(12), 1120-1126.

[8] Douglas, T. S., & Mutsvangwa, T. E. M. (2010). A review of facial image analysis for delineation of the facial phenotype associated with fetal alcohol syndrome. *Am J Med Genet Part A*, 152A(2), 528-536.

[9] Kapoor, S., Khanna, S., & Bhatia, R. (2010). Facial gesture recognition using correlation and mahalanobis distance. *International journal of computer science and information security*, 7(2), 267-272.

[10] Turk, M. A., & Pentland, A. P. (1991). Face recognition using eigenfaces. *IEEE Conf. on Computer Vision and Pattern Recognitio*, 586-591.

[11] Iancu, C., Corcoran, P., & Costache, G. (2007). A review of face recognition techniques for in-camera applications. In Signals, Circuits and Systems, 2007. ISSCS 2007. International Symposium on July (2007)., 1, 1-4.

[12] Aldridge, K. A., Boyadjiev, S. T., Capone, G., et al. (2005). Precision and Error of Three-Dimensional Phenotypic Measures Acquired From 3dMD Photogrammetric Images. *American Journal of Medical Genetics*, 138A(3), 247-253 .

[13] Kau, C. H., Rich, Mond. S., Incrapera, A., English, J., & Xia, J. J. (2007). Three-dimensional surface acquisition systems for the study of facial morphology and their application to maxillofacial surgery. *Int J Med Robotics Comput Assist Surg*, 3(2), 97-110.

[14] Gul, A. B. (2003). Holistic Face Recognition by Dimension Reduction. *Master Thesis. METU.*

[15] Akalin, V. (2003). Face Recognition Using Eigenfaces and Neural Networks. *Master Thesis. METU.*

[16] Tripathi, B. K., & Kalra, P. K. (2010). High dimensional neural networks and applications. In: Prathiar DK., Jain LJ. (ed) Intelligent autonomous systems: foundations and applications. Springer , 215-233.

[17] Calvo, A. R., Rurainsky, J., & Eisert, P. (2009). D-3D Mixed Face Recognition Schemes. In: Girgic M et al. Recent Advances in Multimedia Signal Processing and Communications. Springer , 121-144.

[18] Viola, P. A., & Jones, M. J. (2001). Rapid object detection using a boosted cascade of simple feature. In: Proceedings of the IEEE Computer Society Conference on Computer Vision and Pattern Recognition. Kauai, USA: IEEE , 551-518.

[19] Dalal, A. B., & Phadke, S. R. (2007). Morphometric analysis of face in dysmorphology. *Comput Methods Programs Biomed*, 85(2), 165-72.

[20] Wilkins, L. E., Brown, J. A., Nance, W. E., & Wolf, B. (1983). Clinical heterogeneity in 80 home-reared children with cri du chat syndrome. *J Pediatr*, 102(4), 528-533.

[21] Mclnnes, R., & Michaud, J. L. (2004). Developmental Biology: Frontiers for Clinical Genetics. *Clin Genet*, 65(2), 163-176.

[22] Pathak, J., Pan, H., Wang, J., Kashyap, S., et al. (2011). Evaluating Phenotypic Data Elements for Genetics and Epidemiological Research: Experiences from the eMERGE and PhenX Network Projects. *AMIA Summits Transl Sci Proc.*, 41-45.

Section 2

Business Applications

Chapter 5

Emerging Applications of the New Paradigm of Intelligent Decision Making Process: Hybrid Decision Support Systems for Virtual Enterprise (DSS-VE)

Gabriela Prelipcean and Mircea Boscoianu

Additional information is available at the end of the chapter

http://dx.doi.org/10.5772/3371

1. Introduction

1.1. Introduction in the paradigm of intelligent decision making process

In the aftermath of the recent global crisis, the modern firm should proactively respond to the disruptive changes in the dynamics of markets, new technologies and the new architecture of the competition. Shen, Norrie (1999) proposed the following set of capabilities for the next generation of production systems: the integration of the firm with all its management systems and their partners to better respond to the global competition and to the movements in the markets; distributed structure based on knowledge; heterogeneous environments (software and hardware heterogeneous distributed in the production and operational environment); interoperability opened and capable to integrate new systems in an dynamic way; efficient cooperation with suppliers, partners and clients, integration human-machine; agility (the ability to adapt to a new environment in the case of rapid changing); scalability (additional resources could be easily incorporate) in every point location at every level without affection to the inter-organizational interdependencies; a good tolerance to different types of errors.

In real word it is very difficult to change, to adapt and to innovate in the context of a centralized managed process. It is necessary a new paradigm of intelligent decision making, more generalized, more flexible, more adaptable to change. The classical decomposition in subsystems- elements is not effective and the distributed method, which defines the components and the interactions between components in order to analyze the effects of dynamic interaction, is better in this emerging context.

It is necessary to adopt new methods, new technics and new instruments for decision support capable to:

- structure and enhance decision-making meetings (intelligent decisional planning);
- facilitate communication between decision-making factors and structuring decision-making problems (decision charts, decision trees);
- online analysis of the data and extracting information and knowledge using Data Warehousing (DW), Online Analytic Processing (OLAP), and Data Mining;
- assess the effects of application of alternative decision-making (what-if) using simulation techniques;
- construct and recommend the optimal decision-making alternative using multi-criteria optimization techniques;
- recommend a candidate solution by multi-attribute decision making (MADM);
- suggest decision-making alternatives based on artificial intelligence (expert system ES, artificial neural networks ANN, Case based reasoning CBR, Genetic Algorithms GA, Swarm Intelligence SI or hybrid models).

2. Decision support systems

The decisional support signifies a set of procedures based upon mathematical models on processing data, in the view of assisting the manager on taking decisions in conditions of simplicity, robustness, controllability, adaptability and completeness (Little, 1970). The Decision Making Process (DMP) consists in the outcome of decisional activities carried out by the representative taking decisions, assisted by a decisional team on supporting and/or a Decisional Support System (DSS). According to Nobel Prize laureate H. Simon, the DMP includes the following tasks: informing and up-taking of information, in order to formulate accurately the decisional issue; designing (includes activities in the view of understanding the decisional issue, adopting a new type of running, generating some new potential action ways and building the models); selecting the alternatives and adopting the solution; implementing the decision and evaluating the involvements. The activities and the phases in the H. Simon model emphasize a generic character and cover a large series of situations. The content and ampleness of them depends upon the decisional issue's features and upon the approaching way that was adopted in the view of solving the issue.

2.1. Basic elements of the DSS concept

DSS should cover a significant number of activities and phases of the decisional process. DSS is running in coordination with other components of the global informatics or informational system of the organization, where data or information is transferred. The available Information and computer technologies, ICT, and the designing and implementation

http://dx.doi.org/10.5772/3371

methodologies play an important part within the quality of the chosen solution. The accurate and equilibrated admixture between those three technologies (computerized models, databases and friendly interfaces) signify the technological centre of the DSS.

The typical constraints of a DSS are: a facile user's control adaptability to certain situations / user's characteristics, as well as the level of use during the process of decisions issuing. The controllability refers to the possibility of using the system at any moment and respectively, the possibility of changing the course of running in accordance to the own wish. DSS should be flexible enough to adapt to the deciding representative; by providing trust, the DSS leads towards a synergic evolution of use, in conditions of customization. Agility represents the capability to change and adapt quickly to changing circumstances. Using DSS is intended to support all phases of the decisional process.

Building a DSS starts with the participants (issuers of instruments, building analysts and the end-users), as well as the context elements (the current situation and the changes estimated in the context of the ITC progress) that interact with the organization. In this process, the specialists and end-users participate (analysts, designers or issuers of DSS instruments), working together within a team assigned by DSS. The DSS team will know details about the own products, as well as the competition alternative products; as regards the success of conception, building and implementation of DSS, the following conditions should be met: a better knowledge of the application, access to the knowledge sources, the identification of challenges of decision making process in connection with the end-users particularities, restraining the information instruments and accurate methods for designing an efficient DSS. The DSS team should provide as faster as possible an employable version and easy to adapt on the technological changes.

2.2. The DSS components

DSS is formed of four essential subsystems: the language subsystem, LS, which emphasizes the set of expression forms, by which the user can transmit; the subsystem of presentation, PS, that signifies a set of forms or means by which messages are transferred (from out to DSS) towards the user or third parties (executants of decisions, data sources within organization); the subsystem of the knowledge elements, KES, which includes elements of knowledge purchased or created internally; the subsystem of problem solving – PSS, signifying the set of software modules by which the KES knowledge elements are processed, as result of rendering the input messages. The amplitude and characteristics of these four subsystems and the adopted solutions of information transposing can make a difference between the application systems.

2.2.1. The Knowledge Elements Subsystem – KES

KES includes the knowledge, whichever the user hasn't any ability or time necessary to accumulate it. KES has the mission of simulating the general knowledge volume, specific to the application and decisional situation that an ideal decisional assistant should have.

The primary elements of knowledge are useful on recognizing a decisional situation and serve as "basic material" in order to issue a solution. These can be particularized into the following classes: descriptive knowledge, procedural knowledge (mathematical knowledge of simulation and optimization, as well as the algorithms of the associates solving the issues), the knowledge regarding the reasoning (concerning the governmental rules and justifying the way of using the procedural knowledge simultaneously with those descriptive).

The secondary knowledge elements (linguistic, which serve on understanding the signification of users solicitations, and of potential reports from the decisions executors, or from other data providers; of presentation which describe the way information is sent during the decisions issuance, or eventually, decisions are communicated; assimilative, which use on determining the conditions and on establishing the way the new knowledge elements can be inserted into KES), aiming on supporting the activities of issuing decisions by auxiliary activities, such as: interpretation of the input messages (received from users or third parties); illustration of the output messages issued by the system (towards the users or third parties); maintaining and updating KES. The knowledge stored is characterized by the following: the source (outside DSS or inside the system), specificity (general, applicable to a field, or strictly related to an application), the persistence and completeness (one or more amongst the types of knowledge elements).

2.2.2. The communication subsystem

The communication subsystem can include many solutions in order to take into consideration the following: knowledge and the cognitive style of those interacting with the system and the part these have towards the system (user, manager or data provider). A compromise should be carried out between simplicity in using, and respectively efficiency and performances.

2.2.3. The problem solving system, PSS

The PSS signifies the dynamic part of DSS, which carries out the knowledge processing, and includes the software programs that transpose the processing knowledge capacities (purchasing the knowledge; selecting the already existing knowledge elements, necessary as basis on issuing the decision and issuing new achieved knowledge; presenting the results; managing and updating the KES content).

2.3. An analysis of the possibilities of selection DSS architecture

The DSS- data oriented decision structure (DSS-DO) is focused on the apprehension and diagnosis of decisional issues, identifying the action alternatives and checking the new hypothesis and ideas. The main particularity consists in organizing the knowledge elements subsystem under the form of well structured databases, which sometimes might have significant dimensions. The PSS is transposed in information by means of the software modules, which carry out the data management, the interactive finding of information and various processing, specific to particular applications.

http://dx.doi.org/10.5772/3371

The support subsystems of documents oriented decisions (DSS-DO), based on the descriptive, procedural or reasoning knowledge use serve both the information decisional activities, as well as the activities of evaluating the action alternatives and choosing a solution. The focus is on the abilities of managing the electronic documents and developing the knowledge, and the interest is to realize the classification and indexation of documents.

The support subsystems of models oriented decisions (DSS-MO) appertain on offering solutions on solving the decisional issue model. The set of solution is directly included in its executable form within the logic of the software modules, transposing the subsystem of issue solving, by means of informatics; or, the set of solvers is kept under the form of programs library, that can be modified in the collection of procedural knowledge of the knowledge elements subsystem. The user can modify parameters/ data and can specify the paths of calculus. The flexible solutions allow the selection of the solving algorithm, defining the presentation way, the modification of the algorithms collection. In contradistinction to the data oriented systems and those oriented on documents, the DSS-MO include a relatively reduced volume of descriptive knowledge elements.

Regarding intelligent DSS (IDSS), the focus is on storing, managing and processing of knowledge on reasoning, within the system of knowledge elements, by using the engine of interfaces carrying out, which can be implemented into the system of treating issue. Initially, the knowledge oriented systems were aimed on replacing the models oriented systems, in situations where no enough truthful model could be issued in order to solve the decisional issue, or in situations where such model were too complicated so as to be solved by the help of the already existing algorithms.

The knowledge elements concerning the reasoning and the software modules based on artificial intelligence, and which implement the abilities of processing such knowledge, are seen as an ingredient within the combined structures of the DSS. In this case, the reasoning knowledge can play different tasks: the intelligent processing of the messages expressed within a non-procedural language, the management of other types of knowledge included into KES, using the procedural knowledge within the evaluation and selection of the solution, at the level of human expert competencies.

There are more styles of mixing the systems, by means of integrating the software modules that transpose by the help of ICT the capacities of knowledge processing, and respectively, those referring to communication inside the same informatics instrument. The styles that characterize the integration within various information instruments are the following: a) integration by knowledge conversion (interfacing) or the endowment of the software modules that should communicate with facilities embedded by knowledge export; b) integration, by means of the clipboard memory; c) integration, by means of the common formats.

The patterns that define the integration inside the same information system are: integration by nesting, where one or more software modules are embedded within a single "host" prevailing program; the synergic integration, situation when more knowledge elements represented in various forms can be processed.

Within the context of the combined systems, calling up the classical paradigm of DSS based on tripe structure of components can be useful: dialogue, data or models (DDM). This is an example of combined data and models oriented system, covering a part of the support possibilities for decisions allowed, thus enabling the DSS decomposing in subsystems, and in completing or endowing with new modules, respectively.

2.4. Aspects regarding the construction of DSS architecture

2.4.1. Stages of creating a DSS process

Creating a DSS includes a series of activities that start with generating of the idea on introducing the system within an organization, and ends by achieving the prototype: preparing the projects, the system analysis, designing, implementation and exploitation. The DSS architecture is determined by elements, such as: the central element aimed in the process of building the DSS architecture; the information platform used; the DSS builder; the form of the process (linear, based on the stages of life cycle or in cycles using the prototype); the interaction between the technical processes and those social that took place while creating an DSS.

First of all it is necessary to mention that the idea of introducing a DSS has determined a series of strengthening activities, in order to be transformed into a first specification of the future system (the diagnosis of current situation, establishing the main characteristics of the future system, evaluation of feasibility and design planning). The diagnosis consists in identifying the current issues and presenting the opportunities, as well as the means of changing or improving, respectively. The commitment decision and the resources allotment follows, in accordance to the feasibility study, framing the project within the development politics is taken into account, as well as the company's priorities, the harmonization with the ICT infrastructure, the availability of funds within context of justifying the impact over the organization and preliminary risk management issues. Planning the project includes the orderly list of phases that follow to be developed forwards: the system analysis, the design and implementation, as well as the potential activities of maintenance. For each stage are indicated: the moment of start/ end, the expected results, the responsible persons and the other participants, as well as the allocated resources.

In the system analysis stage, it is necessary to mention data storing and processing, take into consideration the following: the stock-taking and thorough studying of the decisional situations, for which providing the information support is aimed; discovering the particularities of each individual that will become users of the system; identification of some frame elements, such as: the restrictions introduces by the organization in issuing, transmitting and executing the decisions, the existing information infrastructure and the possibilities of combining with other parts of the global information system of the organization; the evaluation of results, of the previous initiatives of introducing the DSS in that organization or from others similar, in order to avoid some potential signalized errors.

The technical design should take into consideration both the ground system, as well as its components as regarded from ITC point of view, the content of defining specifications is transposed into an execution project. The designing process is composed of activities of establishing the DSS structure and of defining each technological component of the system, as well as the way it integrates with the other parts of the global information system of the organization. The designing stage is accomplished by the specification of carrying out the system and integrating it within the organization. The level of describing in details and of defining the components depends upon how this is allowed while using information platform. For most of applications, the component where the designer has the most levels of freedom signifies the data basis, followed by the dialogue subsystem.

In the stage of implementation, the content of technical design is transposed into an information system, by means of the instruments selected, and consists in activities of effective building of DSS into an application and integration within the global information system of the organization, testing and issuance of the documentation, of building the future users and taking organizational measures, necessary to effectively exploit the system. Testing the system by the user is necessary in order to see the way the system carried out will satisfy the direct future beneficiary. This represents the validation of user, named also as acceptance test or operational test, and is able to determine the modification of characteristics.

The exploitation and the progress of DSS are important because the efficiency and the costs on the entire life cycle of the system are essential aspects. The validated system in action is provided with documentation of using and maintenance issued, and can be carried out in current exploitation. The further modifications of the tasks, preferences of users can determine the need of adapting and modernization of the DSS.

2.4.2. The DSS generator

The selection process and the effective use of a DSS generator will influence powerfully both the solution achieved, as well as the way one can reach to it. Within the system analysis, a stock-taking of the DSS generators already existing on the market is aimed. These are selected by means of a limited number of criteria, in the view of filtering those not serving on reaching the requirements included within the functional specification of details, that do not frame within the restrictions imposed by the already existing information infrastructure or in the strategy of developing the global information system of the organization, or that lead towards the unacceptable overreaching of the project budget.

The next stage is placed into the stage of issuing the technical project, when the alternatives selected in the previous stage should be put in order, in the view of performing a selection. In order to solve it, the following became necessary: defining the set of evaluation criteria and of weights associated to them, appreciating the value or the utility of each instrument-candidate, viewed through all the evaluation criteria and applying a method of establishing the classification.

As regards the ordering, a set of evaluation criteria will be used: the completeness, which means that per assembly, the criteria should cover all the issues that can slope the balance towards an alternative or other; the non-redundancy, which imposes a certain issue to be taken into consideration, only by a single evaluation criterion, so that more calculations will not be carried out in a favorable or non-favorable way; the discomposing, which requires that a criterion, seen as general or vague, might be decomposed in more simple independent criteria; the operability, which shows that formulating the criteria should be expressed very clear, in order to be understood by all involved on taking decisions and choosing a solution; the minimalistic feature, consisting in the drawing a limit for the criteria number, so as to solve a dilemma between a fast but superficial analysis, and one that can become non-opportune, because of the attempt on taking in view another perfect solution reaching.

The DSS generator can be used in order tot test some requirements or ideas of designing, which were unclear from the start of the project, and in order to simulate the future user's interest, and of convincing the project's sponsor, after which designing an optimized and flexible system will be carried out by using primary constructive elements. In this way, the DSS generators are ideal means on building a progressive and based on prototype structure.

2.4.3. Data management in DSS

In order to achieve efficient results, quality data, well-structured and organized has become necessary. The set of attributes that characterize the data quality is different from one type of information system to another. In this way, the systems necessary to control in real time the technological processes or to enable fast data access signify the most important feature, while high data precision within computer aided applications is compulsory. The main data models are: the hierarchical model, the network type model and the relational model. Starting from the very beginning, some issues that might occur within a DSS could be identified, being caused by weak quality of data: the necessary data on issuing the decision does not simply exist, since none has thought that such data might be necessary; as consequence, it should be stored; the already existing data within the system are not accurate or are old; data gathered in the system are not consistent with the way of performing activities on issuing decisions, where decisions are being represented accurately. The data storage signifies the name of a specialized database, aimed on satisfying firstly the information necessities of the top managers or of the workers based on knowledge, which develop activities of strategic type within an organization. The data included within the storage come from multiple and various internal and external sources.

The main classes of operations are drawn up by: data storage by its extraction from various sources; the data conversion from the original format into the adopted format, in order to be used within the data storage; ordering the data, by identifying and correcting the conversion errors, and by completing the omissions; the internal derivation of new data from the operative data received and processed, by means of aggregation or synthetizing actions, so that the data storage can include elements that haven't been met within the operative databases; effective loading into the chosen data structure, in order to be used in subsequent interrogations and analysis.

2.4.4. *The portfolio of models used within DSS*

DSS models can be classified in accordance to the following criteria: the aim, the time variable existence, the certainty degree, the generality, the decisional level and the issue type, in this way, the aim can signify: the understanding of decisional situations, the consequences of applying the decisional alternatives and the robustness of recommended solutions.

Depending upon the presence or absence of time variable within the models form, these might be dynamic or static, respectively. Depending upon the certainty degree, deterministic and probabilistic models can be distinguished. Regarding from the generality point of view, a model can be used for a class of decisional issued or only into a single application. In accordance to the decisional level the strategic, tactical and operative models can be emphasized, on assisting and establishing the objectives and necessary resources on log terms. These are, in generally, descriptive, dynamic, deterministic and created accurately, being provided with a high number of generating variables.

Within a DSS, more models and associated solvers can exist. As in the situation of data, models signify one of the sources with organization knowledge elements. In order to manage and exploit them, without being known by the user or the application programs and without the need of explaining in details the physical aspects relative to storing the models, the existence of a management system for the portfolio of models capable to execute tasks analogous with those specific to a databases management system. The characteristics of this Models Management System (MMS) emphasize the existence of some accurate control means, for both the expert user and the new one; the flexibility or possibility of choosing or changing the preference towards the model type during the decision al process; the presence of the reaction able to indicate the stage of developing the models execution, the compatibility with the solutions chosen for the system of databases management system.

The main functions of the MMS refers to the abilities of performing the assimilation of procedural knowledge on designing and selecting, in the view of exploitation, in order to process descriptive knowledge elements, such as: creating some models in the view of storing them within the DSS models database. Creation and assimilation of new models can be accomplished in more ways, meaning: selection performed in the view of storing new models from the set of the already existing products on the market, formulating new models, by the help of designing languages and using the issue's characteristics, the content of some complex models from the already existing building blocks and by integrating building modules, similar to the content, but foregoing by the operation of modifying modules; maintenance of the models base by updating and extension actions; selecting and preparing, in the view of executing the existing models and the algorithms of solving, so as to assist the activities on decisional issues solving; the execution of models and data sets, followed by the evaluation of results and potential taking over other data sets.

All these assume the existence of more elements, such as: a language of designing, aimed on ensuring the creation and loading of models within the models base and by the help of solving algorithms; models database and solving algorithms easy to be accessed; a diagram of treating the models and algorithms, enabling the selection in the view of execution.

2.5. The integration of artificial intelligence (AI) in DSS

In order to increase the decisional performances, DSS can be endowed by means of artificial intelligence techniques. The artificial intelligence techniques are used for both information processing and data visualization, as well as for extracting the information from high data volumes, in the view of searching templates that might be helpful within decisions taking processes.

The Artificial Intelligence (AI) is characterized by a high learning ability, in the view of continuous improvement with or without external helping. The main applications of the AI are the following: the expert systems, the neuronal networks, the logic fuzzy, the genetic algorithms, the intelligent agents and pattern recognition. Programming languages have been especially created, such as LISP and Prolog, in the view of carrying out the research in the field, and even on creating artificial intelligence devices or programs.

One of the candidates to be incorporated in the intelligent decision making paradigm is the intelligent control (Fu, 1970) with the aim to reproduce the most important human intelligence characteristics (adaptation, learning, planning in uncertainty environments) and the capability to interpret a huge quantity of data. Based on the new approaches (artificial neural networks - ANN, fuzzy logic - FL, genetic algorithms - GA, expert systems and hybrid systems), DSS could be reinforced via the biological inspiration (Swarm Intelligence, SI) and could solve an extended category of applications.

FL shapes the rationing of human brain based on the approximate, non-quantitative, non-binary reasoning. Applying the FL method is performed in the following steps: defining the input-output variables, defining subsets intervals, choosing the functions, setting the if-then rules, performing calculations and adjusting the rules.

NN tries to reproduce the structure and functions of the human nervous system (consisting of a large number of interconnected neurons that determine the way in which the information is stored). In ANN the neurons receive inputs from other neurons through a weighted function (with increasing / decreasing signal). These signals are received and collected by the neuron, and if the amount exceeds a certain threshold, the neuron will send its own signal to other neurons. Information is stored in the neuron input weights and the adjustments offer the ability to store different information. The storage capacity of a single neuron is limited, but the set of neurons interconnected in several layers provide superior performance. ANN are used to solve problems of estimation, identification and predictive or problems of complex optimization. Due to independence of operations inside the components, related models have a great potential for parallelism.

Based on the Darwin's principles of genetics and natural selection, GAs are adaptive techniques for heuristic search (Holland, 1975). The biological process of evolution is based on the adaptation to the environment, the capability to survive/ evolve over generations. GA is a complex model that emulate biological evolutionary model to solve/ optimize problems. It includes a set of individual elements represented in the form of binary sequences (population) and a set of biological operators defined on the population. With the support of operators, GA manipulates the most promising sequences evaluated according to an objective

http://dx.doi.org/10.5772/3371

function and improves the solution. GA are used to solve optimization problems (near-optimal solutions), planning or search problems.

The AI has studied new architectures of computing, able to: offer support in situations of unclearness and uncertainty; to use knowledge and the experience on adapting to the environment changes; to understand, to deduce and to analyze new situations; to recognize the relative significance of various elements in the context of fast changing of situations or to detect the ambiguous or contradictory messages.

In the view of achieving an intelligent machine, such amplitudes concerning the intelligence and related behaviors or mechanisms should integrate within the computing system. The intelligent system should be able to offer a fast, soft and adaptable support, endowed by the ability of acting accurately within an uncertain and chaotic field (Meystel, Albus, 2002).

AI based technologies are able to establish both an alternative to the numeric methods, when these fail or cannot be applied due to the qualitative issues preponderance and uncertainty presence, as well as a complement of them, when the limits above mentioned can affect the decisions quality.

The limits of the AI based technologies should be also taken into account. For example the solution could be sensitive to decider's preferences and there is a limited ability of treating small variations of the attributes, with impact on the experiments (since the user does not have access to rules within the knowledge base). There are also technical difficulties specific to various means of knowledge representation and the transmission of the parameters between the software components that implement the numerical methods, and those including the AI components. One of the most known AI based information technology met within the frame of decisional activities assistance is represented by the expert systems (ES). The differentiation between the DSS and ES can be expressed by: borders of the application field, which are evasive and many times variable and unpredictable in the situation of DSS, and limitary and well shaped within the ES; the historical progress that took place, since the beginning of real applications on carry out systems within DSS, respectively, from the study of abstract reasoning, in the attempts of creating some general systems of solving issues within ES; the normative, which is more pronounced within ES; the goal aimed, which consists in increasing the decisions efficiency on DSS and respectively, on growing the efficiency within the process of ES solution achieving; the user's attitude towards the system, which is of acceptance or rejection of solutions and explanations, based on the best knowledge within ES. An ES will usually designate an AI based information technology, while and DSS will involve, more often the idea of an application.

3. Virtual enterprise VE and virtual organization VO

3.1. Definition of concepts

The enterprise modeling is a complex process of building integrated systems of models (process models, data models, resource models) dedicated to the managerial support of a modern firm (Vernadat, 1996). In Petersen (2000), Bernus (1996) is proposed the Enterprise Engineering and Enterprise Integration concept (EEEI), useful in the actual context of a high competitive environment. In Fig 1 is presented the evolution of enterprises in the context of modern partnerships, based on the VE/ VO concepts.

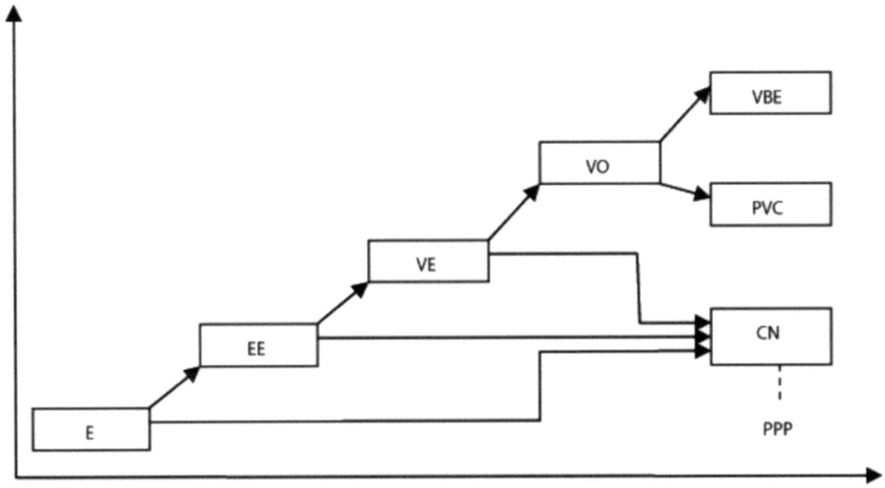

Figure 1. The evolution of enterprises and modern partnerships (based on the VE/VO concept)

The concept of Extended Enterprises (EE)/ Extended Enterprise Engineering (EEE) is often used in the context of virtual enterprise (VE) as a partnership and involves constructive collaboration between the manufacturer, the customer and the supplier. EE is a formation of co-operative enterprises responsible for all operations related to the product (from procurement to end customer, but it also includes maintenance/ service tasks). In Vernadat (1996), there is no distinction between EE and VE, which function based on a cooperation and the use of ICT communications and electronic data interchange, but in Globeman (1999) is proposed a clear distinction based on their lifecycle characteristics. In this case EE is a network for collaboration which offers share core competencies and becomes operational after a specific customer demand via the building of a special purpose vehicle (SPV) named VE. Enterprise Integration (EI) is a holistic approach that provides frameworks and methodologies to integrate complex systems. Totally Integrated Enterprise (TIE) is an extended architecture and taking to consideration the entire customer/ product life cycle. The modern paradigm is related to the collaboration/ partnerships in the context of competition. Collaboration between different types of partners offer opportunities (a better market share, stock reduction, cost reduction, better quality, shorter product development cycles) and enables partners to gain knowledge (innovation, a better understanding of the transformation of future processes/ markets, capability to implement efficient programs/ products). Specman (1998) proposed the transition from coordination to collaboration and Slack (2004) underlines importance of trust, commitment and information sharing among partners. SAP (2002) proposed the conceptive of Adaptive Supply Chain which represents a chain able to have better visibility of requirements and capabilities in the context of flexible, adaptive and robust management, based on a greater speed of information and assets.

There are different definitions of the virtual enterprise VE/ VO concepts. The VE emphasizes a temporary alliance between enterprises, based on cooperation/ partnership and efficient common use of competencies, abilities and resources, capable to respond to business opportunities or to improve the global performances. The VO also signifies an alliance between various organizations, but the objectives are extended beyond the simple profit achieving. According to Katzy (2002), VE is based on the ability to create temporary co-operations and to realize the value of a short business opportunity by using the synergy of the different capabilities of the partners. In Jagdev, Browne (1998), VE is defined as a temporary network of independent companies that are linked using information technology; the focus is on the technology that links the partners rather than the roles of the independent companies. In Byrne (1993) VE is defined as a temporary network of independent companies formed to share skills/ costs and to gain the access to each other's markets. In Garita, Afsarmanesh (2001) VE is represented by an interoperable network of firms that collaborate via ITC elements in order to realize a common objective. In Olegario (2001) VE represents a temporary alliance of independent firms with complementary competencies. In the DAI context, VE is a temporary, cooperative network based on independent, autonomous firms that cooperate in order to exploit a particular market opportunity (Clements, 1997; Fischer, 1996; Oliveira, Rocha, 2000; Ru, Vierke, 1998). Other authors incorporate properties of VEs such as "rapidly configured, multi-disciplinary network of firms" (Ambroszkiewicz, 1998), goal-oriented behavior based on cooperative work (Oliveira, Rocha, 2000), decentralized control of activities, (Szirbik, 1999), and commitment among the autonomous partners (Jain, 1999). The aim of VE is to provide a quick and flexible solution for an unpredicted opportunity. This agile reaction it is more than an action, rather than an institution. The focus is on the agility and adaptability to grasp a new opportunity and it is based on quick innovative solutions. It results that the concept of VE is linked to the following attributes: value created and not added; there is only a temporary cooperation focused on objectives; there is a mechanism capable to facilitate permanent restructuring in flexibility, adaptability and robustness.

Regarding the VO concept, in Davidow, Malone (1992) the interest is to integrate the information throughout the organizational components and to act intelligent based on this information. In Venkatraman, Henderson (1998) VO is based on the "virtualness" strategy with three independent components: virtual encounter (customer interaction), virtual sourcing (asset configuration) and virtual expertise (knowledge leverage). In Fox (1998) VO is defined in the context of strategic alliances.

The Virtual Breeding Environment (VBE) represents an extended cooperation between organizations (cooperation agreements, common operation principles and a common infrastructure), in the view of identifying new opportunities in order to build temporary alliances, able to lead towards achieving better results on mean and long term. The Professional Virtual Community (PVC) combines those virtual community concepts (individuals' networks that uses computer technologies) and professional community (pooling the experience, knowledge and competencies).

In the literature (Camarinha-Matos, Afsarmanesh, 2001; Camarinha-Matos, 1998), there are presented different types of classification for VEs according to the following aspects: duration (lifespan of the organization); the topology of the network; the flexibility of the structure; the level/ type of participation (a partner could participate in just one VE or several VEs simultaneously); the type of coordination (centralized coordination, democratic alliances, federation of partners) where the partners achieve their goals by creating a joint coordination structure; the visibility scope (related to typology and coordination/ dependencies among the partners).

Other authors (Bernus, 1997) identify several different types of VEs: major/ huge scale projects; consortia (for production, research or service as an alliance of partners limited to a common mission); general project group (set up by business executives).

Regarding the main characteristics/ properties of VE we should mention there exists a partnership of organizations that collaborate or a strategic alliance (the partners are aligned at the activities level, but also at the level of their business goals); there is a temporary network with a limited lifetime based on the exploitation of a particular market opportunity or a special customer demand; high level of communication based on advanced ICT technologies capable to support the entire partnership; dynamic sharing of skills, costs and markets; goal-oriented and commitment-based. Wigand (1997) identified the main characteristics (modularity, heterogeneity, time/ space distribution, open-closed and transparency) and the corresponding design principles. Goldman (1995) identified the following characteristics: opportunism, excellence, technology, no borders, and trust. In the modern literature, other authors (Tolle, 2004; Camarinha-Matos, Afsarmanesh, 2005) concluded that the more important characteristics of VE are: a partial mission overlap; customer-centered and mass customization; network of independent companies; semi-stable relations; geographical dispersion; focus on core competencies, and innovation. The recent evolutions demonstrated also the following characteristics: single identity; based on trust; shared loyalty; focus on the use of ICT; the management should understand the essential distinction between strategic and operational levels; capability to stimulate/ integrate innovation.

3.2. Possibilities for evolution and developments

At the foundation core of VE are the proactive exploitation of dynamic competition rather than the transformation of raw material into finished products. In the traditional view, value is created in the form of labor performed and resources consumed both of which can best be achieved under stable conditions (Norman, Ramirez, 1993). In contrast, the VE/ VO are a structure that supports entrepreneurial innovation to create new platforms from competencies, resources and partners that have never existed before. In this case the value is created from new opportunities and new structures should be implemented in order to exploit these opportunities.

In Fine, Whitney (1996) the evolution and the development of VE is linked to outsourcing/ subcontracting features, with focus on the core capabilities by deciding whether to make/ buy a given component/ subsystem. Another branch of literature (Jager, 1998; Wildeman, 1998; Franke, 2001; Tølle, 2004; Camarinha- Matos, Afsarmanesh, 2005) considers VE as an evolution from network organizations with creative combination of attributes from outsourcing, strategic networks and agility.

To understand new opportunities, we first examine potential sources of value identified in the empirical literature. We then discuss virtual operations as a temporary industrial structure designed to exploit these opportunities.

In Figure 2 is presented an intuitive, but practical way for developing a VE solution based on the identification of needs in a context defined by environmental factors and restrictions. The interest is to enhance the capability to respond to different opportunities of the markets by stimulating organizational flexibility. In Figure 2 it is also a suggestive picture that represents the way to model and integrate the VE operation in real business until an efficient decommissioning, coupled with a reliable capacity to recuperate units/ subsystems adaptable for future VEs. This is not a standard form, because VE/VO required an architectural construction and it is a complex innovative process.

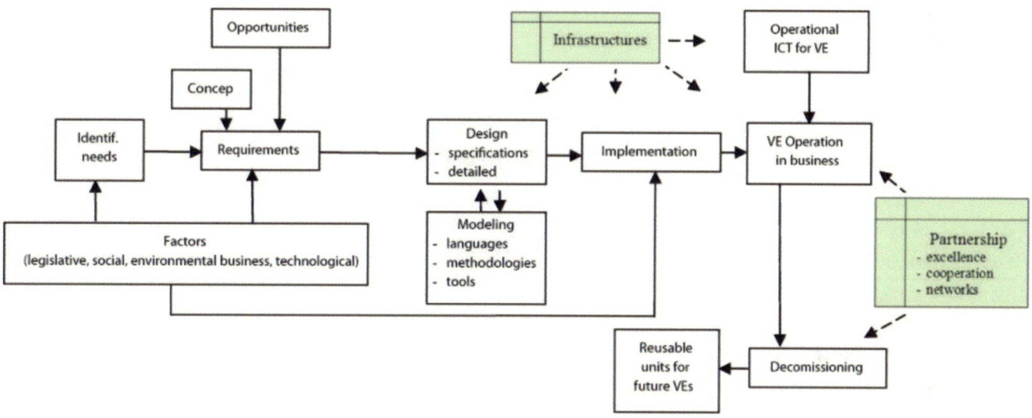

Figure 2. The practical way for developing a VE solution

3.3. Possibilities of modeling VE/ VO architectures

Agent based modeling (ABM) is a more powerful concept better adapted to the actual trends than the classic process of equation based modeling, because the complexity could be modeled by using the interactions between the elements- subsystems. Multi agent systems (MAS) are characterized by: modularity, decentralization, interchangeability, low structured character and complexity. The most interesting applications of ABM/ MAS in production management are represented by SCM (supply change management), addressed to offer better services to clients with lower production costs and VE/ VO which represents a unique interconnected chain of the supply in which the activities realized are oriented to the objective of production. VE/ VO mix the advantages of integrated firms (financial power, availability of resources, production costs) with the advantages of distributed firms (adaptability, flexibility). From the perspective of MSA, VE/ VO represents a group of agents which cooperates in order to realize a unique objective.

Regarding the state of the art in the field of formation/ operation of VEs (Kazi, Hannus, 2002; Zweger, 2002) we should mention different types of architectures which support the formation and operation of VEs and capable to optimize the cooperative functioning of the key components of VEs such as elements that support modeling, set up management, ICT support, reference models, and infrastructures, like GERAM (Generic Enterprise Reference Architecture and Model) and Virtual Enterprise Reference Architecture and Methodology (VERAM).

The modeling of these types of architectures are based on the following features: the lifecycle view (the phases in the lifecycles); genericity (generic, particular and partial levels); modeling strategies (a view which comprise function, information, organization and resources).

The basic steps in the life cycle of a VE are: preliminary configuration of the VE and design phases of the lifecycle; the build of a detailed design and implementation of the phases in the lifecycle; service/ maintenance; decommission VEs during the decommission phase of the lifecycle.

The phases of the development of VEs (Parunak, 1997) are: creation (establishes the goal/ objectives of the future VE according to the market conditions); management/ operation (focused on how to achieve the goals/ objectives); dissolution (ending the relationship among partners and evaluation of the results of this partnership). The design of VE could be divided in four stages: identification of the market opportunity; identification of the core competencies required for taking advantage of the market opportunity; the selection of the partner companies capable of delivering the required core capabilities, and the formation of the VE by operating an intelligent integration of the core capabilities of the partners. In Tolle (2004) the design is subdivided into five phases: identification, concept, requirements, preliminary design and detailed design.

4. Decision Support Systems for Virtual Enterprise (DSS – VE)

A typical DSS-VE system should contain tools, applications and models that can be efficiently used during the formation and operation of VEs but also courses which offer guidelines that indicate how these tools, applications and models should be used in practice (Zweger, 2002; Tolle, 2002). The main subsystems are: modeling (analyze, preparation and (re)-design of the VE's business processes, partner roles, contracts); applications and infrastructures (the components that perform or support the processes in order to provide the technological realization of the VE); methodology (guidelines on modeling); contingency factors ("situational factors" or conditions which affect the set up of the VE and "design parameters" which describe different set- ups for VEs). Other authors have proposed software agents and DAI in order to support the dynamism of VEs, for example multi agent systems (MAS) for SCM (Fox, 1993)

http://dx.doi.org/10.5772/3371

The Distributed Business Process (DBP) is represented by a set of business processes (BP), which emphasize the VE. Since one assumes that BP is carried out by various enterprises, the entity that has started the VE occurrence will coordinate the accurate and efficient functioning of the new business (Rabelo, 1996). In this case, VE signifies an optimal supply chain management (SCM) equipped with extended possibilities of analyses: a better response in the situation of a reduced level of coordination that covers activities carried out on the production flow systems, capable to react; in the situation of a mean coordination level, which emphasizes advanced coordination functions or high level of coordination (based on intelligent coordination functions).

The VE coordinator should understand the aims and capabilities of each enterprise involved, but also the interconections. The new logistics imposed by this new architecture has determined the transformation/ evolution of the logistics toward an integrated flow of materials/ information that should be managed as a single entity, starting from the raw material up to the final consumer. Using the Integrated Logistics (IL), as a basic concept needed to meet the distributed relationships requirements, permits a better understanding of the involvements into the real integration of VE because it focuses on the global level of performance, and not on individual performance (Christopher, 1994; Moeller, 1994; Slats, 1995; Bowersox, Closs, 1996).

The VE functioning can be affected by the occurrence of some unforeseen, but critical events, such as: delaying or modification within the BP chain, changing the BP priorities, communication deficiencies and/or network overloading or falling. In the case of such a critical event, the VE coordinator should take all the measures in order to solve quickly the issue locally, and if such aspect is not reached, the coordinator will not comply with the provisions foreseen in the DBP contract; in this way, a conflict will occur, with impact on the information on DBP, thus affecting the entire production chain. The DBP assumes the existence of interdependencies between subsystems in order to take into account the entire network.

Depending upon the issue's seriousness, the solution might need more throughout and complex analysis. It is essential to take into consideration more evaluations and more factors, especially if we think that usually, an enterprise can carry out more DBP contracts, which can be indirectly affected by the BP under discussion. The complexity of a VE will make almost impossible the individual solving of each issue by a user, meaning that a single user will not have the necessary knowledge and capabilities (regarding from the necessary time and technical experience point of view), or solving each issue by the system, meaning this will not benefit from the experience and "flexibility in business" of the human factor, in order to perform an accurate analysis or to take the optimal decisions.

In other words, DSS should offer the capability to: identify the issue situation; collect and analyze data; establish the causes of an issue; redefine the objectives; generate alternative solutions; compare and to evaluate alternative solutions; chose the optimal solution. DSS should also offer to decision matters the information stored together with a description of both the external competition environment, as well as the way enterprise caries out activities.

The subsystem of underlying the decision and simulating the alternative solutions should respond on the automatic reprogramming, basing on conflict analysis and by using one of the planning-reprogramming strategies. The decision should take into account the execution delays, and should be able to anticipate the potential distortions that might influence the requirement's concluding. The protocol includes a series of interactive steps, by sending messages of recommendation towards providers, by issuing new solutions of making efficient the production process, of selecting partners and of reprogramming the procedures of maintaining the delivering data, as well as real time evaluation of the partial results. There are various possibilities of reprogramming, as following: automatic, semi-automatic and manual. A potential conflict should affect at the very most the BP, under the responsibility of provider under discussion, and only slightly the other VE members.

The Conflict Detection Subsystem is an entity which receives information regarding the production, and it is permanently supervised, in order to check the information accuracy on planning or established terms on deliveries, as well as the execution stages. In the case a conflict is detected, this will be identified and transferred towards the module of taking decisions as answer on those detected.

The control subsystem performs a series of actions as regards the carrying into effect a decision chosen as alternative solution. The user of the VE coordination website will work together with DBPM (regarded as DSS, also) and will be able to simulate an extended set of alternative decisions.

The contract provided within a VE scenario will specify the rights and obligations within the relationships established by enterprises (clauses including the judicial, technical and financial information) and moreover, the responsibilities towards conventional systems, the clauses of supervision (access to information, in the view of monitoring it). The cooperation between enterprises regards the agreement or consensus over the set of information to be provided, so that the remote supervision will be enabled.

Customizing the supervision clauses signifies one of the first procedures than a user should apply immediately after a VE is formed. The user should specify periodically reported information (for instance, the manufacturing data, the produced quantities, the demands status, the information transparency, transferring decisions and in parallel, supplementary documentations or sending the supervision data).

It is important to give some examples of Virtual Breeding Environments (VBEs) as the following: Virtuelle Fabrik (consortium in machine building sector between Switzerland and Germany); Swiss Microtech (micromechanics, collaboration with China); ISOIN (aeronautical cluster); CeBeNetwork (integrated portfolio for aeronautical engineering between France, UK and Germany); ConSEN Euro – Group (cluster of European SMEs in Information Society Technologies); Infranet – Partners (network of SMEs in Internet solution domain). As Professional Virtual Communities (PVCs) we can take into consideration the following examples: Projectwerk (4000 freelancers and SMEs); Elance; freelancer; associations of professionals etc.

http://dx.doi.org/10.5772/3371

5. Conclusions and future work

The current situation in the aftermath of the global crisis and the European debt crisis, markets are highly volatile and very sensitive to the social, political, economical, business, technical, organizational but also other factors dealing with the workforce. The success of a VE solution depends heavily on innovation (including innovation on management) since they are market-oriented organizations. These vehicles should react quickly and reconfigure to satisfy new market demands and customer trends in an agile manner.

Although ontologies specifically for VEs have not been addressed, we believe that ontologies for enterprises, in general, will address issues that need to be addressed by VE ontologies too. It is important to highlight that the need for ontology is mostly due to information exchange among people and computers and to support interoperability, which is one of the most important issues in VEs.

The modern business environment has been characterized by the networking interconnection, the cooperation related to disrupted technologies, where one might emphasize the interest growth on intelligent platforms of common architecture, able to provide valuable elements. The intelligent coordination will require taking into account the entire SCM, within an intelligent organizational environment (Pereira, Klen, 2000).

The modern enterprise should benefit from new, intelligent, adaptive instruments of decision, capable to: solve complex problems; to realize efficient interconnection/ interoperation (modularity); to offer efficient/ quick solutions for the distributed problems in a more and more complex environment with highly volatile markets; to integrate, fuse and filter information from different, distributed informational sources; to offer better performances (speed, security, expandability to operate with information and knowledge); to offer better clarity and simplicity in analysis; to offer scalability and, in general adaptability of the application for an optimal use of resources.

DSS is more than informational product that implement a method for decision making. DSS is based on multitude components in interaction and it integrates informatics modules but also specific techniques for decisions, and communications. The main characteristics of DSS are: applicability, expected benefits, utility and relevance, addressability. The AI ingredients, such as the expert systems, the knowledge based systems, learning abilities networks have been underlying on different types of AI technologies and coul offer better performance on mixing with DSS.

The DSS-VE/VO offers advanced coordination facilities, able to support the means of achieving, providing and managing the information related to production within VE/ VO. This system will embed the SCM and ILM concepts in the context of Integrated Logistics Management (ILM). This system should be modular, allowing to enterprises to operate better within an integrated virtual environment, underlying on subsystems of supervision or monitoring the DBP and DSS execution, meaning the configuration of the supervising provision.

The DSS-VE/VO systems will allow efficient tasks regarding: the supervision of SCM demands, underlying on the supervision clauses associated to contracts; the interactive support on analyzing and solving the conflicts on processing demands by taking reactive decisions; the partners' configuration; the support on re-planning share by means of the basic programming actions within VE; integration with the cooperation platform (data integration; security communications; inter-functionality or interaction). Taking into account the complexity of DSS-VE/VO systems, innovative issues should be investigated, especially towards the line of intelligent coordination.

The future developments of the concepts linked to VE (new assessment models based on ability to add real value, changes in the competition nature between firms, new possibilities for integration/ mixing with DSS) should consider the following future directions of research: the development of VE platforms dedicated for SMEs and startups; the specification of operational characteristics and the analysis of the distributed architectures; the development of the new methods of management, coordination, cooperation and negotiations between VEs; special focus on social aspects regarding the development of VEs. Other aspects to cover in future work should take into account: the coordination functionalities such as distributed resource management and scheduling and the new role of negotiation in a VE as a central task in the formation of a VE/ VO but also in the operation and success of these innovative vehicles.

Author details

Gabriela Prelipcean[1] and Mircea Boscoianu[2]

1 Stefan cel Mare University of Suceava, Romania

2 Henri Coanda Air Force Academy of Brasov, Romania

References

[1] Afsarmanesh, H., Camarinha-Matos, L.M., 2000, A virtual tourism enterprise, Proceedings of WISE 2000 – 1st ACM/IEEE International Conference on Web Information Systems Engineering, Vol. 1, IEEE Computer Society Press, Hong Kong.

[2] Afsarmanesh, H., Camarinha-Matos, LM, 2005. A Framework for Management of Virtual Organization Breeding Environments. 6TH ifip working conference on virtual enterprises, PROVE-05, Valencia, Spain.

[3] Alexakis, S., Kolmel, B., Heep, T., 2004, VO in Industry: State of the Art, in Collaborative Networked Organizations: A Research Agenda for Emerging Business Models", Kluwer.

[4] Ambroszkiewicz, S., Cetnarowicz, K., Radko, B., 1998, Enterprise Formation Mechanisms based on Mobile Agents, In Holsten, A. et al. (eds.), Proc. of the Workshop on Intelligent Agents in Information and Process Management, KI'98, TZI-Bericht, No.9.

[5] Baldo, f., Rabelo, R.J., Vallejos, R.V., 2008, Modeling Performance Indicators' Selection Process for VO Prtners' Suggestions, in Proceedings BASYS'2008 – 8th IFIP Int. Conf. on Information Technology for Balance Automation Systems, pp.67-76, Springer, Heilderberg.

[6] Bernus, P., Nemes, L., 1996, A framework to define a generic enterprise reference architecture and methodology, Computer-Integrated Manufacturing Systems, vol.9, no.3.

[7] Bowersox, D.J., Closs, D.J., Helferich, O.K., 1986, Integration of phisical distribution, materials management and logistical coordination, New York, NY: Macmilan.

[8] Brazier F.M.T., Jonker C.M., Treur J., 2002, Principles of component-based design of intelligent agents. Data and Knowledge Engineering, 41.

[9] Brazier, F. M. T., Dunin-Keplicz, B. M., Jennings, N. R. and Treur, J., 1997, DESIRE: Modelling Multi-Agent Systems in a Compositional Formal Framework. Int. Journal of Cooperative Information Systems, 6, (1).

[10] Byrne, J. A., Brandt, R. and Port, O., 1993, The virtual corporation: the company of the future will be the ultimate in adaptability, Business Week.

[11] Camarinha-Matos, LM and Afsarmanesh, H., 2005, Brief historical perspective for virtual organizations, Virtual Organizations Systems and Practices, Springer, New York, USA.

[12] Camarinha-Matos, LM. and Afsarmanesh, H., 2003, Elements of a base VE infrastructure, Journal of Computers in Industry, Volume 51, Issue 2.

[13] Camarinha-Matos, LM., Afsarmanesh, H., Ollus, M., 2005, Ecolead: A Holistic Approach to Creation and Management of Dynamic Virtual Organizations, in collab. Networks and Their Breeding Environments, Springer, Heilderberg.

[14] Camarinha-Matos, LM; Afsarmanesh, H., 2005, Collaborative networks: A new scientific discipline, In Journal of. Intelligent Manufacturing.

[15] Camarinha-Matos, L.M. and Afsarmanesh, H., 2001, Virtual enterprise modelling and support infrastructures: applying multi-agent system approaches, in M. Luck et al. (Eds.) Multi-agent Systems and Applications, Springer-Verlag.

[16] Camarinha-Matos, LM., Afsarmanesh, H., 1999, The virtual enterprises Concept. In Infrastructures for Virtual Enterprises: networking industrial enterprises, US: Kluwer Academic Publishers.

[17] Camarinha-Matos, L.M., Afsarmanesh, H., Garita, C., Lima, C., 1998, Towards an architecture for virtual enterprises, The Journal of Intelligent Manufacturing, Vol. 9, Issue 2.

[18] Castelfranchi C., Falcone R., 1998, Towards a theory of delegation for agent-based systems, Robotics and Autonomous Systems, 24 (3-4).

[19] Clements, P. E., Papaioannou, T., Edwards. J., 1997, Aglets: Enabling the Virtual Enterprise, In Wright, D et al. (Eds.), Proc. of Mesela '97 - 1st Int'l Conf. on Managing Enterprises - Stakeholders, Engineering, Logistics and Achievement. Mechanical Engineering Publications Ltd.

[20] Cunha, M.M., Putnik, G.D., Carvalho, J.D. and Avila P., A review of environments supporting virtual enterprise integration, Knowledge and technology integration in production and services, Fifth IFIP international Conference on Information technology for Balanced Automation Systems in Manufacturing and Services, Kluwer Academic Publishers, 2002, Cancun, MX.

[21] Cristopher, M.L., 1994, Logistics and supply chain management, Pitman Publishing, London.

[22] Christopher, M., 1994, New directions in Logistics, Logistics and Distribution Planning – strategies for management, ed. by James Cooper, Kogan Page Limited, 2nd edition.

[23] Davidow, W.H., Malone, M.S., 1992, The Virtual Corporation: Structuring and Revitalising the Corporation for the 21st Century, Harper Business.

[24] Dorn, J. Hrastnik, P. and A. Rainer, 2004, Conferences as Virtual organization, Virtual Enterprises and Collaborative Environments, IFIP 5th working conference on virtual enterprises, Kluwer Academic Publishers, Toulouse, France.

[25] Drissen-Silva, M.V., Rabelo, R.J., 2009, A Collaborative Decision Support Framework for Managing the Evolution of Virtual Enterprises, International Journal of Production Research, 47 (17).

[26] Ferber, J., Gutknecht, O., 1998, A meta-model for the analysis and design of organizations in multi-agent systems. In Proceedings of the 3nd International Conference on Multi-Agent Systems (ICMAS-98).

[27] Ferreira, D., Goletz, T. and Ferraz, R., 2000, A workflow-based approach to the integration of enterprise networks, Proceedings CARS& FOF 2000, Port of Spain, Trinidad.

[28] Fischer, K., Muller, J. P., Heimig, I., Scheer, A., 1996, Intelligent Agents in Virtual Enterprises, Proceedings of the First International Conference and Exhibition on The Practical Applications of Intelligent Agents and Multi-Agent Technology, April 1996, London, U.K.

[29] Fox, M.S., Chionglo, J.F. Barbuceanu, M., 1993, The Integrated Supply Chain Management System, University of Toronto, Enterprise Integration Laboratory, Toronto.

[30] Franke, U., 2001, The Concept of Virtual Web Organizations and Its Implications on Changing Market Conditions, Electronic Journal of Organizational Virtualness, Vol. 3 No.4.

[31] Fu, K.S., 1970, Learning Control Systems--Review and Outlook, IEEE Transactions on Automatic Control, No. 15.

[32] Gadomski, A. M., Bologna, S., Di Constanzo, G., Perini, A., Schaerf, M., 2001, Towards intelligent decision support systems for emergency managers: the IDA approach, International Journal Risk Assessment and Management, vol.2, no. 3-4.

[33] Holland, J.H., 1975, Adaptation in Natural and Artificial Systems, University of Michigan Press, Ann Harbor, MI.

[34] Holsaplle, C. W., Whinston, A. B., 1996, Decision Support Systems: A Knowledge-based Approach, West Publishing Company, Minneapolis/St Paul.

[35] Ivanov, D., Arkhipov, A. and Sokolov, B., 2003, Intelligent planning and control of manufacturing supply chains in virtual enterprises, in Proceeding of PRO-VE'03 – Processes and Foundations for Virtual Organizations, Kluwer Academic Publishers, Switzerland.

[36] Jain, A. K., Aparicio IV, M., Singh, M. P., 1999, Agents for Process Coherence in Virtual Enterprises, In Communications of the ACM, March, Vol. 42, No. 3.

[37] Jansson, K., Eschenbacher, J., 2005, Challenges in Virtual Organisations Management – Report on methods for distributed business process management. Tech. Report D32.1. European Collaborative networked Organizations LEADership initiative. FP6 IP 506958.

[38] Janssen, T. L., 1989, Network expert diagnostic system for real-time control, Proceedings of the second international conference on industrial and engineering applications of artificial intelligence and expert systems, Vol. 1 (IEA/AUIE '89).

[39] Katzy, B. R., Schuh, G., 1997, The Virtual Enterprise, in: Molina, A., Sanchez, J. M., Kusiak, A. (eds.), Handbook of Life Cycle Engineering: Concepts, Methods and Tools, New York, Chapman & Hall.

[40] Kazi, A.S., Hannus, M., 2002, Virtual enterprise reference architecture and methodology, eWork and eBusiness in AEC, ECPPM 2002, Slovenia.

[41] Kerschberg, L., 1997, Knowledge rovers: Cooperative intelligent agent support for enterprise information architectures, in P. Kandzia and M. Klusch, Eds., Cooperative Information Agents, First International Workshop, CIA'97, Kiel, Germany, Proceeding, Springer-Verlag.

[42] Kim, C., Son, Y., Kim, T., Kim, K., 2004, A modeling approach for designing a value chain of VE. Virtual Enterprises and collaborative Environments, IFIP 5th working conference on virtual enterprises, Kluwer Academic Publishers, Toulouse, France.

[43] Little, J. D.C., 1970, Models and Managers: The Concept of a Decision Calculus, Management Science, 6, No. 8.

[44] Lopes Cardoso, L., Malucelli, A., Rocha, A.P., Oliveira, E., 2005, Institutional Services for Dynamic Virtual Organizations, In 6th IFIP working conference on virtual enterprises (PRO-VE'05), Valencia, Spain.

[45] Lopes Cardoso, L., Oliveira, E., 2004, Virtual Enterprise Normative Framework Within Electronic Institutions, In Proceedings of the Fifth International Workshop Engineering Societies in the Agents World (ESAW'04), Toulouse, France.

[46] Loss, L., Pereira-Klen, A.A., Rabelo, R.J., 2006, Virtual Organization Management: An Approach Based on Inheritance Information. In Global conference on Sustainable Poduct Deelopment and Life Cycle Engineering. Oct.03-06, Sao Carlos, SP, Brazil.

[47] Luczak et. al., 2005, Realization of the Virtual Enterprise Paradigm in the clothing industry though e-business technology, Virtual Organizations Systems and Practice.

[48] Malhotra, Y., 2000, Knowledge Management and Virtual Organizations, Idea Group Publishing, USA.

[49] Meystel, A.M., Albus, J.S., 2002, Intelligent System: architecture, design and control, John Wiley and Sons.

[50] Negretto, H., Hodik, J., Mulder, W., Ollus, M., Pondrelli, P., Westphal, I., 2008, VO Management Solutions: VO management e-services, in Methods and Tools for Collaborative.Netwoked Organisations, Springer, Heilderberg.

[51] Norman, R., Ramirez, R., 1993, From Value Chain to Value Constellation: Designing Interactive Strategy, Harvard Business Review.

[52] Oliveira, E., Rocha, A.P., 2000, Agents advanced features for negotiation in electronic commerce and virtual organisation formation process, European Perspectives on Agent-Mediated Commerce, Springer-Verlag.

[53] Petersen, S.A., Gruninger, M., 2000, An agent-based model to support the formation of virtual enterprises', International ICSC Symposium on Mobile Agents and Multi-agents in Virtual organisations and E-Commerce (MAMA'2000), Wollongong, Australia.

[54] Prelipcean G., Boscoianu M., 2008, An innovative decision support system for strategic investments in power sector, WSEAS TRANSACTIONS on POWER SYSTEMS, ISSN 1790-5060, Issue 6, volume 3, June 2008.

[55] Prelipcean G., Boscoianu M., 2008, Computational framework for assessing decisions in energy investments based on a mix between real options analysis and artificial neural networks, in Proceedings of the 9th WSEAS International Conference on Mathematics & Computers in Business and Economics (MCBE'80).

[56] Rabelo, R., F Baldo, F., Tramontin, R.J., 2004, Smart configuration of dynamic virtual enterprises, Virtual Enterprises and collaborative Environments, IFIP 5th working conference on virtual enterprises, Kluwer Academic Publishers, Toulouse, France.

[57] Rabelo, R.J., Camarinha-Matos, L.M., Vallejos, R., 2000, Agent-based brokerage for virtual enterprise creation in the moulds industry, in E-business and Virtual Enterprises, Kluwer Academic Publishers.

[58] Rabelo, R. J. Camarinha-Matos, L.M., 1996, Towards Agile Scheduling in Extended Enterprise. In Balanced Automation Systems II - Implementation Challenges for Anthropocentric Manufacturing. (Luis M. Camarinha-Matos and Hamideh Afsarmanesh, (Eds.)), Chapman & Hall.

[59] Rabelo, R.J., Camarinha-Matos, L.M., 1994, Negotiation in multi-agent based dynamic scheduling, International Journal on Robotics and CIM, Vol.11(4).

[60] Rocha, A., Oliveira, E., 1999, An electronic market architecture for the formation of virtual enterprises, in Infrastructures for Virtual Enterprises, Kluwer, Boston.

[61] Slats, P. A., 1995, Logistics Chain Modeling, European Journal of Operational Research, No. 87.

[62] Shen, W., Norrie, D., 1999, Agent-Based Systems for Intelligent Manufacturing: A State of the Art Survey, International Journal of Knowledge and Information Systems 1(2).

[63] Szirbik, N. B., Hammer, D. K., Goossenaerts, J. B. M., Aerts, A. T. M., 1999, Mobile Agent Support for Tracking Products in Virtual Enterprises, AGENT'99, Seattle, USA, May, Workshop Notes, ACM.

[64] Stone, P., Veloso, M., 2000, Multiagent Systems: A Survey from a Machine Learning Perspective, Autonomous Robots, Volume 8, No. 3.

[65] Tølle, M., Bernus, P., 2003, Reference models supporting enterprise networks and virtual enterprises, International Journal of Networking and Virtual Organisations, Vol. 2, No. 1.

[66] Tsakopoulos, S., Bokma, A., Plekhanova, V., 2003, Partner evaluation and selection in virtual enterprises using a profile theory based approach, in Proceeding of PRO-VE'03 – Processes and Foundations for Virtual Organizations, Kluwer Academic Publishers, Switzerland.

[67] Venkatraman, N., Henderson, C., 1998, Real Stategies for Virtual Organising, Sloan Management Review, Issue 40.

[68] Vernadat, F. B., 1996, Enterprise Modeling and Integration Principles and Applications, Chapman and Hall Publishers.

[69] Wigand, R., Picot, A., Reichwald, R., 1998, Information, Organization and Management: Expanding Markets and Corporate Boundaries, Chichester: John Wiley and Sons.

[70] Wildeman, L., 1998, Alliances and networks: the next generation, International Journal Technology Management, Vol. 15.

[71] Wognum, P.M., Faber, C., 2003, Infrastructures for collaboration in virtual organizations, Int. Journal of Computer Applications in Technology, Geneva, Vol. 18, Issue 1-4.

[72] Zweger, A., Tolle, M., Vesterager, J., 2002, VERAM: Virtual Enterprise Reference Architecture and Methodology, Global Engineering and Manufacturing in Enterprise Networks GLOBEMEN, eds. I. Karvonen et. al., Julkaisija Utgivare Publisher, Finland.

Chapter 6

Optimal Control of Integrated Production – Forecasting System

R. Hedjar, L. Tadj and C. Abid

Additional information is available at the end of the chapter

1. Introduction

The production planning problem has received much attention, and many sophisticated models and procedures have been developed to deal with this problem. Many other components of production systems have also been taken into account by researchers in so called integrated systems, in order to achieve a more effective control over the system.

In this work, optimal control theory is used to derive the optimal production rate in a manufacturing system presenting the following features: the demand rate during a certain period depends on the demand rate of the previous period (dependent demand), the demand rate depends on the inventory level, items in inventory are subject to deterioration, and the firm can adopt a periodic or a continuous review policy. Also, we are using the fact that the current demand is related to the previous demand in order to integrate the forecasting component into the production planning problem. The forecast of future demand for the products being produced is needed to plan future activities. Forecasting information is an important input in several areas of manufacturing activity. This problem has been considered in the literature. The proposed approach is different from that of other authors which is mainly based on time-series. In [1], the authors deal with the interaction between forecasting and stock control in the case of non-stationary demand. In [2], the authors assume a distribution for the unknown demand, estimate its parameters and replace the unknown demand parameters by these estimates in the theoretically correct model. In [3], the authors propose an approach to evaluate the impact of interaction between demand forecasting method and stock control policy on the inventory system performances. In [4], the authors present a supply chain management framework based on model predictive control (MPC) and time series forecasting. In [5], the authors consider a data-driven forecasting technique with integrated inventory control for seasonal data and compare it to the traditional Holt-Winters algorithm for random demand with a seasonal trend. In [6], the authors assess the empirical stock control performance of intermittent demand estimation procedures. In [7], the authors study two modifications of the normal distribution, both taking non-negative values only.

Many researchers have investigated the situation where the demand rate is dependent on the level of the on-hand inventory. In [8], the authors consider an inventory model under inflation for deteriorating items with stock-dependent consumption rate and partial backlogging shortages. In [9], the authors examine an inventory model for deteriorating items under stock-dependent demand and two-level trade credit. The reference [10] deals with a supply chain model for deteriorating items with stock-dependent consumption rate and shortages under inflation and permissible delay in payment. In [11], the authors deal with the optimal replenishment policies for non-instantaneous deteriorating items with stock-dependent demand. In [12], the authors investigate an inventory model with stock–dependent demand rate and dual storage facility. In [13], the authors develop a two warehouse inventory model for single vendor multiple retailers with price and stock dependent demand. In [14], the authors asses an integrated vendor-buyer model with stock-dependent demand. In [15], the authors study an EOQ model for perishable items with stock and price dependent demand rate. In [16], the authors develop the optimal replenishment policy for perishable items with stock-dependent selling rate and capacity constraint. In [17], the authors consider an inventory model for Weibull deteriorating items with price dependent demand and time-varying holding cost. In [18], the authors study fuzzy EOQ models for deteriorating items with stock dependent demand and nonlinear holding costs. In [19], the authors approach an extended two-warehouse inventory model for a deteriorating product where the demand rate has been assumed to be a function of the on-hand inventory. In [20], the authors investigate a channel who sells a perishable item that is subject to effects of continuous decay and fixed shelf lifetime, facing a price and stock-level dependent demand rate. In [21], the authors develop a mathematical model to formulate optimal ordering policies for retailer when demand is practically constant and partially dependent on the stock, and the supplier offers progressive credit periods to settle the account. The literature on stock-dependent demand rate is abundant. We have reported some of it here but only a comprehensive survey can summarize and classify it efficiently.

In [22], the authors review the most recent literature on deteriorating inventory models, classifying them on the basis of shelf-life characteristic and demand variations. In [23], the authors introduce an order-level inventory model for a deteriorating item, taking the demand to be dependent on the sale price of the item to determine its optimal selling price and net profit. In [18], the authors formulate an inventory model with imprecise inventory costs for deteriorating items under inflation. Shortages are allowed and the demand rate is taken as a ramp type function of time as well. In [10], the authors model the retailer's cost minimization retail strategy when he confronts with the supplier trade promotion offer of a credit policy under inflationary conditions and inflation-induced demand. In [24], the authors develop two deterministic economic production quantity (EPQ) models for Weibull-distributed deteriorating items with demand rate as a ramp type function of time.

The goal of this chapter is to study the same problem in periodic and continuous review policy context, knowing that the inventory can be reviewed continuously or periodically. In a continuous-review model, the inventory is monitored continually and production/order can be started at any time. In contrast, in periodic-review models, there is a fixed time when the inventory is reviewed and a decision is made whether to produce/order or not.

We assume that the firm has set an inventory goal level, a demand goal rate and a production goal rate, to build the objective function of our model. The inventory goal level is a safety stock that the company wants to keep on hand. The demand goal rate is the amount that the company wishes to sell per unit of time. The production goal rate is the most efficient rate desired by the firm. The objective is to determine the optimal production rate that will keep the inventory level, the demand rate, and the production rate as close as possible to the inventory goal level, the demand goal rate, and the production goal rate, respectively.

Therefore, we deal with a dynamic problem and the solution sought, the optimal production rate, is a function of time. The problem is then represented as an optimal control problem with two state variables, the inventory level and the demand rate, and one control variable, the rate of manufacturing.

The rest of this chapter is organized as follows. In section 2, the notation used is introduced and the dynamics of the system are described for both periodic and continuous review systems. In section 3, the optimal solution is computed for each case. Simulations are conducted in section 4 to verify the results obtained theoretically in section 3. Section 5 summarizes the chapter and outlines some future research directions.

2. Model formulation

2.1. Continuous review integrated production model

Consider a manufacturing firm producing units of an item over some time interval $[0, T]$, where $T>0$. Let $I(t)$, $D(t)$, and $P(t)$ represent the inventory level, the demand rate, and the production rate at time t, respectively. Let $\hat{I}(t)$, $\hat{D}(t)$, and $\hat{P}(t)$ represent the corresponding goals at time t. Also, let h, K, r represent the penalties for each variable to deviate from its goal. Then, the objective function J to minimize is given by

$$\min_{P(t)} J = \frac{1}{2}\int_0^T \{h[I(t) - \hat{I}(t)]^2 + K[D(t) - \hat{D}(t)]^2 + r[P(t) - \hat{P}(t)]^2\}dt \; + \frac{1}{2}\{h_T[I(T) - \hat{I}(T)]^2 + K_T[D(T) - \hat{D}(T)]^2\} \tag{1}$$

In (1), the expression $\frac{1}{2}\{h_T[I(T) - \hat{I}(T)]^2 + K_T[D(T) - \hat{D}(T)]^2\}$ gives the salvage value of the ending state. Using the shift operator defined by $\Delta f(t) = f(t) - \hat{f}(t)$, the objective function is expressed as

$$\min_{P(t)} J = \frac{1}{2}\int_0^T [h\,\Delta^2 I(t) + K\Delta^2 D(t) + r\Delta^2 P(t)]dt + \frac{1}{2}\{h_T \Delta^2 I(T) + K_T \Delta^2 D(T)\} \tag{2}$$

To use a matrix notation, which is more convenient, let $X(t)=\begin{bmatrix}\Delta I(t)\\ \Delta D(t)\end{bmatrix}$ and let $\| X \|_A^2 = X^T AX$. Then, the objective function (2) can be further rewritten as

$$\min_{P(t)} J = \frac{1}{2}\int_0^T [\| X(t)\|_H^2 + r\Delta^2 P(t)]dt + \frac{1}{2}\| X(T)\|_{H_T}^2 \tag{3}$$

where $H = \begin{bmatrix} h & 0 \\ 0 & K \end{bmatrix}$ and $H_T = \begin{bmatrix} h_T & 0 \\ 0 & K_T \end{bmatrix}$.

Two state equations are used to describe the dynamics of our system. The variations of the inventory level and demand rate are governed by the following state equations

$$\frac{d}{dt} I(t) = P(t) - D(t) - \theta I(t) \tag{4}$$

with known initial inventory level $I(0)=I_0$ and

$$\frac{d}{dt} D(t) = aD(t) + bI(t) \tag{5}$$

with known initial demand rate $D(0)=D_0$ and $a<0$ for a stable demand. Since the goals $\hat{I}(t)$, $\hat{D}(t)$, and $\hat{P}(t)$ also follow the dynamics (4)-(5), we can use the shift operator defined above to express the state equations (4) and (5) as

$$\frac{d}{dt}\Delta I(t) = \Delta P(t) - \Delta D(t) - \theta\Delta I(t) \tag{6}$$

and

$$\frac{d}{dt}\Delta D(t) = a\Delta D(t) + b\Delta I(t) \tag{7}$$

The state equations (6)-(7) can also be written in matrix form as

$$\frac{d}{dt} X(t) = AX(t) + B\Delta P(t) \tag{8}$$

where $A = \begin{bmatrix} -\theta & -1 \\ b & a \end{bmatrix}$, $B = \begin{bmatrix} 1 \\ 0 \end{bmatrix}$, with initial condition $X(0) = X_0$.

2.2. Periodic review integrated production model

In the periodic review model, the time interval $[0, T]$ is divided into N subintervals of equal length. During period k, the plant manufactures units of some product at the controllable rate $P(k)$, and the state of the system is represented by the inventory level $I(k)$ and the demand rate $D(k)$.

Assuming that the initial inventory level is $I(0)=I_0$ and that the units in stock deteriorate at a rate θ, the dynamics of the first state variable, the inventory level, are governed by the following difference equation:

$$I(k+1)= \alpha I(k) + P(k) - D(k) \tag{9}$$

where $\alpha=1-\theta$.

Also, and as mentioned in the introduction and previous paragraph, assuming a dependent demand rate and a stock-dependent demand rate with initial value $D(0)=D_0$, the dynamics of the second state variable, the demand rate, are governed by the following difference equation:

$$D(k+1)=a D(k) + b I(k) \tag{10}$$

where a and b are positive constants, with $0<a<1$, for a stable demand.

It is assumed that the firm has set for each period k the following targets: the production goal rate $\hat{P}(k)$, the inventory goal level $\hat{I}(k)$, and the demand goal rate $\hat{D}(k)$. If penalties q_I, q_D, and r are incurred for a variable to deviate from its respective goal, then the objective function to minimize is given by:

$$J(P, I, D)=\frac{1}{2}\sum_{k=0}^{N}\left[q_I\Delta^2 I(k) + q_D\Delta^2 D(k) + r\,\Delta^2 P(k)\right] \tag{11}$$

where the shift operator Δ is defined by $\Delta f(k)=f(k)-\hat{f}(k)$.

Since the target variables satisfy the dynamics (9) and (10), these can be rewritten using the shift operator Δ to get:

$$\Delta I(k+1)=\alpha\,\Delta I(k) + \Delta P(k) - \Delta D(k) \tag{12}$$

$$\Delta D(k+1)=a\,\Delta D(k) + b\Delta I(k) \tag{13}$$

It is more convenient to write the model using a matrix notation. To this end, let

$$Z(k)=\begin{bmatrix} I(k) \\ D(k)\end{bmatrix},\ \hat{Z}(k)=\begin{bmatrix} \hat{I}(k) \\ \hat{D}(k)\end{bmatrix},\ Z_0=\begin{bmatrix} I_0 \\ D_0\end{bmatrix},\ Q=\begin{bmatrix} q_I & 0 \\ 0 & q_D\end{bmatrix}.$$

The objective function (11) becomes

$$J(P,\, I,\, D)=\frac{1}{2}\sum_{k=0}^{N}\left[\|\,\Delta Z(k)\|_{Q}^{2}+r\,\Delta^{2}\,P(k)\right] \tag{14}$$

where $\|\,X\,\|_{A}^{2}=X^{\,T}A\,X$ while the dynamics (12)-(13) become

$$\Delta Z(k+1)=A\;\Delta Z(k)+B\;\Delta P(k) \tag{15}$$

where $A=\begin{bmatrix}\alpha & -1\\ b & a\end{bmatrix}$ and $B=\begin{bmatrix}1\\ 0\end{bmatrix}$.

Thus we need to determine the production rates $P(k)$ at each sample that minimize the objective function (14), subject to the state equation (15).

3. Optimal control

3.1. Optimal control of continuous review model

Given the preceding definitions, the optimal control problem is to minimize the objective function (3) subject to the state equation (8):

$$(\mathrm{P})\quad\begin{cases}\min\limits_{P(t)} J=\frac{1}{2}\int_{0}^{T}\left[\|\,X(t)\|_{H}^{2}+r\Delta^{2}P(t)\right]dt+\frac{1}{2}\|\,X(T)\|_{H_{T}}^{2}\\ \qquad\qquad\text{subject to}\\ \frac{d}{dt}X(t)=A\Delta X(t)+B\Delta P(t),\;\; X(0)=X_{0}\end{cases}$$

To use Pontryagin principle, see for example the reference [25], we introduce the Hamiltonian

$$\mathrm{H}(\Delta P,\, X,\, \Lambda,\, t)=\frac{1}{2}\left[\|\,X(t)\|_{H}^{2}+r\Delta^{2}P(t)\right]+\Lambda^{\mathrm{T}}(t)\left[AX(t)+B\Delta P(t)\right] \tag{16}$$

where $\Lambda(t)=\begin{bmatrix}\lambda_{1}(t)\\ \lambda_{2}(t)\end{bmatrix}$ is the adjoint function associated with the constraint (8). An optimal solution to the control problem (P) satisfies several conditions. The first condition is the control equation $\nabla_{\Delta P(t)}\mathrm{H}(\Delta P,\, X,\, \Lambda,\, t)=0$ which is equivalent to

$$r\Delta P(t)+B^{\,T}\Lambda(\mathrm{t})=0 \tag{17}$$

The second condition is the adjoint equation $\nabla_{\Delta X(t)}\mathrm{H}(\Delta P,\, X,\, \Lambda,\, t)=-\frac{d}{dt}\Lambda(t)$ which is equivalent to

$$-\frac{d}{dt}\Lambda(t)=HX(t)+A^{T}\Lambda(t) \tag{18}$$

The next condition is the state equation $\nabla_{\Lambda(t)}\mathrm{H}(\Delta P,\ X,\ \Lambda,\ t)=\frac{d}{dt}X(t)$ which is equivalent to (8). Finally, the last condition is given by the initial and terminal conditions $X(0)=X_0$ and $\Lambda(T)=H_T X(T)$.

Note that, using the control equation (17), the state equation (8) becomes

$$\frac{d}{dt}X(t)=AX(t)-r^{-1}BB^{T}\Lambda(t) \tag{19}$$

Model Solution

We propose the following two equivalent solution approaches to solve the optimal control problem (P).

3.1.1. First solution approach

In this approach, we need to solve a Riccati equation as we will see below. To use the backward sweep method of Bryson and Ho [26], we let

$$\Lambda(t)=S(t)X(t) \tag{20}$$

where $S(t)=\begin{bmatrix} s_1(t) & 0 \\ 0 & s_2(t) \end{bmatrix}$.

Differentiating (20) with respect to t and then using successively the state equation (19) and the change of variable (20) yields

$$\frac{d}{dt}\Lambda(t)=\left[\frac{d}{dt}S(t)+S(t)A-r^{-1}S(t)BB^{T}S(t)\right]X(t) \tag{21}$$

Also, using the change of variable (20), the adjoint equation (18) becomes

$$\frac{d}{dt}\Lambda(t)=[-H-A^{T}S(t)]X(t) \tag{22}$$

Equating expressions (21) and (22), we obtain the following Riccati equation

$$\frac{d}{dt}S(t)=-H-S(t)A-A^{T}S(t)+r^{-1}S(t)BB^{T}S(t) \tag{23}$$

To solve Riccati equation (23), we use a change of variable to reduce it to a pair of linear matrix equations. Let

$$S(t)=E(t)F^{-1}(t) \tag{24}$$

The Riccati equation (23) becomes

$$\frac{d}{dt}E(t)F^{-1}(t)-E(t)F^{-1}(t)\frac{d}{dt}F(t)F^{-1}(t)=-H-E(t)F^{-1}(t)A-A^{T}E(t)F^{-1}(t)+r^{-1}E(t)F^{-1}(t)BB^{T}E(t)F^{-1}(t) \tag{25}$$

Multiplying this expression from the right by F yields

$$\frac{d}{dt}E(t)-E(t)F^{-1}(t)\frac{d}{dt}F(t)=-HF-E(t)F^{-1}(t)AF-A^{T}E(t)+r^{-1}E(t)F^{-1}(t)BB^{T}E(t) \tag{26}$$

Now, set

$$\frac{d}{dt}E(t)=-HF(t)-A^{T}E(t) \tag{27}$$

Then, we have

$$E(t)F^{-1}(t)\frac{d}{dt}F(t)=E(t)F^{-1}(t)AF(t)-r^{-1}E(t)F^{-1}(t)BB^{T}E(t) \tag{28}$$

Multiplying this expression from the left by $(EF^{-1})^{-1}$ yields

$$\frac{d}{dt}F(t)=AF(t)-r^{-1}BB^{T}E(t) \tag{29}$$

Equations (27) and (29) now give two sets of linear equations

$$\begin{bmatrix}\frac{d}{dt}E(t)\\ \cdots\cdots\cdots\\ \frac{d}{dt}F(t)\end{bmatrix}=\begin{bmatrix}-A^{T} & \vdots & -H\\ \cdots\cdots\cdots & \vdots & \cdots\cdots\cdots\\ -r^{-1}BB^{T} & \vdots & A\end{bmatrix}\begin{bmatrix}E(t)\\ \cdots\cdots\cdots\\ F(t)\end{bmatrix} \tag{30}$$

Call $G(t)=\begin{bmatrix}E(t)\\ F(t)\end{bmatrix}$. The differential equations (30) become of the form

$$\frac{d}{dt}G(t)=\Gamma G(t),\ G(t_0)\text{ given},\ \ \Gamma\text{ constant} \tag{31}$$

where

$$\Gamma=\begin{bmatrix} -A^T & \vdots & -H \\ \cdots\cdots\cdots & \vdots & \cdots\cdots\cdots \\ -r^{-1}BB^T & \vdots & A \end{bmatrix}=\begin{bmatrix} \theta & -b & -h & 0 \\ 1 & -a & 0 & -K \\ -r^{-1} & 0 & -\theta & -1 \\ 0 & 0 & b & a \end{bmatrix}$$

The boundary conditions $S(N)=H$ are equivalent to $E(N)F^{-1}(N)=H$ or $E(N)=H$ and $F(N)=I_4$ where I_4 denotes the identity matrix of order 4. The linear equations (32) can be solved in terms of a matrix exponential. The homogeneous set of equations has the solution

$$G(t)=e^{\Gamma(t-t_0)}\,G(t_0) \tag{32}$$

We recall that for a given a constant matrix Γ, the matrix exponential $e^{\Gamma t}$ is found as $e^{\Gamma t}=Pe^{Dt}P^{-1}$, where D is the diagonal matrix whose elements are the eigenvalues of Γ and P is the matrix whose columns are the corresponding eigenvectors. Thus,

$$G(t)=Pe^{D(t-t_0)}P^{-1}G(t_0) \tag{33}$$

In the next solution approach, which also leads to a set of homogeneous equations, we will show how the constant term $G(t_0)$ is obtained. For this approach, after finding $E(t)$and $F(t)$, the desired result $S(t)$ is obtained by using the change of variable (24). The optimal solutions of the problem (P) are:

$$I(t)=\hat{I}(t)+\Delta I(t),\ D(t)=\hat{D}(t)+\Delta D(t),\ P(t)=\hat{P}(t)+\Delta P(t),$$

where $\Delta I(t)$ and $\Delta I(t)$ are solutions of the linear equation:

$$\frac{d}{dt}\begin{bmatrix}\Delta I(t)\\ \Delta D(t)\end{bmatrix}=\left(A-r^{-1}B^TE(t)F(t)^{-1}\right)\begin{bmatrix}\Delta I(t)\\ \Delta D(t)\end{bmatrix},$$

with initial condition $X(0)=\begin{bmatrix}\Delta I(0)\\ \Delta D(0)\end{bmatrix}$

and

$$\Delta P(t)=-r^{-1}B^TE(t)F(t)^{-1}\begin{bmatrix}\Delta I(t)\\ \Delta D(t)\end{bmatrix}.$$

3.1.2. Second solution approach

This approach avoids the Riccati equation as we will see. The adjoint equation (18) and the state equation (19) are equivalent to the vector-matrix state equation

$$\begin{bmatrix} \frac{d}{dt} X(t) \\ \cdots\cdots\cdots \\ \frac{d}{dt} \Lambda(t) \end{bmatrix} = \begin{bmatrix} A & \vdots & -r^{-1} B B^T \\ \cdots\cdots\cdots & \vdots & \cdots\cdots\cdots \\ -H & \vdots & -A^T \end{bmatrix} \begin{bmatrix} X(t) \\ \Lambda(t) \end{bmatrix} \tag{34}$$

Let $Z(t) = \begin{bmatrix} X(t) \\ \Lambda(t) \end{bmatrix}$. Then, the vector-matrix state equation (32) can be rewritten as

$$\frac{d}{dt} Z(t) = \Phi Z(t) \tag{35}$$

where

$$\Phi = \begin{bmatrix} A & \vdots & -r^{-1} B B^T \\ \cdots\cdots\cdots & \vdots & \cdots\cdots\cdots \\ -H & \vdots & -A^T \end{bmatrix} = \begin{bmatrix} -\theta & -1 & -r^{-1} & 0 \\ b & a & 0 & 0 \\ -h & 0 & \theta & -b \\ 0 & -K & 1 & -a \end{bmatrix}$$

Expression (35) is a set of 4 first-order homogeneous differential equations with constant coefficients. It is similar to (31) and it has a solution similar to (33). We give here the explicit solution.

The matrix Φ has four distinct eigenvalues m_i, $i=1,2,3,4$. The explicit expressions of these eigenvalues are easily obtained using some mathematical software with symbolic computation capabilities such as MATHCAD, MAPLE, or MATLAB. These expressions are lengthy and thus are not reproduced here. The explicit expressions of the corresponding eigenvectors are also obtained using the same software. Then, the solution to (33) is given by

$$Z(t) = \varphi(t) Z(0) \tag{36}$$

Note that the first two components of $Z(t)$ thus computed form the state vector $X(t)$ whose components are $\Delta I(t)$ and $\Delta D(t)$, while the last two components form the co-state vector $\Lambda(t)$ whose components are $\lambda_1(t)$ and $\lambda_2(t)$. In what follows, we show how $\varphi(t)$ and $Z(0)$ are determined using the two initial conditions $I(0)=I_0$, $D(0)=D_0$ and the terminal conditions $\lambda_1(T)=h_T \Delta I(T)$, $\lambda_2(T)=K_T \Delta D(T)$.

To determine $\varphi(t)$, introduce the diagonal matrix $M = diag(m_1, m_2, m_3, m_4)$ and denote by Y the matrix whose columns are the corresponding eigenvectors. Then,

$$\varphi(t) = Y e^{Dt} Y^{-1} = \sum_{i=1}^{4} Y(:, i) Y^{-1}(i, :) e^{m_i t} \tag{37}$$

where $Y(:, i)$ is the ith column of Y and $Y^{-1}(i, :)$ is the ith row of Y^{-1}.

To determine $Z(0)=\begin{bmatrix} X(0) \\ \Lambda(0) \end{bmatrix}$, we recall that $X(0)=\begin{bmatrix} \Delta I(0) \\ \Delta D(0) \end{bmatrix}$ is known while $\Lambda(0)=\begin{bmatrix} \lambda_1(0) \\ \lambda_2(0) \end{bmatrix}$ is not. However, using the final value $\Lambda(T)$, we can find $\Lambda(0)$ as follows. From (36), we have at $t=T$,

$$Z(T)=\varphi(T)Z(0)$$

which can be rewritten as

$$\begin{bmatrix} X(T) \\ \Lambda(T) \end{bmatrix}=\begin{bmatrix} \varphi_1(T) & \varphi_2(T) \\ \varphi_3(T) & \varphi_4(T) \end{bmatrix}\begin{bmatrix} X(0) \\ \Lambda(0) \end{bmatrix}$$

Using the terminal condition

$$\Lambda(T)=H_T X(T)$$

we have

$$\begin{bmatrix} X(T) \\ H_T X(T) \end{bmatrix}=\begin{bmatrix} \varphi_1(T) & \varphi_2(T) \\ \varphi_3(T) & \varphi_4(T) \end{bmatrix}\begin{bmatrix} X(0) \\ \Lambda(0) \end{bmatrix}$$

from which, it follows

$$\Lambda(0)=(H_T\varphi_2(T)-\varphi_4(T))^{-1}(\varphi_3(T)-H_T\varphi_1(T))X(0) \tag{38}$$

Finally, the optimal solutions of the problem (P) using the second method are:
$I(t)=\hat{I}(t)+\Delta I(t)$, $D(t)=\hat{D}(t)+\Delta D(t)$, $P(t)=\hat{P}(t)+\Delta P(t)$,

where $\Delta I(t)$ and $\Delta I(t)$ are solutions of the linear equation:

$$\begin{bmatrix} \Delta I(t) \\ \Delta D(t) \end{bmatrix}=\varphi_1(t)\begin{bmatrix} \Delta I(0) \\ \Delta D(0) \end{bmatrix}+\varphi_2(t)\Lambda(0)$$

$$\Lambda(t)=\varphi_3(t)\begin{bmatrix} \Delta I(0) \\ \Delta D(0) \end{bmatrix}+\varphi_4(t)\Lambda(0)$$

and

$$\Delta P(t)=-r^{-1}B^T\Lambda(t).$$

3.2. Optimal control of periodic review model

Here also we assume that the system state is available during each period k. To use the standard Lagrangian technique, we introduce the discrete Lagrange multiplier vector: $\Lambda(k)=\begin{bmatrix} \lambda_I(k) \\ \lambda_D(k) \end{bmatrix}$

Then, the Lagrangian function is given by

$$\mathsf{L}(P, Z, \Lambda)=\sum_{k=0}^{N}\left\{\tfrac{1}{2}[\| \Delta Z(k)\|_Q^2 + r\ \Delta P(k)^2] + \Lambda(k+1)^T[-\Delta Z(k+1) + A\ \Delta Z(k) + B\ \Delta P(k)]\right\} \tag{39}$$

The necessary optimality conditions are the control equation

$$\frac{\partial \mathsf{L}}{\partial\ \Delta P(k)}=0 \Leftrightarrow r\ \Delta P(k) + B^T \Lambda(k+1)=0 \tag{40}$$

and the adjoint equation

$$\frac{\partial \mathsf{L}}{\partial\ \Delta Z(k)}=0 \Leftrightarrow Q \Delta Z(k) - \Lambda(k) + A^T \Lambda(k+1)=0. \tag{41}$$

In order to solve these equations, we use the backward sweep method of Bryson and Ho (1975), who treat extensively in their book the problem of optimal control and estimation. They detail two methods for solving the Riccati equation arising in linear optimal control problem, the first one being the transition matrix method and the second being the backward sweep method. Let

$$\Lambda(k)=S(k)\ \Delta Z(k), \tag{42}$$

The control equation (40) becomes

$$\begin{aligned}\Delta P(k) &= -r^{-1} B^T \Lambda(k+1), = -r^{-1} B^T S(k+1)\Delta Z(k+1),\\ &= -r^{-1} B^T S(k+1)[\mathrm{A}\ \Delta Z(k) + B\ \Delta P(k)].\end{aligned} \tag{43}$$

Solving for $\Delta P(k)$, we get

$$\Delta P(k)= - V(k+1)\ \Delta Z(k) \tag{44}$$

where

$$V(k+1)=r^{-1}[1 + r^{-1} B^T\ S(k+1)\ B]^{-1} B^T\ S(k+1) A$$

Now the adjoint equation (41) becomes

$$\Lambda(k)=Q\ \Delta Z(k) + A^T \Lambda(k+1) \tag{45}$$

so that

$$\begin{aligned}S(k)\ \Delta \mathrm{Z}(\mathrm{k}) &= \mathrm{Q}\ \Delta \mathrm{Z}(\mathrm{k}) + \mathrm{A}^T S(k+1)\Delta Z(k+1),\\ &= \mathrm{Q}\ \Delta \mathrm{Z}(\mathrm{k}) + \mathrm{A}^T S(k+1)[A\ \Delta Z(k) + B\ \Delta P(k)],\end{aligned} \tag{46}$$

$$=Q\,\Delta Z(k)+A^T S(k+1)[A\,\Delta Z(k)-B\,V(k+1)\Delta Z(k)],$$
$$=\{Q+A^T S(k+1)A-A^T S(k+1)B\,V(k+1)\}\Delta Z(k).$$

Finally, the matrices S can be computed from the backward discrete time Ricatti equation (DTRE) given by the recursive relation

$$S(k)=Q+A^T S(k+1)A-r^{-1}A^T\,S(k+1)B\,[1+r^{-1}B^T S(k+1)B]^{-1}B^T\,S(k+1)A \tag{47}$$

The boundary condition $S(N)=Q$ follows from $\Delta P(N)=0$. Now, to obtain the optimal production rates, we use the change of variable (42) to get from the adjoint equation (41),

$$AS(k+1)\Delta Z(k+1)=S(k)\Delta Z(k)-A\Delta Z(k) \tag{48}$$

so that

$$\Delta Z(k+1)=[AS(k+1)]^{-1}[S(k)-Q]\Delta Z(k) \tag{49}$$

Also, from the dynamics (15), we have the optimal production rates

$$P(k)=\hat{P}(k)-r^{-1}[1+r^{-1}B^T\,S(k+1)B]^{-1}B^T S(k+1)A\,\Delta Z(k) \tag{50}$$

where the optimal state vector $\Delta Z(k)$ is found in expression (49) above and $S(k)$ is found in expression (47).

Parameters		Values
Nonmonetary parameters	Length of planning horizon	$T=2.5$
	Initial inventory level	$I_0=5$
	Initial demand rate	$D_0=2$
	Demand rate coefficient	$a=0.8$
	Inventory level coefficient	$b=1$
	Deterioration rate	$\theta=0.1$
Monetary parameters	Penalty for production rate deviation	$r=0.1$
	Penalty for inventory level deviation	$h=4$
	Penalty for demand rate deviation	$K=10$
	Inventory salvage value	$h_T=100$
	Demand salvage value	$K_T=100$

Table 1. Data for continuous-review model

4. Simulation results

4.1. Simulation of continuous review model

To illustrate numerically the results obtained, firstly we present some simulations for optimal control of the continuous-review integrated production-forecasting system with stock-dependent demand and deteriorating items. The data used in this simulation is presented in Table 1.

Using the MATLAB software, we implemented the results of the previous section and obtained the graphs below. Figures 1, 2 and 3 show the variations of $\Delta I(t)$, $\Delta D(t)$, and $\Delta P(t)$. We observe that they all converge toward zero, as desired.

Using equation (3), the optimal cost is found to be $J = 3047.93$. A sensitivity analysis is performed in order to assess the effect of some of the system parameters on the optimal cost. The analysis is conducted by keeping the values of the parameters at the base values shown in Table 1 and varying successively one parameter at a time. We were interested in the effect on the value of the optimal objective function J of the parameters a, b, and θ, that we varied from 0.1 to 0.9. Table 2 summarizes the results of the sensitivity analysis.

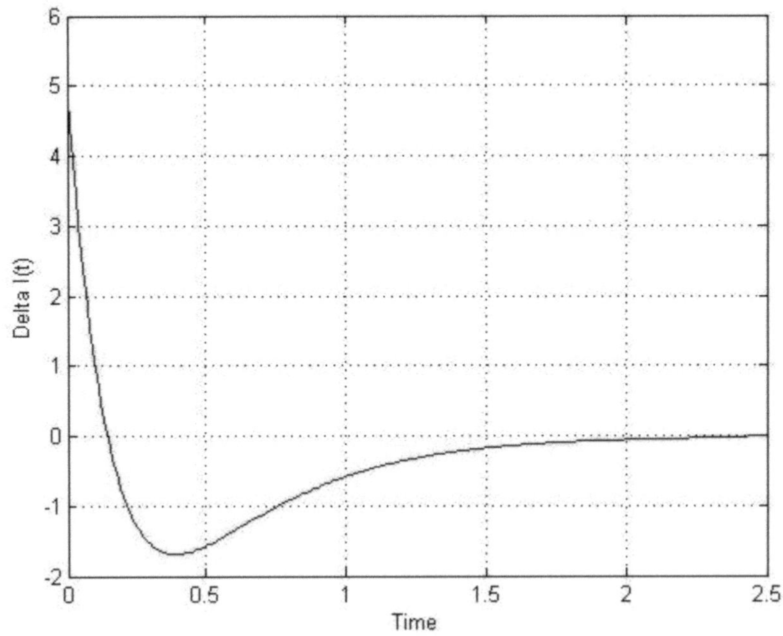

Figure 1. Variation of the optimal inventory level

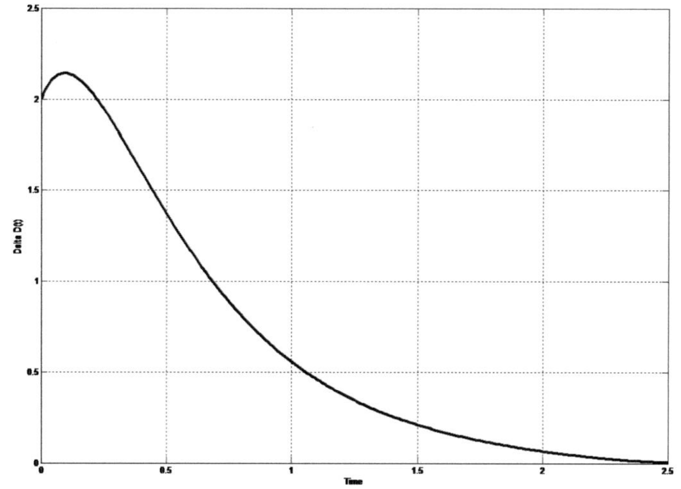

Figure 2. Variations of the optimal demand rate

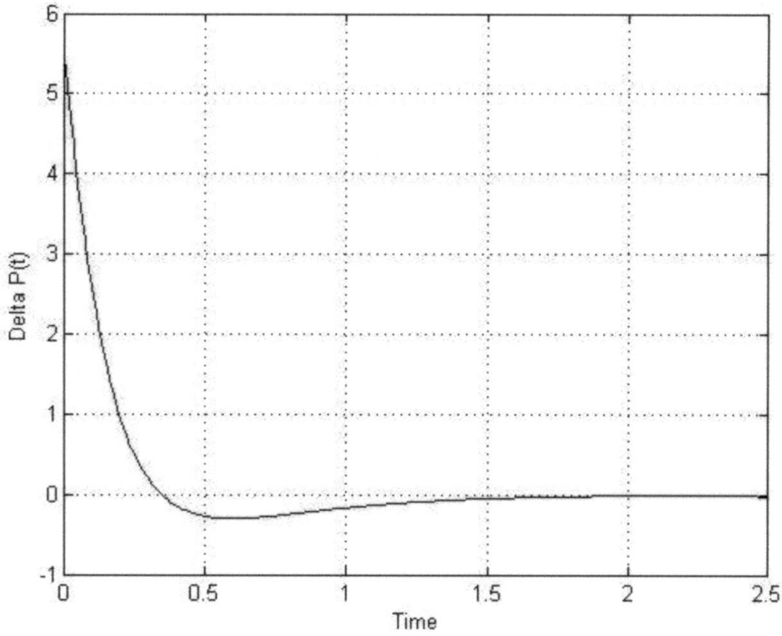

Figure 3. Variations of the optimal production rate

a / b / θ	$J(a)$	$J(b)$	$J(\theta)$
0.1	5822.40	23426.21	3047.93
0.2	489.77	7648.73	463.79
0.3	485.62	5560.00	461.53
0.4	481.57	740.12	459.30
0.5	477.58	659.34	457.09
0.6	473.67	600.85	454.91
0.7	469.84	556.02	452.76
0.8	466.08	520.24	450.63
0.9	462.38	490.83	448.52

Table 2. Sensitivity analysis

As can be seen, the objective function decreases as any of the three parameters increases.

4.2. Simulation of periodic review model

In this second part of the simulation, we illustrate the results obtained on the optimal control of the periodic review integrated production-forecasting system with stock-dependent demand and deteriorating items. Thus, consider the production planning problem for a firm for the next T units of time. Divide this interval into N subintervals of equal length. Assume the product in stock deteriorates at the rate θ. Assume also the variations of the demand rate occur according to the dynamics (10). The firm has set the following targets. For $k=1, \cdots, N$, the goal inventory level and goal demand rate are assumed to be as follows:

$$\hat{I}(k)=5+1.5\, sign\left(sin\left(\frac{2\pi k}{40}\right)\right) \text{ and } \hat{D}(k)=2+0.5\, sign\left(sin\left(\frac{2\pi k}{15}\right)\right)$$

where the sign function of a real number x is defined by

$$sign(x)=\begin{cases} -1 & \text{if } x<0, \\ 0 & \text{if } x=0, \\ 1 & \text{if } x>0. \end{cases}$$

We have to note that the goal inventory level and the goal demand rate were constant in the continuous review case.

The goal production rate is then computed using

$$\hat{P}(k)=\hat{D}(k)+\theta\, \hat{I}(k)$$

where we assume that the inventory goal level is constant over a certain range. The penalties for deviating from these targets are q_I for the inventory level, q_D for the demand rate, and r for the production rate. The data are summarized in Table 3.

Parameters	Values
planning horizon length T	10
number of subintervals N	51
coefficient for demand dynamics a	0.1
coefficient for demand dynamics b	0.2
deterioration rate θ	0.01
deviation cost for inventory level q_I	20
deviation cost for demand rate q_D	15
deviation cost for production rate r	0.01

Table 3. Data for periodic-review model

For the periodic review case, the simulation results are shown in the graphs below. Figure 4 shows the variations of the optimal inventory level and the inventory goal level. We observe that except for the early transient periods, $I(k)$ follows $\hat{I}(k)$very closely.

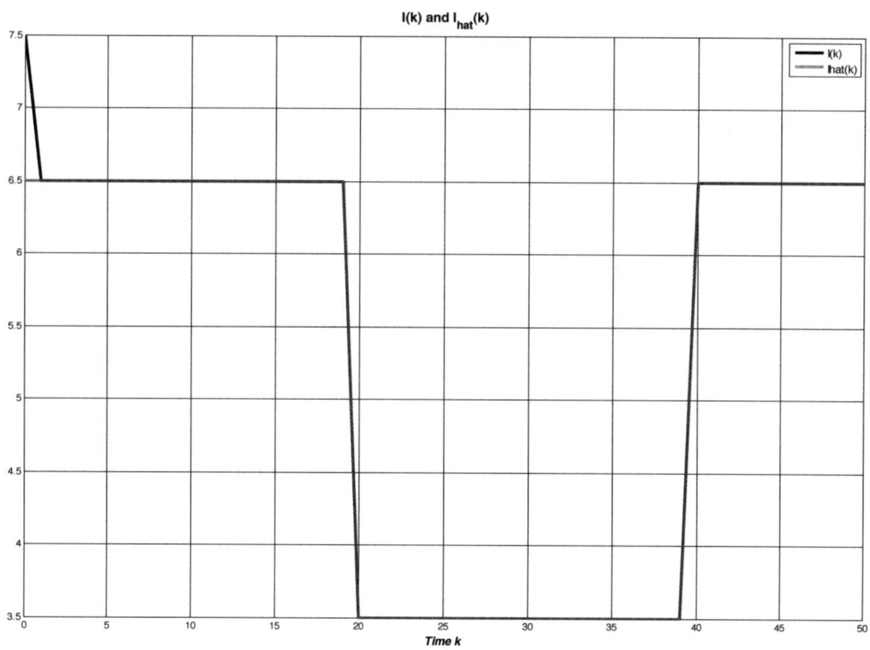

Figure 4. Optimal and inventory goal levels

Figure 5 shows the variations of the optimal demand rate and the demand goal rate. We observe that except for the early transient periods, $D(k)$ follows $\hat{D}(k)$ very closely.

Finally, Figure 6 shows the variations of the optimal production rate and the production goal rate. We again observe that except for the early transient periods, $P(k)$ follows $\hat{P}(k)$ very closely.

The optimal cost is found to be $J = 10.3081$. Here also a sensitivity analysis is performed in order to assess the effect of some of the system parameters on the optimal cost. The analysis is conducted by keeping the values of the parameters at the base values shown in Table 3 and varying successively one parameter at a time. We were interested in the effect on J of the parameters a, b, and θ, that we varied from 0.1 to 0.9. Table 4 summarizes the results of the sensitivity analysis.

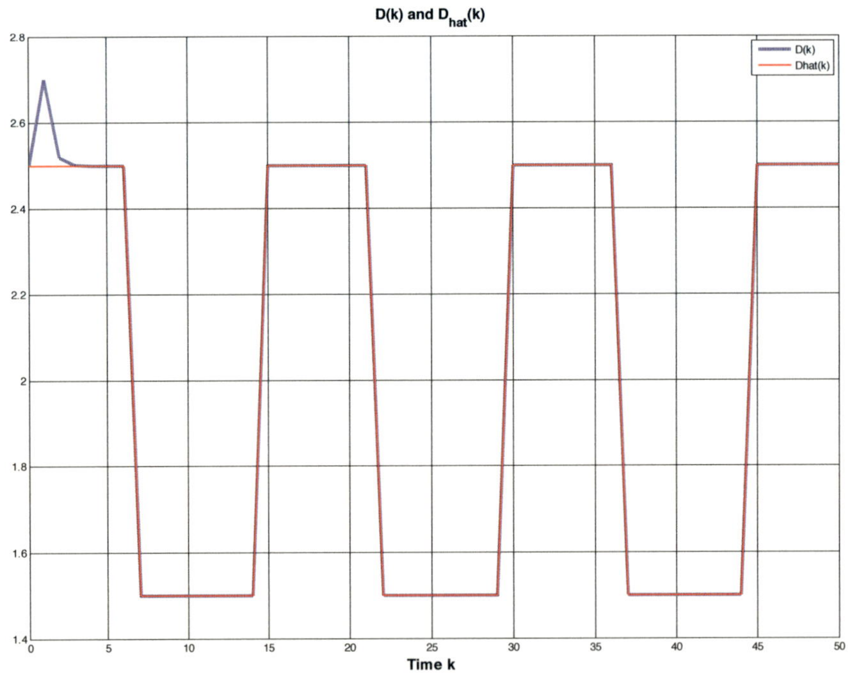

Figure 5. Optimal and demand goal levels

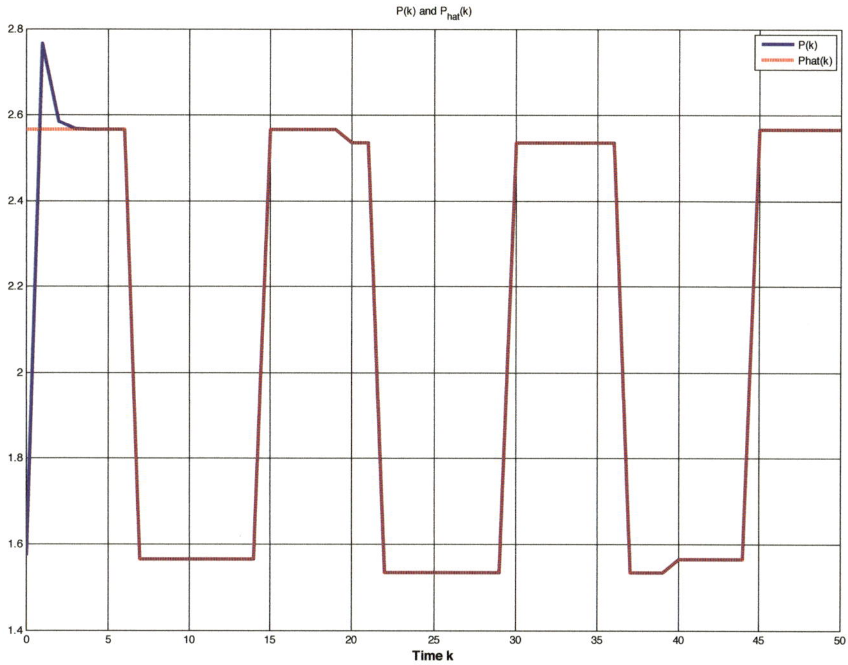

Figure 6. Optimal and production goal rates

a/b/θ	**J(a)**	**J(b)**	**J(θ)**
0.1	10.3081	10.0807	10.3072
0.2	10.3173	10.3081	10.3064
0.3	10.3339	10.6868	10.3056
0.4	10.3601	11.2166	10.3050
0.5	10.4004	11.8973	10.3044
0.6	10.4630	12.7284	10.3036
0.7	10.5651	13.7098	10.3040
0.8	10.7444	14.8413	10.3033
0.9	11.0880	16.1226	10.3032

Table 4. Effect of the parameters a, b and θ on the optimal cost J

The second column of Table 4 shows that the optimal cost increases as a increases. The third column of Table 4 shows that the optimal cost increases also as b increases. The effect of b on J is however more significant than the effect of a. Finally, column 4 of Table 4 shows that the optimal cost decreases as θ increases. The effect of θ is however almost negligible.

5. Conclusion

In this chapter we have used optimal control theory to derive the optimal production rate in a manufacturing system presenting the following features: the demand rate during a certain period depends on the demand rate of the previous period (dependent demand), the demand rate depends on the inventory level, items in inventory are subject to deterioration, and the firm adopts either a continuous or periodic review policy. In contrast to most of the existing research which uses time series forecasting models, we propose a new model, namely, the demand dynamics equation. This model approaches realistic problems by integrating the forecasting component into the production planning problem with deteriorating items and stock dependent demand under continuous-review policy. Simulations were conducted in order to show the performance of the obtained solution. The theoretical and the simulations results allow gaining insights into operational issues and demonstrating the scope for improving stock control systems.

Of course, as with any research work, this study is not without limitations. The main contribution of our model is equation (5) where we use the demand from the previous period to predict the demand in the current period. The main limitation of that equation is that it involves two coefficients. We have assumed in this chapter that the parameters a and b of the demand state equation are known. However, in real life, that may not be the case. We are currently further investigating this model to estimate these parameters in the case when they are unknown, using self-tuning optimal control.

Another research direction would be to use a predictive control strategy where, given the current inventory level, the optimal production rates to be implemented at the beginning of each of the following periods over the control horizon, are determined. Model predictive control (or receding-horizon control) strategies have gained wide-spread acceptance in industry. It is also well-known that these models are interesting alternatives for real-time control of industrial processes. In the case where the above parameters a and b are unknown, the self-tuning predictive control can be applied. The proposed control algorithm estimates online these coefficients and feeds the controller to take the optimal production decision.

Note that our state equations are linear and thus linear model predictive control (LMPC), which is widely used both in academic and industrial fields, can be used. Nonlinear model predictive control (NMPC) can be used in case one of the state equations is nonlinear, for example, if equation (5) were of the form

$$\frac{d}{dt}D(t)=aD(t)+\alpha I(t)^{\beta} \tag{51}$$

NMPC has gained significant interest over the past decade. Various NMPC strategies that lead to stability of the closed-loop have been developed in recent years and key questions such as the efficient solution of the occurring open-loop control problem have been extensively studied.

The case combining unknown coefficients and a nonlinear relationship between the demand rate and the on-hand inventory yields a very complex, highly nonlinear process for which there is no simple mathematical model. The use of fuzzy control seems particularly well appropriate. Fuzzy control is a technique that should be seen as an extension to existing control methods and not their replacement. It provides an extra set of tools which the control engineer has to learn how to use where it makes sense. Nonlinear and partially known systems that pose problems to conventional control techniques can be tackled using fuzzy control.

Acknowledgement

This work has been supported by the Research Center of College of Computer and Information Sciences, King Saud University.

Author details

R. Hedjar[1], L. Tadj[2*] and C. Abid[3]

*Address all correspondence to: Lotfi.Tadj@dal.ca

1 King Saud University, College of Computer and Information Sciences, Department of Computer Engineering, Riyadh, Saudi Arabia

2 Dalhousie University, Faculty of Management, School of Business Administration, Halifax, Nova Scotia, Canada

3 American University in Dubai, College of Business Administration, Department of Management, Dubai, UAE

References

[1] Strijbosch, L.W.G., Syntetos, A.A., Boylan, J.E., and Janssen, E. On the interaction between forecasting and stock control: The case of non-stationary demand. International Journal of Production Economics2011; 133:1, 470-480.

[2] Janssen, E., Strijbosch, L., and Brekelmans, R. Assessing the effects of using demand parameters estimates in inventory control and improving the performance using a correction function.International Journal of Production Economics 2009; 118, 34–42.

[3] Tiacci, L. and Saetta, S. An approach to evaluate the impact of interaction between demand forecasting method and stock control policy on the inventory system performances 2009; International Journal of Production Economics; 118, 63-71.

[4] Doganis, P., Aggelogiannaki, E., and Sarimveis, H. A combined model predictive control and time series forecasting framework for production-inventory systems, International Journal of Production Research 2008; 46:24, 6841-6853.

[5] Metan, G. and Thiele, A. Integrated forecasting and inventory control for seasonal demand: A comparison with the Holt-Winters approach. Technical Report. Department of Industrial and Systems Engineering, Lehigh University, Bethlehem, PA; 2007.

[6] Syntetos, A.A. and Boylan, J.E. On the stock control performance of intermittent demand estimators 2006; International Journal of Production Economics, 103, 36-47.

[7] Strijbosch, L.W.G. and Moors, J.J.A. Modified normal demand distributions in (R,S)-inventory control. European Journal of Operational Research 2006; 172, 201-212.

[8] Yang, H.-L., Teng, J.-T., and Chern, M.-S. An inventory model under inflation for deteriorating items with stock-dependent consumption rate and partial backlogging shortages. International Journal of Production Economics 2010; 123:1, 8-19.

[9] Min, J., Zhou, Y.-W., and Zhao, J. An inventory model for deteriorating items under stock-dependent demand and two-level trade credit. Applied Mathematical Modelling 2010; 34:11, 3273-3285.

[10] Jaggi, C.K. and Khanna, A. Supply chain model for deteriorating items with stock-dependent consumption rate and shortages under inflation and permissible delay in payment. International Journal of Mathematics in Operational Research 2010; 2:4, 491-514.

[11] Chang, C.-T., Teng, J.-T., and Goyal, S.K Optimal replenishment policies for non-instantaneous deteriorating items with stock-dependent demand. International Journal of Production Economics. 2010; 123:1, 62-68.

[12] Choudhury, K.D. and Datta, T.K. An inventory model with stock–dependent demand rate and dual storage facility. Assam University Journal of Science & Technology: Physical Sciences and Technology 2010; 5(2) 53-63.

[13] Panda, D., Maiti, M.K., and Maiti, M. Two-warehouse inventory models for single vendor multiple retailers with price and stock dependent demand. Applied Mathematical Modelling. 2010; 34(11) 3571-3585.

[14] Sajadieh, M.S., Thorstenson, A., and Jokar, M.R.A. An integrated vendor-buyer model with stock-dependent. Transportation Research Part E: Logistics and Transportation Review 2010; 46(6) 963-974.

[15] Khanra, S., Sana, S.S., and Chaudhuri, K. An EOQ model for perishable items with stock and price dependent demand rate, International Journal of Mathematics in Operational Research 2010; 2(3) 320-335.

[16] Hsieh, T.P. and Dye, C.Y. Optimal replenishment policy for perishable items with stock-dependent selling rate and capacity constraint. Computers & Industrial Engineering 2010; 59(2) 251-258.

[17] Tripathy, C.K. and Mishra, U. An inventory model for Weibull deteriorating items with price dependent demand and time-varying holding cost. Applied Mathematical Sciences 2010; 4(44) 2171-2179.

[18] Mahata, G. C. and Goswami, A. Fuzzy EOQ models for deteriorating items with stock dependent demand and nonlinear holding costs, International Journal of Applied Mathematics and Computer Sciences 2009; 5(2) 94-98.

[19] Gayen, M. and Pal A.K. A two-warehouse inventory model for deteriorating items with stock dependent demand rate and holding cost, Journal of Operational Research 2009; 9(2) 153-165.

[20] Chen, L.-T. and Wei, C.-C. Coordinated supply chain mechanism for an item with price and stock dependent demand subject to fixed lifetime and deterioration. In: International Conference on Business and Information, 6-8 July 2009, 6(1) ISSN: 1729-9322.

[21] Soni, H. and Shah, N.H. Ordering policy for stock-dependent demand rate under progressive payment scheme. International Journal of Systems Science. 2009; 40(1) 81-89.

[22] Goyal, S.K. and Giri, B.C. Recent trends in modelling of deteriorating inventory. European Journal of Operational Research 2001; 134, 1-16.

[23] Roy, T. and Chaudhuri, K.S. An inventory model for a deteriorating item with price-dependent demand and special sale. International Journal of Operational Research 2007; 2(2) 173-187.

[24] Manna, S.K. and Chiang, C. Economic production quantity models for deteriorating items with ramp type demand. International Journal of Operational Research 2010; 7(4) 429-444.

[25] Sethi, S.P. and Thompson, G.L. Optimal Control Theory: Applications to Management Science and Economics. 2nd ed., Kluwer Academic Publishers, Dordrecht; 2000.

[26] Bryson, A.E. and Ho, Y.C. Applied Optimal Control. Halsted Press. Washington D.C.;1975.

Section 3

Technological Applications in Management and Forecast

Chapter 7

DairyMGT: A Suite of Decision Support Systems in Dairy Farm Management

Victor E. Cabrera

Additional information is available at the end of the chapter

http://dx.doi.org/10.5772/50801

1. Introduction

Dairy farming is a highly dynamic and integrated production system that requires continuous and intense decision-making. Several dairy farm components that include 1) cattle, 2) crops, 3) soils, 4) weather, 5) management, 6) economics, and 7) environment are extremely interrelated [1]. These components and their sub-components dynamically affect and are affected among them. Therefore, an efficient decision support system (DSS) framework within an integrated systems approach is critical for successful dairy farming management and decision-making [2-5].

This chapter describes the development, application, and adoption of a suite of more than 30 computerized DSS or decision support tools aimed to assist dairy farm managers and dairy farm advisors to improve their continuous decision-making and problem solving abilities. These DSS emerged in response of dairy farm managers' needs and were shaped with their input and feedback [6-7]. No single or special methodology was used to develop each or all of these DSS, but instead a combination and adaptation of methods and empirical techniques with the overarching goal that these DSS were: 1) highly user-friendly, 2) farm and user specific, 3) grounded on the best scientific information available, 4) remaining relevant throughout time, and 5) providing fast, concrete, and simple answer to complex farmers' questions [2, 8-11]. After all, these DSS became innovative tools converting expert information into useful and farm-specific management decisions taking advantage of latest software and computer technologies.

All the DSS object of this chapter are hosted at http://DairyMGT.info, *Tools* section and are categorized within dairy farming management and decision making such as: 1) nutrition and feeding, 2) reproductive efficiency, 3) heifer management and cow replacement, 4) production and productivity, 5) price risk management and financial analysis, and 6) environmental stewardship. Depending on the complexity, the specific purpose, and the requirements of dairy farm decision makers, some DSS are completely online applications, others are Macromedia Flash tools, others are Spreadsheets, and others are self-extractable and installable programs.

This chapter discusses the challenges on the development of these DSS with respect to the trade-offs among user-friendly design, computational detail, accuracy of calculations, and bottom line efficiency performance and effective decision-making. It portrays DSS development strategies, within the computational resources available, that succeeded in their primary objective of providing dairy farm mangers fast and reliable responses to perform efficient and effective decision-making.

The chapter reveals practical and real-life applications of a number of these DSS to demonstrate satisfactory system assessment, acceptable future predictability, adequate scenario evaluation, and, consequently, satisfactory decision-making.

The chapter also covers aspects of DSS dissemination and adoption evaluation, including the inception and development of a dedicated webpage; local, national and international usage, requested presentations, and academic publications.

The chapter also infers the possible role of emerging and evolving new technologies such as smart phones and tablets in the intersection of DSS, real-time applications, and mobile devices, which is a fast growing area of development within the dairy farming industry.

2. Description of DairyMGT.info Decision Support Tools

This section lists and describes the DSS object of this chapter. These DSS are categorized in main areas of dairy farm management, as they appear in the DairyMGT.info: *Tools* webpage.

2.1. Nutrition and Feeding (DairyMGT.info → Tools→ Feeding)

Dairy farmers recognize that the largest item cost in a dairy farm system is feed, whether purchased or farm-grown. Obviously the major source of income in a dairy farm operation is the milk sale. Consequently, managing and optimizing the milk income over feed cost is a critical decision that affects not only economic sustainability, but also has large impacts regarding environmental stewardship[12]. Farmers also recognize that every farm is completely different and that market conditions are constantly changing. Therefore, beyond established farm feeding rations, there is a need for tools to permanently adjust strategic feeding decisions. Take as an example corn grain and its highly volatile price. Corn is a staple feed commodity for dairy farm feeding and consequently its price influences largely diet costs. With sudden corn price swings farmers confront permanently the question of re-considering the amount of corn in the diet. This question can be responded by estimating the marginal value of milk (also depending on highly volatile prices) to corn according to lactation stage and current amount of corn in the diet. The optimal use of corn would occur when the marginal value of milk equals the marginal value of corn, which at research-based feed efficiency levels [13], would solely depend on the ever-changing price relationship of milk and corn. The tool *"Corn Feeding Strategies"* shows these relationships in a graphical, dynamic, and interactive way so dairy farmers can optimize the amount of corn grain in each farm feeding group according to ever-changing market price conditions.

Take as another example the price of the main dairy cattle feed commodities and their relationship with milk price according to feed efficiency changes throughout lactation states. Research data indicate that the use of concentrates (i.e., corn, soybean meal) have a substantially higher impact on milk production during early or mid-lactation than in late lactation [14]. Under this premise, increased use of forages is justified in late lactation to maximize the overall milk income over feed cost, which however depends on ever-changing feed commodity prices. The tool *"Income Over Feed Cost"* graphs interactively the milk income over feed cost weekly for entire lactations and shows the impact of feed commodity prices on the dynamic milk income over feed cost value. Therefore, dairy farmers can fine-tune their feeding strategies to maximize their milk income over feed cost according to lactation states and feed prices swings.

Sometimes dairy farmers need additional help on formulating their diets to optimize feed concentrate supplementation. Research trails indicate that the optimal level of concentrate supplements in a diet could be achieved by using milk production response to crude protein (CP) and its components of rumen un-degradable protein (RUP), and rumen degradable protein (RDP), according to particular cow-group rations [15]. The tool *"Income over Feed Supplement Cost"* performs an optimization according to defined feed ingredients, prices, and CP (RUP, RDP) restrictions to maximize the net return. The tool helps dairy farm decision makers to select the most cost effective concentrate supplements in the diet, especially from the point of view of providing adequate amounts of RUP and RDP, which not only optimizes the net return, but also reduces the amount of nitrogen excretion and hence environmental impacts.

Dairy farmers also want to know what are the best-priced feed ingredient choices in the market. This information would drive farmer feed purchase decisions. The tool called *"FeedVal 2012"* is a dynamic and interactive matrix that finds the estimated price of a feed as an aggregated sum of its individual nutrients values according to the nutrient content and prices of a set of defined feed ingredients available in the market. The tool then compares the actual price of a feed ingredient with its calculated price. The result is a list of ingredients with their relative prices, indicating if an ingredient is a bargain or an expensive proposition.

Another critical factor in the quest for feed efficiency and maximum milk income over feed cost is the analysis of "benchmarking" with respect to feed efficiency, milk income, and feed costs [16]. Results from surveying dairy farm rations and farm prices reveals an impressive difference regarding to feed costs, feed consumption, and overall milk income over feed cost among otherwise similar dairy farms. A large and important opportunity exists then to improve the milk value net of the feed costs by comparing performance among farms. Therefore an online database structure and DSS was developed: *"Dairy Extension Feed Cost Evaluator,"* Figure 1. This tool performs advanced benchmarking analyses for a group of users within a region, state, or country throughout a defined timeline by querying an online database, which is permanently being updated by the users. The tool allows users to "drill-down" the analysis and find out the driving factors for differences, an important step toward improving dairy farm feed efficiency and income over feed cost.

Figure 1. Screen snapshot of DSS *Dairy Extension Feed Cost Evaluator.*

Dairy farmers also require some simpler evaluation tools for feed additives. The tool "*Optigen® Evaluator*" analyzes the economic value of including this slow release urea additive while maintaining diets at the same level of protein and dry matter intake. The tool "*Dairy Ration Feed Additive Break-Even Analysis*" determines any additive's additional milk production needed to justify its economic inclusion in the diet.

Finally, regarding nutrition and diets, there is some evidence that dairy farmers might be over-feeding a large proportion of lactating cows when they feed the same diet ration to a large group of animals. Diets are normally formulated to provide enough nutrients to the most productive animals, which in turn gives extra nutrients to the less productive animals within the same group. Therefore, splitting lactating cows in smaller groups and offering group-specific feeding rations provide more precise nutrient requirements, increase herd's income over feed cost, and decrease nutrient excretion [17]. The tool "*Grouping Strategies for Feeding Lactating Dairy Cattle*" calculates dynamically individual cow nutrient requirements and optimizes cow grouping feeding strategies within particular farm constraints.

2.2. Reproductive Efficiency (DairyMGT.info → Tools→ Reproduction)

Reproductive efficiency plays a critical role in the economics of dairy farming. However, assess the economic value of it is extremely difficult and complex [5]. A first step on understanding the economic impact of reproductive programs is to demonstrate the milk value net of feed cost dependent on the pregnancy time. The tool "*Exploring Pregnancy Timing Impact on Income over Feed Cost*" shows interactively and dynamically a cow's total milk income net of feed costs to a fixed lactation's pregnancy time and defined lactation curves. The tool illustratesand quantifies the economic value of having cows pregnant at the right time.

Dairy farmers are also required to do complex decisions regarding the best reproductive programs for the lactating herd population. New reproductive management strategies, whether they use hormonal synchronization technologies, heat detection methods, or a combination of both, are continuously and permanently evolving. Dairy farmers need not only to keep up-to-date with all these technologies, but also make the best decisions according to their own conditions [5]. Dairy farmers usually know which reproductive programs are more efficient from the reproductive point of view of getting more cows pregnant. Farmers also have a good handle on costs incurred according to reproductive programs. Nonetheless, dairy farmers have difficulty assessing the overall profitability of reproductive programs. Not surprisingly, they have long demanded for a systematic economic analysis to analyze reproductive programs. The tool "*UW-DairyRepro$Plus*" is a complex, still user-friendly, decision support systems that assess the economic value of farm-defined alternative reproductive programs for a particular farm according to prevalent market conditions. These tools allow farmers to be highly specific regarding their current or alternative reproductive programs. Besides reporting the most important reproductive parameters for each alternative program, the tools find the reproductive program with the best economic outcome and calculates the difference in net returns a farm would have when using alternative reproductive programs.

Sex-sorted semen that increases the chance of female offspring is a relatively new technology being widely adopted in the dairy industry. Farm-specific sexed semen's economic value and, moreover, when and how to use it, are critical. The tool "*Economic Value of Sexed Semen for Dairy Heifers*" (Figure 2) finds interactively the gain (or loss) of different reproductive program management strategies that include sexed semen compared with solely using conventional semen [18].

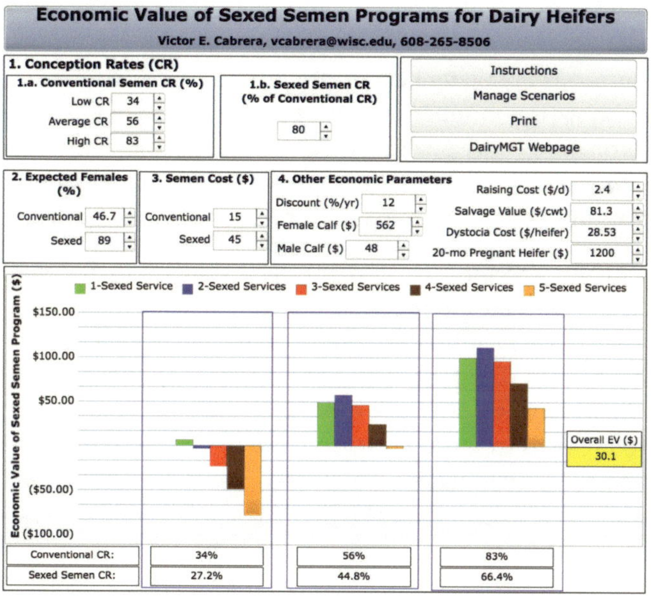

Figure 2. Screen snapshot of DSS *Economic Value of Sexed Semen for Dairy Heifers.*

As important as to find out the value of specific-defined reproductive programs is to explore the value of improving the overall reproductive efficiency. The tool "*Dairy Reproductive Economic Analysis*" is a Markov-chain stochastic dynamic model packed in a simple to use online application. This tool integrates detailed parameters of pregnancy, abortion, and culling risks to perform iterations during 9 lactations until a herd reaches a steady state [19]. Then, the economic value of a reproductive program is determined by using predicted milk production curves, calve value, replacement costs, and other economic figures. The end result is a net return tied to a reproductive performance.

2.3. Heifer Management and Cow Replacement (DairyMGT.info → Tools→ Heifers / Replacement)

Whether farmers raise replacement heifers or not, they benefit from decisions related to this dairy farming enterprise. One first step on the economic decision about heifers is to determine the overall cost associated with rearing heifers according to estimated time to first calving. The tool *"Heifer Break-Even"* calculate the daily and accumulated cost for rearing heifers up to 12 months, 24 months, and beyond 24 months according to farm-defined prices for forages, corn, and soybean meal. Farmers use this tool to decide if to raise their own heifers, use custom-raising heifer services, or simply buy heifer replacements, according to market prices.

When farmers raise heifers on-farm, another decision comes along: to use or not to use accelerated feeding programs for boosting the early development of calves. The tool *"Cost-Benefit of Accelerated Feeding Programs"* gives dairy farmers the opportunity to compare hand-by-hand their current heifers' feeding program with an alternative accelerated feeding program within farm defined conditions. This tool shows economic differences at weaning and calving and calculates the amount of milk amount that would be needed to pay for heifer rearing costs.

In addition to the decisions of raising heifers and if to use accelerated feeding programs, dairy farmers want to know the number of heifers needed to maintain (or increase) the herd size according to farm long-term goals, reproductive efficiency, and heifers' culling rates. The tool *"Heifer Replacement"* calculates the number of replacement animals needed (springer heifers) responding to farm specific data inputs.

Dairy farmers would need to buy (or sell) springing heifers if the number of he replacements is fewer (or greater) than the required number to achieve the goal of maintaining or expand the herd size. Consequently, they need support on estimating the right price to pay (or to sell) springing heifers. The tool *"Value of a Springer"* performs a projection of the net return an animal would have under farm specific conditions. This value indicates the value of a replacement to break-even its costs. Because of the uncertainty in the milk price, milk production, and the productive lifetime, the model presents outcomes under different price and lifetime scenarios, so farmers can make decisions based on their assertion of the future prices and their risk preferences.

Furthermore, dairy farmers need to make critical decisions if to keep or replace a cow from the herd. The optimal decision will depend on which alternative would bring a greater net return in the future. The tool *"The Economic Value of a Dairy Cow"* (Figure 3) is a complex Markov-chain simulation model, still a user-friendly application that calculates interactively the economic value of a cow (or the value of each single cow in a herd) compared with its replacement [20]. Farmers use this value to make more informed decisions if to keep or replace cows. This tool, in addition, calculates the expected herd demographics and the average herd net return for better and additional dairy farm management and decision-making.

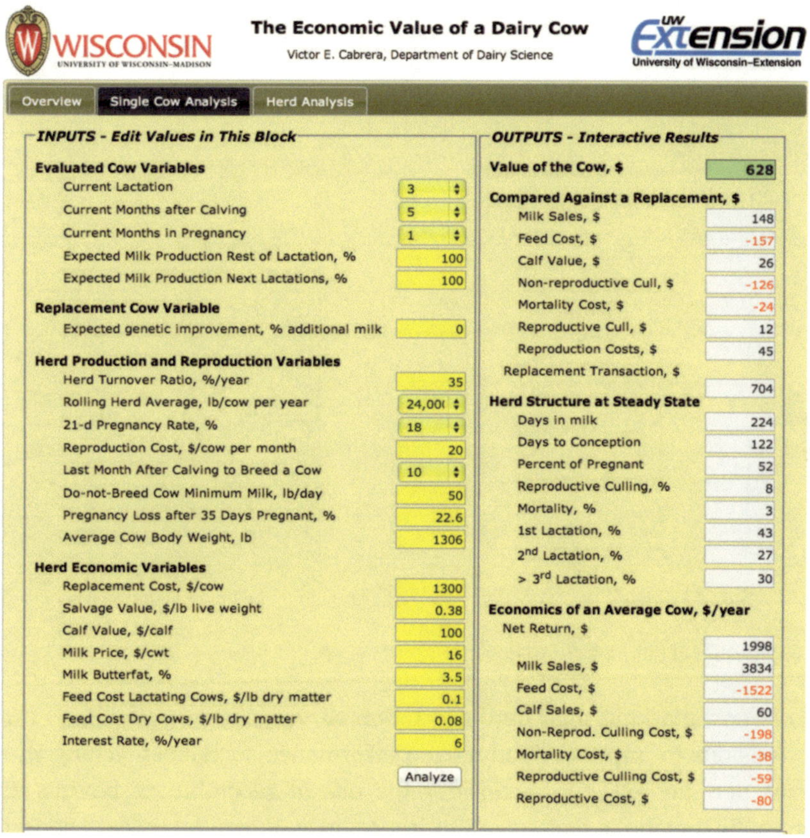

Figure 3. Screen snapshot of DSS *The Economic Value of a Dairy Cow*.

2.4. Production and Productivity (DairyMGT.info → Tools→ Production)

Dairy farmers face several decisions regarding production-related issues. In order to make best decisions, they would like to know how their farm milk production profile compares to other similar farms. Besides milk amount produced per animal, the shape of the herd's lactation curves is critical to pinpoint management weaknesses and strengths of a particular farm. The tool "*Lactation Benchmark Curves for Wisconsin*" displays different parity lactation curves for different production levels herds obtained by processing 3.6 million lactation records. Dairy farmers can define their own lactation curves to assess their production performance compared with the benchmarked records. Similarly, farmers find great benefit of projecting their own lactation curves and compare specific dairy herd cows to the standards of the whole herd, which can be accomplished by using the tool "*Milk Curve Fitter,*" Figure 4.

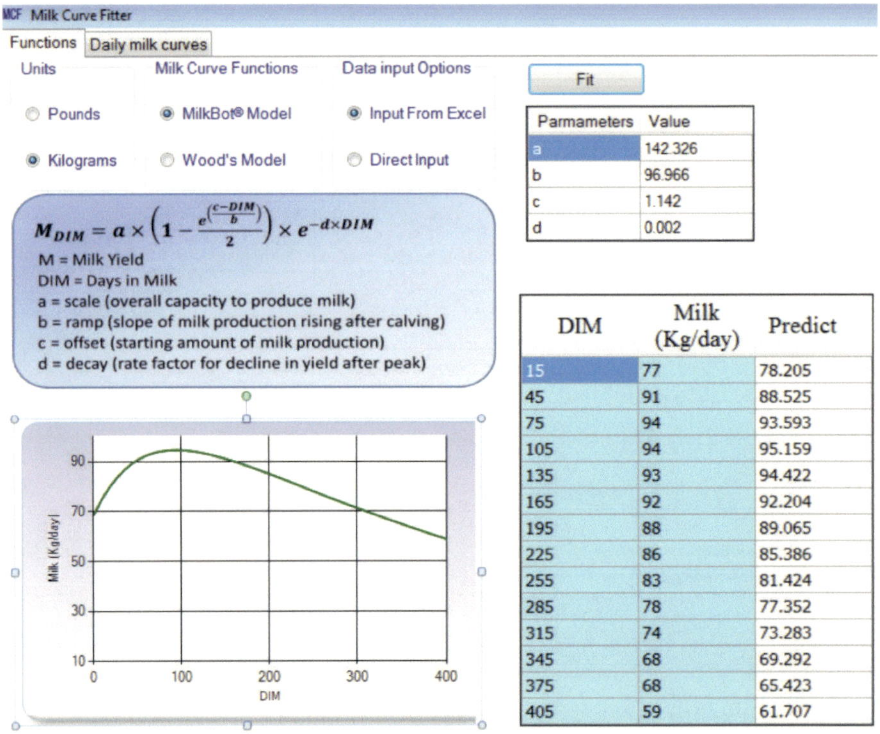

Figure 4. Screen snapshot of DSS *Milk Curve Fitter.*

As a result of benchmarking their herd's lactation curves, dairy farmers may contemplate a new set of decisions to improve productive performance such as switching the number of milking times per day [21] or re-consider the use of recombinant bovine somatotropin (rbST), a synthetic metabolic hormone that improves milk productivity. The tool "*Economic Analysis of Switching from 2X to 3X Milking*" performs a farm-specific partial budgeting analysis of the projected gain (or loss) when a farmer decides to milk 3 times a day instead of 2 times. The tool "*Economic Analysis of using rbST*" displays the economic gain (or loss) of using rbST as an interactive sensitivity analysis according to ever-changing milk price and estimated milk increase because of rbST under specific farm conditions.

Some dairy farmers are also interested in the possibility of either expand or modernize their farm facilities or increase their herd size. Therefore, they require support on important decisions that will drive the future of the dairy farm operation. The tool "*Decision Support System Program for Dairy Production and Expansion*" is a Spreadsheet application that allows dairy farmers to outline their current farm conditions regarding herd structure and market conditions, define a possible plan of expansion or modernization including required loans (for facilities and animals), and project the cash flow of the entire farm up to a period of 54 months in the future.

http://dx.doi.org/10.5772/50801

2.5. Price Risk Management and Financial Assessment (DairyMGT.info → Tools→ Financial)

Unfavorable prices of milk and feed commodities together with increased price volatility create large uncertainty in the dairy farm business. Recent unprecedented uncertain times have prompted to re-visit farm's financial status and look for alternatives to stabilize net returns. It is critical to explore price risk management alternatives such as the relatively new revenue insurance program called Livestock Gross Margin for Dairy (LGM-Dairy) and to assess farm financial performance compared with peers [22].

In brief, the LGM-Dairy can protect the net margin (milk value less feed cost or milk income over feed cost) at a much lower cost than using comparable options in the future markets. The tool "*LGM-Analyzer*" (Figure 5) is an online, easy-to-use, suite of real-time, data intense, simulation, and optimization integrated modules to help on the decision of using LGM-Dairy. The *LGM-Analyzer* not only replicates the official premium calculation from the U.S. Department of Agriculture Risk Management Agency, but also is capable of perform historical sensitivity analysis as well as complex optimizations to minimize the premium cost at a level of target guaranteed income over feed cost. This suite of tools is also capable of comparing the LGM-Dairy with more traditional price risk management tools such as puts (Class III milk) and calls (corn and soybean meal) for feeds as bundled price options. The *LGM-Analyzer* connects live with the dairy and grain-based futures and market (through a structured query language) to determine the premium cost a particular farmer could expect according to a guarantee income over feed cost ("*Premium Estimator*"). Furthermore, a unique module ("*Least Cost Optimizer*") lets the user to minimize the LGM-Dairy premium cost at a defined level of income over feed cost insured. Other tools in the area of analysis of the LGM-Dairy include the "*LGM-Dairy Feed Equivalent,*" a tool to covert feed diet ingredients to corn and soybean meal equivalents needed for a LGM-Dairy contract and the "*Net Guarantee Income over Feed Cost,*" a tool to help dairy farmers determine the income over feed cost to break-even all other costs of production, which should be covered by using LGM-Dairy.

Also, performing a farm's financial benchmark assessment is critical in the process of measuring the financial health of a dairy farm. Moreover, this is usually required by lenders in order to consider loan applications. The "*Wisconsin Dairy Farm Benchmarking Tool*" is a database application that calculates 15 financial ratios including variables of liquidity, solvency, profitability, repayment capacity, and financial efficiency for a group of more than 500 Wisconsin dairy farms during a period of 10 years. The tool then compares each one of these ratios with those of a particular farm. Therefore, farmers can assess their financial health compared with their peers. Furthermore, the tool provides a *DuPont* analysis, in which a farm is compared against the population with respect to revenue and profit generated for every dollar invested. Another related tool, "*Working Capital Decision Support System*" assists dairy farmers in identifying cash flows, project expected incomes and expenses, and identifies cash excesses and shortfalls well in advance of their occurrence.

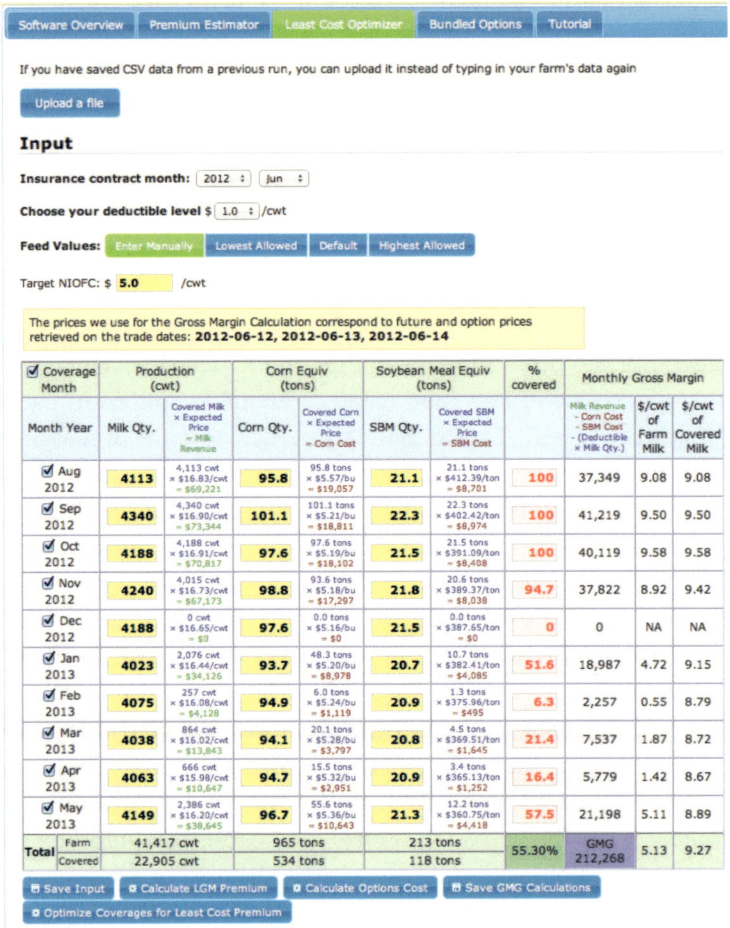

Figure 5. Screen snapshot of DSS *LGM-Analyzer*.

2.6. Environmental Stewardship (DairyMGT.info → Tools→Environment)

The dairy farm business faces important challenges regarding increased environmental scrutiny. An increasingly important dairy farm management task is to maintain a farm nutrient balance and therefore avoid over-concentration of nutrients in or around the farm. Opportunities exist to better utilize nutrients in dairy farming and not only improve the balance of nutrients coming in and going out of the farm, but also decrease fertilizer expenses and therefore environmental concerns. Depending on the farm herd and crop characteristics, additional expenses might be required to comply with environmental regulations. In any case, an economic assessment along with the environmental requirements promotes better decision-making. A series of decision support tools deal with these sensitive aspects of dairy farming. The tool *"Dynamic Dairy Farm Model"* (Figure 6) is an integrated, whole-farm, simulation and optimization model that maximizes the net economic return while minimizing nitrogen leaching to surface and ground water sources. A simplified version of nutrient balance between nitrogen and phosphorus manure excretion for a fast assessment is the tool with name *"Dairy Nutrient Manager."* Also related, the *"Grazing-N"* is an application that balances nitrogen for dairy farms with grazing activities and the *"Seasonal Prediction of Manure Excretion,"* as its name says, helps dairy farmers project seasonally the amount of cow manure (and consequently nutrients in the manure) will be produced and will be needed to be recycled.

Figure 6. Screen snapshot of DSS *Dynamic Dairy Farm Model.*

3. Decision Support Systems Development: Challenges and Trade-offs

A number of methodologies and software applications were used to develop the decision support tools above described (Table 1). The goal always remained to provide solid, but user-friendly DSS tools. The methodology as well as the software application approach followed the tool development and the ultimate goal pursued and not vice versa. It was usual to combine and adapt methodologies within a particular tool development. Following is a succinct description of the most important methodologies used for the DairyMGT.info DSS tools and a discussion of the approaches used for the software applications.

3.1. Methodologies used for the Decision Support System Tools

3.1.1. Partial Budgeting

Partial budgeting compares a current with an alternative technology by balancing the economics of 4 elements that are assessed before and after the adoption of the alternative technology: 1) additional returns (adds), 2) reduced costs (adds), 3) returns foregone (subtracts), and 4) additional costs (subtracts) [23]. Partial budgeting could be a robust methodology when a direct change is expected from the new technology without major interaction with other system components beyond the analyzed variables. Partial budgeting is the underline methodology to assess the break-even level of using feed additives, the economic benefit of milking 3 times a day, the economic evaluation of using rbST, the assessment of corn feeding strategies, and the assessment of income over feed cost by different diets under commodity price changes.

3.1.2. Cost Benefit

The cost benefit methodology is similar to partial budgeting but determines profitability of a new technology over longer periods of time and therefore requires the specification of a discount rate that is used to calculate a net present value [23]. The cost benefit is the underline methodology for calculating the value of adopting accelerated heifer liquid feeding programs and is as a supporting methodology to find out the economic value of sexed semen for dairy heifers, the value of reproductive programs in adult cows, and to assess the net present value of alternative scenarios of possible dairy farm expansion or modernization.

3.1.3. Decision Analysis

The decision analysis is appropriate when probabilistic distributions are important factors in determining the final outcomes [24] as it occurs when analyzing the value of using sexed semen on heifers, comparing the value of reproductive programs in adult cows, or projecting the replacement flow needed to maintain the herd size. In the first two cases, conditional probabilities were used to successively determine populations of pregnant, non-pregnant, and eligible to breed animals along with their respective expected monetary contributions. In the case of the replacement flow tool, transition probabilities are used to dynamically project the herd dynamics across time.

Decision Support System Tool	Underline Methodology	Software Application
Feeding and Nutrition		
Corn Feeding Strategies	Partial Budgeting	Flash[1]
Income Over Feed Cost	Partial Budgeting	Flash
Income over Feed Supplement Cost	Linear Programming	Spreadsheet/ Online[2]

http://dx.doi.org/10.5772/50801

Decision Support System Tool	Underline Methodology	Software Application
FeedVal 2012	Matrix Solution	Online
Dairy Extension Feed Cost Evaluator	Database Management	Online
Optigen® Evaluator	Matrix Solution	Online
Dairy Ration Feed Additive Break-Even Analysis	Partial Budgeting	Flash
Grouping Strategies for Feeding Lactating Dairy Cattle	Mathematical Simulation	Online
Reproductive Efficiency		
Exploring Pregnancy Timing Impact on Income over Feed Cost	Mathematical Simulation	Online
Economic Value of Sexed Semen for Dairy Heifers	Decision Analysis	Flash/Online
UW-DairyRepro$	Decision Analysis	Spreadsheet
Dairy Reproductive Economic Analysis	Markov Chains	Online
Heifer Management and Cow Replacement		
Heifer Break-Even	Enterprise Budgets	Online/Spreadsheet
Cost-Benefit of Accelerated Feeding Programs	Cost Benefit	Flash/Online
Heifer Replacement	Decision Analysis	Spreadsheet/Online
The Economic Value of a Dairy Cow	Markov Chains	Online/Spreadsheet
Production and Productivity		
Milk Curve Fitter	Nonlinear Optimization	Installation[3]
Lactation Benchmark Curves for Wisconsin	Database Management	Flash/Spreadsheet
Economic Analysis of Switching from 2X to 3X Milking	Partial Budgeting	Flash
Economic Analysis of using rbST	Partial Budgeting	Flash
DSS Program for Dairy Production and Expansion	Markov Chains	Spreadsheet
Price Risk Management and Financial Assessment		
LGM-Analyzer	Mathematical Simulation	Online
LGM-Premium Estimator	Mathematical Simulation	Online
LGM-Least Cost Optimizer	Nonlinear Optimization	Online

Decision Support System Tool	Underline Methodology	Software Application
LGM-Dairy Feed Equivalent	Matrix Solution	Online
LGM-Net Guarantee Income Over Feed Cost	Mathematical Simulation	Spreadsheet
Wisconsin Dairy Farm Benchmarking Tool	Database Management	Online/Spreadsheet
Working Capital Decision Support System	Enterprise Budgets	Spreadsheet
Environmental Stewardship		
Dynamic Dairy Farm Model	Markov Chains	Spreadsheet
Dairy Nutrient Manager	Mathematical Simulation	Spreadsheet
Grazing-N	Mathematical Simulation	Spreadsheet
Seasonal Prediction of Manure Excretion	Markov Chains	Spreadsheet

Table 1. Principal methodology and software application of DairyMGT.info decision support system tools.[1]Flash: Macromedia Flash. [2]Online tools use a combination of software including HTML, PHP, JavaScript, C, CSS, and MySQL. [3]Requires software installation in local machine.

3.1.4. Enterprise Budgets

Enterprise budgets are a systematic way to list returns and costs and evaluate profits from inside a specific business enterprise [25] within the dairy farm. This methodology is used to calculatethe heifer break-even by contrasting heifers' rearing costs with potential benefits. This methodology is also used, in more detail, in the tool working capital to project the cash flow of a dairy farm enterprise.

3.1.5. Linear Programming

Linear programming is a mathematical optimization algorithm to maximize or minimize a goal (e.g., maximum profit or minimum costs) within a set of constraints represented as linear relationships [26]. Linear programming is at the core of the tool income over feed supplementation cost in determining the diet composition that results in the maximum net return within a set of constraints of available feed ingredients. Linear programming is also used recursively in the dynamic dairy farm model to maximize the farm net return while minimizing nitrogen leaching.

3.1.6. Markov Chains

Markov chains are a mathematical system that undergoes transitions from one state to the next within a finite space of states as random processes. In dairy farming, Markov chains are widely used for decision-making to predict herd demographics or to project cows' probabilistic life [2, 10, 12, 19-20]. Markov chains are also very useful to implement decision support tools, as these are less computationally demanding than alternative methods. Markov chains are therefore important part of the DairyMGT.info DSS tools and are the backbone structure of the tools: seasonal manure prediction, dynamic dairy farm model, reproductive economic analysis, and the economic value of a dairy cow. Markov chains are also important part of the tools dealing with expansion and modernization and the one comparing the value of different reproductive programs for adult cows.

3.1.7. Mathematical Simulation and Projection

Mathematical simulation and projection is a general description that encompass a group of diverse and integrated empirical techniques and algorithms that have as main goal to represent observed data as it happens in real-life situations when not a single method fits this condition to satisfaction. Mathematical simulation and projection is used in most of the DairyMGT tools. However, it is a core methodology in a group of them. For example, mathematical simulation is used in the grouping tool to calculate feed nutrient requirements for every single cow in a herd; in the timing of pregnancy tool to aggregate the overall milk production and feed consumption a cow will have depending on the time of pregnancy; and in all LGM related tools to generate thousands of replicates and calculate the statistics of net margins that will determine insurance premiums [27]. Also mathematical simulation and projection is important to predict cash flows within the expansion tool and to perform nutrient balances in tools such as dairy dynamic model, dairy nutrient manager, and grazing-N.

3.1.8. Nonlinear Optimization

Nonlinear optimization deals with finding an objective function of maximizing or minimizing a variable within a set of simultaneous constraints, where the objective function or some of the constraints have nonlinear relationships. Nonlinear optimization adds a set of complexity to the implementation of decision support tools because it is computational demanding. However, for some applications it is required. Since finding the global maxima for nonlinear problems it is not always possible, a compromise between finding a satisfactory answer and maintain the applications as user-friendly as possible is needed. Nonlinear optimization is used in the grouping, milk curve fitter, and LGM least cost optimizer tools. For the grouping tool, a nonlinear optimization algorithm groups lactating cows according to nutritional requirements with the objective function of finding the aggregated maximum income over feed cost through recursive iterations by allocating cows to size-defined groups. In the milk curve fitter tool, the user enters farm herd milk production and a nonlinear algorithm minimizes the residual difference between the farm observed data and the predicted data adjusted to a pre-defined milk lactation function such as Wood [28] or MilkBot [29]. The results are coefficients of the defined function that best represent farm-specific lactation curves. The LGM-least cost uses a nonlinear optimization to find out the minimum premium price to a defined target guarantee net income over feed cost according to future projected commodity prices and farm specific conditions, replicating the rules governing the insurance product. The result is the least cost premium for a determined level of coverage within the LGM-Dairy insurance structure [30-31].

3.1.9. Matrix Solution to Multiple Equations

Matrix or algebra simultaneous equation solution is helpful in the area of nutrition and feeding to replace feed ingredients and maintain same level nutritional of the diet and same level of feed intake. It is also useful to value feeds depending on their nutrients content. Each feed ingredient is defined in function of its nutrient contents and its market price. When the number of nutrients equals to the number of feed ingredients (same number of equations as unknowns) the result is an exact value for each nutrient and therefore the predicted value of a feed ingredient is equal to the input value as it is the case in the Optigen Evaluator tool [32]. Similar approach is used for the LGM-feed equivalent, which converts any feed ingredient into equivalents of corn and soybean meal, as it is required for LGM-Dairy insurance contracts. The tool FeedVal 2012 goes beyond and analyzes a set of user-defined matrix between 2 and 50 ingredients and between 2 and 13 nutrients to find out the difference between the feed ingredient market price and the estimated price based on the nutrient composition value of the ingredient.

3.1.10. Database Management and Analysis

Some tools require a database interface and some mechanism of querying the database to retrieve information and to perform analysis dynamically and efficiently. Databases are permanently being updated. Database tools are the lactation benchmark curves and the dairy farm ratio benchmarking. The user does not update these database applications directly, but a server manager. The user queries the database and is able to compare specific farm data with a set of filtered information within the databases. Other type of database application is the feed evaluator tool that registers users in the system and allows them to enter and save their data. The users update the database and the queries retrieve real-time information anytime. Users can then compare their own data against to a filtered group of other farms. A different concept is portrayed in all LGM related tools for which all the data (commodity prices of milk, corn, and soybean meal from the future markets) is retrieved real-time from the official sources anytime the user performs an analysis [29]. The calculation of either LGM premiums or least cost premiums changes depending not only on the user inputs, but also based upon the time of the query. The system saves historical information, so users can also do retrospective analyses.

3.1.11. External Simulation Models

Some tools require to be integrated with more complex, fully developed and established models. That is for example the case of the Dynamic Dairy Farm Model and the Grazing-N tools. In the first case, model requires assessments of crop production (corn, soybean, pastures, etc.), which are performed by using external crop simulation models from the family of Decision Support System for Agrotechnology Transfer [33]. The dynamic dairy farm model feeds the crop simulation model with data of soils, weather, and crop management schemes and the crop simulation models return predicted biomass produced, nutrient utilization, and nitrogen leaching from the soil. The Grazing-N application is integrated with the National Research Council model of nutrient requirement for dairy animals [34] according to a set of characteristics that include age, production, and live weight.

3.2. Software Applications

According to the type of application, the methodologies used in the tool, and, most importantly, the goal of the tool as a DSS, different software application approaches were used (Table 1). Most of the tools have been developed in different software applications with the objective of better meeting user styles and therefore capture larger audiences of users.

Spreadsheet applications are a very popular format among dairy farmers and consultants because of their familiarity with them, the possibility of using the same spreadsheet for further analyses, and the capacity of save and maintain a copy of it in a personal computer. Spreadsheet application was the elected method for a number of DairyMGT.info tools (Table 1). Most of the spreadsheet applications, however,required some type of Visual Basic code embedded into the application (macros).

Other group of tools uses Macromedia Flash as the software application. Macromedia Flash has the advantage of having a nice interactive visual interface connected with a calculator. From the point of view of the user, Flash tools are probably the easiest to use. They havethe additional advantage of becoming stand-alone applications and therefore of being used offline or embedded in Power Point presentations or Portable Document Format (PDF) files. One problem with Flash applications is, however, its limited computational functionality. Flash applications have only a set of limited mathematical functions without the possibility of using macros or combinethemwith code programming. Also Flash applications are not compatible with Apple smart phones and tablets. Current tools that are only Flash applications within the DairyMGT.info DSS tools will eventually be converted also to be online applications.

Other group of tools can be classified in the general category of online tools. These use an array of different software applications. What they all have in common is that these work in any web browser and eventually in any device and in any platform including smart phones, tablets, Apple, Linux, PC, etc. Calculations and analyses are normally performed in the DairyMGT.info web server, so the online tool is only an interface between the device of the user and the server. In general, online tools are very efficient and reliable tools that have the advantage to be always up-to-date: users always experience the latest version of the tool. Other important advantage is that complex processes and mathematical calculations can be managed using a combination of web code such as HTML (hyper text markup language), PHP (hypertext preprocessor), JavaScript (prototype-based scripting language), C (general-purpose language), CSS (style sheet language), MySQL (relational database management system), or others. Another advantage of online tools is that their design layout can be very efficient and solid once the tool is deployed. A drawback for developing online tools, however, is the need of expertise in web-based code writing. Nonetheless, online tools are very efficient and probably a trend to which many of the tools of DairyMGT.info will continue to gravitate.

4. Illustration and Practical Decision-Making

4.1. Group Feeding

The value grouping feeding strategies was analyzed by applying the grouping tool to 30 dairy farms in Wisconsin. Test records were collected and adjusted to datasets consisting of cow identification, lactation, days after calving, milk production, and milk butterfat for each cow in each farm. The aim of this exercise was to demonstrate the value of grouping compared to no grouping without knowing studied farms' actual feeding strategies. Therefore, same procedure and assumptions were followed on each analyzed farm: 1) comparison of no grouping versus 3 same-size groups, 2) prices at \$15.89/45.4 kg milk, \$0.14337/0.454 kg CP, and \$0.1174/4.19 mega joules (MJ) net energy, 3) average body weight of 500 kg for first lactation cows and 590 kg for cows in second and later lactations, 4) requirements of CP and net energy at the 83rd percentile level of the group (mean + 1 standard deviation), and 5) a cluster grouping criterion (grouping cows depending on their CP and net energy requirements for maintenance and milk production).

Evaluations clearly and consistently demonstrated that the income over feed cost (IOFC) in all analyzed farms was greater for the 3 feeding groups strategy than the no groping strategy (Table 2).

	Number of lactating cows on analyzed farms (n = 30)	No grouping IOFC	3 same-size feeding groups IOFC	Additional IOFC of doing 3 same-size feeding groups
		--------------------$/cow per year----------------------		
Mean	788	2,311	2,707	396
Minimum	<200	697	1,059	161
Maximum	>1,000	2,967	3,285	580

Table 2. Comparison of income over feed cost (IOFC) of no grouping versus 3 same-size feeding groups for Wisconsin dairy farms assessed by the tool: *Grouping Strategies for Feeding Lactating Dairy Cattle*.

The analysis indicated that farms could realize between \$161 and \$580/cow per year (mean = \$396) of additional IOFC by switching from no grouping to 3 same-size feeding groups using the cluster criterion for grouping. These values represented an increase of between 7 and 52% of farm calculated IOFC. It was concluded then that grouping would have important economic implications in farm profitability and that further analysis should be done at farm-specific level and in a permanent basis by using the *Grouping Strategies for Feeding Lactating Dairy Cattle* DSS tool.

4.2. Sexed Semen

The *Economic Value of Sexed Semen for Dairy Heifers* tool was used for general conditions of Wisconsin dairy farms based on data of a sample of 309 dairy farms and 38 custom heifer growers, a survey performed by county extension agents [35]. At the time of the analysis, using the aggregated data of the 347 operations, the average economic benefit of using sexed semen, as calculated by the tool, was $30 per heifer. Results confirmed that most of these farmers were using optimally this new technology. They were using it for first and second service only, which was the same optimal strategy found by the tool [35]. A main conclusion of this analysis was that the sexed semen technology has an economic benefit, but it would be mostly recommended when the conception rate of the sexed semen is at least 80% of the conventional semen, the value of the heifer calf is high, and when the price of the sexed semen is twice or less than that of the conventional semen. Due that the conception rate of both the conventional and sexed semen and the market prices are important determinant parameters, a main recommendation was that the analysis should be performed on a farm-specific basis and on a permanent basis, for which the decision support tool plays an important role.

4.3. Dairy Reproductive Economic Analysis

Published data along with dairy farm records were collected and summarized to create a representative farm to assess the value of improving reproductive efficiency measured as improving the 21-day pregnancy rate using the tool *Dairy Reproductive Economic Analysis*. Data consisted of detailed information on transition probabilities arrays of replacement and abortion risks; definition of lactation curves, and several economic parameters. Then, the DSS was used multiple times to represent incremental gains in reproductive efficiency.

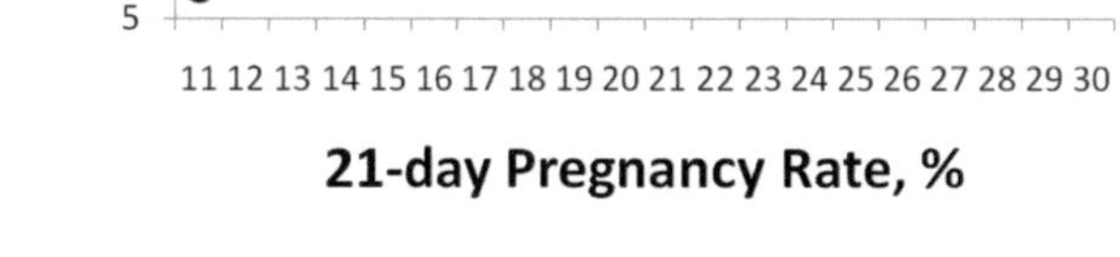

Figure 7. Projected net economic gain of improving 21-day pregnancy rate from a baseline of 10% assessed by the tool: *Dairy Reproductive Economic Analysis*.

Figure 7 portrays a marginally decreasing trend of economic gain with respect to 21-day pregnancy rate: the higher the original 21-d pregnancy rate, the lower the gain. Nonetheless the tool shows clearly that even at 30% 21-day pregnancy rate, an extremely (and unusual) good pregnancy rate, there is still an opportunity of additional gains because of improved reproductive efficiency. The tool, furthermore presents the main factors from which the additional value comes (in order): higher milk income over feed cost, lower culling costs, higher calf revenues, and lower reproductive costs. These results are being used in a large extension undertaking to promote improved reproductive efficiency in hundreds of dairy farms, but always with the final recommendation that specific farm data and information from current market conditions should be used with the DSS tool to have a more precise assessment.

4.4. Decision Support System for Expansion

Three hundred dairy farms completed a mailed questionnaire regarding their desires and needs of expansion or modernization [36]. Seventy eight percent of farms (26% of respondents) indicated that were planning to expand or modernize their installations and listed as the most important reason of doing that the expected increase on farm net return. Importantly, they acknowledge largely the uncertainty of the process of expansion as a large hindrance and therefore they asked for decision support tools that would allow them project systematically their options and analyze scenarios. More than 20 of these farmers were then contacted and offered to perform those projections by using the tool *Decision Support System Program for Dairy Production and Expansion*. The overall outcome was that all farmers visited agreed that the tool represented reasonably well their farm sand therefore they would trust its future projections. Further analyses were used to confirm or reject their pre-conceived evaluations and to assist farmers to make more informed decisions throughout the process of expansion or modernization. More than 10 farmers did some adjustments in their expansion or modernization process because of the tool and all of them indicated will continue using the DSS tool throughout their expansion or modernization operation.

4.5. The Economic Value of a Dairy Cow

Representative data from Wisconsin farms were collected from official sources, farm records, and market reports to become a baseline scenario [20] from which users could select modifications according to their own conditions. Results of these data contained in the tool *Economic Value of a Dairy Cow* indicated that the expected milk production of the cow was the single most important factor for replacement decisions. The impacts of increasing or decreasing up to 20% (120 to 80 in Table 3) the average milk production of a cow, a reasonable assumption, are portrayed in Table 3. It is evident that the milk production expectancy of following lactations is a much more important factor for pregnant cows whereas the impact of milk production expectancy of this lactation and future lactations are similarly important factors for non-pregnant cows.

Although these numbers are good indicators for farm decision-making, the need of using the tool with specific farm conditions and under current market condition could not be over emphasized.

This tool *Economic Value of a Dairy Cow* was also used to value the animal farm assets in a farm. The tool was first set with all parameters concerning to the specific farm and with economic variables representing the market conditions. Followed, the farmer created a list of all cows in the farm including their current state (lactation, month after calving, and pregnancy status) and, importantly, their projected milk production. Then, a cow value was calculated for every single animal in the herd. Finally, the calculated salvage value was added to the cow value. The farmer was then able to use these data for continued monetary support from a financial institution.

Expected Milk Production (% of the average cow)		Cow Value of a 2-month pregnant, 8-month after calving cow, $			Cow Value of a non-pregnant, 7-month after calving cow, $		
Rest of Lactation[1]	Successive Lactations[2]	1st Lactation	2nd Lactation	3rd Lactation	1st Lactation	2nd Lactation	3rd Lactation
120	120	2,458	2,038	2,002	1,973	1,485	1,462
120	100	1,045	877	829	1,109	857	814
120	80	-380	-284	-345	244	230	165
100	120	1,891	1,499	1,477	1,184	796	809
100	**100**	**479**	**338**	**304**	**320**	**168**	**161**
100	80	-934	-823	-870	-545	-460	-487
80	120	1,325	961	952	395	106	157
80	100	-88	-200	-221	-469	-521	-491
80	80	-1,501	-1,361	-1,395	1,344	1,149	-1,139

Table 3. Impact of expected milk production on the cow value of a 2-month pregnant, 8-month after calving cow and a non-pregnant, 7-month after calving cow assessed by the tool *Economic Value of a Dairy Cow*. Bolded values represent the cow with average production in the herd (100%). [1]Cow's expected milk production (% of the average cow) from the current state to the end of the present lactation. [2]Cow's expected milk production (% of the average cow) in all successive lactations.

4.6. The LGM-Dairy Least Cost

During the months LGM-Dairy revenue insurance program was offered in year 2011, the average savings when using the LGM-Dairy Least Cost tool was 27.8% (Table 4). The tool was used during those months to assess the premium cost for a 200-cow farm producing 31 kg milk/cow per day. Based on experience and expertise with a number of dairy farmers and consultants in Wisconsin, the strategy was to insure a minimum income over feed cost of $5/46.4 kg milk during the effective insurance period that is 10 month s per contract (starting 2 months after the contract month).

Considering that the level of insurance protection is exactly the same whether to paying the regular premium or a least cost premium in Table 3, the savings are substantial. The main difference between regular and least cost premiums is the allocation of milk and feed being insured according to the covered months in the future. In the regular premium, the default situation is to assign the same level of milk quantity for protection every month. The least cost optimization, however, finds a better allocation that based on the underline simulated data determines a better plan that results in a much lower premium, but the same level of protection.

Month	Regular Premium, $	Least Cost Premium, $	Savings on Premium, %
January	4,384	3,389	22.7
February	4,904	3,429	30.1
March	5,209	3,863	25.8
October	4,019	2,685	33.2
November	4,216	3,064	27.3

Table 4. Savings on premiums when insuring net margins using the LGM-Dairy insurance program during the year 2011 assessed by the tool *LGM-Dairy Least Cost* using default amounts of corn and soybean meal as feed insured and assuming a reasonable insurance deductible of $1/46.4 kg milk for a 200-cow dairy farm producing 31 kg milk/cow per day.

4.7. Dynamic Dairy Farm Model

The *Dynamic Dairy Farm Model* was applied on a typical North Florida dairy farm of 400 cows with a production of 7,711 kg/cow per year having 62 ha of crop fields and pastures. A dual optimization including maximization of profit while relaxing N leaching indicated that the nitrogen leaching ranged between 4,800 to 5,000 kg/year whereas the profit would change between $70,000 and $70,600 (Figure 8) [2]. Furthermore, strategies to reduce nitrogen leaching would compromise profit. Depending on the farm goals and environmental regulations, the *Dynamic Dairy Farm Model* proved to be an effective tool to screen options and study whole farm management strategies. As in previous cases, farm specific conditions along with current market conditions need to carefully be defined before doing those assessments.

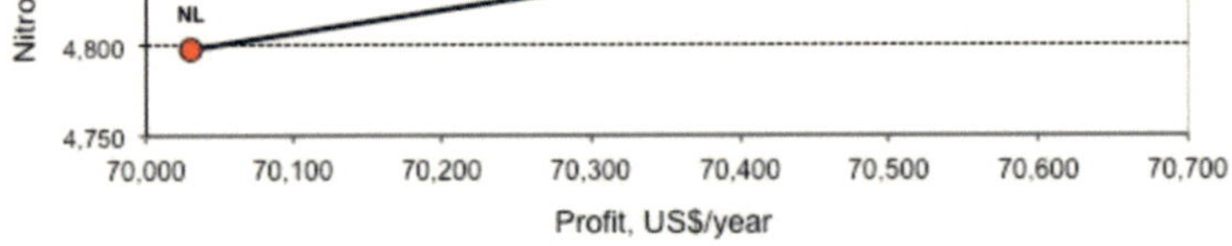

Figure 8. Dual optimization of profit maximization by relaxing nitrogen leaching assessed by using the tool *Dynamic Dairy Farm Model*. NL is average nitrogen leaching and SD is standard deviation.

5. Evaluation of Dissemination and Adoption: Potential Impact

Following is some evidence that indicates the DairyMGT.info Website has become the place-to-go for decision-making tools related to dairy farm management in Wisconsin and a trusted reference with increased visibility in other states and internationally. The DairyMGT website was officially launched at the end of 2009. A predecesor webpage existed since June 2008. between April 2012, and a rate of when email registration was required. According to *Google Analytics (http://www.google.com/analytics/)* the Wisconsin Dairy Management domain (DairyMGT.info or DairyMGT.uwex.edu) received 45,307 page views during the year period ending on April 30, 2012. Fifty nine percent were visitors from the U.S.A. and the rest from other 135 countries. From these, the most important countries were: India (5.5%), Australia (3.3%), Argentina (2.6%), Canada (1.9%), Mexico (1.8%), Kenya (1.6%), United Kingdom (1.5%), Italy (1.5%), Turkey (1.3%), Brazil (1.2%), Peru (1.2%), South Africa (1.0%), Pakistan (1.0%), and Spain (1.0%). Inside the U.S.A., visitors came from all states, but 63% of them were from Wisconsin. Other important states were: California (7.4%), Minnesota (3.1%), Illinois (2.8%), New York (2.6%), Iowa (1.6%), Texas (1.5%), Florida (1.3%), Pennsylvania (1.3%), Michigan (1.3%), and Washington (1.0%).

During the same period of time, May 2011 to April 2012, 1,635 users of decision support tools elected to register their emails on the DairyMGT.info system. A thousand and fifty five did it during the months of 2011, a period in which email registration was optional. During January-to April 2012 a rate of 5 emails registrations a day was recorded. During the one year period May 2011 to April 2012 there were 9,336 downloads of the top 25 DSS tools as shown in Table 5.

Rank	Decision Support Tool	Downloads
1	The Wisconsin Dairy Farm Ratio Benchmarking Tool	1,280
2	LGM-Dairy Insurance Related Tools	1,279
3	Dairy Reproductive Economic Analysis	1,030
4	Corn Feeding Strategies	655
5	UW-DairyRepro$: A Reproductive Economic Analysis Tool	592
6	Optigen® Evaluator	482
7	Economic Analysis of Switching from 2X to 3X Milking	479
8	Lactation Benchmark Curves for Wisconsin	454
9	Grouping Strategies for Feeding Lactating Dairy Cattle	432
10	Heifer Break-Even	346
11	Milk Curve Fitter	313
12	The Economic Value of a Dairy Cow	312
13	Decision Support System Program for Dairy Production and Expansion	252
14	Economic Value of Sexed Semen Programs for Dairy Heifers	245

Rank	Decision Support Tool	Downloads
15	Dairy Ration Feed Additive Break-Even Analysis	240
16	Herd Structure Simulation	228
17	Milk Component Price Analysis	218
18	Heifer Replacement	215
19	Exploring Timing of Pregnancy Impact on Income Over Feed Cost	196
20	Dynamic Dairy Farm Model	156
21	Cost-Benefit of Accelerated Liquid Feeding Program for Dairy Calves	113
22	Dairy Nutrient Manager	98
23	Grazing-N: Application that Balances Nitrogen in Grazing Systems	97
24	Economic Evaluation of using rbST	90
25	Seasonal Prediction of Manure Excretion	48

Table 5. Ranking of the most downloaded tools of DairyMGT.info Decision Support System tools during the period May 2011-April 2012.

A number of tools have been adjusted and translated to other languages to better represent conditions in other regions or in other countries following user inquiries and requests. This was the case for the tools: *Economic Value of Sexed Semen for Dairy Heifers, UW-DairyRepro$: A Reproductive Economic Analysis Tool, Value of a Springer*, and *Income Over Feed Supplement Cost* translated to Spanish and adjusted to Argentinian conditions. The *Economic Value of Sexed Semen for Dairy Heifers* tool was in addition translated to Chinese.

Another evidence of DairyMGT.info DSS demand is the world wide requests for talks regarding these tools. During the past 4 years (May 2008 to April 2012) 168 talks have been given regarding DairyMGT.info tools, a rate of 3.33 talks per month. These talks had a total attendance of about 6,500 people. One hundred and twelve of these talks were in Wisconsin (3,200 people); 25 in other states (1,700 people), and the rest, 31, in other countries such as Mexico, Chile, Peru, Argentina, Honduras, and Nicaragua (1,600 people).

Evidence of adoption together with functionality and benefits of the DSS tools can also be measured by comments and feedback reported by users and other stakeholders. Some anonymous test imonials about DairyMGT.info DSS Tools are listed below.

- "The Income over Feed Supplement Cost is a very useful tool that allows me to find out the best ingredients to buy and provide clear and practical advise in a number of clients I work with" – A dairy farm nutritionist.

- "I have used the tool 2X to 3X milking with a number of farms and consultants and it has always been well received. It does an excellent job of determining the economic impact of switching milking frequencies." – A county Extension agent.

http://dx.doi.org/10.5772/50801

- "The Optigen tool is a very simple application, yet it makes a quite powerful impact because it opens a realm of opportunities in the field." – A dairy industry service provider.
- "...the Sexed Semen evaluator brings very useful information and it is a tool that people can really use and apply within field situations. This is a very useful tool" – A veterinarian attending dairy farms.
- "I think that the information and spins of using the Income over Feed Cost database tool are great and powerful" – A dairy farm consultant.
- "The tools related to economic evaluations of reproductive programs in dairy cattle are going to be incredibly useful." – A dairy Extension specialist.
- "The State of Wisconsin has led the nation in number of contracts and milk insured under the LGM-Dairy program, which reflects, at least in part, the usage and practical application of the LGM-Dairy Analyzer tool of the UW-Madison" – An Extension specialist. "[The LGM-Dairy Analyzer] ...is having a direct and measurable impact [in our dairy industry]" – A University administrator.
- "We are defining reproductive strategies for our herd and we found invaluable the use of the [DairyMGT.info] management tools in our planning design. We specially appreciate the clarity of the applications and the simplicity of concepts that make these tools very practical and applicable." – A dairy farm manager of several dairy farms.
- "The [DairyMGT.info] decision support tools have really helped out our dairy farm in may aspects including financials, replacements, reproduction, and even nutrition." – A senior dairy science student and dairy farmer.
- "These [DairyMGT.info tools] are a collection of the most practical tools I have ever seen." – A well-established county Extension agent.

6. Future Developments: Keep Up with Technology and Needs

A number of emerging and evolving technologies are today available to dairy farmers more than ever. These include the use of smart phones, tablets and similar hardware devices; more efficient software resources; and improved data networks. There is no doubt the trend of fast technological improvement in the area of computer, software, and gadget development will continue even at a faster pace. Progressive farmers and an increasing proportion of Extension agents and dairy farm consultants are already using these technologies. New technologies bring challenges to keep information systems up-to-date, but at the same time bring great opportunities for improved DSS development.

One important advantage of smart phones and tablets is their portability along with connectivity. Nowadays farmers enjoy voice and, importantly, data network and therefore the capability to save and retrieve data eventually from anywhere at anytime. For example, a farmer can have complete information of a cow (e.g., age, lactation, pregnancy status, production history, today's production, genetic background, health incidence, etc.) at the time the cow is being registered through a smart phone system whether the cow is in a corral, in the milking parlor, or out in the field grazing. This gives the farmer the opportunity to make critic a land time-sensitive decisions right away. This could be one of the major benefits of smart phones and tablets applications. Decision support systems have to be integrated with these new technologies and need to take advantage of these important advantages.

One drawback, however, of smart phones and tablet applications is their restricted screen size and some hardware and software limitations. Applications need to be especially designed for smart phones and tablets. Normally, the information entered and retrieved would need to be summarized or would require additional layers of navigation. Extra design details could, though, lead to more compact, more intuitive, and overall more efficient DSS.

There is a trade-off of functionality and payback. The industry seems to favor both types: application for conventional computers and laptops in addition to those applications for smart phones and tablets. The decision-maker selects what type of tool to use for a particular situation. From the developmental standpoint, this is an additional challenge that requires additional work and expertise.

Important considerations regarding upcoming and developmental technologies are the increasing need for integration of DSS with information systems currently used in a farm. Most of the farmers are already using some type of software or information systems for operational management such as feeding, general record keeping, reproductive synchronization programs, identification, heat devices, or others. The DSS portrayed in this chapter and similar have the opportunity of becoming a bridge among these information systems. Decision support systems can use live information from farm records and provide predictions that go beyond the simple record keeping summaries. Farmer expertise combined with real-time DSS projections using farm record keeping systems is a powerful combination for efficient and effective decision-making in dairy farm management.

7. Conclusion

More than 30 computerized decision support system tools have been developed to assist dairy farmers in their continuous decision-making needs. All these tools are openly available at http://DairyMGT.info under the *Tools* section. Tools are grouped in major management areas of dairy farming such as feeding and nutrition, reproductive efficiency, heifer management and replacement, production and productivity, price risk management and financial assessment, and environmental stewardship. A number of methodologies and combinations of methodologies as well as different software applications were used to develop these decision support systems with the ultimate goal to always provide solid, but still user-friendly management tools for dairy practical farm decision-making. Methodologies included partial budgeting, cost benefit, decision analysis, enterprise budgets, linear programming, Markov chains, mathematical simulation and projection, nonlinear optimization, matrix solution, database management, and use of external simulation models. Software used to develop the tools included Macromedia Flash, HTML, PHP, JavaScript,

C, CSS, MySQL, Spreadsheet applications, and executable programs. The DSS have proven to be effective decision-making tools for improved dairy farming operation. Large dissemination and impact of these DSS tools can be verified by having 9,336 downloads of these DSS tools during the one-year period between May 2011 and April 2012 and the request of 168 talks with 6,500 people in attendance across the world during the 4-year period between May 2008 and April 2012.

Acknowledgements

The development and maintenance of the DairyMGT.info tools has been possible by the partial support of several extra-mural grants: Agriculture and Food Research Initiative from the USDA National Institute of Food and Agriculture Competitive Grants No.: 2010-51300-20534, 2010-85122-20612, 2011-68004-30340 and several Hatch grants to V.E.C from the College of Agriculture and Life Sciences at the University of Wisconsin-Madison. Acknowledgement is extended to a number of people involved at different levels in the development of these tools; Collaborators: B.W. Gould, R.D. Shaver, M.A. Wattiaux, L. Armentano, J. Vanderlin, K. Bolton; Students: J.O. Giordano, J. Janowski, M. Valvekar, E. Demarchi, A. Kalantari; Programmers: A. Kalantari, N. Suryanarayana, K. Nathella, V. Vats, A. Gola.

Author details

Victor E. Cabrera*

Address all correspondence to: vcabrera@wisc.edu

Department of Dairy Science, University of Wisconsin-Madison, U.S.A.

References

[1] Rotz, Corson., Chianese, Montes. F., Hafner, S. D., & Coiner, C. U. (2011). The Integrated Farm System Model: Reference Manual Version 3.5. USDA Agricultural Research Service. http://www.ars.usda.gov/SP2UserFiles/Place/19020000/ifsmreference.pdf (accessed 5 May 2012).

[2] Cabrera, V. E., Hildebrand, P. E., Jones, J. W., Letson, D., & de Vries, A. (2006). An Integrated North Florida Dairy Farm Model to Reduce Environmental Impacts under Seasonal Climate Variability. *Agriculture Ecosystems & Environment*, 113, 82-97.

[3] Groenendaal, H., Galligan, D. T., & Mulder, H. A. (2004). An Economic Spreadsheet Model to Determine Optimal Breeding and Replacement Decisions for Dairy Cattle. *Journal of Dairy Science*, 87, 2146-2157.

[4] Meadows, C., Rajala, Schultz P. J., & Frazer, G. S. (2005). A Spreadsheet-Based Model Demonstrating the Nonuniform Economic Effects of Varying Reproductive Performance in Ohio Dairy Herds. *Journal of Dairy Science*, 88(3), 1244-1254.

[5] Giordano, J. O., Fricke, P. M., Wiltbank, M. C., & Cabrera, V. E. (2011). An Economic Decision-Making Support System for Selection of Reproductive Management Programs on Dairy Farms. *Journal of Dairy Science*, 94, 6216-6232.

[6] Cabrera, V. E., Breuer, N. E., & Hildebrand, P. E. (2008). Participatory Modeling in Dairy Farm Systems: A Method for Building Consensual Environmental Sustainability Using Seasonal Climate Forecasts. *Climatic Change*, 89, 395-409.

[7] Breuer, N. E., Cabrera, V. E., Ingram, K. T., Broad, K., & Hildebrand, P. E. (2008). AgClimate: A Case Study in Participatory Decision Support System Development. *Climate Change*, 87, 385-403.

[8] Cabrera, V. E., Breuer, N. E., Hildebrand, P. E., & Letson, D. (2005). The Dynamic North Florida Dairy Farm Model: A User-Friendly Computerized Tool for Increasing Profits while Minimizing Environmental Impacts. *Computer and Electronics in Agriculture*, 86, 207-222.

[9] Fraisse, C. W., Bellow, J. G., Breuer, N. E., Cabrera, V. E., Hatch, L., Hogenboom, G., Ingram, K., O'Brien, J. W., Paz, J. J., & Zierden, D. (2006). AgClimate: A Climate Forecast Information System for Agricultural Risk Management in the Southeastern USA. *Computer and Electronics in Agriculture*, 53, 13-27.

[10] Cabrera, V. E., de Vries, A., & Hildebrand, P. E. (2006). Manure Nitrogen Production in North Florida Dairy Farms: A Comparison of Three Models. *Journal of Dairy Science*, 89, 1830-1841.

[11] Cabrera, V. E., Jagtap, S., & Hildebrand, P. E. (2007). Strategies to Limit (Minimize) Nitrogen Leaching on Dairy Farms Driven by Seasonal Climate Forecasts. *Agriculture Ecosystems & Environment*, 122, 479-489.

[12] Cabrera, V. E. (2010). A Large Markovian Linear Program for Replacement Policies to Optimize Dairy Herd Net Income for Diets and Nitrogen Excretion. *Journal of Dairy Science*, 93, 394-406.

[13] Earleywine, T. J. (2001). Profitable Dietary Grain Concentrations and Grouping Strategies in Dairy Herds. *PhD Thesis*, Madison, University of Wisconsin-Madison.

[14] Tessmann, N. J., Radloff, H. D., Kleinmans, J., Dhiman, T. R., & Satter, L. D. (1991). Milk Production Response to Dietary Forage:Grain Ration. *Journal of Dairy Science*, 74, 2696-2707.

[15] Cabrera, V. E., Shaver, R. D., & Wattiaux, M. A. (2009). Optimizing Income over Feed Supplement Cost. Dubuque, IA. *Four-State Dairy Nutrition and Management Conference*.

[16] Cabrera, V. E., Shaver, R. D., & Dyk, P. (2010). The Four-State Dairy Extension Feed Evaluator. Dubuque, IA. *Four-State Dairy Nutrition and Management Conference.*

[17] Cabrera, V. E., Contreras, F., Shaver, R. D., & Armentano, L. (2012). Grouping Strategies for Feeding Lactating Dairy Cattle. Dubuque, IA. *Four-State Dairy Nutrition and Management Conference.*

[18] CabreraV. E. (2009). When to Use Gender Biased Semen: Economics. *Dairy Cattle Reproductive Council Annual Convention.Boise, ID and St. Paul, MN.*

[19] Giordano, J. O., Kalantari, A., Fricke, P. M., Wiltbank, M. C., & Cabrera, V. E. (2012). A Daily Herd Markov-Chain Model to Study the Reproductive and Economic Impact of Reproductive Programs Combining Timed Artificial Insemination and Estrous Detection. *Journal of Dairy Science: in press.*

[20] Cabrera, V. E. (2012). A Simple Formulation of the Replacement Problem: A Practical Tool to Assess the Economic Value of a Cow, the Value of a New Pregnancy, and the Cost of a Pregnancy Loss. *Journal of Dairy Science: in press.*

[21] Erdman, R. A., & Varner, M. (1995). Fixed Yield Responses to Increased Milking Frequency. *Journal of Dairy Science*, 78, 1199-1203.

[22] Risk Management Agency (2008). Livestock Gross Margin for Dairy Cattle Handbook Washington DC USDA RMA http://www.rma.usda.gov/handbooks/20000/2009/09lgm-dairy-handbook.pdf (accessed 14 May 2012).

[23] Huirne, R. B. M., & Dijkhuizen, A. A. (1997). Basic Methods of Economic Analysis. *In: Dijkhuizen AA, Morris RS (ed.) Animal Health Economics: Principles and Applications.*, Sidney, University of Sidney, 25-41.

[24] Gregory, G. (1988). *Decision Analysis*, New York, Plenum.

[25] Warren, M. F. (1986). *Financial Management for Farmers*, London, Hutchinson.

[26] Cabrera, V. E., & Hildebrand, P. E. (2012). Linear Programming for Dairy Herd Simulation and Optimization: An Integrated Approach for Decision Making. *In: Zoltan AM (ed.) New Frontiers in Theory and Applications*, New York, Nova, 193-212.

[27] Gould, B. W., & Cabrera, V. E. (2011). USDA's Livestock Gross Margin Insurance for Dairy: What is it and how it can be Used for Risk Management University of Wisconsin Department of Agricultural and Applied Economics http://future.aae.wisc.edu/lgm-dairy/lgmdairymanual.pdf (accessed 10 May 2012).

[28] Wood, P. D. P. (1976). Algebraic Models of the Lactation Curves for Milk, Fat, and Protein Production, with estimates of seasonal variation. *Animal Production*, 22, 35-40.

[29] Ehrlich, J L. (2011). Quantifying Shape of Lactation Curves, and Benchmark Curves for Common Dairy Breeds and Parities. *The Bovine Practitioner*, 45(1), 88-94.

[30] Valvekar, M., Cabrera, V. E., & Gould, B. W. (2010). Identifying Optimal Strategies for Guaranteeing Target Dairy Income Over Feed Cost. *Journal of Dairy Science*, 93, 3350-3357.

[31] Valvekar, M., Chavas, J. P., Gould, B. W., & Cabrera, V. E. (2011). Revenue Risk Management, Risk Aversion and the Use of LGM-Dairy Insurance. *Agricultural Systems*, 104, 671-678.

[32] Inostroza, J. F., Shaver, R. D., Cabrera, V. E., & Tricarico, J. M. (2010). Effect of Diets Containing a Controlled-Release Urea Product on Milk Yield, Composition and Component Yields in Commercial Wisconsin Dairy Herds and Economic Implications. *Professional Animal Scientist*, 26, 175-180.

[33] Tsuji, G. Y., Hoogenboom, G., & Thornton, P. K. (1998). *Understanding Options for Agricultural Production*, London, Kluwer Academic Pub.

[34] National Research Council. (2001). *Nutrient Requirement for Dairy Cattle* (Seventh Revised Edition), Washington DC, The National Academies Press.

[35] Sterry, R., Brusveen, D., Cabrera, V. E., Weigel, K., & Fricke, P. (2009, 25 March). Why They Use Sexed Semen. *Hoard's Dairyman Magazine*, 25.

[36] Cabrera, V. E., & Janowski, J. M. (2011). Wisconsin Dairy Business and Production Survey: Comparison between Farms Planning to Expand and Farms not Planning to Expand. Journal of Extension: 3RIB1 http://www.joe.org/joe/2011june/rb1.php (accessed 10 May 2012).

Chapter 8

Designing Effective Forecasting Decision Support Systems: Aligning Task Complexity and Technology Support

Monica Adya and Edward J. Lusk

Additional information is available at the end of the chapter

http://dx.doi.org/10.5772/51255

1. Introduction and Motivation

Forecasting is critical to successful execution of an organization's operational and strategic functions such as for delivery of a cost effective and efficient supply chain [1]. The complex and dynamic organizational environment that defines much of today's forecasting function is often supported by a range of technology solutions, or forecasting decision support systems (FDSS). Typically, FDSS integrate managerial judgment, quantitative methods, and databases to aid the forecaster in accessing, organizing, and analyzing forecasting related data and judgments [1-2]. Forecasting task complexity can negatively impact forecast reliability, accuracy, and performance [3-4]. Specifically, it can influence two elements of forecaster behavior – deriving forecasts and judgmental adjustment of these forecasts [5]. In executing these functions, forecasters may utilize different heuristics for complex series as opposed to simple ones in order to mitigate cognitive demands [6-7]. Because selection and execution of these heuristics can be influenced by forecaster experience and knowledge-base, integrating time series complexity into Forecasting Support Systems (FSS) design can bring greater objectivity to forecast generation, while simultaneously providing meaningful guidance to forecasters [1].

Advances in design and use of FDSS, however, have been slow to come because of the following range of problems that limit their usefulness in the forecasting domain. Firstly, FDSS are expensive to create, operationalize, and calibrate and therefore, require significant organizational investment. Second, and most significantly, forecasts generated by such expensive FSS are often subjected to judgmental adjustments. Such adjustments may be driven by forecaster confidence, or lack thereof, in FDSS capabilities as well as forecaster's sense of ownership once they make judgmental adjustments as opposed to just accepting outputs of a forecasting model. Third, forecaster confidence in FDSS and its outcomes is influenced by numerous system abilities such as strength of and confidence in explanations provided about forecast creation [8], information presentation [9], data about the systems past success rate [10], support from analogical forecasting tasks [11], and ability to decompose the forecasting problem [12] to mention a few. Lastly, the functionality and processes underlying FDSS are sometimes difficult to align with the experiential thinking of forecasters [11], i.e. If such support systems adaptively support complex and simple tasks according to task demands, forecasters may be less tempted to make judgmental adjustments [11, 13-14].

The above discussions and supporting literature reaffirm that the level of agreement between a task and the functionalities of the supporting technologies, i.e. the task-technology fit (TTF), can determine individual performance on tasks [15-19]. TTF studies suggest that the extent to which a technology supports individuals in performance of their portfolio of tasks can determine the degree of success in the execution of their tasks through both improved performance and better system utilization [15, 20]. In a sense then, TTF provides important justifications for discretionary use of FDSS for simple and complex tasks. Under conditions where FDSS perform well empirically, it would likely be worth committing the time and resources to utilizing the FDSS. In contrast, where FDSS do not perform effectively or performs as effectively as human judgment, such commitment of time and resources to parameterize the FDSS may not be warranted. It has been asserted that certain functionalities of a technology are better suited for specific types of processes or tasks [17]. To this end, improved alignment between FDSS and FDSS-supported tasks, essentially better Forecasting Task-Technology Fit (FTTF), can mitigate the factors driving forecasters to make *ad hoc* adjustments of questionable validity done for rationalizing their worth [19].

In this study, we specifically examine the issue of forecasting task complexity and commensurate FDSS support to provide a framework for FSS design and implementation using the TTF as an underlying motivator. In doing so, we achieve the following:

a. Develop a characterization of complex and simple time series forecasting tasks. Herein, we rely on historical patterns and domain-based features of time series to develop discrete task profiles along a simple to complex continuum.

b. Review evidence from the empirical literature regarding forecasting task complexity and its implications for FDSS design and suggest designs that would benefit the forecasting process.

c. Develop an agenda for research and discuss practice-related issues with regard to balancing forecasting utility with efficiency given the costs of FDSS.

2. Literature Review

2.1. Task-Technology Fit

TTF theory defines tasks as actions carried out by individuals to process inputs into outputs [20] and task profile as aspects of these tasks that might require users to rely on information

http://dx.doi.org/10.5772/51255

technology. Technologies are defined as any set of tools, such as FDSS, required for executing these tasks. The fit between tasks and technologies, then, refers to the "degree to which a technology assists an individual in performing his or her portfolio of tasks" [20]. In the usual case, TTF theory is implemented at two levels: (a) an organizational level that examines the presence of data, processes, and high-level system features (e.g. system reliability) to fulfill the broad needs of a decision domain, and (b) a context level that examines the presence of system features specific to a decision context e.g. system capabilities for time series forecasting or group decision making. Studies in both contexts develop TTF concepts from three perspectives: identification of (a) a task profile [15] i.e. tasks specific to the domain of study; (b) technology features or needs specific to a task profile; and (c) impact of TTF on individual performance. We discuss these findings in the next sections.

Most TTF studies characterize tasks based on organizational level decision support needs such as information and data quality, access, procedures surrounding data access, and system reliability [19-21] characterized tasks in terms of non-routineness, defined as lack of analyzable search behavior, and interdependence with other organizational units. Later a dummy variable was added to capture managerial factors as a determinant of user evaluation of information system use [20]. Recently, an increasing number of studies have examined tasks more contextually i.e. specific to the domain of study. Most commonly, these studies classified tasks according to their complexity [22-23]. Also characterized tasks were characterized on the basis of complexity and proposed a task classification that ranged from simple to fuzzy tasks [23]. In group decision making, [15] extended this classification to further define task complexity in group decision making. These studies define task complexity as having four dimensions: *outcome multiplicity* suggesting more than one desired outcome, *solution scheme multiplicity* suggesting more than one possible approach to achieving task goal, *conflicting interdependence* which can occur when adopting one solution scheme conflicts with another, and *outcome uncertainty* defined as the extent of uncertainty regarding a desired outcome from a solution scheme. Others found that task support for virtually-linked teams often translated into those related to conflict management, motivation/confidence building, and affect management [17]. Other applications of TTF theory appear in mobile-commerce for the insurance industry [24], consumer participation in e-commerce [25]), and software maintenance and support [16]) among others. In the forecasting domain, surprisingly we found only one TTF study [19], that adapted organizational level factors to the forecasting domain by examining needs related to forecasting procedures.

In the TTF framework, technological support has been characterized most often in terms of hardware, software, network capabilities, and features of the support system. Others, for instance, developed technology characteristics based upon input from an independent panel of IS experts [20-21]. These technology capabilities included relationships between DSS and its user, quality of support, timeliness of support, and reliability of system among others. Further, some relied on the same technology characteristics for considering adoption of Personal Digital Assistants (PDAs) in the insurance industry [24]. In keeping with the underlying emphasis of TTF, i.e. fit between tasks and technologies, context-dependent studies have focused on specific capabilities for the domain of interest. For instance, others examined richness of communication media for resolving conflict between virtual teams and motivating positive team work [17]. And some proposed that technologies supporting group decision making must be capable of providing communications support and structuring group interaction processes along with supporting information processing needs of the group [15]. Finally, [19] leveraged the framework of [20] to the forecasting domain by focusing more significantly on system functionality and capabilities—specifically focusing on data, methods, and forecasting effectiveness.

TTF studies have most commonly examined two outcomes of alignment between task and technology – system utilization and task performance. It was found that there was a suggestive relationship between TTF and system utilization and a strong positive connection with performance but mediated by utilization [20]. In contrast, it was suggested that TTF strongly predicted customer intention to purchase from an e-commerce site [25]. Also it was confirmed that a strong relationship between performance on certain insurance tasks and use of mobile devices exists [24]. Finally others found that FSS characteristics, specifically forecasting procedures included in the FSS, to be positively related to perceptions of TTF which, in turn, positively related to forecasting performance. In general, these results confirm a strong association between performance and alignment between task needs and supporting technologies [19]. This is a critical linkage for our study.

2.2. Adapting TTF to the Forecasting Domain

Time series extrapolation calls for quantitative methods to forecast the variable of interest with the assumption that behaviors from the past will continue in the future [2]. Time series forecasting is also found to improve with use of domain knowledge such as for series decomposition [26]. In essence, successful time series extrapolation relies upon recognizing idiosyncratic aspects of the series as defined by patterns in the historical data as well as domain knowledge likely to emerge through unknown future generating processes. Considering this, the implementation of time series task classifications using TTF theory is best achieved by following the context-specific approach discussed earlier as this perspective emphasizes conditions that impact the contextual usefulness of FSS. In other words, if for the task that a forecaster must execute, the time series, serves as input into the FDSS, task characterizations may best emerge from the features of the series being processed. For purposes of this paper, we follow recommendations by [15, 23] to classify decision tasks, specifically time series, along a simple to complex continuum.

2.2.1. Complexity in Time Series Forecasting

Complexity is inherent in the forecasting process [12]. While it can be argued that all one needs is a forecasting method and adequate data, a non-trivial view of the forecasting process suggested by [2] provides a more realistic perspective—that of decomposition. Each stage of the forecasting process entails coordinated action that requires use of judgment and analytical skills, inputs from multiple organizational units, as well as validation and integrity checks. When decomposed into its components, the forecasting process integrates domain knowledge, historical data, causal forces acting upon the domain, as well as physical characteristics of the process producing the measured realizations that are to be forecast [12].

Of interest in our study, however, is characterization of complexity in the context of the task i.e. the time series being forecast. Forecasting literature has provided some interpretations of complex time series. Most commonly, time series are defined as complex if the underlying processes that generate them are such [27]. Chaotic time series, as opposed to "noise driven series", wherein observations drawn at different points in time follow a non-linear relationship with past observations of variables [28] have also been referred to as complex series. More recently, studies have characterized complexity in terms of time series composition. For instance, [26] describe complex time series as those where forecasters expect conflicting underlying causal forces, i.e. underlying forces will push the series in different directions in the forecast period. In essence, such series can be represented as a composite of multiple series where the challenge is to determine the overall effect or momentum of these multi-directional forces whose net effect could be static i.e., no movement due to offsetting causal forces.

Most views presented above define complexity in terms of either specific patterns in historical data (e.g. variation or volatility) or underlying processes and influences (e.g. causal forces). This constrained view of time series complexity is surprising considering the taxonomy of time series features available in existing literature. Time series features often captured in empirical literature include stationarity or non-stationarity of series [29-31]. Stock market forecasting studies have often relied on capturing features like volatility persistence, leptokurtosis, and technical predictability of stock related series [32-33] classified time series in terms of three features – irrelevant early data (where the generating process has fundamentally and irrevocably changed such that it creates a misleading impression of the future), outliers, and functional form. Although focused on assessing judgmental confidence intervals, some have characterized time series in terms of trend, level, seasonality, and noise [34]. These features provided 57% of the explanation for confidence intervals chosen by forecasters, suggesting that possibly a finer breakdown of series characterizations may be worth consideration.

For purposes of this paper, we rely on a more extensive taxonomy of time series characterizations suggested by [35-37] to classify time series along the continuum of simple to complex tasks. Their classification is particularly relevant because it captures not merely a range of patterns in historical data but also underlying generating processes and judgmental expectations about the future based on domain knowledge. Initially it was suggested that there were 18 such features [35] and these were later expanded to 28 by [36 - 37]. For purposes of this paper, we use a subset of these 28 features, particularly in the context of the four feature sets discussed earlier in this paragraph. These time series features are described at length in Table A in the Appendix and in [35].

2.2.2. Time Series Task Characterizations

As mentioned previously, some have classified tasks along a simple to fuzzy (complex) continuum such that system features could be developed in alignment with the task [15, 23]– in essence, TTF. Table 1 defines the key tasks types and their characteristics proposed in [15].

Task Categorization	Description
Simple Tasks	Low uncertainty; low conflicting interdependence; clear solution
Problem Tasks	Multiple solution schemes to a well-specified outcome. Needs involve finding optimal way of achieving the outcome.
Decision Tasks	Finding solutions that meet needs of multiple conflicting outcomes. Selecting best option from several available.
Judgment Tasks	Conflicting and probabilistic nature of task related information. Need to integrate diverse sources of information, predict future states.
Fuzzy Tasks	Multiple desired states and multiple ways of getting to them. Unstructured problems that require effort to understand. High information load, uncertainty, and information diversity. Minimal focus for the task executor.

Table 1. Overview of Suggested Task Characterizations [15].

In Table 2, we offer a simplified adaptation of this taxonomy for the forecasting domain and classify series as simple, moderately complex, and complex. Time series features in [35], hereafter referred to as C&A, were used to develop the complexity taxonomy. The C&A's feature set is particularly relevant because it captures not merely a range of visible patterns in historical data that can influence judgmental forecasting processes (e.g. outliers, trends, and level discontinuities), but also recognizes underlying generating processes and domain-based expectations about the future. These features, described in Table A in the Appendix, could broadly be categorized into four clusters: (a) *uncertainty* defined by variation around the trend and directional inconsistencies between long and recent trend, (b) *instability* characterized by unusual time series patterns such as irrelevant early data, level discontinuities, outliers, and unusual observations, (c) *domain knowledge* defined as availability (or lack thereof) of useful domain knowledge and underlying functional form of the series i.e. multiplicative or additive, and (d) *structure*, the presence or lack of a significant trend i.e., a perceptible signal. In forecasting literature, these features are the most comprehensive attempt to characterize series for use in an FSS, Rule-based Forecasting (RBF). RBF studies have extensively validated these features, first in C&A on 126 time series, then in [38] across 458 time series, and finally on 3003 M3 competition series [36]. Considering this, we relied on a subset of these 28 features (see Table A - Appendix and C&A) for development and validation of our taxonomy. The four feature clusters discussed above were used for classification as they have the potential of destabilizing a time series (C&A). Table 2 below provides a conceptual view of the details of this classification.

Using features from C&A, time series tasks can be classified into four categories with simple and complex forecasting tasks being the two ends of this continuum. *Simple forecasting tasks* represent low instability and uncertainty, demonstrate relatively clear structure in their underlying trend patterns, and do not rely on significant domain knowledge to generate useful forecasts. In most instances, demographic series such as percentage of male births tend to regress towards a known mean [37], have slow but steady trends, and variations that are rare, unusual, and easily accounted for, thereby making them easier to forecast. Alternatively, domain knowledge is clear and non-conflicting. Such tasks are expected to pose low cognitive load on the forecaster because confounding features and underlying processes are few and, consequently evident.

Series Characteristics	**Simple Time Series**	**Moderately Complex Time Series**	**Complex Time Series**
Instability Recent run not long Near a previous extreme Irrelevant early data Changing basic trend Suspicious pattern Outliers present Level discontinuities Unusual last observation	Few or no instability features present	Some instability features present	Many instability features present
Uncertainty Coefficient of variation > 0.2 Difference between basic and recent trend	Low variation about the trend Recent and basic trends agree	Medium to high variation about the trend Recent and basic trends may disagree	High variation about the trend Recent and basic trends disagree
Structure Significant basic trend Clear direction of trend (up or down)	Insignificant trend No or low trend	Significant trend Clear direction	Significant trend Lack of clarity in direction due to confounding features
Presence of Domain Knowledge Causal forces Functional Form	Additive or multiplicative series Simple, consistent causal forces	Multiplicative series Multiple causal forces	Multiplicative series Unknown or inconsistent causal forces

Table 2. Time Series Task Classification Based on Series Features.

At the other end of the continuum, by contrast, *complex forecasting tasks* are characterized by greater instability and uncertainty, do not demonstrate a clear generating structure, and may require "systematic" integration of a complex set of domain knowledge features that send conflicting signals [26]. For instance, forecasting monetary exchange rates is made challenging by the low signal to noise ratio and the non-ergodic nature of the process caused by numerous undetermined underlying drivers [37]. Such series may pose greater cognitive demand on the forecasters who may find it difficult to isolate features such as trends and instabilities and recognize underlying processes.

Moderately complex time series will fall somewhere along the continuum (see Table 2). These tasks demonstrate some instability, variation about the trend may be higher than for simple series, and/or recent and basic trends may conflict. The structure of such series demonstrates a more complex interplay of domain knowledge than for simple series, thereby lending multiple possible solution schemes depending upon interpretation and application of domain knowledge. An example of decomposition of UK Highway deaths illustrated these conflicting scenario possibilities where the decomposition of the series yielded two conflicting elements of domain knowledge – growth in traffic volume and decay in decline in death rate [39]. Decomposing the time series into its components helped improve forecasts for the target series.

2.2.3. *Judgmental Accuracy on Complex and Simple Forecasting Tasks*

In earlier sections, we have mentioned the dearth of studies in forecasting on complexity and its implications on performance and outcomes. Consequently, we have relied on general studies in other domains to highlight implications of complexity in forecasting complex versus simple tasks. Most fundamentally, [23] defines simple tasks as those that are not complex. In general, more complex tasks require greater support [15] and richer information presentation [40-43]. Complex tasks increase cognitive overload and place greater information processing requirements on the user, thereby reducing performance [44-45]. Under such situations, decision makers choose "satisficing" but suboptimal alternatives [46] thereby lowering decision accuracy. When task complexity does not match abilities of the decision maker, motivation and consequently, performance may decline [47]. Using a Lens model approach, [48] attributed poor judgment in complex task settings to limitations in participants' ability to execute judgment strategies as opposed to their knowledge about the task domain, essentially a lack of experiential acuity. This could be attributable to loss in perceived self-efficacy and efficiency in application of analytical strategies.

In the forecasting domain, studies have uncovered confounding effects in situations that manifest uncertainty and instability. For instance, [34] found that as the trend, seasonality, and noise increased in a time series, forecasters indicated wider confidence intervals, and hence uncertainty, in their forecasts. Further, [49] also found that while forecasters successfully identified instability in time series, their forecasts were less accurate than statistical forecasts when such instabilities were present. Considering this, even experienced forecasters may find lowered performance in complex settings. These multidisciplinary findings then suggest:

- *Practical Proposition 1:* Judgmental forecasts of complex time series will be less accurate than judgmental forecasts of simple time series.
- *Practical Proposition 2:* Judgmental forecasts of moderately complex time series will be less accurate than judgmental forecasts of simple time series but more accurate than those for complex time series.

FDSS, through effective design, can allay the cognitive and human information processing demands that task complexity can place on the decision maker, and thereby potentially increase system use and confidence. DSS range from simple decision aiding such as using visual, as opposed to text-based, presentations to complex intelligent systems that adaptively perceive and respond to the decision context. The alignment between task needs and technology support, however, needs reflection. If misaligned, decision maker performance can

http://dx.doi.org/10.5772/51255

be compromised. For instance, [50] evaluated a DSS for treatment of severe head injury patients by comparing physician expert opinions with results generated by the DSS. The study concluded that the tool was not accurate enough to support complex decisions in high-stress environments. Similarly, [51] found that providing certain types of cognitive support for real-time dynamic decision making can degrade performance and designing systems for such tasks is challenging. Based on these studies, the following can be proposed:

- *Practical Proposition 3:* FDSS generated forecasts for complex time series will be more accurate than judgmental forecasts of complex time series.
- *Practical Proposition 4:* FDSS generated forecasts for complex time series will be more accurate than judgmental forecasts of moderately complex time series.
- *Practical Proposition 5:* FDSS generated forecasts for simple time series will be as accurate as judgmental forecasts of simple time series.

2.2.4. Judgmental Adjustment of FDSS Generated Forecasts

While existing forecasting literature has yielded several recommendations for forecast adjustment, once again, this area suffers from lack of sufficient empirical findings regarding adjustment of forecasts for complex and simple tasks. Here too, we rely on multidisciplinary studies and findings from our own studies [52] to support our propositions. Forecasting literature, for instance, has suggested that statistically generated forecasts should be adjusted based on relevant domain knowledge and contextual information that practitioners gain through their work environment. Others [53-54] demonstrated that familiarity with the specific factors being forecast was most significant in determining accuracy. Judgmental adjustments should also be applied to statistically generated forecasts under highly uncertain situations or when changes are expected in the forecasting environment, i.e. under conditions of instability. Both uncertainty and instability, according to our earlier framework in Table 2, lend complexity to the forecasting environment.

Managerial involvement in the forecasting process, primarily in the form of judgmental adjustments, has been questioned in terms of value added benefits. For instance, [55] suggest that benefits of managerial adjustment in stable series may not be justified as automatic statistical forecasts may be sufficiently accurate. In contrast, they recommend high levels of managerial involvement in data that has high uncertainty, in a sense, high complexity surrounding it.

In our own empirical studies comparing FDSS and judgmental forecasting behaviors [52], we find that when given FDSS-generated forecasts, forecaster adjustments to simple series harm forecast accuracy but improve accuracy of complex series when compared to unadjusted FDSS forecasts. Furthermore, when given simple series, forecasters react to complex series by assuming forecast values to be too low and, in response, adjust forecasts more optimistically than necessary. In contrast, they view the forecasts for simpler series to be aggressive and accordingly overcompensate by suppressing the forecasts. Accordingly, we propose:

- *Practical Proposition 6:* Forecasters will adjust complex series more optimistically than simple series whose forecasts will be suppressed.

- *Practical Proposition 7:* Adjustments to FDSS-generated forecasts for simple series will harm forecast accuracy.
- *Practical Proposition 8:* Adjustments to FDSS-generated forecasts for complex series, if executed correctly, can improve forecast accuracy.

As a caveat to the last proposition above, judgmental adjustments to complex forecasts may be best supported by FDSS in a way that the adjustments are structured [53] and validated automatically through improvements in forecast accuracy [35, 39]. In the following sections, we rely on the TTF framework and other DSS studies to propose ways in which FDSS could be best designed to adaptively support simple to complex tasks.

3. Implications for FSS Design and Research: Putting Theory into Practice

In conjunction with the decision maker, DSS have been shown to generate better decisions than humans alone by supplementing the decision makers' abilities [56], aiding one or more of phases of intelligence, design, and choice in decision making [57], facilitating problem solving, assisting with unstructured or semi-structured problems [58-59], providing expert guidance [60], and managing knowledge. Our discussion above raises additional issues pertinent to FDSS design with emphasis on overcoming inefficiencies such as bias, irrationality, sub-optimization, and over-simplification that underlie judgmental adjustments. Since a growing body of research is focusing attention on specific DSS features such as information presentation, model building and generation, and integration of dynamic knowledge, in this section we view DSS design from the perspective of making directive and non-directive changes in forecaster behavior regarding application of adjustments. Such behavioral changes can be brought about in two ways: (a) by guiding and correcting forecaster behavior during task structuring and execution and (b) by encouraging evaluative analysis of decision processes through structured learning [61].

Our empirical research has raised two key observations related to forecaster behavior and implications for FSS design:

I. Forecasters will make adjustments to forecasts even when provided highly accurate forecasts. However, the direction and magnitude of these adjustments may be defined by complexity of the forecasting tasks. Considering this, FSS should offer system features in congruence with adjustment behaviors.

II. Design of FSS must necessarily factor in, and adapt to, forecasting task complexity.

Elaborating on these findings, we make several propositions for FSS design in the next few sections.

3.1. Design FSS that Adapt to Task Complexity

For years, DSS designers have proposed designing systems that adapt to decision makers [62-63] and align with their natural thinking. Adaptive DSS support judgment by adjusting to high level cognitive needs of decision makers, context of decision making, and task characteristics [64]. The FTTF framework proposed in this paper provides a task-based approach to such adaptive systems. As a time series is initially input into the FSS, automated feature detection routines can categorize time series along the simple to complex continuum. Task profiles gathered in this way could be used to customize levels of *restrictiveness* and *decisional guidance* for simple versus complex tasks.

Restrictiveness is the "degree to which, and the manner in which, a DSS limits its users' decision making process to a subset of all possible processes" [65, p. 52]. For example, a DSS may restrict access to certain data sets or ability to make judgmental inputs and adjustments to the system. Restrictiveness can be desirable when the intention is to limit harmful decision choices and interventions. However, general IS literature has largely recommended limited use of restrictive features in DSS [1, 61, 65-66]. Excessive restrictiveness can result in user frustration and system disuse [65, 67]. It can also be difficult for the designer to determine *a-priori* which decision processes will be useful for a particular situation [1]. However, when users are poorly trained [1], known to make bad decision choices, or when underlying conditions are stable, restrictive DSS features can be beneficial.

Decisional guidance is "the degree to which, and the manner in which, a DSS guides its users in constructing and executing the decision-making processes by assisting them in choosing and using its operators" [65, p. 57]), can be informative or suggestive. *Informative guidance* provides factual and unbiased information such as visual or text based display of data thereby empowering the user to choose the best course of action. *Suggestive guidance*, on the other hand, recommends an ideal course of action to the user such as by comparing available methods and recommending the one deemed to be most suited to the task at hand. Also [1] provide an excellent and extensive review of decisional guidance features for FSS that we recommend highly. To complement their recommendations, in the next few paragraphs, we provide additional design guidelines emergent from the theme of this study.

A.1 Restrict Where Harmful Judgment can be Applied: When unrestricted, forecasters are free to apply adjustments at many levels in the forecasting process such as toward data to be used or excluded, models to be applied and those to be ignored, and changes to decision outcomes. Similarly, as we demonstrated in our Study 2 [52], inexperienced forecasters may attempt to overcome their limited knowledge of underlying decision processes by making adjustments to the final outcomes [1]. FSS can restrict where such judgmental adjustments are permitted. Specifically, judgment is best utilized as input into the forecasting process or within the context of a validated knowledge base rather than as an adjustment to the final decision outcome [55].

A.2 Restrict FSS Display Based on Task Complexity: Since complex tasks pose significant demands on human cognitive and information processing capabilities, FSS displays for such tasks can be restricted as opposed to simple tasks that can benefit from decisional guidance. Since simple tasks create lower cognitive strain, performance on such tasks can potentially be improved by increasing user awareness of the forecasting cues such as by displaying features underlying the time series, generating processes, forecasts from alternative methods, and forecasting knowledge underlying the final forecasts. For instance, [49] found that making available the long-term trend of a time series improved forecaster accuracy since it allowed them to overlook distracting patterns and apply knowledge more consistently.

As decision makers have a tendency to trade off accuracy in favor of cost efficiency, *informative* and *suggestive* guidance could be displayed prominently such that the forecaster does not have to drill down to make such trade-off decisions [68]. However, this same information presented to the forecaster for complex tasks can result in greater information overload, cognitive strain, and over-reaction. Indeed, [69] confirm that in complex task settings, decision makers tended to ignore suggestive advice and focused on informative guidance. To reduce this cognitive load, several of the above discussed features could be hidden and made available as layered drill-down options. Such adaptive support can reduce information overload and related information processing challenges in the context of complex tasks [66], and is replicable across different contexts and organizational settings.

A.3 Provide and Adapt Task Decomposition According to Task Complexity: Individual decision maker's working memory is limited and consequently, complex tasks broken into simple "chunks" can be more effectively executed when compared to tasks not so simplified [12]. Cognitive overload may be avoided through effective and efficient design materials [44] ranging from better information presentation to providing greater structure to the learning environment [70] such as through use of decomposition strategies to simplify the subject domain. Decomposition is found to improve performance over unaided and intuitive judgment [71-72] by breaking down a complex, holistic task into a set of easier tasks which are more accurately executed than the more holistic task [1]. Others [73] also found that DSS users were able to leverage more information when they used decomposition for forecasting tasks. While there are neurological explanations for why decomposition is effective [74-75], from a psychological perspective, decomposition allows the decision maker to optimize the problem solving domain into manageable chunks so that information processing for each chunk can be minimal and relevant while cognitive overload is minimized [70, 76-77].

Although it can be argued that decomposition can be a restrictive DSS feature when its use is forced upon the decision maker [1], most often, a user may not focus on the benefits of decomposing a task or may not recognize how to proceed with decomposition. To this end, we suggest that decomposition be implemented in both restrictive and decisional guidance mode. Specifically, we use the framework by [12] who suggests that decomposition can be applied at three levels: *decomposition via transformation*, i.e. identifying characteristics of the forecasting task and domain; *decomposition for simplification*, i.e. understanding components of the forecasting process from problem formulation to forecast use (Armstrong, 2001 [2]); and *decomposition for method selection* i.e. applying forecasting knowledge and rules to selecting fitting methods. Herein, we propose *transformational decomposition* should be a restrictive feature in FSS. This decomposition of time series into its features can enhance forecaster ability to recognize meaningful patterns as opposed to random ones.

In the same vein, *simplification* of the problem domain could follow restrictive design by using the forecasting process presented in Figure 1 to design FSS modules. In such a design, then, the flow of activities presented in Figure 1 could be used to restrict more rapid convergence on forecast methods and use. In contrast, the evaluative component of this given process can lend itself to decisional guidance in numerous ways discussed later in this section. Decomposition by simplification can also be implemented by narrowing task demand for complex decisions. For instance, [49] recommend that forecasts should not be required for multiple time periods because forecasters tend to anchor long-term forecasts to short-term forecasts. Our data indirectly suggests that complex series generate higher errors and such anchoring and adjustment can compound errors across the long-term.

Finally, *decomposition for method selection* could largely be implemented as decisional guidance. Users may be prompted with forecasts from multiple relevant methods (selected using rules applied to time series features) to consider use of alternative methods and processes. Suggestive guidance on how to proceed with method selection and combination could be useful for simple tasks.

As decision situations become complex, guidance may need to be modified to minimal levels as such situations are already characterized by information overload. Adding suggestive guidance to this mix can lead to the FSS itself complicating the decision situation. Forecasters may become increasingly frustrated with interventions from such guidance and consequently engage in deleterious decision making behaviors. These suggestions are supported by [69] who found that for highly complex tasks, subjects who were provided with suggestive guidance performed poorly at the task when compared to those who were provided informational guidance or no decision support. Specifically, we suggest that for complex tasks, informational guidance be provided such that users can determine best strategy on their own or ignore the additional information as desired.

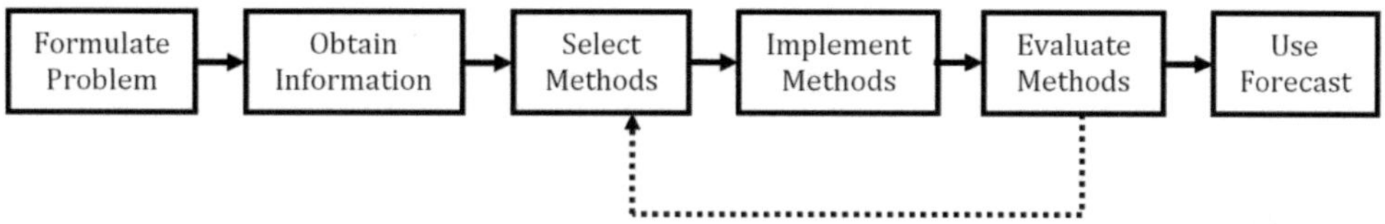

Figure 1. Components of the Forecasting Process as Presented in [2].

A.4 Provide In-Task Feedback for Simple Tasks and Shift to Post-Task Feedback on Complex Tasks: Feedback is intended to promote learning and behavior modification with the assumption that organizational practices encourage such review. Broadly speaking, evaluative feedback can be offered to forecasters at two stages – *during task execution* and *post task execution* – the former being critical to effective forecasting and the latter being beneficial for fostering reflection and learning [1]. Suggestive and informational feedback regarding impact of their current actions on other aspects of the forecasting environment may contain the extent to which a series of poor adjustments may be executed. However, feedback during execution of complex tasks can frustrate the user. Forecasters facing complex tasks may not have the time or cognitive resources to reflect adequately upon the impact of their adjustments on the environment [78] and consequently fail to consider control actions that can impact the forecasting environment. Indeed, corrective process-based feedback has been found to be transient and shallow [79-80] and inadequately contributes to long term behavior modification [81].

To this end, FSS developers may primarily focus on post-execution feedback for complex tasks. Post-task feedback has been found to improve decision quality [82] and attainment of challenging goals [83], particularly when the feedback is informative [69]. Further, [1] suggest four forms of post-task feedback: *outcome feedback*, result of outcomes from the forecasting task; *performance feedback*, assessment of performance such as forecast accuracy; *cognitive process feedback*, effectiveness of forecasting process deployed; *task properties feedback*, information about the task e.g. presence of conflicting underlying series. Considering that the intention of post-execution is to foster learning, holistic learning is possible for instance, by providing informative guidance on the above aspects complemented with the ability to drill down to the suggestive components, may be most beneficial to forecasters.

Simple tasks, in contrast, do not require the same level of feedback and support as complex tasks. Moreover, these tasks are cognitively less demanding. Consequently, in-task feedback may not be detrimental and may be designed to provide the user with guidance such as by displaying features of the time series and discussing their impact on forecasts, providing original series contrasted with series that have been cleansed of distracting features such as outliers and irrelevant early data, and providing forecasting guidance in form of rules and relevant methods. As a case in point, RBF rules that pertain to a specific set of features present in the task being executed could be displayed such that the user can recognize the knowledge that has gone into generating the forecast.

A.5 Restrict Data and Models According to Task Complexity: Restrictiveness may be relaxed for simpler tasks by increasing the range of available data and models. FSS can shift to making some desirable processes easy to use while making other, less desirable alternatives, more difficult [1]. Automating and thereby simplifying the application of desirable strategies can serve to reduce the effort associated with executing the more desirable strategies [84] and thereby reduce the need for making damaging judgmental adjustments to the decision process [13].

A.6 Restrict to Impose Standards and Best Practices: Finally, restrictions can be applied when certain organizational best practices and standards need to be applied in the forecasting process. For instance, a critical issue in supply chain forecasting is an escalation of forecasting adjustments as a forecast moves down the supply chain, thereby contributing to the bullwhip effect [85]. Embedding restraints in the forecasting system that contain the magnitude and directionality of adjustments may potentially reduce the risks associated with overcompensating for each element of the supply chain. This is particularly true for complex data where forecasters may overemphasize random patterns in the data or simple series where forecasters may want to overcompensate for seemingly aggressive forecasts. These restraints may be in the form of boundaries or confidence intervals which adapt to the nature of the complexity being presented to the forecaster.

3.2. Design FDSS to Increase Forecaster Confidence

Earlier, we discussed judgmental adjustments as a mechanism for forecasters to develop ownership of the forecasts. If FSS can be designed with features that enhance forecaster confidence in its abilities, possibly the compulsion to make judgmental adjustments may be mitigated. Most studies have focused on DSS use and satisfaction and suggested user attitudes towards DSS and their satisfaction with DSS as indicators of DSS use [86-87]. However, our concern in this paper extends beyond use since forecasters may use an FSS to generate forecasts and still make judgmental adjustments. Confidence in the system can be enhanced by making its abilities transparent to the forecaster by making the FDSS and its features fully disclosed [35]. Furthermore, a well validated FDSS that has demonstrated stability across time and multiple data sets can potentially improve confidence [88]. This validation is particularly simple to implement in FDSS due to the well-defined and universally accepted success measure, forecast accuracy. Confidence in an FDSS may also be enhanced by highlighting the credibility of knowledge underlying it. When transparent to forecasters, use of expert knowledge, empirically validated findings, and methodical calibrations can potentially enhance forecaster confidence in system abilities, and thereby mitigate the need for adjustments. Finally, user involvement in systems design and development has been shown to increase user satisfaction with and commitment to the system and its outcomes [89-91]. For instance, [92] found that forecasters involved in defining features of the FSS such as display and models indicated greater satisfaction with FSS forecasts, even though their overall accuracy was lower than those who were constrained in their involvement.

3.3. Implications for Practical Design Research

In the sections above, we have offered numerous suggestions regarding FSS design. While some of these have been researched and validated, most require further research attention particularly in light of the simple-complex task classification that forms the foundation of our paper. To this end, we first suggest that our proposed task classification be tested on a broader time series base to (a) determine if the application of this framework is generalizable to a larger set of time series, and (b) whether the patterns of judgmental performance and adjustments we observed across the two studies [52] hold ground in a larger context. If our results are proven across a broader base, implications for FSS design are numerous in terms of recommendations addressed earlier.

Beyond confirmation of the FTTF framework, there are numerous opportunities for examining FSS design issues. Most importantly, our proposition has been that FSS should be designed to not only enhance forecaster support for task execution but also to promote effective behavior modification during and post execution. Such learning and modification will occur over long term system utilization, features supporting feedback and learning in FSS should occur early in the design process. This has implications for finding the ideal balance between restrictive and decisional guidance features and identifying the decision making stage to which these are best applied. As [69] suggest, increased decisional guidance during problem formulation can have an adverse effect on judgmental task performance but providing feedback at the right opportunity can improve performance. In response, much research is required to identify aspects of forecaster behavior that are amenable to behavior modification and those that are not, nature of desirable support, and stage of forecasting process where these support features are best applied.

4. Summary and Conclusions

The practical implications of our chapter are, indeed, numerous from the eight practical propositions to the six design FSS aspects regarding adaptations to Task Complexity and issues having to do with forecaster confidence. We summarize these here next. First, fitting technology support to task characteristics can provide a useful mechanism for identifying gaps between system functionality and user needs. Understanding task characteristics and corresponding support needs will enable FDSS designers to create systems that better suit and adapt to user needs. Second, a methodical integration of task and support technologies can lead to greater user commitment, thereby reducing forecaster's tendency to make deleterious *ad hoc* adjustments. Task-technology fit can enable identification of functions for which human intervention can be problematic and thereby restrict or guide selection towards improved choice [65, 93]. For instance, systems that complement limitations of human information processing (HIP) may improve decision maker performance [40] because they mitigate cognitive overload that constrains human performance on complex tasks [94]. Finally, a well-designed and optimally utilized FSS has a strong positive impact on individual performance and system adoption [20]. From an organizational perspective, this can have measurable positive implications for return on investments [95-96].

From a forecasting perspective, this study has yielded several insights to forecaster behavior and implications for FDSS design. We find that little has been done in the forecasting literature by way of developing a formal taxonomy for forecasting tasks. The principal reason for this is that a taxonomy for forecasting tasks essentially depends upon a codification of series complexity. We have endeavored to begin this classification work [52]. Our framework provides an initial attempt to do so in the domain of time series forecasting. Researchers in various other domains may find explorations of similar classifications to be beneficial in making recommendations for systems design in their own domains. Further, we find that forecasters' behaviors regarding direction and magnitude of these adjustments is impacted by complexity of the forecasting task, thereby underscoring the value of parsing out simple from complex tasks. Finally, considering the above contributions, we recommend the need for congruence between system features and task features. Our research, in some aspects, is exploratory in nature and further work is required to solidify this research stream.

Appendices

Feature	Description and Implementation as in C&A	Operationalization
Coefficient of Variation (CV)	Standard deviation divided by the mean for the trend adjusted data.	Automatic identification - C&A
Regression T-Statistic (T-Stat)	The t-statistic for linear regression. If T-statistic is greater than abs(2), the series is classified as having a significant basic trend.	Automatic identification - C&A

http://dx.doi.org/10.5772/51255

Feature	Description and Implementation as in C&A	Operationalization
Functional Form (FF)	Expected pattern of the trend of the series. Can be multiplicative or additive.	Judgmental identification - C&A*
Basic Trend (BT)	Direction of trend after fitting linear regression to past data.	Automatic identification - C&A
Recent Trend (RT)	The direction of trend that results from fitting Holt's to past data.	Automatic identification - C&A
Near a Previous Extreme (Ext.)	A last observation that is 90% more than the highest or 110% lower than lowest observation.	Automatic identification - C&A
Outliers (Out.)	Isolated observation near a 2 std. deviation band of linear regress.	Automatic identification - C&A
Recent Run Not Long (RR)	The last six period-to-period movements are not in same direction.	Judgmental identification - C&A
Changing Basic Trend (CB)	Underlying trend that is changing over the long run.	Judgmental identification - C&A*
Irrelevant Early Data (Irr.)	Early portion of the series results from a substantially different underlying process.	Judgmental identification - C&A
Unusual Last Observation (ULO)	Last observation deviates substantially from previous data.	Judgmental identification - C&A*
Suspicious Pattern (Sus.)	Series that show a substantial change in recent pattern.	Judgmental identification - C&A
Level Discontinuities (LD)	Changes in the level of the series (steps)	Judgmental identification - C&A*
Causal Forces (CF)	The net directional effect of the principal factors acting on the series. *Growth* exerts an upward force. *Decay* exerts a downward force. *Supporting* forces push in direction of historical trend. *Opposing* forces work against the trend. *Regressing* forces work towards a mean. When uncertain, forces should be *unknown*.	Judgmental identification - C&A
Trend Conflict (TC)	If recent trend conflicts with causal forces, e.g. recent trend is growing while causal forces are decay, then a trend conflict is flagged.	Judgmental assessment for this study
Trend Variation (TV)	Standard deviation divided by the mean for the trend adjusted data. If coefficient is >0.2, the series is flagged as being uncertain.	Automatic identification - C&A

Table A.

Author details

Monica Adya[1] and Edward J. Lusk[1*]

*Address all correspondence to: luskej@plattsburgh.edu

1 Department of Management Marquette University Milwaukee, WI, USA

Department of Accounting SUNY; Plattsburgh Plattsburgh, NY USA and Emeritus: Department of Statistics The Wharton School: University of Pennsylvania Philadelphia, PA, USA

References

[1] Fildes, R., Goodwin, P., & Lawrence, M. (2006). The Design Features of Forecasting Support Systems and Their Effectiveness. *Decision Support Systems*, 42, 351-361.

[2] Armstrong, J. S. (2001). Extrapolation of Time-series and Cross-sectional Data. *In: JS Armstrong (Ed.) Principles of Forecasting: A Handbook for Researchers and Practitioners*, Boston, Kluwer Academic Press.

[3] Clemen, R. T. (1989). Combining Forecasts: A Review and Annotated Bibliography. *International Journal of Forecasting*, 5, 559-583.

[4] Remus, W. (1987). A Study of the Impact of Graphical and Tabular Displays and Their Interactions with Environmental Complexity. *Management Science*, 33, 1200-1205.

[5] Önkal, D., Goodwin, P., Thomson, M., Gönül, S., & Pollock, A. (2009). The Relative Influence of Advice from Human Experts and Statistical Methods on Forecast Adjustments. *Behavioral Decision Making*, 22, 390-409.

[6] Bystrom, K., & Jarvelin, K. (1995). Task Complexity Affects Information Seeking and Use. *Information Processing & Management*, 31, 191-215.

[7] Wood, R. E., Atkins, P., & Tabernero, C. (2000). Self-efficacy and Strategy on Complex Tasks. *Applied Psychology: An International Review*, 49, 330-466.

[8] Gönül, M. S., Önkal, D., & Lawrence, M. (2006). The Effects of Structural Characteristics of Explanations on Use of a DSS. *Decision Support Systems*, 42, 1481-1493.

[9] Lawrence, M., & O'Connor, M. (1992). Exploring Judgmental Forecasting. *International Journal of Forecasting*, 8, 15-26.

[10] Jiang, J. J., Muhanna, W. A., & Pick, R. A. (1996). The Impact of Model Performance History Information on Users' Confidence in Decision Models: An Experimental Examination. *Computers in Human Behavior*, 12, 193-207.

[11] Lee, W. Y., Goodwin, P., Fildes, R., Nikolopoulos, K., & Lawrence, M. (2007). Providing Support for the Use of Analogies in Demand Forecasting Tasks. *International Journal of Forecasting*, 23, 377-390.

[12] Adya, M., Lusk, E. J., & Belhadjali, M. (2009). Decomposition as a Complex-skill Acquisition Strategy in Management Education: A Case Study in Business Forecasting. *Decision Sciences Journal of Innovative Education*, 7, 9-36.

[13] Goodwin, P. (2000). Improving the Voluntary Integration of Statistical Forecasts and Judgment. *International Journal of Forecasting*, 16, 85-99.

[14] Lim, J. S., & O'Connor, M. (1996). Judgmental Forecasting with Interactive Forecasting Support Systems. *Decision Support Systems*, 16, 339-358.

[15] Zigurs, I., & Buckland, B. K. (1998). The Theory of Task/Technology Fit and Group Support Systems Effectiveness. *MIS Quarterly*, 22, 313-334.

[16] Dishaw, M. T., & Strong, D. M. (1998). Supporting Software Maintenance with Software Engineering Tools: A Computed Task-technology Fit Analysis. *Journal of Systems and Software*, 44, 107-120.

[17] Maruping, L. M., & Agarwal, R. (2004). Managing Team Interpersonal Processes Through the Task-Technology Fit Perspective. *Journal of Applied Psychology*, 89, 975-990.

[18] Mathieson, K., & Keil, M. (1998). Beyond the Interface: Ease of Use and the Task/Technology Fit. *Information & Management*, 34, 221-230.

[19] Smith, C., & Mentzer, J. (2010). Forecasting Task-technology fit: The Influence of Individuals, Systems and Procedures on Forecast Performance. *International Journal of Forecasting*, 26, 144-161.

[20] Goodhue, D. L., & Thompson, R. L. (1995). Task-Technology Fit and Individual Performance. . MIS Quarterly , 19, 213-236.

[21] Goodhue, D. L. (1995). Understanding User Evaluations of Information Systems. *Management Science*, 41, 1827-1844.

[22] Shaw, M. E. (1954). Some Effects of Problem Complexity Upon Problem Solution Efficiency in Different Communication Nets. *Journal of Experimental Psychology*, 48, 211-217.

[23] Campbell, D. J. (1988). Task Complexity: A Review and Analysis. *Academy of Management Review*, 13, 40-52.

[24] Lee, C. C., Cheng, H. K., & Cheng, H. H. (2005). An Empirical Study of Mobile Commerce in Insurance Industry: Task-technology Fit and Individual Differences. *Decision Support Systems*, 43, 95-110.

[25] Klopping, I., & Mc Kinney, E. (2004). Extending the Technology Acceptance Model and the Task-Technology Fit Model to Consumer e-commerce. *Information Technology Learning and Performance Journal*, 22, 35-48.

[26] Armstrong, J. S., Collopy, F., & Yokum, J. T. (2005). Decomposition by Casual Forces: A Procedure for Forecasting Complex Time Series. *International Journal of Forecasting*, 21, 25-36.

[27] Rossana, R. J., & Seater, J. J. (1995). Temporal Aggregation and Economic Time Series. *Journal of Business & Economic Statistics*, 13, 441-452.

[28] Johnes, G., Kalinoglou, A., & Manasova, A. (2005). Chaos and the dancing stars: Non-linearity and entrepreneurship. *Journal of Entreprenuership*, 1, 1-19.

[29] Lee, D., & Schmidt, P. (1996). On the Power of KPSS Test of Stationarity Against Fractionally-Integrated Alternatives. *Journal of Econometrics*, 73, 285-302.

[30] Mac, Kinnon. J. G. (1994). Approximate Asymptotic Distribution Functions for Unit-root and Co-integration Tests. *Journal of Business and Economic Statistics*, 12, 167-176.

[31] MacKinnon, J. G. (1996). Numerical Distribution Functions for Unit-root and co-integration tests. *Journal of Applied Econometrics*, 11, 601-618.

[32] LeBaron, B., Arthur, W. B., & Palmer, R. (1999). Time Series Properties of an Artificial Stock Market. *Journal of Economic Dynamics & Control*, 23, 1487-1516.

[33] Vokurka, R. J., Flores, B. E., & Pearce, S. L. (1996). Automatic Feature Identification and Graphical Support in Rule-based Forecasting: A comparison. *International Journal of Forecasting*, 12, 495-512.

[34] O'Connor, M., & Lawrence, M. (1992). Time Series Characteristics and the Widths of Judgmental Confidence Intervals. *International Journal of Forecasting*, 7, 413-420.

[35] Collopy, F., & Armstrong, J. S. (1992). Rule-based Forecasting: Development and Validation of an Expert Systems Approach to Combining Time Series Extrapolations. *Management Science*, 38, 1394-1414.

[36] Adya, M., Armstrong, J. S., Collopy, F., & Kennedy, M. (2000). An Application of Rule-based Forecasting to a Situation Lacking Domain Knowledge. *International Journal of Forecasting*, 16, 477-484.

[37] Armstrong, J. S., Adya, M., & Collopy, F. (2001). Rule-based Forecasting: Using Judgment in Time-Series Extrapolation. *In: JS Armstrong (Ed.) Principles of Forecasting: A Handbook for Researchers and Practitioners*, Boston, Kluwer Academic Press.

[38] Adya, M. (1997). Critical Issues in the Implementation of Rule-based Forecasting Systems: Refinement, Evaluation, and Validation. *PhD Dissertation*, The Weatherhead School of Management, Case Western Reserve University, Cleveland, OH, USA.

[39] Armstrong, J. S., & Collopy, F. (1992). The Selection of Error Measures for Generalizing About Forecasting Methods: Empirical Comparisons. *International Journal of Forecasting*, 8, 69-80.

[40] Robey, D., & Taggert, W. (1982). Human Information Processing in Information and Decision Support Systems. *MIS Quarterly*, 6, 61-73.

[41] Marsden, J., Pakath, R., & Wibowo, K. (2002). Decision Making Under Time Pressure with Different Information Sources and Performance-based Financial Incentives. *Decision Support Systems*, 34, 75-97.

[42] Vila, J., & Beccue, B. (1995). Effect of Visualization on the Decision Maker When Using Analytic Hierarchy Process. *Proceedings of the 20th Hawaii Conference on System Sciences, HI.*

[43] Benbasat, I., & Lim, L. (1992). The Effects of Group, Task, Context, and Technology Variables on the Usefulness of Group Support Systems: A Meta-analysis of Experimental Studies. *Small Group Research*, 24, 430-462.

[44] Kester, L., Kirschner, P. A., & van Merrienboer, J. J. G. (2005). The Management of Complex Skill Overload During Complex Cognitive Skill Acquisition by Means of Computer Simulated Problem Solving. *British Journal of Educational Psychology*, 75, 71-85.

[45] Carley, K. M., & Zhiang, L. (1997). A Theoretical Study of Organizational Performance Under Information Distortion. *Management Science*, 43, 976-997.

[46] Payne, J. W., Bettman, J. R., & Johnson, E. J. (1993). *The adaptive decision maker*, Cambridge University Press, Cambridge, England.

[47] Katz, I., & Assor, A. (2007). When Choice Motivates and When It Does Not. *Educational Psychology Review*, 19, 429-442.

[48] Bisantz, A. M., Llinas, J., Seong, Y., Finger, R., & Jiam, J. (2000). *Empirical Investigations of Trust-related System Vulnerabilities in Aided, Adversarial Decision-making*, Department of Industrial Engineering, SUNY Buffalo.

[49] Welch, E., Bretschneider, S., & Rohrbaugh, J. (1998). Accuracy of Judgmental Extrapolation of Time Series Data: Characteristics, Causes, and Remediation Strategies for Forecasting. *International Journal of Forecasting*, 14, 95-110.

[50] Dora, C. S., Sarkar, M., Sundaresh, S., Harmanec, D., Yeo, T., Poh, K., & Leong, T. (2001). Building Decision Support Systems for Treating Severe Head Injuries. Tucson, AZ. *Proceedings of the 2001 IEEE International Conference on Systems, Man and Cybernetics.*

[51] Lerch, F. J., & Harter, D. E. (2001). Cognitive Support for Real-time Dynamic Decision-making. *Information Systems Research*, 12, 63-82.

[52] Adya, M., & Lusk, E. J. (2012). Development and Validation of a Time Series Complexity Taxonomy: Implications for Conditioning Forecasting Support Systems. *Working Paper*.

[53] Edmondson, R. H., Lawrence, M. J., & O'Connor, M. J. (1988). The Use of Non-time Series Information in Sales Forecasting: A Case Study. *Journal of Forecasting*, 7, 201-211.

[54] Sanders, N. R., & Ritzman, L. P. (1992). The Need for Contextual and Technical Knowledge in Judgmental Forecasting. *Journal of Behavioral Decision Making*, 5, 39-52.

[55] Sanders, N., & Ritzman, L. (2001). Judgmental Adjustments of Statistical Forecasts. *In JS. Armstrong (Ed.), Principles of Forecasting: A Handbook for Researchers and Practitioners*, Kluwer Academic Publishers, Norwell, MA.

[56] Holsapple, C., & Winston, A. (1996). *Decision Support Systems: A Knowledge-Based Approach*, St. Paul, MN, West Publishing.

[57] Simon, H. (1997). *Models of Bounded Rationality*, 3, New York, NY, MIT Press.

[58] Keen, P. G. W., & Morton, M. S. (1978). *Decision Support Systems: An Organizational Perspective*, Addison-Wesley, Reading, PA.

[59] Keen, P. G. W. (1981). Information Systems and Organizational Change. *Communications of the ACM*, 24, 24-33.

[60] Leidner, D. E., & Elam, J. J. (1993). Executive Information Systems: The Impact on Executive Decision Making. *Journal of Management Information Systems*, 10, 139-155.

[61] Silver, M. J. (1991). Decisional Guidance for Computer-based Support. *MIS Quarterly*, 15, 105-133.

[62] Alavi, M. (1982). An Assessment of the Concept of Decision Support Systems as Viewed by Senior-level Executives. *MIS Quarterly*, 6, 1-10.

[63] Lamberti, D. M., & Wallace, W. A. (1990). Intelligent Interface Design: An Empirical Assessment of Knowledge Presentation in Expert Systems. *MIS Quarterly*, 14, 279-311.

[64] Fazlollahi, B., & Parikh, Verma. S. (1997). Adaptive Decision Support Systems. *Decision Support Systems*, 20, 297-315.

[65] Silver, M. J. (1990). Decision Support Systems: Directed and Non-directed Change. *Information Systems Research*, 1, 47-70.

[66] Xiao, B., & Benbasat, I. (2007). E-commerce Product Recommendation Agents: Use, Characteristics, and Impact. *MIS Quarterly*, 31, 137-209.

[67] Gettity, T. P. (1971). The Design of Man-machine Decision Systems: An Application to Portfolio Management. *Sloan Management Review*, 12, 59-75.

[68] Vessey, I. (1994). The effect of information presentation on decision making: A cost-benefit analysis. *Information & Management*, 27, 103-119.

[69] Montezami, A. R., Wang, F., Nainar, S. M. K., & Bart, C. K. (1996). On the effectiveness of decisional guidance. *Decision Support Systems*, 18, 181-198.

[70] Lee, F. J., & Anderson, J. R. (2001). Does Learning a Complex Task Have to be Complex? *A Study in Learning Decomposition. Cognitive Psychology*, 42, 267-316.

[71] MacGregor, D. G. (2001). Decomposition for Judgmental Forecasting and Estimation. *In JS Armstrong (Ed.), Principles of forecasting: A Handbook for Researchers and Practitioners*, 107-123, Norwell, MA, Kluwer Academic Publishers.

[72] Plous, S. (1993). *The Psychology of Human Judgment and Decision Making*, New York, McGraw Hill.

[73] Webby, R., O'Connor, M., & Lawrence, M. (2001). Judgmental Time Series Forecasting Using Domain Knowledge. *In J.S. Armstrong (Ed.) Principles of Forecasting: A Handbook for Researchers and Practitioners*, Kluwer Academic Publishers, Norwell, MA.

[74] Ghahramani, Z., & Wolper, D. M. (1997). Modular Decomposition in Visiomotor Learning. *Nature*, 386, 392-395.

[75] Jordan, M. I., & Jacobs, R. A. (1994). Hierarchical Mixture of Experts and the EM Algorithm. *Neurological Computing*, 6, 181-214.

[76] Card, S. K., Moran, T. P., & Newell, A. (1983). *The Psychology of Human-computer Interaction*, Hillsdale, NJ, Earlbaum.

[77] Newell, A., & Rosenbloom, P. S. (1981). Mechanisms of Skill Acquisition and the Law of Practice. *In J. R. Anderson (Ed.), Cognitive Skills and their Acquisition*, 1-55, Hillsdale, NJ, Earlbaum.

[78] Sterman, J. D. (1989). Misperceptions of Feedback in Dynamic Decision Making. *Organizational Behavior and Human Decision Processes*, 43, 301-335.

[79] Goodman, J. S., Wood, R. E., & Hendrickx, M. (2004). Feedback Specificity, Exploration, and Learning. *Journal of Applied Psychology*, 89, 248-262.

[80] De Nisi, A. S., & Kluger, A. N. (2000). Feedback Effectiveness: Can 360-degree Appraisals be Improved? *Academy of Management Executive*, 14, 129-139.

[81] Kayande, U. A., de Bruyn, A., Lilien, G., Rangaswamy, A., & Van Bruggen, G. (2006). The Effect of Feedback and Learning on Decision-support System Adoption. Athens. *In Avlonitis, GJ., Papavassiliou, N, Papastathopoulou, P. (Eds.) Proceedings of the 35th EMAC Conference*, European Marketing Academy, Brussels.

[82] Singh, D. T. (1998). Incorporating Cognitive Aids into Decision Support Systems: The Case of the Strategy Execution Process. *Decision Support Systems*, 24, 145-163.

[83] Bandura, A., & Cervone, D. (1983). Self-evaluative and Self-efficacy Mechanisms Governing the Motivational Effects of Goal Systems. *Journal of Personality and Social Psychology*, 41, 586-598.

[84] Todd, P., & Benbasat, I. (1999). Evaluating the Impact of DSS, Cognitive Effort, and Incentives on Strategy Selection. *Information Systems Research*, 10, 356-374.

[85] Chen, F., Drezner, Z., Ryan, J. K., & Simchi-Levi, D. (2000). Quantifying the Bullwhip Effect in a Simple Supply Chain: The Impact of Forecasting, Lead times, and Information. *Management Science*, 46, 436-443.

[86] Eierman, M., Niederman, F., & Adams, C. (1995). DSS Theory: A Model of Constructs and Relationships. *Decision Support Systems*, 14, 1-26.

[87] Guimaraes, T., Igbaria, M., & Lu, M. (1992). The Determinants of DSS Success: An Integrated model. *Decision Sciences*, 23, 409-430.

[88] Grabowski, M., & Sanborn, S. (2001). Evaluation of Embedded Intelligent Real-time Systems. *Decision Sciences*, 32, 95-124.

[89] De Lone, W., & Mc Lean, E. (1992). Information Systems Success: The Quest for the Dependent Variable. *Information Systems Research*, 3, 60-95.

[90] Lawrence, M., & Low, G. (1993). Exploring Individual Satisfaction Within Use-led Development. *MIS Quarterly*, 17, 195-208.

[91] Seddon, P. (1997). A Re-specification and Extension of the DeLone and McLean Model of IS Success. *Information Systems Research*, 8, 240-253.

[92] Lawrence, M., Goodwin, P., & Fildes, R. (2002). Influence of User Participation on DSS Use and Decision Accuracy. *Omega*, 30, 381-392.

[93] Goodwin, P., Fildes, R., Lawrence, M., & Stephens, G. (2011). Restrictiveness and Guidance in Support Systems. *Omega*, 39, 242-253.

[94] Jarvenpaa, S. L. (1989). The Effect of Task Demands and Graphic Format on Information Processing Strategies. *Management Science*, 35, 285-303.

[95] Bannister, F., & Remenyi, D. (2000). Acts of Faith: Instinct, Value and IT Investment Decisions. *Journal of Information Technology*, 15, 231-241.

[96] Lin, C., Huang, Y., & Burns, J. (2007). Realising B2B e-commerce Benefits: The Link with IT Maturity, Evaluation Practices, and B2BEC Adoption Readiness. *European Journal of Information Systems*, 16, 806-819.

Chapter 9

Comparison of Multicriteria Analysis Techniques for Environmental Decision Making on Industrial Location

M.T. Lamelas, O. Marinoni, J. de la Riva and
A. Hoppe

Additional information is available at the end of the chapter

http://dx.doi.org/10.5772/51222

Introduction

European legislation calls for a well-planned sustainable development. As such, it has to include a social, economic as well as an environmental dimension. According to Agenda 21 (http://www.un.org/esa/dsd/agenda21/), countries should undertake efforts to build up a comprehensive national inventory of their land resources in order to establish land information systems. The overall objective is to provide information for the improvement or the restructuring of land-use decision processes including the consideration of socio-economic and environmental issues.

In the last decades conflicts caused by competing land uses have increased, particularly in urban areas. Consequently, a lot of research has been done aiming to develop methods and tools that assist complex spatial decision problems. The development of Spatial Decision Support Systems (SDSS) has turned out to be very beneficial in assisting to the solution of complex land-use problems [1, 3].

In addition, any planning process must focus on a mix of hard (objective) and soft (subjective) information. The former are derived from reported facts, quantitative estimates, and systematic opinion surveys. The soft information denotes the opinions (preferences, priorities, judgments, etc.) of the interest groups and decision makers. The idea of combining the objective and subjective elements of the planning process in a computer based system lies at the core of the concept of SDSS [1, 3].

SDSS can be defined as an interactive, computer-based system designed to support a user or a group of users in achieving a greater degree of effectiveness in decision making when solving a semi-structured spatial decision problem [3]. SDSS also refers to the combination of GIS and sophisticated decision support methodologies, e.g. in terms of multicriteria analysis techniques [3, 6], and are therefore suitable to manage sustainable development of urban areas.

Although the development of multicriteria analysis began mainly in the '70s (the first scientific meeting devoted entirely to decisionmaking was held in 1972 in South Carolina) its origins can be dated back to the eighteenth century [4]. Reflections on French policies in the action of judges and their translation into policy (social choice), led people like Condorcet to deepen in decision taken supported in several criteria [4].

In the last two decades of the twentieth century there was an increased trend of integration of Multicriteria Evaluation techniques (MCE) and Geographic Information Systems (GIS), trying to solve some of the analytical shortcomings of GIS "For example see [4, 7, 15]". Wallenius et al. [16], made a study of the evolution in the use of MCE techniques from 1992 to 2006, showing that the use of multiattribute techniques has increased 4.2 times during this period. In recent years, there has also been a great effort in the integration of MCE and GIS techniques on the Internet "For example see [17, 20]".

Since we consider land-use decision making in general as an intrinsic multicriteria decision problem, in our opinion these are valid methodologies to support the land-use decision process by means of a land-use suitability analysis.

Land-use suitability analysis aims to identify the most appropriate spatial pattern for future land uses according to specified requirements or preferences [3, 21, 22]. GIS-based land-use suitability analyses have been applied in a wide variety of situations, including ecological and geological approaches, suitability for agricultural activities, environmental impact assessment, site selection for facilities, and regional planning [3, 6, 11, 17, 21,23, 28].

Different attempts to classify Multicriteria Decision Making (MCDM) methods by diverse authors exist in the literature [4, 6, 7, 11, 26, 29]. The majority of them agree that additive decision rules are the best known and most widely used Multiattribute Decision Making (MADM) methods in GIS based decision making. Some of the techniques more commonly described in literature are: Simple Additive Weighting (SAW), Ordered Weighting Averaging (OWA) technique, the Analytical Hierarchy Process (AHP), ideal point methods (e.g. TOPSIS), concordance methods or outranking techniques (e.g. PROMETHEE, Electre).

Nevertheless, the integration of these techniques continues to pose certain problems or difficulties at the time of developing specific applications. Among the most notable drawbacks are [4]:

- The impracticality of applying pairwise comparison techniques as PROMETHEE with long series of data due to limitations posed by existing informatics systems.
- The difficulty on the implementation of some MCE methods, thereby leading to a difficult analysis of the results, as well as an ignorance of the internal procedure of the methods by non-specialist users.
- The need to generate data processing software attached to the GIS, based on algorithms that describe MCE methods, which naturally implies that many users of these systems cannot access these methods.

In this chapter, we compare the results obtained by the application of two distinctive land-use suitability analyses to the location of industrial sites, applying two different multicriteria analysis techniques. The multicriteria analysis employed has been performed in a raster environment and been used for two objectives. During the site search analysis each pixel was considered a potential location alternative. This analysis used a SAW method which signifies a weighted summation. It can thus easily be performed in GIS [24, 25, 30, 31]. A site selection analysis then used the PROMETHEE-2 methodology [32] and a set of predefined alternatives [30, 33]. All of the techniques used in the project were coded and integrated within ArcGIS by Marinoni [5, 34].

A problem in the application of multicriteria analysis is the definition of weights for a given set of criteria. A variety of approaches does exist, see for example [26], and the probably best known weight evaluation method is the AHP [35], which we have used in our case as well.

Another problem is the specification of the criteria performance scores which are often subjective in their determination. Data which have been measured directly will certainly be regarded as more reliable than data which have been estimated, interpolated, taken from a map or simply interpreted. Thus, the method of criteria data collection plays a central role [5]. A stochastic approach which takes account of the uncertainty of input values and which is presented at a last step in this chapter could be a way out of this dilemma.

1. Background and Methodology

1.1. Study area and project background

Zaragoza city and its surroundings are located in the Ebro corridor, a highly dynamic economic area within the Iberian Peninsula. The climate in this area is semi-arid with mean annual precipitation of about 350 mm and a mean annual temperature of about 15° C.This city is crossed by the cited Ebro river and two of its main tributaries, the Gállego and Huerva rivers (Figure 1). Geologically, Quaternary alluvial terraces of the Ebro river were deposited above Tertiary gypsum formations, forming a covered karst area with intense karstification processes. The Quaternary materials are an important source of sand and gravel which are needed for civil engineering purposes. In addition, it hosts important groundwater reservoirs, used for domestic, industrial and agricultural purposes.

The availability of these resources has been one of the reasons of the fast development of the city in the last decades. But this fast development has also led to negative interactions with the environment and man-made infrastructure. Intense irrigation triggered land subsidence which in turn caused costly damage and/or destruction of infrastructure such as roads, buildings, gas and water supply networks [36]. Many infrastructures that have been built occupy areas where soils of high fertility had naturally developed, making these areas inaccessible to agriculture. Also, many ecologically important areas have been harmed and an increased contamination of the aquifer has been observed [37].

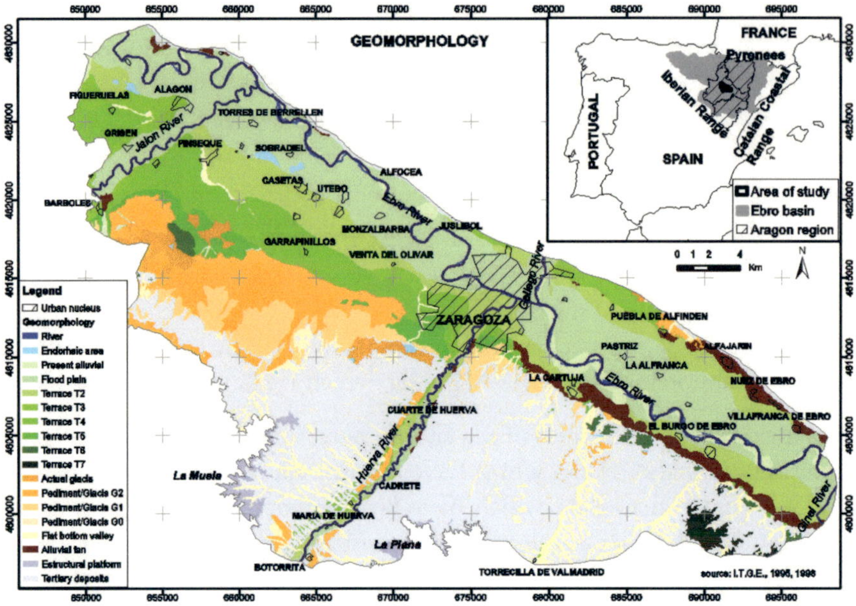

Figure 1. Location and geomorphology of study area.

Based on the above, the area surrounding Zaragoza, which represents a rapidly growing urban area, merits closer investigation in terms of geoscientific factors. Thus, a research project was initiated to develop a methodological workflow which will facilitate the sustainable development in the surroundings of a growing city. Our main objective was to perform a land-use suitability analysis to identify the most appropriate future land-use patterns. Therefore a variety of tasks needed to be performed such as:

- Characterization of the study area and collection, analysis and processing of the available information for its introduction into a GIS environment.
- Geo-hazards and geo-resources detection, description and modelling with the help of GIS and 3D techniques.
- Land-use suitability analysis by means of SDSS.

Here, we report on the land-use suitability analysis to find most suitable locations for industrial facilities. As mentioned above, we compare the results obtained by the application of two distinctive multicriteria analysis techniques for environmental decision making on industrial location. For more details on the general project workflow and geo-resources and geo-hazards modellingsee [24, 25, 30, 31, 33, 37, 39].

1.2. Methodology

It is important to differentiate between the site selection problem and the site search problem. The aim of site selection analysis is to identify the best location for a particular activity from a given set of potential (feasible) sites. Where there is no predetermined set of candidate sites, the problem is referred to as site search analysis [3].

In terms of the MCE methods applied, the main advantage of the SAW approach can be considered its low degree of complexity as which made it attractive to be used for the site search analysis in this project. It is precisely this simplicity that makes weighted summation actually quite widely applied in real-world settings [8, 40, 42].

The site selection analysis has been performed by the implementation of PROMETHEE-2 which belongs to the 'family' of outranking techniques. Since the mentioned techniques require pairwise or global comparisons among alternatives, these methods become impractical for applications where the number of alternatives ranges in the tens or hundreds of thousands (Pereira and Duckstein, 1993). For a more detailed description of both methodologies see [24, 25, 30, 33, 35, 36].

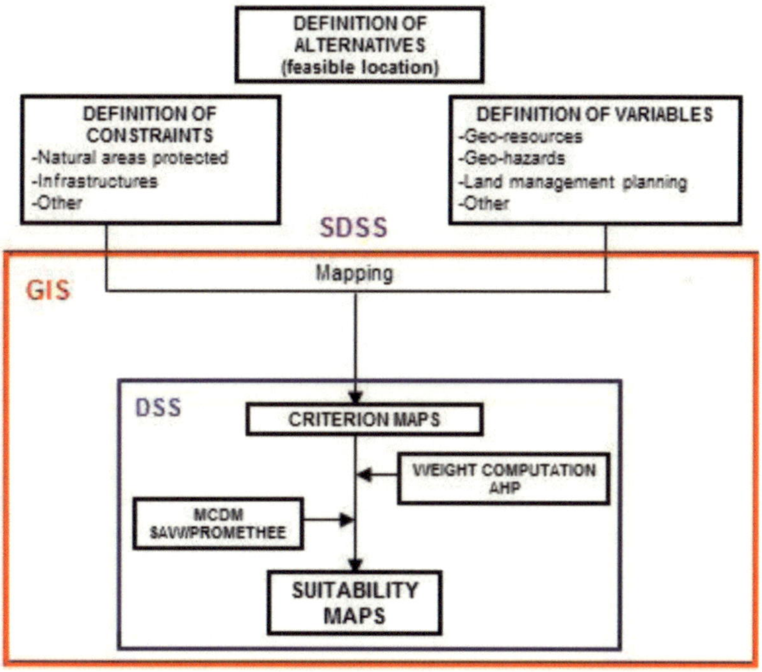

Figure 2. Workflow of the land-use suitability analysis.

In order to perform both site search and site selection, several steps needed to be covered. These included (Figure 2):

- Definition of alternatives (decision options): feasible location areas.

- Definition of constraints: areas with land-use restrictions.
- Definition of important factors in the decision process: identification of criteria.
- Determination of criteria weights

The criteria weights were determined with the AHP. This technique represents another MCE method and involves pairwise comparison of criteria where preferences between criteria are expressed on a numerical scale usually ranging from 1 (equal importance) to 9 (strongly more important). This preference information is used to compute the weights by means of an eigenvalue computation where the normalized eigenvector of the maximum eigenvalue characterizes the vector of weights. Empirical applications suggest that this pairwise comparison method is one of the most effective techniques for spatial decisionmaking approaches based on GIS [15, 43]. There exist many well-documented examples of application of this method with success [44, 46].

It is well known that the input data to the GIS multicriteria evaluation procedures usually present the property of inaccuracy, imprecision, and ambiguity. In spite of this knowledge, the methods typically assume that the input data are precise and accurate. Some efforts have been made to deal with this problem by combining the GIS multicriteria procedures with sensitivity analysis [47] and error propagation analysis [48]. Another approach is to use methods based upon fuzzy logic [3].

In many situations it is hard to choose the input values for multicriteria analysis procedures, since the criteria values for the different alternatives usually do not have a single realization, but can obtain a range of possible values [5]. Performing a multicriteria analysis with the mean values produces some kind of mean result, but the uncertainty in either the input values or the result cannot be quantified. A solution to this dead-end is a stochastic approach, which utilizes probability distributions for the input parameters instead of single values. A stochastic multicriteria analysis implies that the analysis is performed multiple times with varying input values for the criteria involved. These criteria input values (or performance scores) are drawn from probability distributions that are inferred from empirical criteria populations (e.g pixels on a map, expert knowledge). Such an approach uses the whole range of possible criteria value outcomes and extreme events are according to their low outcome probabilities realistically represented as rare events. In a last step we explored the influence of criteria weightsby conducting a sensitivity analysis.

1.2.1. Site search analysis

Within the site search analysis, every pixel was considered a decision alternative. Constraints depict the areas where industry is and will not be allowed. These restrictions are generally characterized by the existence of other land uses (e.g. urbanareas), the protection of natural areas and land management planning. These restrictions are (Figure 3):

- Natura 2000 network areas: natural reserve of the oxbows in La Cartuja (map provided by the Aragon Government).

http://dx.doi.org/10.5772/51222

- Urbanized areas: obtained from the topographic map scale 1:25,000 from the National Geographical Institute (IGN, *Instituto Geográfico Nacional*), imported to ArcGIS and updated.
- Infrastructures (roads, rail roads, canals) and their area of protection: also extracted from the topographic maps. The area of protection of roads and train rails was delineated as defined by the Spanish Roads Law and according to the Spanish Railway Sector Law, respectively.
- Other restrictive planning: Zaragoza Land Management Planning (PGOUZ, *Plan General de Ordenación Urbana de Zaragoza*), mapping provided by Zaragoza Council, and natural resources planning of the thickets and oxbows of the Ebro river, provided by the Aragon Government.
- Cattle tracks: tracks traditionally used by the seasonal migration of livestock which are protected by law, provided by the Aragon Government.
- Industrial areas where no space is left for new industries. Provided by the Aragon Institute of Public Works (IAF,*Instituto Aragonés de Fomento*) from the Aragon Government.

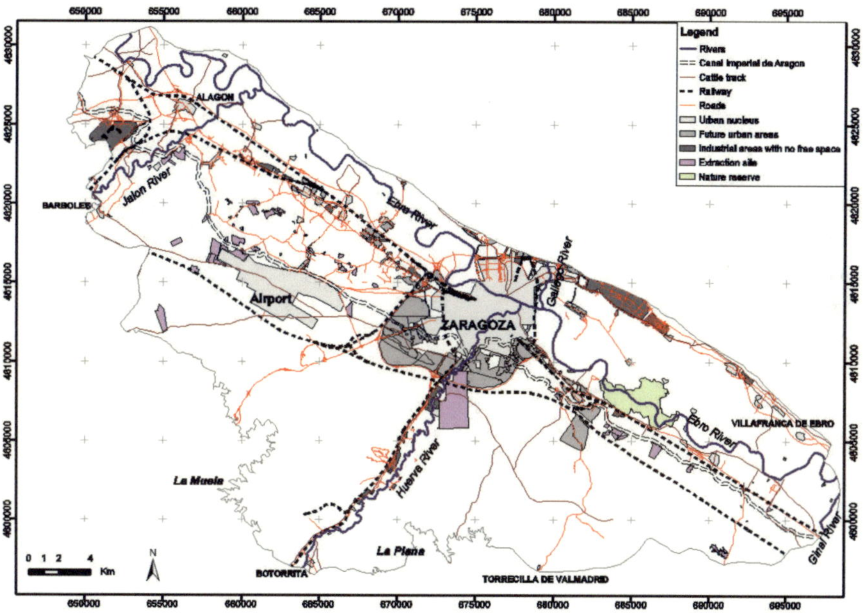

Figure 3. Industrial restrictions.

A variety of social, economic and environmental factors were taken into consideration. Figure 4 shows the mapping of all the variables that were considered relevant for industrial development. Areas considered less suitable are kept in red while a higher suitability is shown in green.These variables are:

- Important areas from the environment point of view: natural areas included in the Natura network 2000 as SPAs (Special Protection Areas for birds), and the SACs (Special Conservation Areas), habitats, points of geological interest and other areas which mapping has been provided mainly by the Aragon Government.
- Doline (sinkhole) susceptibility: model developed within the project using a quantitative method, a logistic regression technique [38].
- Groundwater protection: a model developed also within the project, performed with Gocad [37] and applying a methodology by the German Geological Survey [49].
- Flooding hazard: a flooding hazard mapping developed along the Ebro river [50] was digitised and introduced in the land-use suitability analysis. This model shows the different periods of return of flood events.
- Agricultural capability of the soils: mapping developed within the project [39] applying the Cervatana Model [51].
- Slope of the terrain: developed from the DEM (resolution 20x20 m) from the Ministry of Agriculture (*SIG oleícola*).
- Geotechnical characteristics of the subsoil: different geomorphological units with better or worse geotechnical characteristics, described according to the PGOUZ. This classification has been applied to the geomorphological units derived from the geological map, scale 1:50,000, from National Geological Survey (IGME, *Instituto Geológico y Minero de España*).

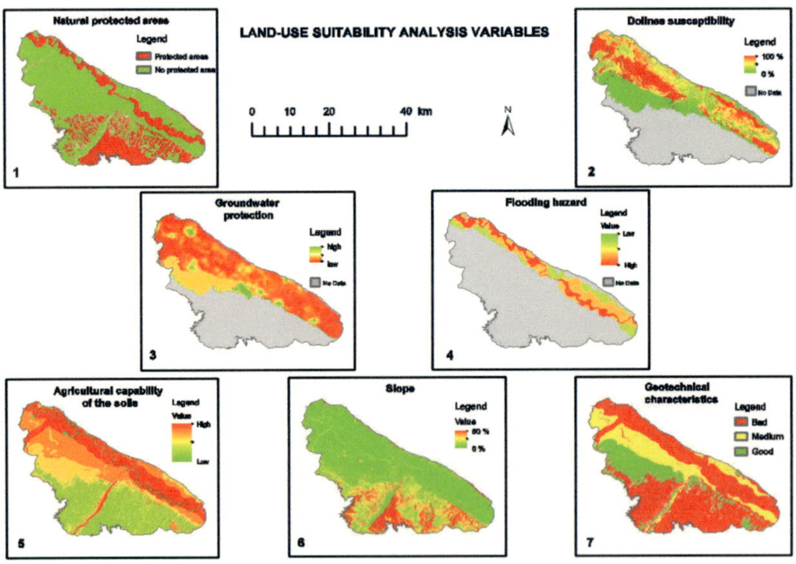

Figure 4. Variable mapping. 1) natural protected areas, 2) doline susceptibility, 3) groundwater protection, 4) flooding hazard, 5) agricultural capability of the soils, 6) slope percentage, 7) geotechnical characteristics.

Many multicriteria methods, as the SAW methodology, require criteria standardization to bring all of them to a common scale. The classification ensures that the weights properly reflect the importance of a criterion.The standardization method used here may be classified as a subjective scales approach [26] since the variables are classified in subjective ranges. These ranges can be selected following standards, legal requirements, or the classes already determined in the geo-resources and geo-hazards models used as criteria in the decision process. Six categories were selected considering the adaptation of these classes to the variables to be introduced. For more details on the standardization approach see [25, 30, 31].

Weights for criteria are assigned with the help of the AHP. An AHP extension was specifically developed for the ArcGIS environment at the Institute of Applied Geosciences of the Technische Universität Darmstadt [34]. This tool can be downloaded from the ESRI web page (http://arcscripts.esri.com/). For more details on the AHP performance see [25, 30, 31]. In a last step all classified raster files (criteria) are multiplied by its corresponding weight and summed up.

1.2.2. *Site selection analyst*

The main objective of a site selection analysis is the ranking of feasible alternatives. Generally, outranking methods, such as PROMETHEE-2, require pairwise or global comparisons among alternatives. Here location alternatives are represented by industrial areas, as defined in the Aragon Institute of Public Works (IAF) database, which signify spaces for the establishment of new industries. Geometrically, these alternatives represent a polygon each. A total of twenty seven industrial areas were evaluated for the site selection analysis.

As alternatives are directly compared along their criteria values, the application of outranking methods does not require a transformation or standardization of criteria values. The restrictions (constraints) and criteria are the same used for the site search analysis. Alternatives located completely in restrictions areas were eliminated from the analysis. However, there exist some industrial polygons, representing one alternative, located partially in restricted areas, as these polygons are partially occupied or crossed by a road or a cattle track. It has implied the inclusion of the constraints as an additional criterion in the decision process. The criterion representative of use restrictions was then reclassified into two different values; zero in the area where industry is forbidden or not possible due to the presence of other uses, and one in areas where this use is permitted or feasible.

It is important to define whether a higher value of a particular criterion leads to an improvement or to a decrease in land-use suitability. In the case of industrial development, an increase in the value of all criteria, with the exception of groundwater protection and geotechnical characteristics, implies a suitability decrease. For example, a higher groundwater protection value implies an increase in suitability to industrial use location while an increase in doline development susceptibility implies a decrease in industrial use location suitability.

Geometrically, every alternative is a polygon so that within each polygon a variety of criteria values (pixels in the criteria layers) are to be found. The question then arises which of the multiple criteria realization to use for the multicriteria analysis evaluation. Therefore, a multicriteria GIS extension was developed to draw site specific values (minimum, maximum, mean etc.) for raster cell populations that lie within the polygonal outline of a location alternative. For our analysis the mean value was used for all criteria since, in our opinion, this value better symbolizes all alternative values. Minimum and maximum values are usually rare events with a low probability of occurrence.

PROMETHEE-2 methodology uses preference function, which is a function of the difference between two alternatives for any criterion [32]. Six types of functions based on the notions of criteria, are proposed. For more details on preference functions see [5, 30, 32].

We exclusively used the "usual criterion" preference function that is based on the simple difference of values between alternatives as this function helps to discriminate best between available alternatives which we wanted to achieve.

The pair comparison of alternatives produces a preference matrix for each criterion (Figure 5). Having calculated the preference matrices along each criterion, a first aggregation is performed by multiplying each preference value by a weighting factor w (expressing the weight or importance of a criterion), and building the sum of these products [5]. This results in a preference index, Π (see Figure 5). The AHP has also been integrated in this tool and used for criteria weighting.

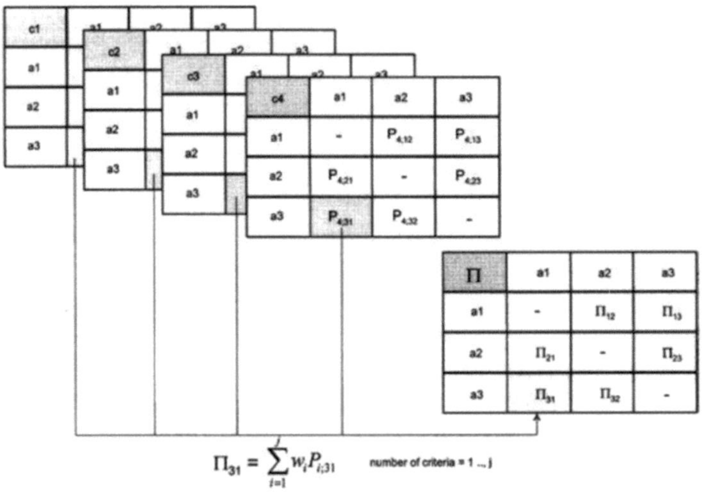

Figure 5. Schematic calculation of the preference index Π. Source [5].

The final ranking of alternatives is performed by calculating the net flow Φ (a1) for every alternative, a, which is a subtraction between the leaving flow and the entering flow. The higher the net flow is, the higher is the preference of an alternative over the others (Table 1).The leaving flow Φ+ (a1) represents a measure of the outranking character of a1 (how a1 is outranking all the other alternatives). Symmetrically, the entering flow Φ- (a1) is giving the outranked character of a1 (how a1 is dominated by all the other actions).

1.2.3. Stochastic PROMETHEE-2

The stochastic PROMETHEE-2 approach requires the assignment of theoretical distribution types to every criterion of the available alternatives. Distribution models were inferred based upon the criteria value populations (pixel values) within each location alternative (polygon) along all criteria. The software used to fit distribution types and to perform distribution fitting test was @Risk [52]. In a next step the distribution models were used within a Monte Carlo Simulation (MCS). The number of iterations *n* was set to 5000.

Starting a MCS with *n* iterations for the specified distributions produces *n* realizations for every cell of the input matrix [5]. Figure 6 shows the principle of one iteration cycle.Values are randomly drawn between 0 and 1 and input values (criteria performance scores) are determined using the inferred theoretical model distribution. With *n* being 5000, the multicriteria analysis is repeated 5000 times. The results may then be used to establish a rank distribution for a specific alternative or a distribution of alternatives for a specific rank (see Figure 7 for a four hypothetical scenarios demonstration).

Π	a1	a2	a3	Φ+(ax)	Φ(ax)	Rank
a1	-	0.25	0.75	1.0	0	2
a2	0.75	-	0.75	1.5	1	1
a3	0.25	0.25	-	0.5	-1	3
Φ-(ax)	1	0.5	1.5			

Table 1. Example of possible preference indices, leaving, entering and net flow calculations and final ranking.Slightly modified after [5].

However, the alternative possessing the highestnumber of first ranks may not necessarily be the best [5]. Therefore, it was suggested calculating a dimensionless mean stochastic rank MSR for every alternative.

$$MSR\ Aj,\ m = \frac{1}{n}\sum_{i=1}^{n}(Ri * i)\forall\ j = 1, \dots, n \tag{1}$$

where:

m: number of iterations

A_j: j^{th} alternative

n: number of available alternatives

R_i: rank count for the ith rank

In order to compare mean stochastic ranks of simulations with different iteration counts, the MSR value must be standardized which leads to the stochastic rank index SI [5]:

$$SI\ Aj,\ m = \frac{MSR\ Aj,\ m - MSR\ min,\ m}{MSR\ max,\ m - MSR\ min,\ m} \tag{2}$$

where:

m: number of iterations

SI_{Aj}: stochastic rank index for the jth alternative

MSR_{Aj}: MSR for the jth alternative

MSR_{min}: the lowest possible MSR value

MSR_{max}: the largest possible MSR value

The more the SI value approaches 0, the better the alternative.

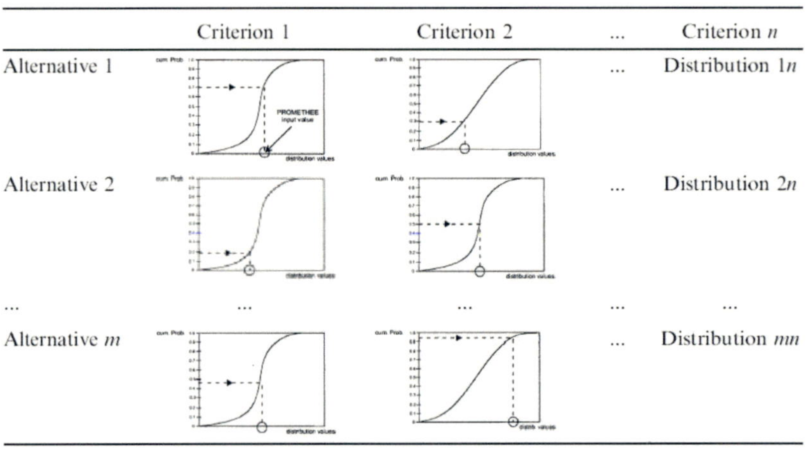

Figure 6. PROMETHEE input value determination for one iteration cycle. Source: [5].

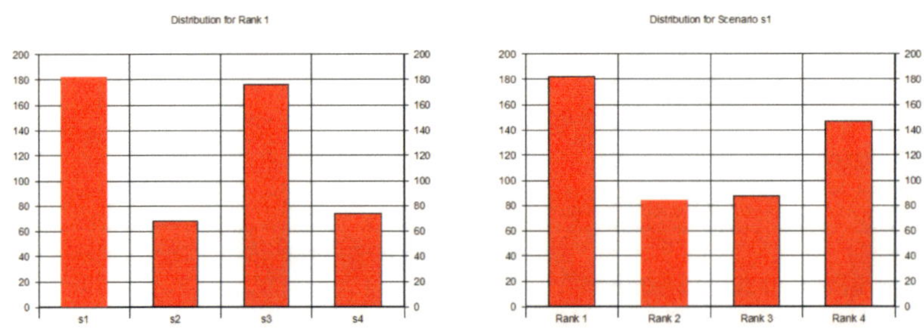

Figure 7. Left: example distribution of 4 scenarios (s1,..., s4) for rank 1. Right: rank distribution for scenario 1. Source: [5].

2. Results and validation

2.1. Site search analysis

The criteria preference values have been assigned by the authors after discussions with experts from different stakeholder groups from the Zaragoza City Council and the Ebro River Authority (CHE, *Confederación Hidrográfica del Ebro*). The highest preference values (and therefore the highest weights) were given to the groundwater protection and environmentally high value areas (Table 2). Hazard criteria were considered less important as some of the encountered geological hazards (land subsidence and sinkhole development) can be mitigated or avoided by applying more suitable (but more costly) construction techniques.

The validation of a model consists in checking whether the structure of the model is suitable for the purpose and if it achieves an acceptable level of accuracy in predictions. In the case of explanatory or predictive models, validation is usually carried out by checking the degree of agreement between the data produced by the model and data from the real world [4]. In the case of our project in order to validate the model has been verified that the result follows the preferences in the assignation of the weights to the criteria.

Preference matrix	A	B	C	D	E	F	G	Weight
A	1.00	2.00	3.00	1.00	5.00	8.00	6.00	0.2288
B	0.50	1.00	2.00	0.50	3.00	7.00	4.00	0.1736
C	0.33	0.50	1.00	0.33	2.00	6.00	3.00	0.1131
D	1.00	2.00	3.00	1.00	5.00	8.00	6.00	0.2288
E	0.20	0.33	0.50	0.20	1.00	4.00	2.00	0.0678
F	0.13	0.14	0.17	0.13	0.25	1.00	0.50	0.0251
G	0.17	0.25	0.33	0.17	0.50	2.00	1.00	0.0427

Table 2. Pairwise comparison matrix, criteria weights for site searchanalysis.A) Groundwater protection, B) Doline susceptibility, C)Flooding hazard, D)Location of natural areas, E) Agricultural capability of soils, F) Slope percentage, G) Geotechnical characteristics.

Figure 8 shows the final results of the land-use suitability analysis for new industrial development. The lefthand side of figure 8 shows the suitability map under sustainability. The grey sections indicate the areas where industrial locationis not possible due to the constraints. Although the suitability analysis sometimes presents good values, the constraints imply that these areas cannot be exploited due to any restriction.The most suitable locations for industrial development are on the pediments or glacis (Figure 1) and Tertiary materials outside environmental protected areas where the groundwater vulnerability and flood risk is lower. The least suitable locations are the floodplains with high groundwater vulnerability and flood risk, environmentally protected areas around the river bed and other areas in the higher terraces which present more susceptibility to doline development.

To test the robustness of the results, a sensitivity analysis of the model has been performed where higher weights were given to economic aspects. The highest weights were assigned to doline susceptibility and flooding hazard, which might cause the destruction of future industrial sites (Table 3). Slope and geotechnical characteristics of the soils were also assigned high values as a more technically difficult terrain will increase the construction budget. Figure 8 shows the results of this last approach where the best locations for industry were identified to be the pediments and slopes in Tertiary sediments. The least favorable locations are on the flood plain and low river terraces, where sinkhole susceptibility shows higher values. In fact, in order to measure the correlation between both results the Pearson coefficient of correlation between both raster images has been calculated giving a value of 0.874, significant at a 0.01 level, implying a high agreement between both results.

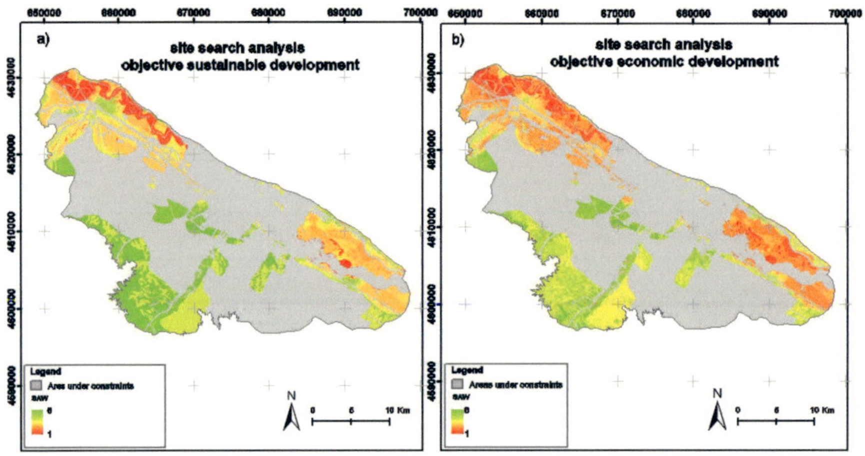

Figure 8. Result of a) site search analysis under sustainability and b) sensitivity analysis for industrial development site search analysis (objective economic development).

2.2. Site selection analysis

As a consequence of the introduction of a new criterion depicting restriction of use or constraints as explained in section 2.2.2., the criteria weights used for the site search analysis are not valid implying a new calculation of them using the AHP. Table 4 shows the preference matrix and criteria weights of the site selection analysis for industrial development. The criteria preference values are the same as for the site search analysis (Table 2) under the sustainability scenario, however the constraints obtained the highest preference values and as a consequence the highest weight, in order to avoid the outranking of alternatives located partially in forbidden areas.

The preference indices and the leaving and entering flow generated after the application of PROMETHEE-2 methodology are presented in Table 5. Figure 9 shows the location of the alternatives of the site selection analysis. The best alternatives are generally located south of

http://dx.doi.org/10.5772/51222

Zaragoza city, outside the alluvial sector (i.e. alternatives 25, 26 and 27). In contrast, the worst locations are the alluvial areas in the surroundings of El Burgo de Ebro (i.e. alternatives 4 and 18), the industrial areas in the north of Zaragoza city (i.e. alternatives 16 and 17), and the Logroño Road Corridor, upstream of Zaragoza (i.e. alternative 8).

Preference matrix	A	B	C	D	E	F	G	Weight
A	1.00	0.25	0.33	2.00	5.00	0.33	0.33	0.0735
B	4.00	1.00	4.00	5.00	8.00	2.00	3.00	0.3492
C	3.00	0.25	1.00	4.00	7.00	1.00	2.00	0.1774
D	0.50	0.20	0.25	1.00	4.00	0.25	0.25	0.0505
E	0.20	0.13	0.14	0.25	1.00	0.14	0.14	0.0224
F	3.00	0.50	1.00	4.00	7.00	1.00	2.00	0.1892
G	3.00	0.33	0.50	4.00	7.00	0.50	1.00	0.1378

Table 3. Pairwise comparison matrix, criteria weights for site search analysis under economic aspects.A) Groundwater protection, B) Doline susceptibility, C)Flooding hazard, D)Location of natural areas, E) Agricultural capability of soils, F) Slope percentage, G) Geotechnical characteristics.

Preference matrix	A	B	C	D	E	F	G	H	Weight
A	1.00	2.00	3.00	1.00	5.00	8.00	6.00	0.50	0.197
B	0.50	1.00	2.00	0.50	3.00	7.00	4.00	0.33	0.121
C	0.33	0.50	1.00	0.33	2.00	6.00	3.00	0.25	0.087
D	1.00	2.00	3.00	1.00	5.00	8.00	6.00	0.50	0.197
E	0.20	0.33	0.50	0.20	1.00	4.00	2.00	0.17	0.048
F	0.13	0.14	0.17	0.13	0.25	1.00	0.50	0.11	0.020
G	0.17	0.25	0.20	0.17	0.50	2.00	1.00	0.14	0.030
H	2.00	3.00	4.00	2.00	6.00	9.00	7.00	1.00	0.300

Table 4. Pairwise comparison matrix, criteria weights for site selection analysis.A) Groundwater protection, B) Doline susceptibility, C)Flooding hazard, D)Location of natural areas, E) Agricultural capability of soils, F) Slope percentage, G) Geotechnical characteristics, H) Constraints.

2.3. Stochastic PROMETHEE-2

In the stochastic approach, distribution types have to be assigned to every alternative and criterion and a MCS is performed over a MCE method (here PROMETHEE-2) meaning that the multicriteria analysis is performed a specified number of times (here: 5000; hence stochastic PROMETHEE-2). It should be noted that, due to local/regional variability, the local distributions of a criterion are highly likely to be different for each location alternative. Thus, although it seems reasonable, at first sight, to determine one distribution type for one criterion, if location dependent statistical analyses indicate varying distribution types, then varying types should be assigned to one criterion.

Alt	Φ-	Φ+	Φ	Rank PROMETHEE	SI	Rank stochastic	SAW Mean value
1	13.69	12.22	-1.48	14	0.41	10	3.95
2	13.41	8.74	-4.67	20	0.75	22	3.09
3	13.65	8.62	-5.03	22	0.65	19	3.26
4	15.76	8.50	-7.25	25	0.50	13	3.95
5	12.77	9.28	-3.49	16	0.70	21	3.25
6	7.48	12.93	5.45	8	0.27	7	4.60
7	6.42	17.08	10.66	4	0.06	1	5.38
8	13.31	6.91	-6.40	24	0.69	20	3.55
9	11.97	8.25	-3.72	17	0.56	14	3.75
10	12.30	8.11	-4.18	18	0.63	17	3.32
11	9.49	10.92	1.44	10	0.42	11	3.69
12	13.30	8.96	-4.34	19	0.63	18	3.79
13	8.99	11.42	2.44	9	0.56	15	3.57
14	8.61	15.29	6.69	7	0.19	5	4.66
15	10.74	9.97	-0.77	12	0.60	16	4.76
16	15.17	4.93	-10.25	26	0.95	27	3.61
17	13.40	7.00	-6.40	23	0.88	26	3.75
18	19.37	6.63	-12.75	27	0.86	25	2.55
19	11.97	8.74	-3.24	15	0.45	12	4.32
20	12.74	7.78	-4.96	21	0.76	24	3.9
21	10.83	9.58	-1.25	13	0.76	23	3.83
22	5.25	15.16	9.91	5	0.33	8	4.68
23	4.90	15.82	10.92	3	0.21	6	5.68
24	10.13	9.98	-0.15	11	0.39	9	5.61
25	5.78	17.63	11.85	1	0.11	4	4.88
26	6.18	17.32	11.14	2	0.10	3	4.80
27	7.22	17.04	9.83	6	0.07	2	5.32

Table 5. Leaving floe, entering flow, net flow and rank for site selection analysis, stochastic rank index and final rank for stochastic approach, and mean value in SAW methodology for every alternative of location.

http://dx.doi.org/10.5772/51222

Table 6 show the distribution types assigned to every alternative and criterion for the suitability analyses. Distribution fitting tests were performed to confirm/reject a modeled distribution type. The software used was @Risk [52]. If physical properties can only have non-negative values distribution types can (and should) be selected such that this feature is reflected, for example by choosing an exponential distribution.

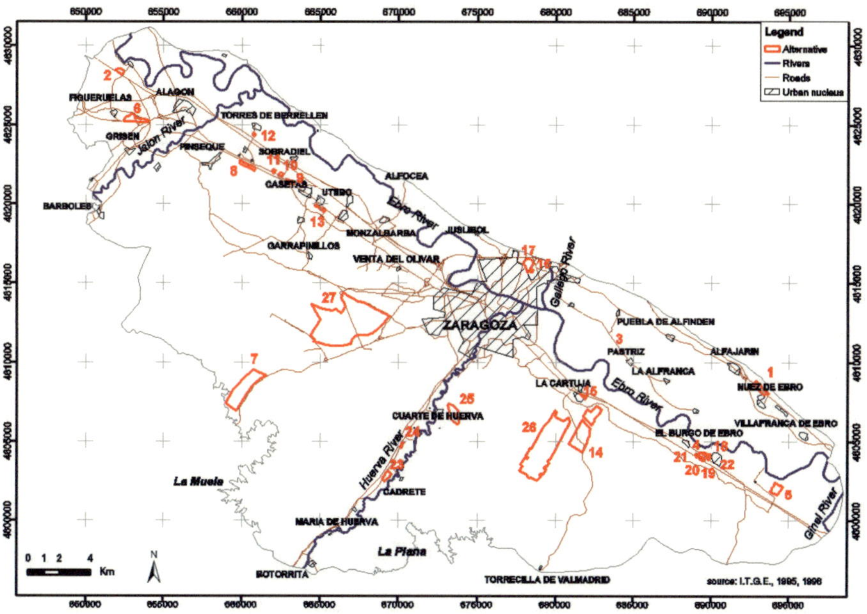

Figure 9. Location of alternatives for site selection analysis.

The more commonly used distributions for continuous variables (i.e. slope percentage) are normal and lognormal, but also logistic and exponential distributions are present in some variable (i.e. groundwater protection and/or doline susceptibility).

A binomial distribution was selected for categorical variables having two possible outcomes.If there are more than two categories (possible outcomes) the use of a categorical distribution can be problematic, implying the inclusion in the decision process of categories not present in the alternative. For example, if one alternative presented values 1 and 4 in agricultural capability criterion, the distribution selected by the fitting test would have given values 2 and 3 to this alternative, which are not present in the real world. Thus, instead of assigning a distribution, the percentage of cases (p value in Table 6) in every category was calculated and used as the probability of occurrence of every category. This was also the case for some continuous variables, which presented few different values, thus complicating the distribution selection (i.e. alternative 3 in doline susceptibility criterion). In these cases, the percentage or probability of occurrence of every value was introduced in the analysis.

In the case of the criterion "susceptibility to doline development", difficulties were experienced as some alternatives showed continuous values close to value 0 (see Figure 10). Since it was not possible to apply the percentage of values in these cases, a decision was made to apply an exponential distribution in order to avoid the introduction of negative values in the suitability analysis, even though the adopted solution was not absolutely satisfactory. Finally, some alternatives presented the same value for the whole alternative (unique value in the tables). Some representative examples of the selected distribution types can be seen in Figures 10. The bars symbolize the original (empirical) values retrieved from the pixels within each location alternative; the solid line the fitted theoretical distribution model.

Al.	A	B	C	D	E	F	G	H	Al.	A	B	C	D	E	F	G	H
1	p	ln	p	p	p	ln	u	b	**15**	p	ln	u	u	p	ln	p	b
2	l	n	p	p	p	ln	u	b	**16**	e	p	u	u	u	ln	p	u
3	e	p	u	u	u	n	u	b	**17**	l	n	u	u	u	ln	p	b
4	l	n	u	p	p	ln	p	b	**18**	l	ln	u	p	p	e	p	b
5	l	ln	p	u	u	ln	u	b	**19**	l	e	u	u	p	ln	p	b
6	l	ln	u	u	p	ln	u	b	**20**	l	ln	u	u	u	n	p	b
7	u	u	u	p	iu	ln	p	b	**21**	p	e	u	u	p	n	u	b
8	l	e	u	u	u	ln	u	b	**22**	l	n	u	u	p	n	u	b
9	p	e	u	u	u	ln	u	b	**23**	p	p	u	u	p	ln	p	b
10	l	e	u	u	p	ln	u	b	**24**	p	p	u	u	u	n	u	u
11	e	u	u	u	p	ln	u	b	**25**	u	u	u	p	p	n	u	u
12	l	p	u	p	u	l	u	b	**26**	u	u	u	p	p	ln	p	b
13	p	e	u	u	p	n	u	b	**27**	p	e	u	p	p	ln	p	b
14	p	u	u	p	p	ln	p	b									

Table 6. Distribution types for every alternative and criterion for industrial settlements suitability analysis. Al.) Alternative, A) Groundwater protection, B) Doline susceptibility, C) Flooding hazard, D) Location of natural areas, E) Agricultural capability of soils, F) Slope percentage, G) Geotechnical characteristics, H) Constraints. p) percentage, ln) lognormal, u) unique value, b) binomial, l) logistic, n) normal, e)exponential, iu) Intuniform

The results of the site selection suitability analysis based on stochastic PROMETHEE-2 can be seen in Table 5. In general, there are few differences in the SI values and total flows between the first rankings: alternatives 7, 25, 23, 26 and 27 (Figure 9). In addition, all these alternatives are located in the areas with higher suitability values in the site search analysis (SAW mean value in Table 5). Nevertheless, alternative 24 presents a high mean value in the SAW methodology but is ranked 11 and 9 in the PROMETHEE-2 and the stochastic approach. This is due to the fact that the major part of this polygon is located in a restricted area. In fact, the worst rankings, alternative 16, 17 and 18, are located partially inside restricted areas. However, in the case of alternative 24 the weight assigned to the constraint

http://dx.doi.org/10.5772/51222

factor in PROMETHEE-2 and the stochastic approach it was not enough to rank this alternative in the last positions. Besides, the first rank changes from alternative number 25 to alternative number 7, in the PROMETHEE-2 and the stochastic approach, respectively. This is the consequence of assigning a unique mean value in the PROMETHEE-2 approach to the alternatives. Figure 11 saws the values of the SAW methodology for both alternatives. It can be observed how, although both alternatives present similar mean value, alternative 7 present homogeneous high values, implying more percentage of high values in its distribution, while alternative 25 present a variety of suitability values, implying a less percentage of high suitability values. The stochastic approach overcomes this handicap by simulating values along the whole range of values inside the distribution assigned to the alternatives.

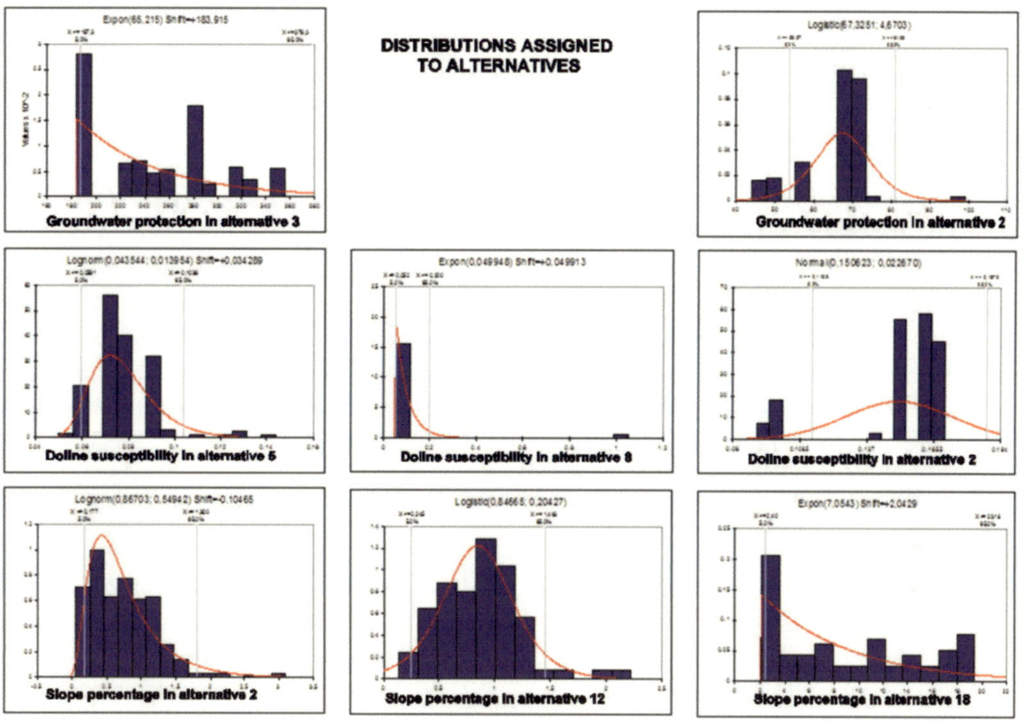

Figure 10. Examples of distributions assigned to alternatives.

3. Discussion and conclusions

The industrial use suitability map developed with the SAW and AHP methods integrated in a GIS for the surroundings of Zaragoza, is a substantial aid in the land-use management of this city. Besides, an additional benefit is achieved by integrating geoscientific aspects in the land-use decision process, as demanded by Agenda 21.

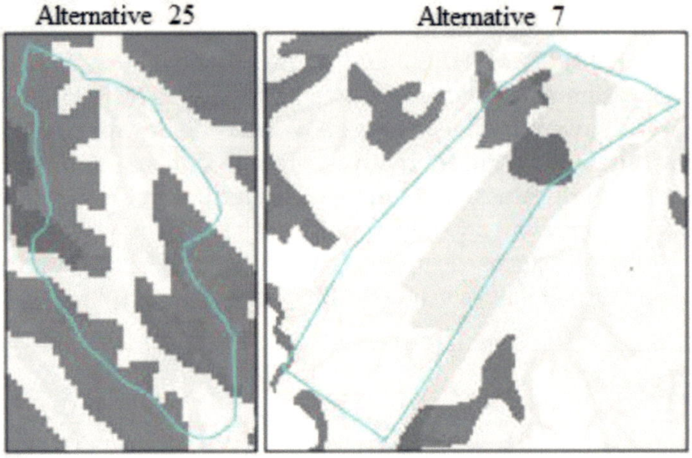

Figure 11. SAW values for alternatives 7 and 25.

A fundamental problem of decision theory is how to derive weights of criteria. One disadvantage of the AHP method is the inherent subjectivity of assigning preference values between criteria. The weights derived from these preference values have usually a profound effect on the results of the suitability analysis. However, in our particular case, in the industrial suitability analysis, there were no strong differences between the results of the site search analysis performed under the concept of sustainable development or the site search analysis performed under the concept of economic development, although different weights were assigned to the criteria in both approaches.

If differences are greater, a possible solution is to establish a set of suitability maps and to combine these to select the most suitable areas.

After some talks with different managers in the administration and following the approach under sustainability aspects, our results suggest that the best location for new industries is on the pediments and Tertiary sediments outside the natural protected areas, where the groundwater vulnerability and flood risk is lower, although the geotechnical characteristics of the terrain are less favorable, according to the PGOUZ. The least favorable location embodies the floodplain with high groundwater vulnerability values and the natural protected areas around the river bed, and other areas in the higher terraces which are more susceptible to doline development.

An advantage of outranking methods as PROMETHEE-2 is the fact that criteria do not need standardization or transformation processes which reduces subjectivity. However, in a spatial multicriteria analysis decisions still need to be made, as for example what characteristic value (from the population of pixels within a location alternative polygon) to use for a subsequent multicriteria analysis (e.g.maximum, minimum, mean, etc.). If using PROMETHEE-2 more decisions needs to be made in regards to the selection of the preference function as well as which set of criteria weights to use.

It is important to notice the similarity of the results after applying the site search analysis and the site selection analysis. In general, the highest rank positions are present in alternatives located in areas where the site search analysis also presented the highest suitability values. Some differences can be observed in alternatives located in areas with restrictions, as in the site selection analysis constrains are included as criteria. This is the case of alternative 24 which presented a high mean value in the SAW methodology but present a rank 11 and 9 in the PROMETHEE-2 and the stochastic approach. In this case, the weight assigned to the constraint factor in PROMETHEE-2 and the stochastic approach it was not enough to rank this alternative in the last positions. Thus, a higher weight should be given to the constraint factor in the site selection approaches.

Performing a PROMETHEE-2 with the mean values produces a mean result, but the uncertainty in either the input values or the result cannot be quantified. The stochastic approach helps approaching this problem by using probability distributions for the input parameters, instead of single values. For spatial multicriteria analysis in a variable data environment it is our recommendation to use stochastic approaches although, in this case, the process was not absolutely integrated in the GIS, and as a consequence it is very time consuming.

Acknowledgements

This research was funded by the Deutsche Forschungsgemeinschaft (DFG, Ho 804/7-1+2). We also greatly acknowledge support of the Ebro River Authority (CHE), the Aragón Region Authority and the Zaragoza Council.

Author details

M.T. Lamelas[1*], O. Marinoni[2], J. de la Riva[1] and A. Hoppe[3]

*Address all correspondence to: tlamelas@unizar.es

1 Department of Geography and Land Management, Faculty of Arts, University of Zaragoza, Zaragoza, Spain

2 CSIRO Ecosystem Sciences, Brisbane, Australia

3 Institute of Applied Geosciences, Technische Universität Darmstadt, Darmstadt, Germany

References

[1] Booty, W. G., Lam, D. C., Wong, I. W., & Siconolfi, P. (2001). Design and implementation of an environmental decision support system. *Environmental Modelling and Software*, 16, 453-458.

[2] Shim, J. P., Warkentin, M., Courtney, J. F., Power, D. J., Sharda, R., & Carlsson, C. (2002). Past, present and future of decision support technology. *Decision Support Systems*, 33, 111-126.

[3] Malczewski, J. (2004). GIS-based land-use suitability analysis: a critical overview. *Progress in Planning*, 62, 3-65.

[4] Gómez-Delgado, M., & Barredo, J. I. (2005). Sistemas de Información Geográfica y evaluación multicriterio en la ordenación del territorio. *Paracuellos de Jiloca: RA-MA Editorial.*

[5] Marinoni, O. (2005). A stochastic spatial decision support system based on PROMETHEE. *International Journal of Geographical Information Science*, 19(1), 51-68.

[6] Jankowski, P. (1995). Integrating geographical information systems and multiple criteria decision-making. *International Journal of Geographical Information Systems*, 9, 251-273.

[7] Voogd, H. (1983). Multicriteria evaluation for urban and regional planning. *London: Pion Limited.*

[8] Janssen, R., & Rietveld, P. (1990). Multicriteria analysis and GIS: An Application to Agricultural Land-use in the Netherlands. *Scholten H. and Stillwell J. (eds.) Geographical Information Systems for Urban and Regional Planning. Dordrecht: Kluwer.*

[9] Carver, S.J. (1991). Integrating multi-criteria evaluation with geographical information systems. *International Journal of Geographical Information Systems*, 5, 321-339.

[10] Can, A. (1993). Residential quality assessment, Alternative approaches using GIS. *Fischer M. and Nijkamp P. (eds.) Geographic information systems, spatial modelling and policy evaluation*, Berlín, Springer-Verlang.

[11] Pereira, J. M. C., & Duckstein, L. (1993). A multiple criteria decision-making approach to GIS-based land suitability evaluation. *International Journal of Geographical Information Systems*, 7, 407-422.

[12] Barredo, J., & Bosque, J. (1995). Integración de evaluación multicriterio y sistemas de información geográfica para la evaluación de la capacidad de acogida del territorio y la asignación de usos del suelo. *AESIG (ed.) Actas del IV Congreso Español de Sistemas de información Geográfica. Barcelona:AESIG*, 191-200.

[13] Bosque, J., Diaz, M. A., Gómez, M., Rodríguez, V.M., Rodríguez, A. E., & Vela, A. (1999). Un procedimiento basado en un SIG, para localizar centros de tratamiento de residuos. *Anales de Geografía de la Universidad Complutense*, 9, 295-323.

[14] Thill, J.C. (1999). Spatial Multicriteria Decision Making and Analysis. *A geographic information science approach. Aldershot:Ashgate.*

[15] Eastman, J.R., Kyem, P.A., Toledano, J., & Jin, W. (1993). Gis and Decision Making. *Ginebra: United Nations institute for Training and Research.*

[16] Wallenius, J., Dyer, J. S., Fishburn, P. C., Steuer, R. E., Zionts, S., & Deb, K. (2008). Multiple Criteria Decision Making, Multiattribute Utility Theory: Recent accomplishments and what lies ahead. *Management science*, 54(7), 1336-1349.

[17] Carver, S.J. (1999). Developing Web-based GIS/MCE: Improving access to data and spatial decision support tools. *Thill J.C. (eds) Multicriteria decision-making and analysis: A geographic information science approach. New York:Ashgate*, 49-76.

[18] Rinner, C., & Malczewski, J. (2002). Web-enabled spatial decision analysis using ordered Weighted averaging (OWA). *Journal of Geographical Systems*, 4(4), 385-403.

[19] Zhu, X., & Dale, A. P. (2003). A Web-based decision analysis tool for natural resource and environmental management. *Environmental Modelling & Software 2001*, 16, 251-262.

[20] Rinner, C. Web-based spatial decision support: status and research directions. *Journal of Geographic Information and Decision Analysis*, 7(1), 14-31.

[21] Collins, M. G., Steiner, F. R., & Rushman, M. (2001). Land-use suitability analysis in the United States: Historical development and promising technological achievements. *Environmental Management*, 28, 611-621.

[22] Hopkins, L.D. (1977). Methods for generating land suitability: a comparative evaluation. Journal of American Institute of Planners , 43, 387-491.

[23] Hoppe, A., Lang, S., Lerch, C., & Marinoni, O. (2006). Geology and a spatial decision support system for the surroundings of urban areas: An example from southern Hesse (Germany). *Zeitschrift der Deutschen Gesellschaftfür Geowissenschaften*, 157, 135-146.

[24] Lamelas, M. T., Marinoni, O., de la Riva, J., & Hoppe, A. (2006). The use of Spatial Decision Support Systems for sand and gravel extraction suitability in the context of a sustainable development in the surroundings of Zaragoza (Spain). *Instituto Cartográfico de Cataluña (ed) Proceedings of the 5th European Congress on Regional Geoscientific Cartography and Information Systems. Barcelona*, 180-183.

[25] Lamelas, M. T., Marinoni, O., Hoppe, A., & de la Riva, J. (1999). Suitability analysis for sand and gravel extraction site location in the context of a sustainable development in the surroundings of Zaragoza (Spain). *Environmental Geology 2008*, 55(8), 1673-1686.

[26] Malczewski, J. *GIS and Multicritera decision analysis*, New York, Wiley.

[27] Marinoni, O., & Hoppe, A. (2006). Using the Analytic Hierarchy Process to Support the Sustainable Use of Geo-Resources in Metropolitan Areas. *Journal of Systems Science and Systems Engineering*, 15(2), 154-164.

[28] Sharifi, M. A., & Retsios, V. (2004). Site selection for waste disposal through spatial multiple criteria decision analysis. *Journal of telecommunications and information technology*, 3-11.

[29] Vincke, P. (1986). Analysis of multicriteria decision aid in Europe. *European Journal of Operational Research*, 25, 160-168.

[30] Lamelas, M.T. (2007). Geo-resources and geo-hazards in the context of a sustainable development in the periphery of urban areas, exemplary of a part of the Ebro Basin in the surroundings of Zaragoza (Spain). *PhD thesis. TechnischeUniversität Darmstadt*, http://elib.tu-darmstadt.de/diss/000794, (accessed June, 2012).

[31] Lamelas, M. T., Marinoni, O., de la Riva, J., & Hoppe, A. (2010). Sustainable spatial decision making in a complex 3d environment: an auditable decision support workflow based on multicriteria analysis. *Sanders M.H. and Clark Ph.D. (eds.) Geomorphology: Processes, Taxonomy and Applications (Series: Earth Sciences in the 21st Century)*, New York, Nova Science Publishers, 1-44.

[32] Brans, J. P., Vincke, P., & Mareschal, B. (1986). How to select and how to rank projects: The PROMETHEE method. *European Journal of Operational Research*, 24, 228-238.

[33] Lamelas, M. T. (2009). Esquema metodológico para la toma de decisiones sobre el uso sostenible del suelo: Aplicación a la localización de suelo industrial. *GeoFocus*, 9, 28-66, http://geofocus.rediris.es/2009/Articulo2_2009.pdf, (accessed June, 2012).

[34] Marinoni, O. (2004). Implementation of the analytical hierarchy process with VBA in ArcGIS. *Computers and Geosciences*, 30, 637-646.

[35] Saaty, T.L. (1977). A scaling method for priorities in hierarchical structures. *Journal of Mathematical Psychology*, 15, 231-281.

[36] Soriano, M. A., & Simón, J. L. (1995). Alluvial dolines in the central Ebro basin, Spain: a spatial and developmental hazard analysis. *Geomorphology*, 11, 295-309.

[37] Lamelas, M. T., Marinoni, O., Hoppe, A., & de la Riva, J. (2007). Groundwater vulnerability map for the Ebro alluvial aquifer between Jalón and Ginel tributaries (Spain). *Environmental Geology*, 53, 861-878.

[38] Lamelas, M. T., Marinoni, O., Hoppe, A., & de la Riva, J. (2008). Dolines probability map using logistic regression and GIS technology in the central Ebro Basin (Spain). *Environmental Geology*, 54, 963-977.

[39] Lamelas, M. T., Marinoni, O., Hoppe, A., & de la Riva, J. (2009). Modelling environmental variables for geohazards and georesources assessment to support sustainable land-use decisions in Zaragoza (Spain). *Geomorphology*, 111, 88-103.

[40] Eastman, J.R. (1997). IDRISI for Windows, Version 2.0: Tutorial exercises. *Graduated School of Geography. Worcester: Clark Unversity.*

[41] Heywood, I., Cornelius, S., & Carver, S. (2002). An introduction to geographical information Systems. *Harlow: Prentice Hall.*

[42] Malczewski, J., & Rinner, C. (2005). Exploring multicriteria decision strategies in GIS with linguistic quantifiers: A case study of residential quality evaluation. *Journal of Geographical Systems*, 7, 249-268.

[43] Malczewski, J., Moreno-Sánchez, R., Bojorquez-Tapia, L. A., & Ongay-Delhumeau, E. (1997). Environmental conflict analysis in the Cape Region, Mexico. *Journal of Environmental Planning and Management*, 40(3), 349-374.

[44] Banai, R. (1993). Fuzziness in geographical information systems: contributions from the analytic hierarchy process. *International Journal Geographical Information Systems*, 7(4), 315-329.

[45] Banai-kashani, R. (1989). A new method for site suitability analysis: the analytical hierarchy process. *Environmental management*, 13, 685-693.

[46] Malczewski, J. (1996). A GIS-based approach to multiple criteria group decision-making. *International Journal of Geographical Information Systems*, 10(8), 955-971.

[47] Lodwick, W. A., Monson, W., & Svoboda, L. (1990). Attribute error and sensitivity analysis of map operations in geographical information systems: suitability analysis. *International Journal of Geographical Information Systems*, 4(4), 413-428.

[48] Hevelink, G. B. M., Burrough, P. A., & Stein, A. (1989). Propagation of errors in spatial modelling with GIS. *International Journal of GeographicalInformationSystems*, 3(4), 303-322.

[49] Hölting, B., Haertlé, T., Hohberger, K. H., Nachtigall, K. H., Villinger, E., Weinzierl, W., & Wrobel, J. P. (1995). KonzeptzurErmittlung der Schutzfunktion der Grundwasserüberdeckung. *Geologisches Jahrbuch C*, 63, 5-24.

[50] Ollero, A. (1996). *El curso medio del Ebro.Zaragoza: Consejo de Protección de la Naturaleza de Aragón.*

[51] De la Rosa, D., & Magaldi, D. (1982). *Rasgos metodológicos de un sistema de evaluación de tierras para regiones mediterráneas Madrid:Sociedad Española de la Ciencia del Suelo.*

[52] Palisade Corporation. (2002). *Risk 4.5.2. Advanced risk analysis for spreadsheets*, New York, Newfield.

Chapter 10

Semi-Automatic Semantic Data Classification Expert System to Produce Thematic Maps

Luciene Stamato Delazari,
André Luiz Alencar de Mendonça,
João Vitor Meza Bravo, Mônica Cristina de Castro,
Pâmela Andressa Lunelli,
Marcio Augusto Reolon Schmidt and
Maria Engracinda dos Santos Ferreira

Additional information is available at the end of the chapter

http://dx.doi.org/10.5772/51848

1. Introduction

This chapter presents an expert system, designed to classify semantic information in a geographic database, aiming to assist non-expert map-makers. Despite the fact that GIS science has been discussing how to deal with ordinary users and their relationship with map production, especially due to the popularization of GIS (*Geographic Information Systems*) software and webmapping technologies, there are still issues concerning map production and its quality. Some of these issues are related to data classification methods, knowledge about levels of measurement and, thus, to map symbolization itself. In Brazil, this subject can be of special interest to municipality and state government departments, NGOs and institutions which use maps for planning and for decision-making support. At least in part, problems seem to occur because of the ease of GIS use, together with employees' lack of education in cartography. In this context, an expert system seems to be a proper choice to ensure that ordinary users can take correct decisions in the map-making process.

Specifically in thematic map production, there are potential ways to ensure that correct choices will be suggested for users, and these range from long-term training to artificial intelligence techniques. In this context, Schmidt & Delazari [1] developed an expert system to classify data, comparing text information on class names with a file that contains a word classification, called the "system dictionary". Originally, this software was built to assist Social Assistance Department users, from Parana state in Brazil, in their activities of social data insertion and classification. Currently, this system has evolved to a web environment and is publicly available, which reinforces the need for automatic assistance in order to avoid mistakes that could impair the data analysis and, consequently, the decision-making based on this analytical process.

This chapter is divided into three main sections. The first addresses the motivations for creation of the expert system, considering thematic maps generation and issues related to non-specialist users and uses. Topics discussed in this section are: ways of providing user assistance in data classification and map symbolization according to map design rules; how users can achieve reasonable understanding of GIS and spatial data as trained users, for correct use of geospatial tools; and, since there is no unique and permanent set of rules for thematic map-making, what are the main aspects to consider when developing user assistance for building good maps.

The second section describes the expert system's theoretical proposition, regarding users and the data to be mapped, and examples of rules to establish and implement in order to achieve proper data classification results. The use of IF-THEN rules for this case study is a noteworthy project element, being initially defined as a stationary software code to support recognition of database entries. The algorithm proceeds with an evaluation of the level of measurement that best suits the data representation process. This data is then classified and stored in the knowledge base. When the total amount of classes are stored, rules indicate the most suitable color ramps, among those available, in order to match the data characteristics. To insert new information, the expert system automatically examines and tests the data type; numerical data are classified to a numerical level of measurement; nominal and ordinal data are classified according to the knowledge base and the system dictionary. When using non-numerical data – semantic classification – the level of measurement choice is more complex due to its subjective nature and requires greater attention.

Lastly, the third part will enclose the project overview demonstrating the code development for the current web environment paradigm and what could be the potential new improved functionality of this system, developed to assist users in building social maps. The results are presented together with a discussion about general aspects of system architecture, interface design and the expert system itself, with a functional point of view, in particular, on how a system can guide users in such activities.

2. Background

Originally, the objective of Social Atlas was to support the *Secretaria de Estado do Trabalho, Emprego e Promoção Social* (SETP). In Parana state, in Brazil, this bureau defines social assistance policies and their execution, besides acting as a government manager, defining the allocation of financial resources. SETP technicians, in 2000, needed to know how counties were organized in terms of Municipal Councils and Public Funds, in order to implant social laws recently approved at that time. For this reason, Delazari [2] started to work on an electronic Atlas prototype, called Social Atlas. The objective of Social Atlas was to be a tool for carrying out spatial analysis and generating maps, by means of user interaction. This was based on the needs of this bureau, specifically under the context of LOAS (Portuguese acronym for Organic law for social assistance) (Schmidt & Delazari [1]).

The original system users were social scientists who had little or no knowledge of cartography or of any other methods to manipulate or represent spatial data. The proposed system must lead users by map generation tasks, avoiding any mistakes which might impair analysis. Since research data includes nominal and ordinal information collected for each county in Paraná, it is mandatory to implement functions that make it possible to choose between different options for data representation and also give users the possibility of using different data classification methods.

In the visual analysis of geographic information, acquiring knowledge is possible if graphic solutions defined for each map provide efficient visualization of the characteristics of geographic phenomena. Graphic solutions may represent the spatial phenomenon behavior, and emphasize important characteristics for each analysis moment. As stated by Fairbarn [3], "maybe the most important change in mapping, in the past ten years, was the appearance of a user who is also a map producer". Regardless of the fact that producing map knowledge still seems to be a cartographer's responsibility, it is impossible to expect that every map built will have a cartographer as part of its genesis.

The main issue in this context is how to enable ordinary users to produce good quality maps which respect cartographic design principles. In other words, map software should offer a set of tools to guide the choice of all the steps in the map production process. There are two possible options: first, to use tutorials which guide users through the stages of map creation (Yufen [4]), or second, by means of expert systems, which automate basic decisions about the mapping process (Wang & Ormeling; Artimo; Su; Zhan & Buttenfield [5-8]).

The choice of an expert system was influenced by factors related to facility of development, knowledge about software, diversity of functions to be implemented and availability of *software* resources. Among other minor differences between expert systems (ES) and conventional systems, it is possible to rely on the ability of an ES to simulate human reasoning, inference and judgment, and derive conclusions and heuristics based on a specific domain of knowledge. This means an ES is a computer software that operates with symbolic objects (symbols), and relationships between objects (Chee & Power [9]), while conventional software generate results through algorithms, which manipulate numbers and character. According to Hemingway et. al. [10], the structure of an expert system has significant advantages over the traditional software, because once the information is correctly inserted into the knowledge base, this may be updated, modified and supplemented. In a general way, an expert system can be conceived as a four-module system that acts as an information manager. These modules include a user interface, a set of rules, a knowledge base and the inference motor (Figure 1)

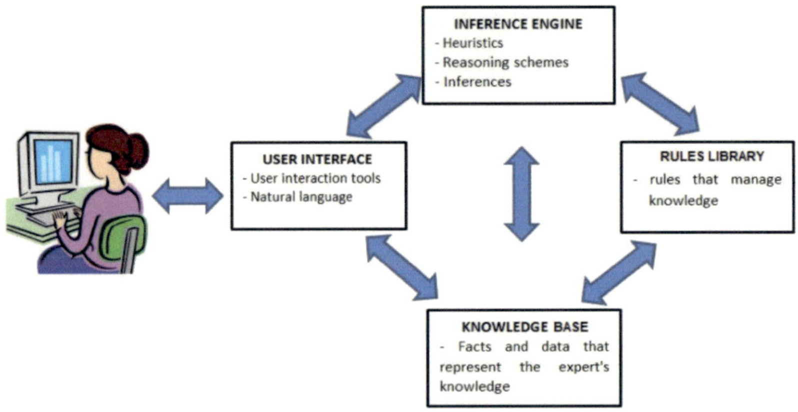

Figure 1. Basic structure of an expert system; Source: Adapted from Mendes [11].

The inference engine is an essential element for an expert system, since it works as the engine control that evaluates and applies rules. In the process of problem-solving, these rules must be in accordance with the information existing in the working memory (Araki[12]). According to Russell & Norvig [13], automated inference engines can be grouped into four categories: theorem proofs and logic programming languages; production systems; "frame" systems or semantic networks; and descriptive logic systems. The inference engine uses forward chaining, a method which seeks to validate the assumptions in the rules and to complete the actions (consequences), not only as a logical conclusion. The intermediate results are validated as assumptions and deduced conclusions are stored in a working memory (Russell & Norvig [13]).

The rules library and the working memory form the so-called 'knowledge base', representing the knowledge captured from a human expert on the problem domain. When an issue is submitted to the system evaluation, this rules library interacts with the user and the inference engine, allowing identification of the problem, possible solutions for it and the whole process that leads to conclusions. Much of the effort to develop an expert system relies on the elicitation of knowledge, i.e., how to capture and use the human knowledge in a computer application.

Rule-based systems are feasible for problems in which the solution process can be written in the form of 'IF-THEN' rules and for which the problem has no easy solution. According to Araki [12], when a system based on rules is created, it is necessary to consider the following:

- A set of facts to represent the memory of the initial work. This can be any relevant information related to the system's initial state;
- A set of rules, a library built to deal with the set of facts. This should include any action that should be within the scope of the problem;
- A condition stipulating that a solution was found or that no solution exists.

The set of facts describes the relevant characteristics of the phenomena, in the expert's point of view. Sometimes, even the expert does not realize all the features that he/she uses to make a decision. At this step, qualitative research tools such as questionnaires and interviews help to identify nuances involved in the particular decision-making process by the human expert, and, from them, it is possible to select key facts in order to build the initial working memory.

To define a set of rules, structures can be designed using the IF-THEN <condition> <action>, where:

<condition>, calls a conditional proposition. This condition provides a test the outcome of which depends on the current state of the knowledge basis. Typically, it is possible to test the presence or absence of certain information;

<action> performs some action, defined in a rule, and may even change the current state of the knowledge base, adding, modifying or removing units which are present in the knowledge basis.

Using an IF-THEN structure will cause the system to examine the condition of all ES rules and determine a subset of rules whose conditions are satisfied by the analysis of the working memory. The choice of the rule to be triggered is based on a strategy of conflict resolution. When the rule is triggered, actions specified in the THEN clause are carried out. These actions can modify the working memory, the rules library, or another specification included by the system programmer. The loop of rules is then triggered and actions will continue until there are no more conditions to be met or there is an action that terminates the program flow.

In cartography, the use of expert systems can have a wide field of applications. Understanding the basic concepts of data classification, level of measurement and visual variables in the process of map design is a major problem for casual GIS users. It is not unusual to find maps with continuous color ramps representing discrete data, map projection problems, complex symbols with no important information, and "noisy" visualization, facts that make interpretation almost impossible (Schmidt & Delazari[1]).

According to Schmidt & Delazari [1] there is a need to develop research on how to assist users in designing maps with GIS tools. The scientific literature presents some study cases on software and specific use and user issues. For automatic visualization, other researchers (Casner; Roth et al.; Senay & Ignatus [14 - 16]) investigated how to eliminate the need to specify, design and develop different visualizations for GIS software outputs, allowing users to focus their attention on determining and describing the information to be represented. Other initiatives are CommonGIS (Fraunhofer [17]) and Geoda™ (Anselin et al[18]). Those systems focus on HCI – Human Computer Interaction - through an interactive training assistance and EDA (Exploratory Data Analysis) assistance tool. CommonGIS adapts the interface as users explore the tool and acquire knowledge about the system. The exploration is guided by an expert system giving users hints and options. Geoda™ emphasizes data mining and spatial statistics, and includes functionality ranging from simple mapping to exploratory data analysis, using an interactive environment and combining maps with statistical graphics (Anselin et al. [18]).

Yet according to Schmidt & Delazari [1], if casual users do not understand map design concepts properly, it is important to determine how to help them to classify attributes and symbolize maps according to the principles of cartography. At the same time, it seems to be essential for cartographers to ensure that these users will achieve a minimum level of understanding of the correct use of GIS. If there are no map design principles for the digital environment, mainly because cartographers do not know exactly what can be adopted from traditional map design theory, what should be taken into account to make these principles feasible for ordinary users? In this context, the expert system application seems to be a plausible solution, regarding the characteristics discussed above.

2.1. The Social Atlas expert system

The expert system was built as an automated information manager placed between the database and the representation device, implemented with MapObjects (ESRI) (Figure 2). The ES controls the data flow in two situations: insertion of new data and carrying out SQL queries. When new information is added, the system goes to the knowledge base in order to try to find a similar configuration, concerning class names. If not all can be found, the rules library breaks it down into isolated words to try to find any kind of order in the dictionary. The same procedure occurs when an SQL is inserted in the system but, in this case, the information existing in the knowledge base is filtered by the rules and presented on a thematic map.

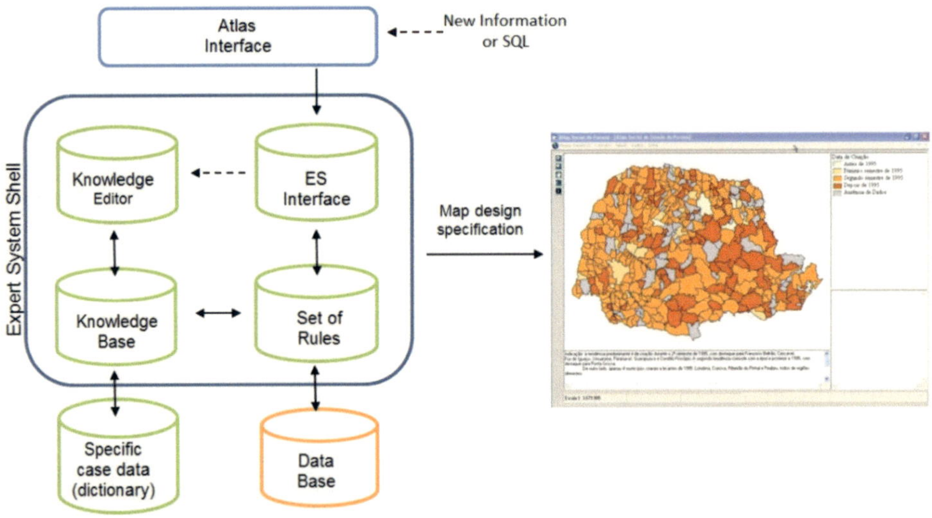

Figure 2. Expert system information flow

Initial memory, or initial facts, is the name given to information located in the database. This is collected by technicians of the SETP bureau for implementation of LOAS. Data is organized into three themes, or major groups, which separate information in terms of its characteristics. There are 26 different types of information in these three themes. Each one has its own classification and number of classes defined by the original map design from Delazari [2] and its condition is related to defining the data's level of measurement and knowledge base rank.

The rules library, unlike other expert systems, is embedded in the software, and the parameters of the rules are updated by use, and can be accessed by the user. The set of rules tries to identify which kind of data has been inserted. Through application of production rules, described as IF-THEN, the expert system tests the type of data to insert new information. Numerical data is classified by its numerical level. Social Atlas does not distinguish between the interval or ratio level of the measurement, because, in this case, the map design does not consider it (Schmidt & Delazari [1]).

Nominal and ordinal data can be stored in the same knowledge base but the rules to deal with them are quite different and their functioning is based on ordering elements from the knowledge base. Therefore, any feature that indicates order, associated with class names, has to be searched for in the knowledge base. When dealing with semantic classification, the choice between one or another level of measurement demands attention, because correct order is a subjective concept. Data indicating temporal or any kind of order can be considered as ordinal data and needs to be evaluated in detail. For example, for LOAS implementation it is important to know County Council's creation data. Classes are "first semester of 1995", "before 1995", "second semester of 1995", "after 1995" and "no available data". The expert system searches the whole class, e.g. first semester of 1995, for possible ordering of categories (Schmidt & Delazari [1]).

If it is not possible to define them, category names are broken into a list of words, using a 'word-wrap' function. The position of each word in the sentence is stored as an index of words. Then the list of words is compared to the dictionary and the ES tries to classify the first word of each class, and then the second word of each class, and so on, trying to establish a hierarchical relationship between class names. This dictionary keeps words in a more generic sense, giving local and global ordering based on the index order of the words that compound the class names. Inside the dictionary there are words and prepositions like "until", "before", "between", "among" and "after", and they also work as a specific working memory, keeping all the words used for classification.

The dictionary functions as a full resource for carrying out efficient classifications. In this context, if a previous classification has been deleted and a new one with a similar name is inserted, the system is able to estimate a possible order for the new classification. The stopping condition, in this case, is defined if an order is or is not associated with the class names, or words associated with them. In this way, when ordering is found, for all categories, the rule library will choose the required visual schemes (color ramps, in the case of choropleth maps) to represent geographic phenomena. Also, the knowledge base must assemble the new classification.

However, as the system can be relatively weak in the early stages of professional use due to the uncertainty of the initial memory and dictionary, some cases of failure or partial success may occur. In these cases, the system asks the user if the order is correct. Then the system stores the user classification, feeds the dictionary and carries out the map symbolization. As long as specialists keep supplying the knowledge base with more information, the vocabulary becomes more extensive and the system can deal with complex situations. Also, user confirmation becomes unnecessary. Thus, the system becomes a more powerful tool, especially when experienced technicians build the knowledge base and dictionary, and distribute them along with the Social Atlas.

As a last point about the ES, there is a special level of access to allow users to edit the knowledge base and database in general. Different modifications can be made to the database and this will modify the final representation aspect, and also change the knowledge base or even the dictionary. The first is a common task performed in order to update available data in the database. In this case, any information deleted or inserted will pass through the Expert System. This step is necessary to update the knowledge base and the dictionary, and to keep the ES and the database synchronized.

The interaction with the ES occurs inside the Social Atlas interface (Figure 3). The dialog box is accessed from the Edition of Social Atlas menu. All other steps of the expert system run under this dialog box and users do not come into direct contact with the data or its classification. Themes are shown in the Themes Dialog box. Data, i.e., column name, is supplied by the Class Dialog box on the left. In this dialog box the class names are supplied and appear at the right hand side. Clicking on the 'confirm' button makes the system carry on with classification, as described previously. In the event of failure, the right hand side buttons are enabled and a message box pops up asking the user for intervention. Users sometimes require additional information storage as text. This action can be done in the 'Additional Information' field at the bottom of the dialog box.

3. New interface design and code development

For cartographers and professional mapmakers, it seems to be hard to think about code development and its relationship to the map production process itself. There are several varieties of GIS software which can help to store and process spatial data to produce high quality geographic representations. However, it cannot be denied that web environments are changing the way map use and users are understood and considered in cartographic activities. Since the web is the lair of interactivity, one mandatory issue is about the way in which casual and ordinary users rely on geographic data to produce thematic maps. Also, there is a major issue about how cartographers can act in this environment to ensure that these users are able to rely on these self-produced maps to take decisions and to analyze geographic phenomena efficiently.

Web applications, just like offline software, are dependent on programming languages and, besides the fact that websites are usually easier to design and to get working, because of common server specifications and widely known browser architecture (which includes client-side features that are constantly evolving), there are some critical issues in developing map applications for the web. Thus, if a cartographer wants to help any user on the world-wide web to make good maps by means of developing an automatic or expert system for it, there is a need to first understand and analyze how web architecture can be handled. This section presents a potential way to figure out this issue, by means of presenting the *"how it works"* on the current "Atlas Social do Paraná" (Delazari [2]) version, presented on http://www.cartografia.ufpr.br/atlas/english[1]. Since the development process was carried out exclusively by cartographers and not by system analysts, perhaps the proposed solution is not as elegant as it could be, but discussions raised by it can be useful for interactive map designers and are currently defined as the main focus of this implementation.

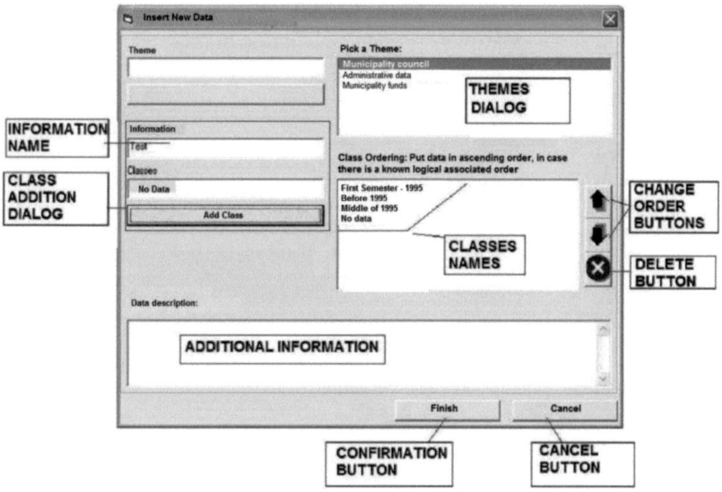

Figure 3. Original expert system interface; Source: Schmidt & Delazari [1]

Describing how an automatic system is developed can serve as the starting point for many related projects. The case study presented here is on the adoption of an automatic system inside the already existing "Atlas Social do Paraná". As previously described, the Atlas comprises a huge amount of social data for the last two decades, which makes it a powerful tool, not only for government planners or public administrators, but also for ordinary citizens, all of them possibly using the atlas to gain a full understanding of social perspectives of Paraná state in Brazil.

Since the Atlas was developed initially as an offline product, the web version has to manage the following issues:

1 All php codes are available for download in the same page.

a. How to make the Atlas database easy to update and query by data producers who are not experts in either cartography or informatics;

b. How to make the Atlas usable in the web, combining cartographic aspects and interface design in order to best suit the audience needs;

c. How to make the Atlas structure serviceable to provide the user with the ability to produce maps on demand, using his own data and preserving the representation quality.

System functionality	Choosing thematic data (U,S)
	Choosing area units for mapping (U,S)
	Choosing level of measurement (S)
	Choosing method for data classification (S)
	Choosing number of classes (U,S)
	Choosing color ramp (U,S)
	Storing user's choices (S)
	Displaying thematic data table with statistics (U,S)
	Printing maps module (U, S)
	Searching location by text (U,S)
	Uploading own data to build maps (U,S)
	Finding address (U,S)
	Where am I (U,S)
Webmap interface functionality	Zooming and panning (U,S)
	Next and back zoom buttons (U,S)
	Querying by click (U,S)
	Legend support (U,S)
	Scale (U,S)
	Latitude and longitude location (U,S)
	Measuring areas and distances (U,S)

Table 1. Interface functionality - 'U' indicates its presence on User version and 'S' indicates its presence on Specialist version

The expert system described in the last section also had to be redesigned in order to deal with new database organization and its interface was rebuilt to consider the use of two groups of web users: specialists and general users. In the first group are the users who will build the expert database by choosing variables to construct their maps and evaluate them. The second group is those who will take advantage of this database to build their own maps, whether using data from the Atlas or using any other spatial data with attributes. Al-

http://dx.doi.org/10.5772/51848

so, the system interface needed to be redrawn in order to consider the browsers' actual style of navigation and the limitation of using only one window and less than 90% of the display area for map application in general.

Many of the answers to the issues presented were discussed during the process of implementing the Atlas. However, the interface design and website functionality were the first set of decisions to be taken, and guided further design on the database, server architecture and web services, used to make spatial data representations available on the internet. The list of interface functionalities can be divided into two steps: the system functionality itself and the webmap interface (Table 1). The initial effort on this new version was designed to build only choropleth maps, but its structure would deal with other mapping techniques, on demand.

3.1. Database and server structure

The first step in designing the current database consisted of defining the former entities and relationships, implemented by DBMS PostgreSQL. The existing data structure – considering spatial data and attributes data to be represented in maps - was first considered from the point of view of common GIS software architecture: producing feature data by surveying, transforming it on spatial files and joining relational tables with area units to produce map symbology on specific themes. Problems arise when there are changes to spatial data, such as when a new municipality or new administration area is created, or when data producers need to load new data or to rectify existing data, since using a form specially built for updating data is required, apart from performance and software compiling issues.

Thus, the next step was to define the database structure for spatial data. The new version of the atlas comprises the introduction of a spatial database paradigm, with spatial data organized as tables with associated geometry information and foreign keys, in order to be related to any thematic data to be added to the database. The use of the *Postgis* spatial extension, *PostgreSQL* support for spatial data, was mandatory in the design of the database structure. Spatial data were built separately from attribute data and divided into types of area units. Since official data from the Atlas has to be from Paraná state only, there are only two spatial subsets: one for municipalities and associated data, and the other for census sectors, official area units from the Brazilian official census. One advantage of the use of this kind of database organization is that associated data like regions, micro-regions and macro-regions can be used as area units (Figure 4), using dissolve operations by means of SQL queries[2,] and using names as attribute fields on joining attributes with spatial area units. By means of using the same Brazilian official geocode for census sectors and for municipalities, it is possible to guarantee that joining the attribute information will be an effective choice for updating the database and maintaining consistency between spatial and attribute data.

The system architecture's first criterion was the use of open source and free software where possible. It was also decided that the spatial database must be available remotely, together with the instance for the spatial data server and the web server itself, in the same physical server. Based on this, the architecture (Figure 5) was defined with an *Apache* and *Tomcat*

---

2 Select ST_UNION(the_geom) … group by 'mesoregion'

webserver, along with instances of *Geoserver* as the mapserver, *PostgreSQL* as the DBMS, PHP to process server-side data, to produce XML (SLD) symbology and to query database and Javascript libraries (*jquery*, *Ext* and *GeoExt*, *Openlayers*) to deal with client-side functionality, like div display, map zoom and map legends. Last, *Curl* was used to establish the communication between PHP and *Geoserver* Rest API, which facilitates the transaction between web servers, making possible to perform map server administration tasks remotely.

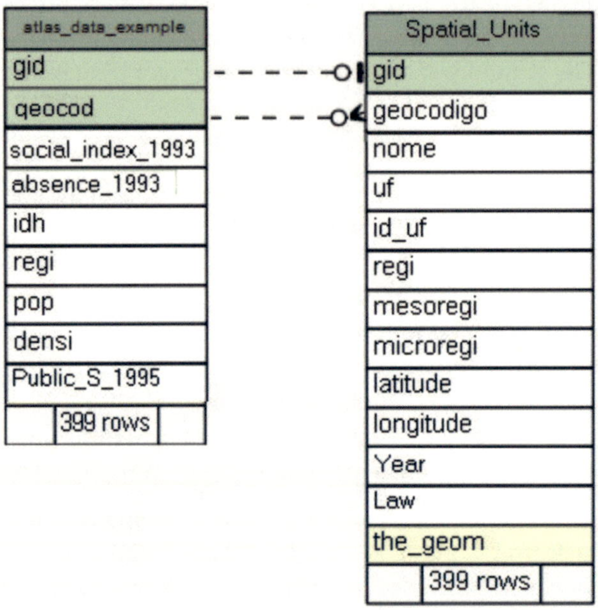

Figure 4. Example of database table's relationship for spatial features and attributes

The PHP language is used to process server-side data, being necessary to the expert system code, since it deals with the database access, together with the creation of rules to create symbols based on users' input. The PHP code is part of the web page code itself, since a ".php" file can also handle *html* and *javascript* code and is a well-documented and easy-to-use language, which offsets its lack of consistency and predictability. PHP connects the database using the pgsql extension, and a piece of code (Figure 6) can connect the database, set the default encoding to prevent from incorrectly displaying accents and make a simple query to return the average for some column, being the resultant row stored in a vector PHP array. For security reasons, it seems important to maintain the connection information (host, name of database, user and password) in a separate file, which must be included[3] in the main PHP file.

Another server-side task that must be taken into account involves publishing spatial data on the web. To accomplish this, the server must be an OGC (Open Geospatial Consortium)

3 Include names_and_passwords_file.php; //line included in the beginning of PHP code

specs compliant, capable of putting data on the internet throughout web services. The chosen one was the *Geoserver* mapserver, a *Java*-based tool to publish spatial data, which was installed using a war file, and configured to optimize performance in a production environment [19]. Since there is no need for vector analysis or satellite imagery, the choice was to publish data using WMS requisitions in the map server. The use of this web service displays a set of image tiles to frame the spatial data and its symbology in the user's client. Also, it uses a simple set of *xml* rules to construct symbols that can be used to get on-demand data classification and symbols choice.

code1.php

```php
<?php
session_start();
$SQL_DSN = "host=".$_SESSION[SQL_SERVER]." dbname=".$_SESSION[SQL_DATABASE]." user=".$_SESSION[SQL_USER]."
password=".$_SESSION[SQL_PASSWORD];
$connection = pg_connect($SQL_DSN) or die ("Não foi possível Conectar ao Banco de Dados");
pg_set_client_encoding($connection, "LATIN1");
$theme = "population_2012";
$average_sql = pg_exec($connection, "Select  avg($theme) from \"$_SESSION[SQL_TABLE]\"");
$average = pg_fetch_array($average_sql,0);
?>
```

Figure 5. Piece of PHP code showing the connection and simple query to the database

3.2. On-demand map symbology

The SLD (Styled Layer Descriptor) is an XML-based file format used to transmit symbols, according to OGC specification on WMS symbology. Traditionally, this file contains parameters which are used together with features stored in a geospatial server, comprising symbolization information, such as color to be used in a point symbol or the thickness value for lines. These parameters are applied to one or more layers stored in the map server and displayed in a static environment, i.e., once generated there is no possibility to change these parameters except by generating a new SLD file for each different map. The SLD construction is often accomplished through direct insertion of the algorithm on the server, usually by means of writing it from a GIS software. The concept of on-demand map symbology is presented here as an algorithm which already possesses variables to build the SLD file to be applied to a map according to users' input, being the file stored in a server folder and read by WMS requisition.

3.2.1. SLD file structure

The file structure for SLD specification is based on rules. These mold the set of styles which symbolize a feature. In choropleth maps, for example, each rule makes it possible to generate a different color value applied to an area feature, resulting from a data classification algorithm. To apply color values to spatial data features, the system's database provides a color table (Figure 6) based on what is suggested by the "Colorbrewer" software (ColorBrewer [20]). Several possible color ramps are stored in the database and their names are then accessed by PHP code, as a list of different options for the user. The fields for the colors table are also designed to make the process of data classification easier. For each class, there is a set of 'x' different *html* colors, 'x' being the number of classes. The field “num_color”, which varies together with the “html_color” value, since the color changes as the number of class elements change, is defined from '1' – to be applied to features contained in first class – to 'x'.

To build the map and construct the SLD file, users have to choose the number of classes, the level of measurement and, if the level of measurement is numeric, the data classification method to be used. These variables are merged to *xml* declarations along the PHP file with a string concatenation operator, and are used in the process of data classification (Figure 7), which defines the final SLD file, written in the server and made a default for the WMS layer, by means of setting the parameter *<IsDefault>1</IsDefault>*. Thus, the map server just serves the WMS layer. The symbology is prepared on the server by PHP code and is accessed directly by the *openlayers* map library to build the map in the client side. It is overwritten automatically when the server executes a new classification method. The iterative process is based on users' choice built in PHP variables, accessing database views. The database can be fed to create as many classes or symbol properties as necessary for users' data needs.

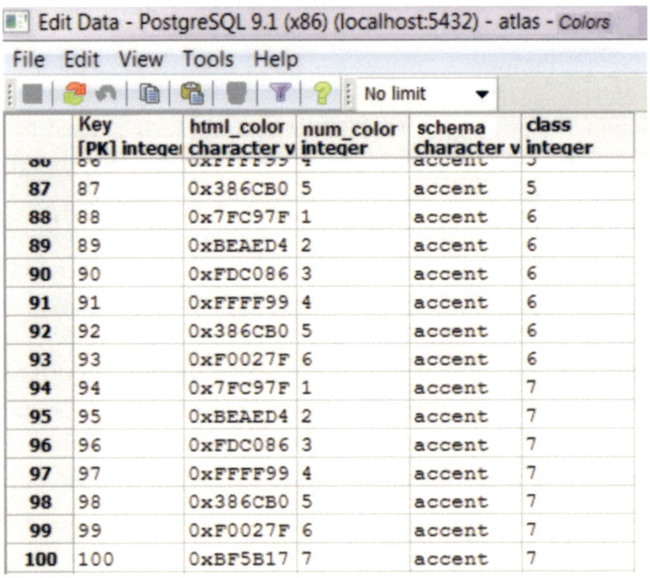

	Key [PK] integer	html_color character v	num_color integer	schema character v	class integer
87	87	0x386CB0	5	accent	5
88	88	0x7FC97F	1	accent	6
89	89	0xBEAED4	2	accent	6
90	90	0xFDC086	3	accent	6
91	91	0xFFFF99	4	accent	6
92	92	0x386CB0	5	accent	6
93	93	0xF0027F	6	accent	6
94	94	0x7FC97F	1	accent	7
95	95	0xBEAED4	2	accent	7
96	96	0xFDC086	3	accent	7
97	97	0xFFFF99	4	accent	7
98	98	0x386CB0	5	accent	7
99	99	0xF0027F	6	accent	7
100	100	0xBF5B17	7	accent	7

Figure 6. Part of color table in the database

3.3. Functionality and interface design

User interaction with a computer system always occurs through the use of an interface. There are several issues about map-related systems and their interface, especially for web use (Nivala [21]), since these interfaces deal with issues related both to computational interfaces and map users and use. Besides that, there are new technologies which allow data organization to be done dynamically, in a way that reduces the amount of decisions and interactions by users, when generating a cartographic representation. This can make interface use easier and also raise performance for functional approaches (de Mendonça & Delazari [22]).

```
<?php
if ($level_measurement=='numeric') //for numeric data only
{
    if ($method== 'equal_int') //Equal Interval data classification method
    {
        $namemethod = 'Equal Interval'; //for legend purposes
        $max_sql = pg_query($connection, "SELECT max($theme) as maximo FROM $SQL_TABLE");
        $min_sql = pg_query($connection, "SELECT min($theme) as minimo FROM $SQL_TABLE");
        $max = pg_fetch_array($max, 0); //maximum theme value
        $min = pg_fetch_array($min, 0); //maximum theme value
        $interval = (($maximo[0]-$minimo[0])/$classes);
        $color_sql = pg_query($connection, "SELECT html_color FROM colors WHERE schema = '$schema'
        and classes = '$classes' and num_color = '1'");
        $color = pg_fetch_array($cor, 0); //color to be used for the first class
        $linferior = $minimo[0];
        $lsuperior = $minimo[0] + $interval;
        //here the Sld is formed. all variables are defined before as strings, cointaning the mandatory
        //elements for a SLD file
        $SLD_EI = $cabecalho . $pre . $rule_beggining . $linferior . "-" . $lsuperior . $rule_quant_1 .
        $theme . $rule_quant_2 . $linferior . $rule_quant_3 . $theme .
        $rule_quant_4 . $lsuperior . $rule_quant_5 . |
        $color[0] .$rule_end;
//'for' iteration, for next classes
        for ($i=2; $i<=$classes ;$i++)
            {
            $j = $i-1;
            $linferior = $min[0] + ($j*$interval);
            $lsuperior = $min[0] + (($i)*$interval);
            $color_sql = pg_query($connection, "SELECT html_color as cor FROM colors WHERE schema =
            '$schema' and classes = '$classes' and num_color= '$i'");
            $color = pg_fetch_array($color_sql, 0);
//using the previously sld, which has the symbol definition for the first element
//the rest of elements are filled in this iteraction, according to the number of classes
            $SLD_EI = $SLD_EI . $rule_beggining . $linferior . "-" . $lsuperior . $rule_quant_1 .
            $theme . $rule_quant_2 . $linferior .  $rule_quant_3 . $theme. $rule_quant_4 . $lsuperior .
            $rule_quant_5 . $color[0] . $rule_end;
            }
            $SLD_EI = $SLD_EI . $closure; //finish the sld file
//from here, sld file is written on server
            $mysld = "testFile.sld";
            $fh = fopen($meusld, 'w') or die ("Cannot creat file, contact webadmin");
            fwrite($fh, $SLD_EI);
            fclose($fh);
    }
}
?>
```

Figure 7. Example for PHP code on Equal Interval Data Classification method

The interface for specialists and atlas' users was planned to be clean and to manage only essential functionality, but since there was a desire to implement an expert system, with a knowledge base fed by specialists, the decision was to make slight changes on functionality, in order to avail specialist knowledge. Thus, specialist users can identify themselves with a login role, in order to contribute to the knowledge database on data classification and symbolization decisions. Users, then, can take advantage of specialists' choices on similar data to make their own decisions. The interface functionalities for this two group of distinct users can be divided by map-interface functions and web interface itself, accessed by login roles: "specialist" and "user".

Inspired by the 'openstreetmap' project interface, the main interface for "Atlas Social do Paraná" (Figure 8) incorporated on its server a javascript map library – *openlayers* – integrated to a window and *css* management *javascript* library – Jquery. Both of them make possible to call predetermined functions to display maps, their symbology and hide or show functional windows on the interface, in which users can input data or make choices about the map production process in terms of forms. Making forms (only one allowed per tab) and the table associated with the chosen theme, available on the same page as the map is then considered a major decision in interface design. Based on this, a small and simple flow that expresses the common use for the website was devised to be followed by both casual users (Figure 9a) and specialists (Figure 9b).

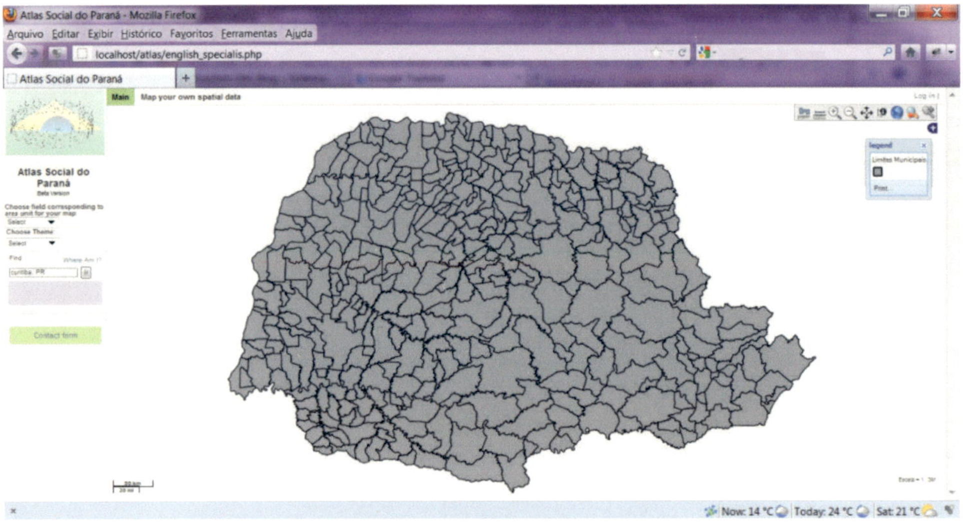

Figure 8. General Initial Atlas interface

3.4. Storing user's own data

One of the main functions of the new Atlas is the ability of reading and storing user's data in the database. Every Atlas page has the option of upload user's spatial data, by using a *html div*, powered by *jquery* (Figure 10). In order to make this possible, it's important to configure the web server to accept uploaded data. In the current Atlas architecture, it is also important to ensure that the PHP installation is able to save temporary uploaded files in a suitable server folder and to allow *Curl* to call *Geoserver Rest API* in order to write the new layer in the map server. All upload and store steps are called by PHP files, included in the main upload form action page. The algorithm to allow user data upload (Figure 11) considers that user's data will be available for 4 hours in the database, when a trigger is activated to clean all new inserted data. After displaying user's data, the system now will use this as default table, to be used for every subsequent query.

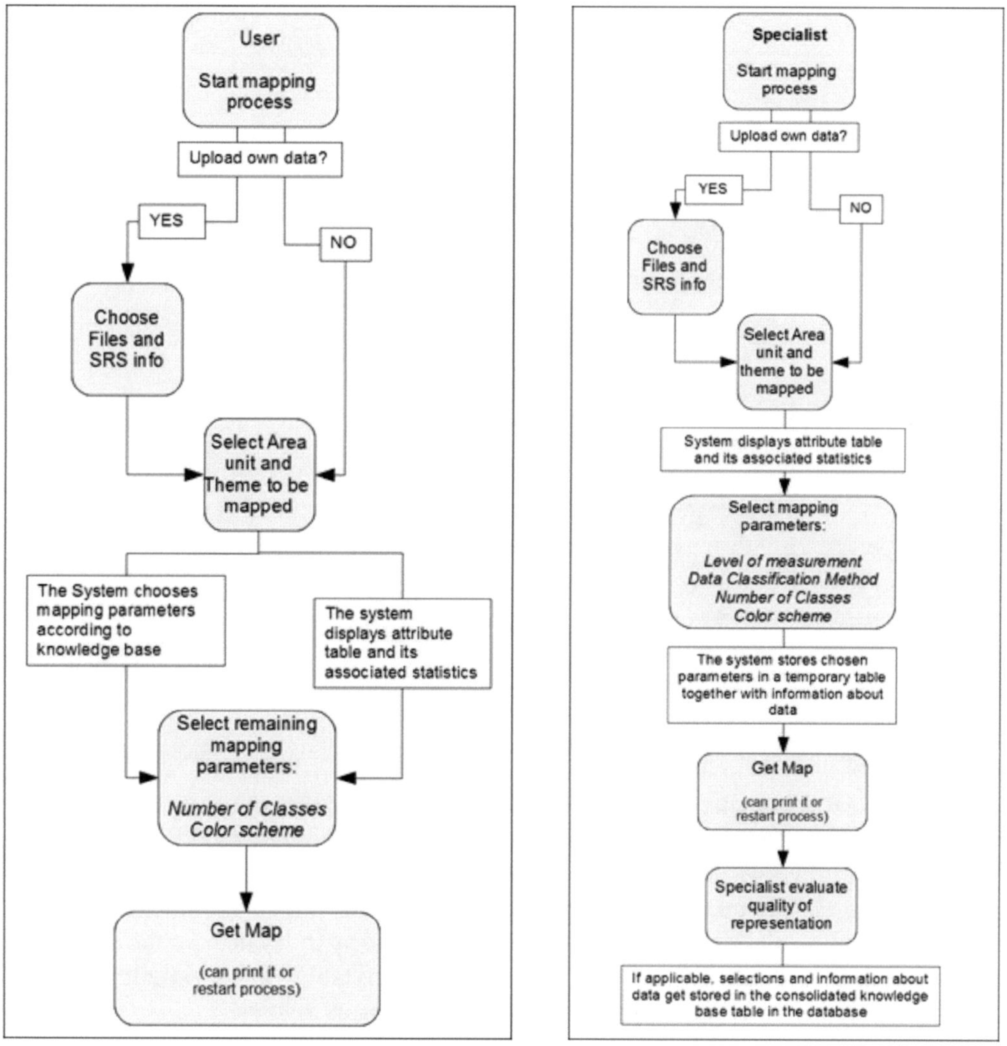

Figure 9. (a - left): Expected interface use flow; (b - right): Expected flow for specialists

3.5. Expert system functionality

The expert system comprises a PHP set of pages which access the database in order to compare specialists' decisions with measurements about the data itself. There is a table in the database that stores every level of measurement decision, data classification method, number of classes and color ramp made by a specialist logged into the website. According to the comparison between what is chosen by them and the data characteristics, it is possible for the system to learn the occurrence of patterns. To learn, in this case, is to store these patterns in the consolidated table of specialists' decisions and using this knowledge base to ordinary users. So, it will often occur when common users upload data that is similar to the ones used by specialists' before.

Figure 10. Detail on the form used to upload *shapefiles*

In order to make this knowledge functional, some metrics are defined for any kind of data uploaded by a user or the Atlas original data. These metrics can be divided among the four possible decisions made by a specialist, plus the final evaluation of the produced map. At least three different specialists must take the same decision, based on relevant data characteristics matching exactly, and transmit the most positive feedback allowed by the system for the built map, in order for a decision to be stored into a consolidated decisions table. At first experimental build, the expert system can learn behavior related to two decisions, as follows.

3.5.1. Level of measurement

For this system, the level of measurement of data is simplified into numeric, ordinal and nominal types. To classify data in one of these three, the expert system needs first to identify the name of the column that stores what has been mapped and the distinct values found in this column. Second, it is important to identify what type of data is being classified, in terms of databases' data types. The system makes the following assumptions:

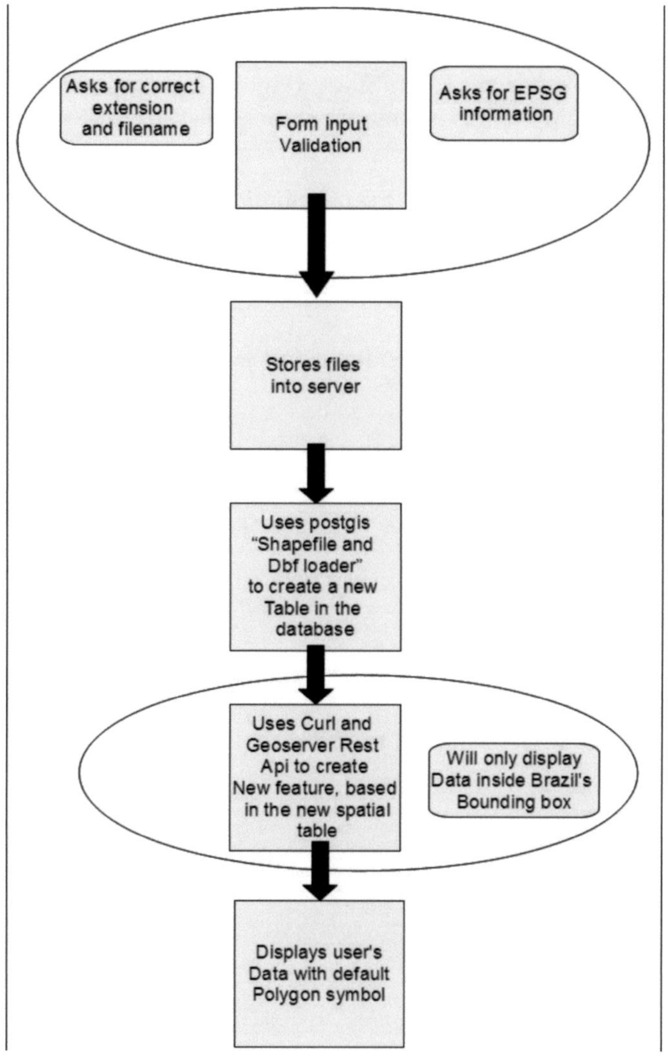

Figure 11. Schema for the algorithm that provide upload and store user's spatial data

- Numerical data are always composed of numeric, integer, float or similar formats;
- Nominal and ordinal data are always text, character varying or other similar formats;
- Numerical data can be stored as text or in a similar format, since when the data is exploded, at least 2 or more characters in the sequence match. When this case occurs, the system should be asked to convert text into numbers, in the user's own database;
- Ordinal data must be compared to the database field corresponding to the knowledge base for the ordinal text group.
- All other cases must be considered as nominal data.

3.5.2. Data classification method

For numerical data only, the expert system measures statistics for the theme data: standard deviation, variance, mean, deviance from mean (Figure 12). These are all taken in order to measure kurtosis (Dent [23]), which is a metric to measure the flatness of a distribution. The following assumptions are considered:

- When kurtosis is between 2.5 and 3.5, the distribution is normal. Equal interval and quintile methods are then suggested to be used;
- When kurtosis is below 2.5, the distribution is considered flat and a standard deviation method is recommended;
- When kurtosis is above 3.5, the distribution is full of peaks. In this case, maximum breaks or Jenks methods fit the data better.

Avg : 67,9767| Std. Deviation: 105,5881| Variance: 11148,8390

State	Pop_Density (hab/km²)	Deviance
Acre	4.8	-63,1767
Alagoas	112.39	44,4133
Amazonas	4.68	-63,2967
Amapa	2.21	-65,7667
Bahia	24.83	-43,1467
Ceara	56.76	-11,2167
Distrito Federal	441.74	373,7633
Espirito Santo	76.23	8,2533
Goias	17.65	-50,3267
Maranhao	19.78	-48,1967
Minas Gerais	3.36	-64,6167
Mato Grosso do Sul	6.85	-61,1267
Mato Grosso	33.4	-34,5767
Para	52.37	-15,6067
Paraiba	66.74	-1,2367
Pernambuco	6.08	-61,8967
Piaui	89.47	21,4933
Parana	12.4	-55,5767
Rio de Janeiro	366.01	298,0333
Rio Grande do Norte	60	-7,9767
Rondonia	37.96	-30,0167
Roraima	6.56	-61,4167
Rio Grande do Sul	2.01	-65,9667
Santa Catarina	65.54	-2,4367
Sergipe	94.38	26,4033
Sao Paulo	166.19	98,2133
Tocantins	4.98	-62,9967

Kurtosis : 8.2466865045365

Figure 12. Example of generated theme table and associated statistics

3.5.3. Feedback on map quality

This is simply asking the specialist: "How would you classify the quality of the representation generated?" Answers can vary from 0 to 10, and only higher grades should be assumed as maps that should have their decisions against data to be considered as knowledge base. Using this metric will ensure that the consolidated table has only the best representations, according to specialists.

Based on results, there are important remarks about the proposed interface design and code implementation. First, user testing is part of the development process, and only doing it can ensure the interface acceptability and usability. However, the proposed framework provides clear step-by-step guidance in order to allow users to produce thematic maps. First informal pre-tests show that the interface has no usability gaps and that the expert system suggestions seems to be an desirable aid, especially for those unfamiliar with cartography and map production environments. Second, there are known limitations on this first web version. In production environments, this software must allow DBMS configuration for multiple database access. Also SLD specification needs to be improved to support more complex mapping techniques. Last, more research on which information about data could be analyzed in order to define more adequate criteria for the system's decisions.

4. Conclusion and further work

An expert system development should consider the subject particularities. In the case of maps, use and users are mandatory issues to be taken into account when designing data storage and analysis and also the way to interact with them. The presented ES can manage not only the LOAS data, users and framework, but is now designed to cover an unpredictable amount of uses, since users can upload and analyze their own data. The system's interface was also carefully discussed in order to present to users the most practical and simple way to interact with complex map design decisions. Usability pre-tests have been carried out, and current feedback is positive.

After testing this first version of the online Atlas, it is intended to develop additional functionalities in order to improve the expert system concept that has been started with this research, as well as the interface use experience. The main objective is to make this system a reference, not only for LOAS technicians but also for ordinary internet users who need to get their data symbolized according to map design expertise.

Currently, users have the option to upload their own data, both geometry and attributes. There is work in progress for the system to recognize if the mapping method is suitable for the data characteristics. One aspect that can be discussed, regarding the analysis of numeric data types, is a mapping technique chosen against relative or absolute data. Here, absolute data are considered those not related to any other data, e.g. people counting; relative data are related to any other data and can be related to area units, e.g. population density. Besides the importance of this classification, there is no formal way to discover if data are absolute or relative. A possible solution for this problem could be to ask the user a set of questions in order to verify this information. After this questionnaire, the system would suggest the most suitable method for data classification and, consequently, the choice of mapping technique.

Another issue that has to be considered is the number of classes. This first version allows the user (with no distinction between common users and specialists) to choose this parameter without restriction. However, this is an important decision that can affect map understanding and legibility, since it can mask the whole distribution, given the number of elements per class and the relationship among the theme elements. To prevent incorrect choices, it is necessary also that system suggests to users a suitable number of classes. This parameter is then decided considering the number of elements in the raw data, i.e., the number of elements in the sample and their metrics, as median or standard deviation.

Acknowledgments

This work was funded by CNPq (The National Council for Scientific and Technological Development, grant n. 306862/2011-5).

Author details

Luciene Stamato Delazari[1*], André Luiz Alencar de Mendonça[1], João Vitor Meza Bravo[1], Mônica Cristina de Castro[1], Pâmela Andressa Lunelli[1], Marcio Augusto Reolon Schmidt[2] and Maria Engracinda dos Santos Ferreira[3]

1 Federal University of Parana, Geodetic Science Program, Curitiba, Paraná, Brazil

2 Federal University of Uberlândia, Brazil

3 Federal Institute of Sergipe, Brazil

References

[1] Expert system to classify semantic information to improve map design. In: The World's Geo-Spatial Solutions: Proceedings of the 24th International Cartographic Conference, ICA/ICC2009, Santiago, Chile.

[2] Delazari, L. S. Modelagem e implementação de um Atlas Eletrônico Interativo utilizando métodos de visualização cartográfica. Ph D Thesis. Escola Politécnica da Universidade de São Paulo- Departamento de Engenharia de Transportes. São Paulo: (2004).

[3] Fairbain, D. J. The Frontier of cartography: mapping a changing discipline. Photogrammetric Record (1994). , 14(84), 903-915.

[4] Yufen, C. Visual cognition experiments on electronic maps. In: Proceedings of the 19th International Cartographic Conference, ICA, (1999). Ottawa, Canada.

[5] Wang, Z., & Ormeling, F. (1996). The representation of quantitative and ordinal information. *The Cartographic Journal*, 33(2), 87-91.

[6] Artimo, K. The bridge between cartographic and geographic information systems. In: MacEachren, A.M.; Taylor, D.R.F (ed). Visualization in modern cartography. Grã-Bretanha: Pergamon, (1994). , 45-61.

[7] Su, B. A. Generalized frame for cartographic knowledge representation. In: Proceedings of the 17th International Cartographic Conference, ICA, (1995). Barcelona, Spain.

[8] Zhan, F. R., & Buttenfield, B. P. Object-oriented knowledge-based symbol selection for visualizing statistical information. International Journal of Geographic Information Systems (1995). , 9(3), 293-315.

[9] Chee, W. J., Power, M. A., Expert, Systems., & Maintainability, . Reliabity and Maintainability Symposium. In: Proceedings of IEEE. (1990).

[10] Hemingway, D. E., Katzberg, J. D., & Vandenberghe, D. G. A. Technology Management Methodology Implemented Using Expert Systems. In: Proceedings of Conference on Communications, Power and Computing- WESCANEX 97, (1997). Winnipeg.

[11] Ciência da Informação ; 26(1). Available from: http://www.scielo.br/scielo.php?script=sci_arttext&pid=S &lng=en&nrm=isoaccessed 24 October 2006)

[12] Araki, H. Fusão de informações espectrais, altimétrica e de dados auxiliares na classificação de imagens de alta resolução especiaesis PhD Thesis. Federal University of Paraná. Curitiba; (2005).

[13] Russell, S. J.; Norvig, P. Artificial intelligence: a modern approach. New Jersey: Prentice-Hall, 1995.

[14] Casner, S. M. A. Task-Analytic Approach to the Automated Design of Graphic Presentations. ACM Transactions on Graphics (TOG) archive (1991). , 10(2), 111-151.

[15] Roth, S. F., Kolojejchick, J., Mattis, J., & Goldstein, J. Interactive Graphic Design Using Automatic Presentation Knowledge. In: Conference on Human Factors in Computing Systems, (1994). Boston, Massachusetts.

[16] Senay, H., & Ignatius, E. A Knowledge-Based System For Visualization Design Computer Graphics And Applications. IEEE(1994). , 14(6), 36-47.

[17] Fraunhofer Institute for Intelligent Analysis and Information Systems IAIS. (2012). http://http://www.iais.fraunhofer.de/index.php?id=1863&L=1 (accessed 12 March 2012).

[18] Anselin, L., Syabri, I., & Kho, Y. (2004). GeoDa: An Introduction to Spatial Data Analysis. GeoDa Center for Geospatial Analysis and Computation. College of Liberal Arts and Sciences. Available at: https://geodacenter.asu.edu/research/publications (accessed in 24 November 2007).

[19] Official documentation of geoserver project.http://docs.geoserver.org/.accessed in 25 June (2012).

[20] ColorBrewer 2.0. http://colorbrewer2.org/ (accessed in 17May (2012).

[21] Nivala, A. M. Usability Perspectives for the Design of Interactive Maps. PhD Thesis, Department of Computer Science and Engineering, Helsinki University of Technology, Helsinki, Finland; (2007).

[22] de Mendonça, A. L. A., & Delazari, L. S. Remote Evaluation of the Execution of Spatial Analysis Tasks with Interactive Web Maps: A Functional and Quantitative Approach. Cartographic Journal, The, February (2012). , 49(1), 7-20.

[23] Dent, B. D. (1999). Cartography: Thematic Map Design. WCB McGraw-Hill. Nova York, EUA.

Chapter 11

Towards Developing a Decision Support System for Electricity Load Forecast

Connor Wright, Christine W. Chan and Paul Laforge

Additional information is available at the end of the chapter

http://dx.doi.org/10.5772/51306

1. Introduction

Short-term load forecasting (STLF) is an essential procedure for effective and efficient real-time operations planning and control of generation within a power system. It provides the basis for unit-commitment and power system planning procedures, maintenance scheduling, system security assessment, and trading schedules. It establishes the generation, capacity, and spinning reserve schedules which are posted to the market. Without optimal load forecasts, additional expenses due to uneconomic dispatch, over/under purchasing, and reliability uncertainty can cost a utility millions of dollars [1].

Many approaches have been considered for STLF. The benefits of increased computational power and data storage have enhanced the capabilities of artificial intelligence methods for data analysis within the power industry [1]. Yet, even with the advancements of technology, industry forecasts are often based on a traditional similar day forecasting methodology or rigid statistical models with reduced variable modifiers for forecasting aggregated system load.

Power systems with a large spatial presence provide an increased challenge for load forecasters, as they often face large diversity within their load centres as well as diverse weather conditions. These geographically separated load centres often behave independently and add considerable complexity to the system dynamics and forecasting procedure.

This chapter investigates forecasting of electrical demand at an electric utility within the province of Saskatchewan, Canada and proposes a multi-region load forecasting system based on weather-related demand variables. The control area examined consists of over 157,000 kilometres of power lines with transmission voltages of 72, 138, and 230KV. The control area was apportioned into twelve load centres, consisting primarily of conforming loads. These conforming loads were cities and rural load clusters not including large industrial customers. Their demand profile conforms to seasonal and weather influences and, thus, maybe referred to as conforming loads.

The chapter is organized as follows: Section 2 introduces the current load forecasting system used at this utility and describes challenges associated with developing a new decision support system. Section 3 discusses the weather diversity of the load centres and the load-weather patterns observed. Section 4 presents the load diversity analysis of the load centres. Section 5 identifies the methodology of the research as well as the load forecasting models examined, which consist of (1) a similar day aggregate model developed in conjunction with the utility's load forecasting experts, (2) an ANN aggregate model, and (3) an ANN multi-region model. Section 6 describes the modelling processes and the performance evaluation methods. Section 7 presents the case study of predicting the hourly energy consumption throughout the 2011 year. The predicted results generated from each of the three models are also presented, which demonstrate the superior performance of the proposed multi-region load forecasting system over the aggregate load forecasting models. Section 8 presents some conclusions on the models examined.

2. Development and Implementation Challenges

Electric demand forecasting is a daily procedure required for efficient and effective grid operations, North American Electric Reliability Corporation (NERC) compliance, and planning procedures. The current practice of making forecasts typically involves system operators manually generating the forecast using similar day-based methodologies. The forecast methods vary depending on the individual operator, and hence are highly inconsistent. There is a tacit reluctance to embrace new technology among operators and the adoption of any new tools, such as decision support systems, would not happen unless they have passed stringent benchmarking criteria and scrutiny. The challenges in developing and implementing a new forecasting system are described in this section.

2.1. Load Forecasting Overview

Load forecasting is the science of predicting human energy usage in response to externalities. It is an essential procedure for effective and efficient real-time operations planning and control of generation within a power system. It provides the basis for unit-commitment and power system planning procedures (such as generation commitment schemes, contingency planning procedures, and temporary operating guidelines), maintenance scheduling, system security assessment (identifying stability concerns with unit-commitment and maintenance schemes), and trading schedules (market-posted generation/interconnection plans). It establishes the generation, capacity, and spinning reserve schedules which are posted to the market. Without optimal load forecasts, additional expenses due to uneconomic dispatch, over/under purchasing, and reliability uncertainty can cost a utility millions of dollars. A one percent reduction in load forecast uncertainty can mean the difference between forecasting an energy emergency or efficient system operation. Therefore a reduction in load forecast uncertainty provides considerable economic, reliability, and planning benefits [2].

Electric load is the demand for electricity by a population, which results from cultural and economic biases and is influenced by externalities [3]. Common drivers for electric loads include: end use relationships (appliances, industries, etc.); time of day; weather; and econometric data.

The accuracy of the predicted demand can impact a variety of power systems operations, such as:

- The dispatch plan of generation units may not be optimal, resulting in economic losses.
- Energy trading schedules may miss advantageous purchasing or selling options.
- Maintenance scheduling may suffer missed opportunities for preventative maintenance.
- System security may misidentify system stability on prospective generation plans.

Since electrical energy cannot yet be efficiently stored in bulk quantities, reliable forecasts are essential to provide efficient scheduling for an electric utility. The increasing regulatory presence in the electricity industry places increased importance on the need for accurate and efficient demand forecasting [4].

Load forecasting is traditionally divided into three categories: long term forecasts, predicting several months to several years into the future; medium term forecasts, predicting one or more weeks into the future; and short term forecasts, predicting several minutes to one week into the future. The focus of this chapter is on short term load forecasting.

Short term load forecasting is conducted not only for efficient operations and planning, but also to comply with regulations imposed by NERC. These forecasts predict either power demand, for real-time forecasting or peak forecasting in megawatts, or energy demand, for hourly or daily forecasting in megawatt-hours. Regardless of the class of load forecasting model utilized, understanding the relationship between electric demand and forecast drivers is essential for providing accurate and reproducible load forecasts.

Recent findings from NERC's Load Forecasting Working Group have identified substantial inconsistencies in forecasting methodologies such that the reported data are not comparable [4]. While it is difficult to standardize forecasting methods across all regions, NERC has encouraged the collection and reporting of load data to include greater detail with respect to demand-side management in terms of regional diversity factors and non-member loads in forecasts. These suggestions indicated weaknesses in current practices of load forecast reporting, specifically, consideration for regional diversity and mixed aggregation methods were acknowledged as high-priority issues.

2.2. Existing Industry Model

Within the utility examined, load forecasting has been conducted based on a similar day aggregate load model, which was constructed based on expert knowledge elicited from operators, engineers, and/or analysts. The model supports forecasting future demand by comparing the demand of historically similar days. It exploits common electric load periodicity of three fundamental frequencies: (1) diurnal, in which the minima are found in the early morning and midday and maxima at mid-morning and evening; (2) weekly, in which demand is lowest during the weekends and approximately the same from Tuesday to Thursday; and (3) seasonal, in which heating and cooling needs increase electrical demand during the winter and summer months [5]. Furthermore, holidays and special events are treated as aberrant occurrences and modelled separately. These periodic load behaviours were analyzed and provided the basis for a sequence of representative days, which are adjusted for load growth and predicted weather phenomena.

The model consists of three components: base load, weather-influenced load, and special load. Base load considers the minimal load experienced throughout a day: an example of a base load application is lighting systems, whose usage is determined by the time of day. Weather-influenced load is the specific deviation from the averaged climactic conditions of the historically representative days. Common weather-influenced load typically pertains to heating and cooling devices such as furnaces and air conditioners. Special load includes the residual load use unaccounted for in the other load categories and is the most difficult to model. For example, special loads include the use of Christmas lights in winter or the outage of a major industrial customer. The weather-influenced loads usually rely on temperature variables, but a variety of forecast approaches exist from utility to utility [4].

Similar day models for load forecasting are often preferred for their simplicity. Operators are able to construct a forecast without a custom-made interface and manipulate data to examine the sensitivity of the system to simulated changes in weather. The models tend to be intuitive to even the most novice operators and can be easily adjusted when unforeseen weather changes occur.

While simple and easy-to-construct, similar day models are often poor at reflecting diversity among regional load forecasts. The diversity of metering infrastructure complicates this model's accuracy as behind-the-meter generation often involves an aggregate estimate. This aggregate estimate ignores specific load details which may be unavailable. Furthermore, similar day models tend to use actual loads instead of weather-normalized loads; thereby reducing the ability of the model to predict electrical usage in a diverse weather environment. An additional weakness of the approach is that load uncertainty is difficult to model. Uncertainty in metering cannot be assessed as system load is an aggregate calculation and masks individual metering errors.

Despite the massive advancements of technology, many power utilities have yet to embrace the new opportunities available in enhanced metering, process automation, and control schemes based on artificial intelligence techniques. Within the grid control centre, short term load forecasting remains a manual procedure, which makes use of similar day-based models for aggregate load forecasting. Every day the tagging desk operator manually prepares a day-ahead forecast, which consists of hourly electric demand forecasts. The operator can use weather forecasts for multiple regions, or forecast as many as four major load regions to produce an aggregate system load. When a complete forecast has been generated, it is compared against similar competing models. The power system supervisor selects the best model based on his or her subjective criteria, and the forecast is posted to the market. Figure 1 illustrates the procedure of STLF based on the traditional similar day model. The operator accesses the historical loads database, runs a pre-processing command to normalize the loads (e.g. by eliminating factors of load growth year-over-year), filters the dataset according to weather variables and load modifiers, and applies data transforms and regression analysis to the dataset filtered by operator-selected input dates. Finally, the output forecast is produced.

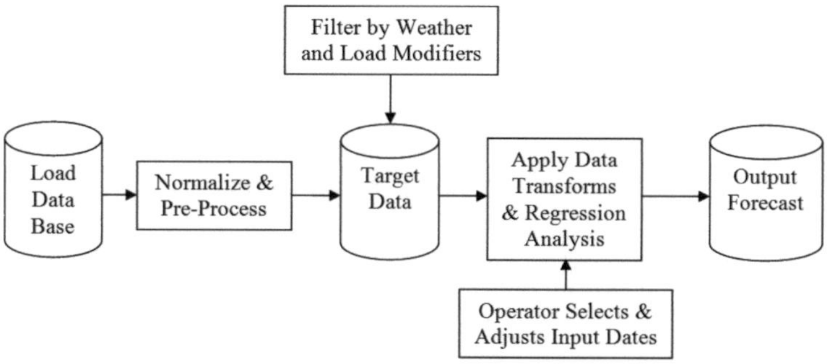

Figure 1. Traditional Similar Day Procedure.

Grid personnel tend to be reluctant to adopt new tools or models due to the long-standing process for creation and evaluation of forecasts. It seems that a surprisingly high-degree of statistical accuracy and simulation evidence is required for grid personnel to consider implementation of new models. Hence, a central challenge in developing a new load forecasting model is to supply substantial evidence to support its claims of accuracy, which is not limited to model performance. In this chapter, we propose that empirical evidence to support the case for multi-region forecasts is essential for grid operations personnel to adopt new modelling techniques. This evidence for the weather and load diversity in the control area will be presented in sections 3 and 4, while section 7 will provide evidence in terms of assessment results on model performance for the case study.

3. Analysis of Regional Weather

Given its large geographic area, northerly latitude, and distance from any major body of water, the province of Saskatchewan is prone to considerable weather diversity. The province transitions its climates from humid continental in the south to subarctic in the north. Precipitation patterns vary considerably, typically decreasing from northeast to southwest. The summers are hot and dry while the winters are frigid.

Wind chill statistics for each of the twelve load centres examined in this chapter were analyzed and compared. Regional weather data were recorded and analyzed from January 2005 to November 2011. Sufficient weather diversity was identified within the analysis for all the load centres to warrant adopting a multi-region approach to modelling. Thirteen weather variables were analyzed, which included: temperature (°C), relative humidity (%), pressure (millibars), wind direction (compass degrees), wind speed (km/hr), wind gust (km/hr), cloud cover (%), normal cloud cover (%), cloud ceiling (metres), visibility (km), low-lying cloud coverage (%), middle-lying cloud coverage (%), and high-lying cloud coverage (%). Based on sensitivity and statistical analysis conducted independently on the thirteen quantitative weather variables, only the variables of temperature, humidity, and wind speed were identified as statistically significant factors for explaining load variation due to weather. These three variables were included in the prediction models and the other weather-related variables were ignored because insignificant improvement was found from their inclusion in the model.

3.1. The Weather of Saskatchewan

Saskatchewan is a land-locked prairie province, bordered east and west by the provinces of Manitoba and Alberta, respectively. Its northern border connects with that of the Northwest Territories and its southern border is divided between the American states of Montana and North Dakota. Saskatchewan is a land of geographic diversity.

Containing an area of 651,900 square kilometres [6], Saskatchewan is immense. Much of Saskatchewan lies within the Great Plains and Interior Plains regions of North America, which comprise nearly half of the area of Saskatchewan, while the Canadian Shield dominates the northern half of the province.

Over 52% of Saskatchewan is covered by boreal forest, largely in the north, while arable land in the south represents roughly half of Saskatchewan's total land area [6]. Due to its geography and location, Saskatchewan is further differentiated by its climate.

The dominant climates of Saskatchewan include: semi-arid in the southwest, humid continental in the south and central, and sub-arctic in the north [6]. The south is typically drier and the north is typically colder. Due to its northern location, distance from any major bodies of water, and relatively flat topography, Saskatchewan has a radical climate.

Summers are hot and short, though temperatures exceeding 32°C are not uncommon during the day, but the nights may quickly cool to near freezing. Humidity decreases from northeast to southwest due to the pacific westerlies. Winters are cold and long; often temperatures do not exceed -17°C for weeks at a time. The average summer temperature for the cities of Saskatchewan see highs of 25°C and lows of 11°C; while the average winter highs and lows are -12°C and -23°C respectively [6].

3.2. Weather-Diversity Analysis

To assess weather-diversity across Saskatchewan, climactic differences across the regions examined were empirically identified. Wind chill statistics for each of the twelve load centres were analyzed and compared. Table 1 contrasts the mean, maximum, and minimum temperatures observed in each of the load centres throughout the period of investigation, which is from January 2005 to December 2011.

http://dx.doi.org/10.5772/51306

Region Code	Mean (°C)	Maximum (°C)	Minimum (°C)
Area01	-1.48	36.66	-53.88
Area02	-1.59	36.89	-52.77
Area03	-1.48	36.53	-53.89
Area04	-1.52	34.46	-51.66
Area05	0.11	38.33	-50.23
Area06	-1.58	36.61	-52.85
Area07	-1.67	35.09	-51.11
Area08	2.56	41.66	-46.66
Area09	-2.68	33.89	-52.22
Area10	-2.65	33.88	-52.28
Area11	-1.51	34.44	-52.77
Area12	-2.04	32.77	-52.23
Regional Average	-1.29	35.93	-51.87

Table 1. Wind Chill Temperature Statistics Across Load Centres.

	Summer Average Daily Wind Chill		Winter Average Daily Wind Chill	
Region Code	**Max (°C)**	**Min (°C)**	**Max (°C)**	**Min (°C)**
Area01	18.77	5.05	-11.11	-23.92
Area02	19.66	4.68	-11.21	-24.75
Area03	19.87	5.02	-11.38	-24.95
Area04	17.71	4.83	-10.51	-23.21
Area05	20.35	5.69	-8.56	-21.47
Area06	20.71	4.14	-11.17	-24.53
Area07	18.38	5.98	-11.87	-23.92
Area08	22.84	7.84	-5.26	-18.89
Area09	16.70	7.04	-13.32	-25.16
Area10	17.16	6.88	-13.45	-25.05
Area11	19.52	5.85	-11.81	-24.91
Area12	17.06	4.28	-11.25	-23.01
Regional Average	19.06	5.61	-10.89	-23.64

Table 2. Average Daily Wind Chill Temperatures During Summer and Winter Months (Jan. 2005 – Nov. 2011).

It can be observed from the dataset that the regions experience different weather conditions at different times such that the temperature distributions and the variances in temperature are not the same. Table 2 lists the seasonal average daily variation of wind chill temperatures experienced by each of the twelve load centres during the period of investigation from January 2005 to December 2011. Significant temperature variation exists among the twelve regions and individual load centres experience a considerable range of temperatures in an average day.

Thus, it can be seen from Tables 1 and 2 that the weather experienced in each of the twelve regions vary considerably. Weather diversity was evidenced by the seasonal differences, daily wind chill ranges, and distribution of wind chill temperatures among the regions. The evidence for weather diversity supports our proposal for the development of a multi-region model.

4. Analysis of Load-Diversity

Since load centres in diverse regions experience different weather conditions throughout a day, the electrical demands of these load centres, which are dependent on weather, also vary. Hence, the electricity demand of the load centres cannot be analyzed with a single aggregate model. Instead, the aggregate demand for electricity is best explained using multi-region modelling. This section presents an analysis of the twelve conforming load centres and weather data of the control region.

4.1. Aggregate and Multi-Region Load Modelling

The two approaches for developing load forecasting models include building aggregate models and multi-region models. An aggregate model does not differentiate between load sectors or physical locations. The strength of this approach is that it provides better analysis for load growth trends and is easier to use. An aggregate model performs well for a small geographic area which can include dense and undifferentiated load categories, such as in a suburb. This model type does not support assessing where and when electrical demand will occur throughout the system. As a consequence, aggregate models do not provide adequate inputs for analysis of grid integrity, and statistical modifiers are often applied on the model outputs so as to provide an average assessment of system response [7].

A multi-region model offers a more discrete analysis for distinct loads or load clusters. This model type is useful for large geographic areas where regionalized load profile trends differ considerably, which often results from economic or weather diversity within the forecast area. The benefit of these models is their ability to provide higher resolution prediction results within the grid, contributing to analysis of grid integrity. However multi-region models are more difficult to construct and operate, as the number of inputs grows with each additional region to the model. Irrespective of whether the aggregate or multi-region approach is adopted, constructing a load forecasting model involves considerations of four aspects: trend, cyclicality, seasonality, and a random white noise error [8].

http://dx.doi.org/10.5772/51306

To illustrate the load diversity among the regions, the region code, average load, and peak load for the twelve load centres from the period of January 2005 to December 2011 are listed in Table 3.

Region Code	Average Load (MW-hour)	Peak Load (MW-minute)
Area01	205.73	345
Area02	181.46	349
Area03	35.59	60
Area04	36.54	71
Area05	36.48	67
Area06	71.33	221
Area07	25.34	45
Area08	23.86	65
Area09	17.04	74
Area10	14.23	65
Area11	43.93	154
Area12	9.44	16
Aggregate System Load	700.97	1154

Table 3. Region Code, Average Load, and Peak Load (January 2005 to December 2011).

It can be seen from Table 3 that the peak load for most load centres tends to be twice the average load, which indicates that considerable load swings are possible within each load centre. The aggregate load model approach would not be able to represent the possible load swings within each centre.

To demonstrate the seasonal trends in electricity demand of the load centres, the hourly aggregate electricity demands of the load centres over four years are shown in Figure 2. In this figure, it can be seen that these seasonal patterns correspond to periodic daily, weekly, and monthly variations. Peaks are found in the winter and summer months, while troughs are found in the spring and autumn months. Limited load growth is found during this period, but a considerable variance is possible within each season, which usually results from significant weather diversity.

The dark black line in Figure 2 indicates the seasonal trends of the system. Peaks are found in the winter and summer months and troughs in spring and autumn. These seasonal patterns correspond to periodic daily, weekly, and monthly variation. Limited load growth is found during this period, but a considerable variance is possible within each season, which usually results from considerable weather diversity.

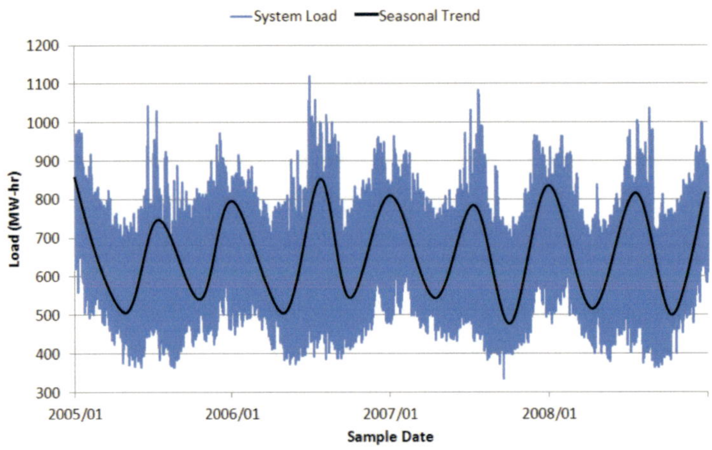

Figure 2. Hourly Aggregate Electricity Demands of Load Centres from January 1, 2005 to December 31, 2008.

4.2. Regional Peaking Responses Versus System Peaking Response

Demand for electricity is not static and varies according to a multitude of variables. Load centres will peak at certain periods during the day, usually conforming to business cycle and weather-related influences. The system peak response is the aggregate peak of the values of all the load centres within a control area, which may occur at a different time from the peak response of an individual load centre. A significant difference in peak response between regions and the system constitutes evidence for a diverse load environment. This evidence can provide motivation for the development of multi-region models.

To determine whether the observed load swings of the studied load centres occurred within the same time frame of the aggregate system response, the coincidence factor C [7, 9] is adopted, which is defined as,

$$C = \frac{\sum_i P_i}{P_A} \tag{1}$$

Where, P_i is the peak load of a single load centre, and P_A is the system peak load.

The coincidence factor describes the degree of discrepancy between regional peaking responses versus system peaking response. If C is greater than 1 and continues to appreciate across an increasing timeline, the load centres peak at different times than the aggregate system load, which provides evidence for the existence of load diversity among the regions. If C is greater than 1 but remains consistent, an aggregate model can be used to accurately predict load swings. In a somewhat consistent or non-diverse system, C will oscillate about 0 and a multi-region model is likely to be of little value in predicting load swings.

http://dx.doi.org/10.5772/51306

The load diversity among the twelve load centres was calculated by comparing the peak load of each load centre to the system peak load across an increasing time interval: beginning with a daily peak to a thirty-one day peak for the period of January 1, 2011 to January 31, 2011. The results of this calculation are shown in Figure 3.

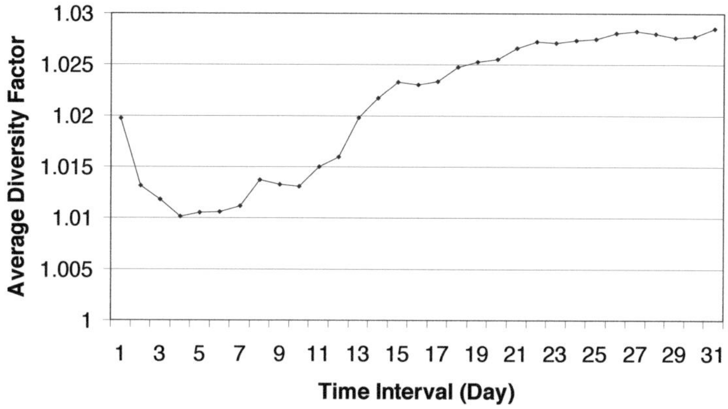

Figure 3. Average Load Diversity Factor Applied to an Increasing Time Interval (January 1, 2011 to January 31, 2011).

It can be seen from Figure 3 that the results of the diversity factor calculation are greater than 1 and its value increases over greater calculation time intervals. Both facts provide evidence for the existence of load diversity amongst the load centres examined. Considering the data presented in Table 3 and Figure 3, it is reasonable to conclude significant load diversity exists throughout the control region. Therefore, both the weather and load diversity observed within the control area provide justification for the development of multi-region forecasting models. The performance of both aggregate and multi-region models will be statistically benchmarked to identify the best model type and structure for STLF in Saskatchewan.

5. Load Forecasting Models

Three load forecasting models were developed: (1) Similar Day Aggregate Load Model, (2) ANN Aggregate Load Model, and (3) ANN Multi-Region Load Model. The similar day aggregate load model provides the industry benchmark. The ANN aggregate load model serves as the baseline to show the performance enhancement achieved by the ANN approach. The ANN multi-region load model demonstrates the performance enhancement achieved by the multi-region approach. All models were evaluated according to the same performance evaluation methods, which will be described in section 6. The models were tested with the same case study, which will be presented in section 7. A comparison of the characteristics of the models is presented in Table 4 and a comparison of the input variables to the models is presented in Table 5. The research methodology and modelling process for each of the three models will be described in this section.

Model Name	Model Type	Methodology	Model Output	Training Type
Aggregate Similar Day Model	Similar Day	Aggregate	Aggregate electrical demand	Knowledge Discovery in Databases
Aggregate ANN Model	ANN	Aggregate	Aggregate electrical demand	Supervised training
Multi-Region ANN Model	ANN	Multi-Region	Aggregate electrical demand	Supervised training

Table 4. Summary of Model Properties and Methodologies.

		Area01	Area02	Area03	Area04	Area05	Area06	Area07	Area08	Area09	Area10	Area11	Area12	System
Aggregate Similar Day	**Past Hour Load**													X
	Air Temp.	X	X											
	Rel. Humidity													
	Wind Speed													
Aggregate ANN	**Past Hour Load**													X
	Air Temp.	X	X											
	Rel. Humidity	X	X											
	Wind Speed	X	X											
Multi-Region ANN	**Past Hour Load**	X	X	X	X	X	X	X	X	X	X	X	X	
	Air Temp.	X	X	X	X	X	X	X	X	X	X	X	X	
	Rel. Humidity	X	X	X	X	X	X	X	X	X	X	X	X	
	Wind Speed	X	X	X	X	X	X	X	X	X	X	X	X	

Table 5. Summary of Model Inputs.

5.1. Development of a Similar Day Model

The domain expertise for this research project was drawn from the grid control operating staff of the Saskatchewan utility, including the power system supervisors, capacity management engineers, and system operators. They were consulted to identify load patterns, select predictive parameters, and assist in development and pre-processing of both the load and weather datasets.

The load history of the control area and temperature variables from Area01 and Area02 are the generalized inputs to the automated similar day model. These variables are used as index for searching a Supervisory Control and Data Acquisition (SCADA) database to obtain the best-fit days, weighted according to the temporal distance from the forecasted day. Most similar day models are aggregated load models, driven by one or more regional temperature forecasts, typically corresponding to the weather of the largest load centres. They do not require training data in the sense that the model learns automatically. Instead the system combines historical data with expert predictions. Figure 1 illustrates the traditional forecast procedure based on the similar day model.

After consultation with experts including system operators and capacity management engineers, a similar day-based load forecasting model was developed. An examination of the hourly observations of system load over the period of 2005 – 2010 revealed that the data patterns can be summarized into four day types. The four day types with their associated electric demand behaviour and external influencing variables were represented in a parameterized rule base, shown in Table 6. This rule base can be used in conjunction with a database that consists of parameter values derived from the SCADA database so as to obtain the best-fit days, weighted according to the temporal distance from the target day for which the load is predicted. The weather variables were further subjected to sensitivity analysis to quantify each parameter's influence on the aggregate load. The sensitivity analysis served to confirm significances of the parameters identified by the experts and the less significant ones were omitted from the input dataset.

Data Module	Controller Module	View Module
Updates and processes knowledge databases; Communicates with SCADA database, updating data entries and database filtering; Responds to data requests issued by controller module with ADO Recordset; and Pre-filters data requests initiated by controller module.	Provides interface between user and data module; Accepts input from user; Translates user forecast queries into well-formatted SQL, which is then sent to the data module; Instructs data module and view to perform actions based on user input; Initiates data requests to the data module; Retrieves data from the data module; Negotiates weighting of best-fit days with the data module through parameterized rule base; Transforms data from data module and sends results to the view module; and Creates, opens, closes, and deletes projects.	Receives data and commands from the controller module; Modifies the user interface to accommodate new data or applications requested by the user; and Acts as the graphical user interface, while hiding non-essential information from the user.

Table 6. Functions of Similar Day System Modules.

The input variables filtered the dataset to select normalized aggregate load which was further modified to correspond with the user-defined load pattern logic. The load pattern logic was generalized from the parameterized rule base. The implemented similar day model consists of three modules: data, control, and view. The functions of the similar day modules are listed in Table 6, while Figure 4 provides a screenshot of the application as viewed by the user through the view module. An example of the similar day model rule base is provided in Figure 5.

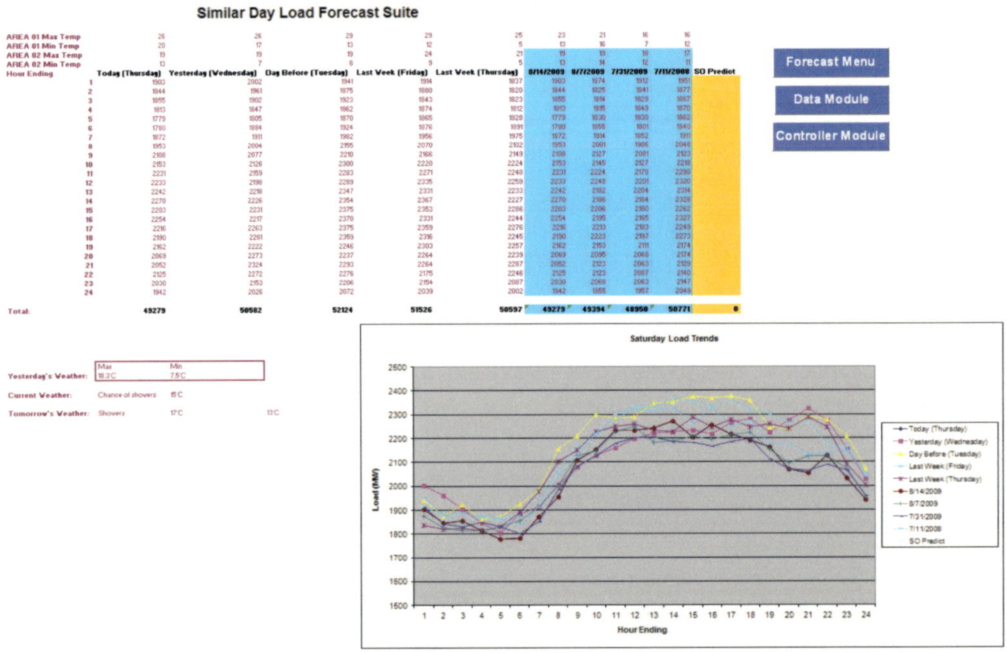

Figure 4. Screenshot of Similar Day Load Forecast Application.

The data module leverages a database of normalized aggregated loads, pre-filtered to correspond with identified hourly and weekday groups. The module encapsulates the data storage and interface between the application and the database. The responsibilities of this module are: responding to data requests issued by the control module, updating and processing data entries within the database, and performing data filtering.

The control module provides the interface between the user and the data. The controller accepts input from the user and instructs the data and view to perform actions based on those inputs. Its responsibilities include: initiating data requests to the data model from the user, retrieving data from the data model, and outputting the data to the view module. The controller translates the user's input into a well-formatted SQL query, which is then applied to the database. The database responds with an ActiveX Data Object (ADO) Recordset, which is then translated by the control module and output to the view module. The control module also creates, opens, closes, and deletes projects, including load pattern changes instigated by the user.

The view module receives data and commands from the control module, which directs the view module to modify the user interface to accommodate new data or applications requested by the user. All data transactions outside of this module are opaque to the user. The view module constitutes the graphical user interface of the aggregate similar day forecasting system, outputting data to the user for consideration.

In order to evaluate and modify the pattern set chosen by the user, a training dataset was used as initial testing data for model tuning. Initial results obtained during preliminary testing approximated those of the experts. However to further improve predictive accuracy, experts can be given the option to modify the model if a weather phenomenon such as a heat wave or a cold snap is forecasted. When the pattern set has been configured and stored in the data model module, the user can view the results of the pattern set against the test set.

```
OldSystemTotal <= 504.5 : LM1 (984/38.979%)
OldSystemTotal >  504.5 :
|   Area01_Temp <= -12.5 : LM2 (250/41.514%)
|   Area01_Temp >  -12.5 :
|   |   OldSystemTotal <= 543.5 :
|   |   |   Area02_Temp <= -1.5 : LM3 (150/33.03%)
|   |   |   Area02_Temp >  -1.5 :
|   |   |   |   Area01_Temp <= 14.5 : LM4 (118/35.034%)
|   |   |   |   Area01_Temp >  14.5 : LM5 (30/46.886%)
|   |   OldSystemTotal >  543.5 :
|   |   |   OldSystemTotal <= 588.5 : LM6 (160/39.104%)
|   |   |   OldSystemTotal >  588.5 :
|   |   |   |   OldSystemTotal <= 661.5 : LM7 (53/39.982%)
|   |   |   |   OldSystemTotal >  661.5 : LM8 (14/34.646%)
```

Figure 5. Example of Similar Day Model Represented in a Decision Tree Structure.

5.2. Limitations of a Similar Day Model

While extensively used, similar day models are susceptible to the following limitations:

- As they are based on expert knowledge, similar day models may be difficult to develop given the possibility of expert contradictions and bias [10];
- Similar day models rely on the expert to be correct in the knowledge engineering and training stages;
- Linear models tend to be produced by similar day models that do not account for dynamic environments [10];
- The prediction capabilities of a similar day model are only as good as the historical data and degree of specificity in the operators' reasoning knowledge, which has been captured and represented in the similar day model; and
- For the same reason, similar day models tend to be restricted to aggregate models due to the extensive knowledge acquisition required for developing a multi-region model [10].

5.3. Development of ANN Models

In order to deal with the considerable load diversity presented in Table 3 and Figure 3, as well as the weather diversity presented in Tables 1 and 2 and Figure 1, a new modelling structure consisting of individual load centre models fed by many weather region specific weather variables was developed. The multi-region model is used to forecast regional loads individually, then the results may be aggregated to forecast system load.

The ANN models were all created and evaluated using the Weka data mining software package. Weka, version 3.75, is a data mining tool, written in Java, and produced by the University of Waikato under the Waikato Environment for Knowledge Analysis. It is a collection of machine learning algorithms, statistical tools, and data transforms for data mining tasks, including: data pre-processing, classification, regression, clustering, association rules, and visualization.

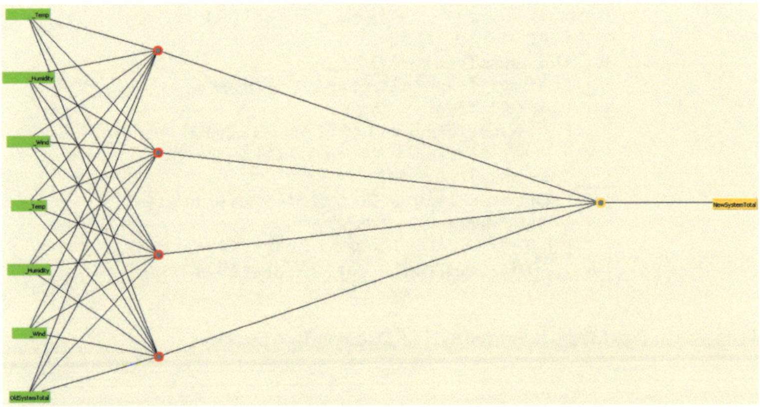

Figure 6. (Left) Topology of Aggregate ANN Model.

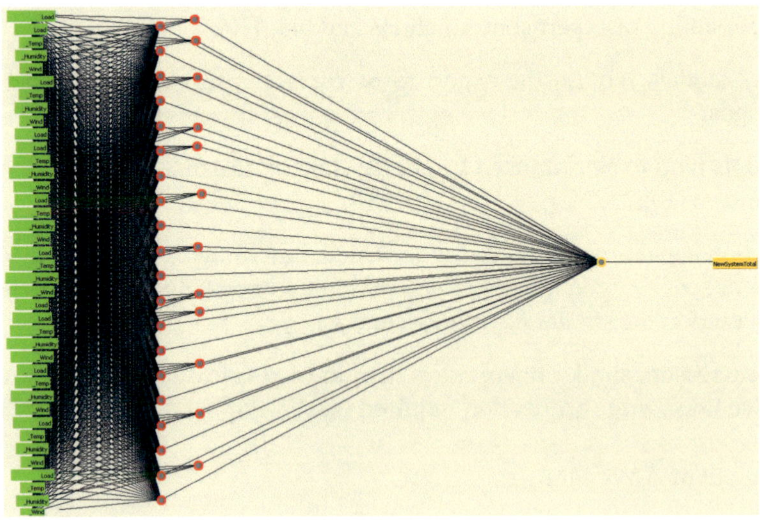

Figure 7. (Right) Topology of Multi-Region ANN Model.

The ANN models utilize the three weather variable categories of: ambient air temperature, relative humidity, and wind speed. Each of the implemented ANN models holds a unique topology. This topology was manually configured for each of the models using the Weka Perceptron GUI. Figure 6 shows the topology of the Aggregate ANN model and Figure 7 shows the topology of the Multi-Region ANN model.

Each ANN model utilized a common training history and the same weather inputs; however, the Aggregate ANN model only used weather variables from the two largest regions, whereas the multi-region model used weather variables from all twelve regions.

In this research, a multi-layer (3 layered) perceptron classifier was chosen for the ANN model. This network architecture was chosen due to its conceptual simplicity, computational efficiency, and its ability to train by both supervised and unsupervised learning. The classifier uses backpropagation, binary classification, and a sigmoid activation function. The Aggregate ANN model used 7 inputs, while the multi-region model used a total of 48 inputs. The ANN model inputs are summarized in Table 5.

After the architecture and topology of the neural networks were determined, optimization of model coefficients was achieved by systematically varying model parameters and observing the response of each network. Both the Aggregate ANN model and the Multi-Region ANN model provided the single output of the forecasted system load, and the inputs were the conditional variables of weather and system load. Through a process of trial and error, the model configurations were updated until optimum values were realized.

5.4. Limitations of an ANN Model

Despite their learning capabilities, ANNs are subject to a number of limitations, including:

- The size of the training set tends to be proportional to the accuracy of predictions, and a large training set is required. Since the network can become over-trained, care must be taken by the designer to tune the network and terminate the training at appropriate moments.

- The training set must cover the range of all possible events which the network is expected to predict. Common events may dampen the response to critical, yet rare, scenarios. Yet in order to respond appropriately to these critical scenarios, transformations of the dataset may be required. Unfortunately the insufficient exposure to scenarios is only revealed after the network has been trained and tested. Therefore the designer must be cognizant of the contents of the training set.

- Benchmarking efforts for neural network performance are difficult since the model may be optimized to locate local, rather than global, minima/maxima [8].

- Network layers and connections are often implemented on a trial and error basis. While domain knowledge is an important aspect of any modelling efforts, neural networks often expose unconventional connections which lead to significant performance enhancements. Linear connections are often redundant when using an ANN [8].

The ANN models developed during this research were subject to the aforementioned limitations; however, efforts were taken to mitigate these impediments. The training set met or exceeded the size of similar STLF ANN models [1, 3, 7, 9, 10] and contained a number of scenarios, both common and diverse with respect to weather conditions and load response. The benchmarking process considered a case study of the 2011 year across all hours and weekdays, which exceeded the evaluation events used in similar STLF ANN models [1, 3, 7, 9] and utilized five statistical measures for model benchmarking, further described in section 6. Finally a systematic analysis of model optimization was enacted. Parameters were changed methodologically and performance was noted. Ultimately, the best modelling parameters were chosen based upon the analytical review of the model configurations.

6. Modelling Process and Performance Evaluation Methods

The three models were supplied with datasets for training/knowledge elicitation. No statutory holidays and adjacent days were used in either the training or testing processes of the model application. The testing dataset was not included in the modelling process and was kept entirely separate from the training sets. The weather data was not the forecast data, but the actual hourly-averaged weather recordings, so as to minimize error due to weather forecasts.

Energy and peak load forecasting was performed for weather-induced demand and profile-conformance. Aggregated versus individual load forecasting were evaluated and contrasted. Load and weather trends were identified and amalgamated into load forecasting methods for further optimization.

Databases of weather and electric loads were constructed and backfilled to January 1, 2005. Load calculations were created, monitored, and evaluated for integrity. A total of 12 conforming load centres were analyzed. Real time and historical weather reports were stored and updated for 10 weather stations.

Load variables were assessed according to their weather-sensitivity and profile-conformance. Sensitivity analysis combined with statistical methods was used to identify weather-induced demand variables. Load forecasting was evaluated with an expert-based Aggregate Similar Day model, an aggregate artificial neural network model, and a multi-region artificial neural network model.

For the purposes of this research, assessments of performance using the following statistical methods: correlation, Mean Absolute Error (MAE), Root Mean Squared Error (RMSE), Relative Absolute Error (RAE), and Root Relative Squared Error (RRSE). These methods assessed the forecasting models by the overall prediction accuracy and consistency.

Correlation performance was calculated by computing the correlation coefficient, which is a measurement of the statistical similarity of the predictor to the prediction. The coefficient is defined from 1, indicating perfectly correlated results, to 0, indicating no correlation present, to -1, indicating perfectly negatively correlated results. Correlation assesses errors different than any other method used in this research for benchmarking. Its scale is independent and untransformed, even if the output is scaled. Its assessment tracks the behaviour of the model, rather than its error [11]. Thus, a large correlation value is desirable, whereas a low error value is also desirable.

Correlation is defined as:

$$Correlation = \frac{S_{PA}}{\sqrt{S_P S_A}}$$

$$S_P = S_{PA} = \frac{\sum_i^n (p_i - \bar{p})(a_i - \bar{a})}{n-1} \quad S_P \frac{\sum_i^n (p_i - \bar{p})^{\hat{2}}}{n-1} and\, S_A = \frac{\sum_i^n (a_i - \bar{a})^2}{n-1} \tag{2}$$

Where a_i is the actual value; p_i is the predicted value; $\bar{a}$ is the mean value of the actual; and n is the total number of values predicted.

Accuracy performance of the three load forecasting systems was established by comparing MAE and RMSE results.

MAE is defined as:

$$MAE = \sum_{i=1}^{n} (| p_i - a_i |) / n \tag{3}$$

Where a_i is the actual value; p_i is the predicted value; and n is the total number of values predicted. MAE is the magnitude of individual errors, irrespective of their sign. MAE does not exaggerate the effect of outliers, treating all errors equally according to their magnitude. MAE, however, does mask the tendency of a model to over or under predict values.

RMSE is defined as:

$$RMSE = \sqrt{\frac{\sum_i^n (p_i - a_i)^2}{n}} \tag{4}$$

Where a_i is the actual value; p_i is the predicted value; and n is the total number of values predicted.

RMSE, like MAE, does not exaggerate large errors as is the case in squared error and root squared error measurements. By computing the square root in RMSE, the dimensionality of the prediction is reduced to that of the predictor [11]. These two methods equally consider all prediction errors.

In order to evaluate the consistency of the predictions, RAE and RRSE are utilized. RAE normalizes the total absolute error of the predictor against the average results to provide a distance-weighted result.

RAE is defined as:

$$REA = \sum_{i}^{n} \frac{|p_i - a_i|}{|a_i - \bar{a}|} \tag{5}$$

Where a_i is the actual value; p_i is the predicted value; $\bar{a}$ is the mean value of the actual; and n is the total number of values predicted.

The RRE, like RAE, evaluates the relative distance of magnitude errors. Outliers are emphasized and, like RMSE, the dimensionality of the prediction equals that of the predictor.

RRSE is defined as:

$$RRSE = \sqrt{\frac{\sum_{i}^{n}(p_i - a_i)^2}{\sum_{i}^{n}(a_i - \bar{a})^2}} \tag{6}$$

Where a_i is the actual value; p_i is the predicted value; $\bar{a}$ is the mean value of the actual; and n is the total number of values predicted.

The best model is one that has the highest correlation and the lowest error rates. The success rate must be evaluated according to each of the aforementioned benchmarking methods. Consistency is equally important to accuracy, a highly variable model may be correct sometimes, but has considerable uncertainty for future planning efforts. In the next section, the case study and the performance results are discussed with reference to the statistical performance indicators of: correlation, MAE, RMSE, RAE, and RRSE.

7. Case Study

Each of the models was evaluated according to the same testing dataset consisting of non-holiday loads from January 2nd, 2011 to December 30th, 2011. Each model had access to a training dataset (see Table 5 for a summary of model inputs) using the same hourly and weekday groups for modelling. The aggregate models were restricted to historical aggregate loads rather than regional loads, and the weather from the two largest load centres, whereas the multi-region model had full access to the training dataset.

This section presents the case study of predicting the hourly energy consumption throughout the 2011 year and an analysis of the prediction results generated from each of the three models. For the purposes of evaluation, historically recorded weather variables were used, rather than predicted weather variables such as a forecaster would use in reality. A summary of the prediction results, assessed with the benchmarking methods identified in section 6, and grouped by classification period (next day and next hour) are presented in Tables 7 and 8.

http://dx.doi.org/10.5772/51306

	Similar Day	Aggregate ANN	Multi-Region ANN
Correlation	0.7282	0.7819	0.8131
MAE (MWhr)	33.1111	31.3465	32.2332
RMSE (MWhr)	43.8135	41.0459	41.2891
RAE (%)	49.15%	46.98%	47.91%
RRSE (%)	46.36%	49.61%	49.44%

Table 7. Average Model Performance – Next Day.

It can be seen from Table 7 that for next day predictions, the performance of the aggregate models closely approximated the multi-region model. Of the two aggregate models, the Aggregate ANN model outperformed the Similar Day model in all categories, except for the RRSE. The Aggregate ANN model demonstrated a greater ability to track the behaviour of the load, produce more accurate predictions, and had greater consistency than the Similar Day model. However, the Similar Day model produced a better RRSE, which indicates it is slightly better at modelling behaviours, than the Aggregate ANN model.

	Similar Day	Aggregate ANN	Multi-Region ANN
Correlation	0.7697	0.9359	0.9469
MAE (MWhr)	24.6104	16.9821	15.8962
RMSE (MWhr)	31.4624	21.7404	20.5349
RAE (%)	38.11%	26.30%	24.49%
RRSE (%)	39.45%	27.22%	25.50%

Table 8. Average Model Performance – Next Hour.

It can be seen from Table 8 that for next hour predictions the performance of the Multi-Region ANN model, as compared to the aggregate models, was superior across all metrics. According to all the metrics, the Multi-Region ANN model was the most accurate and consistent for next hour predictions, and the Similar Day model was the least accurate and consistent.

The Multi-Region ANN model performed best overall for next hour intervals, but was second to the Aggregate ANN model for next day intervals. This was because the perceptron generalizes the data it receives into a single model. If this generalization was not achieved then the model becomes over trained and relies too heavily on the training set. Since weather is much more dynamic from one day to the next versus hour to hour, the Multi-Region ANN model was able to generalize weather/load responses for next hour conditions. However for next day conditions, the Multi-Region ANN model was unable to sufficiently generalize the impact from all its weather inputs and, consequently, was over-trained. The Aggregate ANN model was best able to generalize relationships for next day forecasts as its reduced input set enables it to better reflect changes in the major load centres, which significantly affected system demand. The Multi-Region ANN model was a more dynamic model in its response to varying weather conditions, but this only applies for same day forecasts.

The Similar Day model performed worst overall for both next day and next hour intervals. Since the Similar Day model operates by finding comparable days for inclusion into a weighted average, its performance will deteriorate during abnormal load/weather days. Its RRSE performance during next day predictions was second best to the Aggregate ANN model. As the Similar Day model is predicated upon the assumption that the past may be used to predict the future, the model relies significantly on direct load modelling; that is, the simple predictor of aggregate system load has a greater influence on the model's calculations than the ANN models which model weather and load equally.

Comparing next day and next hour performance identified that model performance across all benchmark metrics improved when the time interval was shortened. This was expected as the previous hour's energy demand has a high correlation with the next hour's energy demand. Next hour predictions require a high ability to adapt to weather and load changes. The ANN models performed better than the Similar Day method across all metrics. Next day predictions require greater generalization of behaviour as the load value of the previous day does not have as great a correlation as compared to the load value of the previous hour.

When considering the performance of individual hour groups, the situation becomes more complicated. The multi-region model, in general, resulted in the lowest MAE and highest correlation; however, during next day predictions, the aggregate models often had better MAE and RMSE performance. Figures 8 and 9 illustrate the behaviour of the models for next day and next hour predictions within specific hourly groupings.

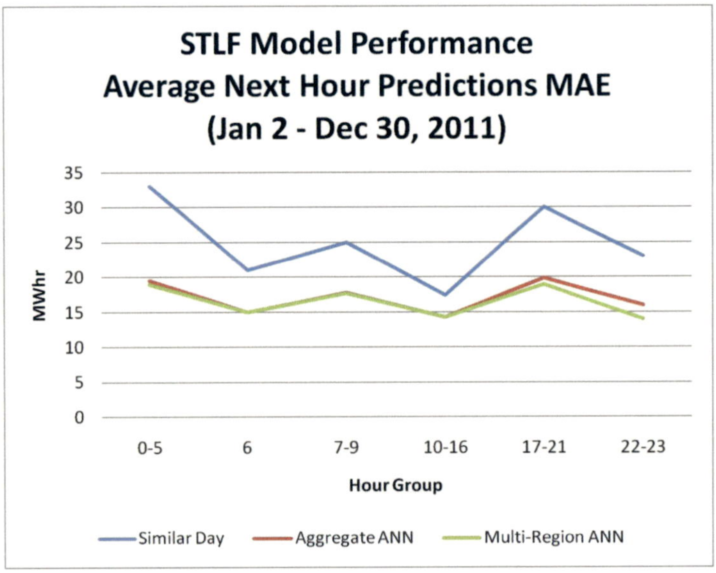

Figure 8. STLF Model MAE Performance in Next Hour Predictions.

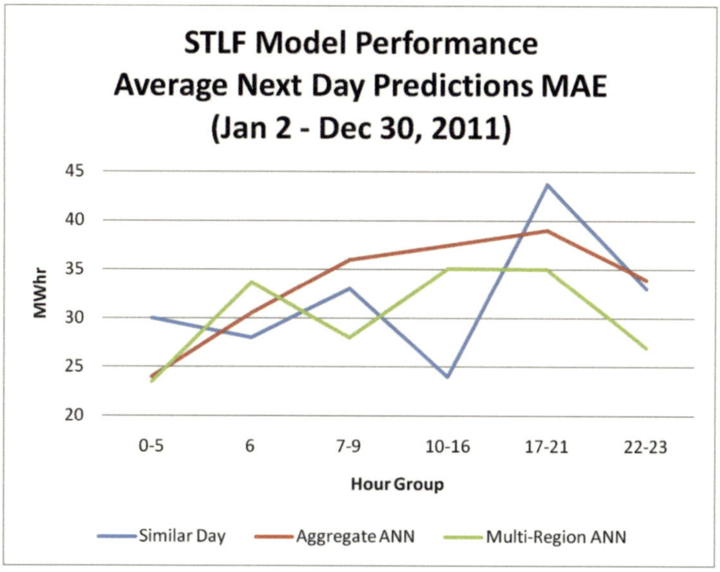

Figure 9. STLF Model MAE Performance in Next Day Predictions.

It can be seen from Figure 8, that the prediction accuracy of the Aggregate ANN model and the Multi-Region ANN model are very similar. This is likely because their topologies are similar. In addition, these models are consistent in their errors across all hours. The similar profile of accuracy across the three models indicates certain hour groups are more difficult to forecast than others. The performance of the Similar Day model is best during off peak periods, as the greatest error associated with the model is found during the hour group of 17 – 21. This observation may be generalized for all the models as peak error was often found during the morning peak or evening peak periods, which suggests the impact of temperature on electrical demand is weakest during peak periods. When these results were shown to the experts, they noted the demands describing the peak periods are often attributed to the business cycle and the temperature would likely exert a less significant influence. In general, the experts identified the results of the hour group of 22 – 23 to be the most accurate. They suggested this hour group should be extended to include hours 22 – 23 and 0 – 3 as these periods typically have high baseload and temperature-dependency. A comparison of the models' abilities in describing the behaviours of loads is shown in Figures 10 and 11.

The Aggregate ANN model and the Multi-Region Grouped ANN model are similar in both their correlation coefficients and predictive accuracy. The Similar Day model has the lowest correlation across all hours, and demonstrates low correlation at both peak periods.

As a conclusion, the multi-region model proved to be the best overall model, in terms of predictive accuracy and consistency. The Similar Day model was the easiest to build and offered to the operators an intuitive explanation for load behavior. However, it also performed the worst among the three models analyzed. The performances of the Aggregate ANN and Multi-Region ANN models were similar due to their topological similarities. This suggests that forecast environments with a considerable weather and load diversity should adopt a multi-region model for prediction of load instead of grouping the regions into a single ANN model. It can be observed that peak periods were the most difficult for the models to predict, and the forecast results have low accuracies.

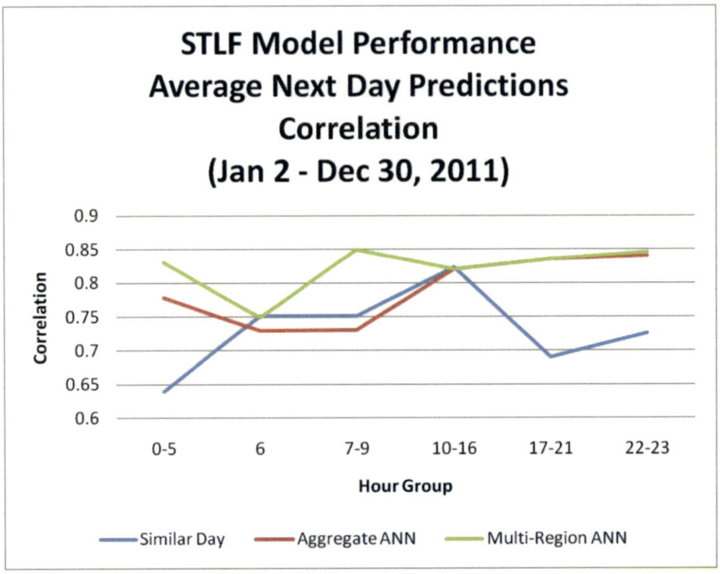

Figure 10. STLF Model Correlation Performance in Next Day Predictions.

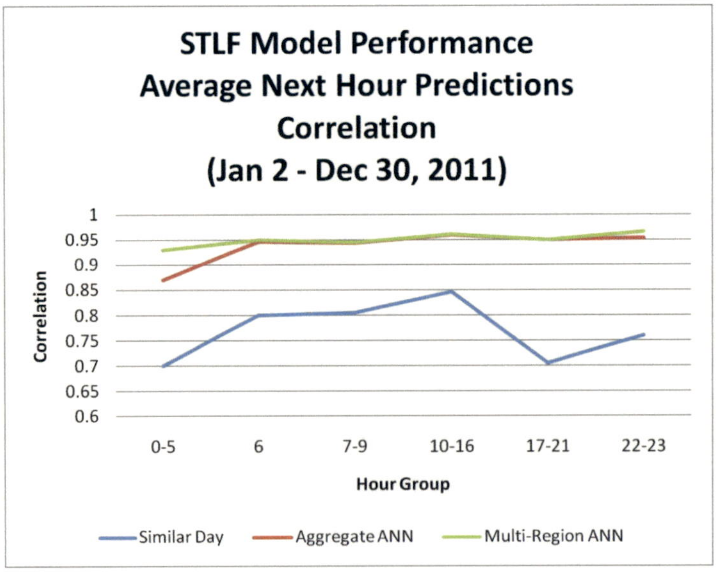

Figure 11. STLF Model Correlation Performance in Next Hour Predictions.

8. Conclusions and Future Work

Load forecasting continues to grow in importance within the electric utility industry. To date, no known study has been published which examines load forecasting within the province of Saskatchewan and/or within the control area examined. The increased importance of energy and environmental concerns, coupled with enhanced regulatory presence, has renewed interest in developing an accurate and easy-to-use load forecasting system within the control area.

The general objective of this research is to conduct load forecasting for a large geographic area which has considerable weather and load diversity. The specific research objective is to develop data-driven hourly prediction models for multi-region short term load forecasting (STLF) for twelve conforming load centres within the control area in the province of Saskatchewan, Canada. Since the load centres experience considerable diversity in terms of both weather and load, a multi-region based approach is needed and the ANN modelling approach was adopted for developing the models.

Due to their simplicity, ease of analysis, and long adoption history, many load forecasting systems currently used are based on a similar day methodology. However, the research results show that the multi-region ANN model improved prediction performance over the aggregate-based short term load forecasting ANN model and the similar day aggregate model in forecasting short term aggregate loads in next hour forecasts as well as next day forecasts. All models examined were weather-driven forecasting systems. The performance of the models was evaluated using the dataset from the 2011 year. Based on the measurements of Correlation, MAE, RMSE, RAE, and RRSE, it can be concluded that the ANN-based models provide superior prediction performance over existing similar-day forecasting systems. The developed models are able to reduce STLF inaccuracies and may be applicable for modelling other system concerns, such as system reliability.

Operational staff of grid control centres often adopt similar day models due to their simplicity and intuitive development, while paying less attention to the impacts of weather changes to electricity demand. This chapter has demonstrated the superior performance of the ANN-based models over the similar day models. This finding suggests that artificial-intelligence-based methods can potentially be used for enhancing performance of load forecasting in the operational environment. Future efforts in developing artificial intelligence-based forecasting systems can include efforts towards building more intuitive user interfaces, so as to promote greater user-adoption.

We believe that merging the ANN models with other methods such as fuzzy logic, support vector regression, and time series considerations can provide enhanced consistency for modelling reduced load interval datasets. Further analysis of heat wave theory and other weather trend electricity demand drivers is necessary for these methods to become applicable for conducting both short and medium term load forecasts. The results and methods of this work will be compared against other artificial intelligence models and statistical methods to identify further areas of improvement. Future work in this field is required to decrease forecast time intervals in order to provide a real-time operating model for intelligent automated unit-commitment algorithms, which operate at 15 minute intervals. Further efforts in weather trend analysis, such as heat wave theory will be investigated in order to quantitatively describe other weather-load trends.

Acknowledgements

We are grateful for the generous support of Research Grants from Natural Sciences and Engineering Research Council (NSERC) and the Canada Research Chair Program.

Author details

Connor Wright, Christine W. Chan* and Paul Laforge

*Address all correspondence to: Christine.Chan@uregina.ca

Energy Informatics Laboratory, Faculty of Engineering and Applied Science, University of Regina, Saskatchewan, Canada

References

[1] Salim, N. A. (2009, November 16 - November 18, 2009). Case Study of Short Term Load Forecasting for Weekends. UPM Serdang, Malaysia. *In: Proceedings of 2009 IEEE Student Conference on Research and Development.*

[2] Wood, A. (1996). *Power Generation, Operation, and Control* (2nd ed.), New York, Wiley-Interscience, John Wiley & Sons, Inc.

[3] Sargent, A. (1994). Estimation of diversity and kWHR-to-peak-kW factors from load research data. *Power Systems, IEEE Transactions on*, 9(3), 1450-1456.

[4] North American Electric Reliability Corporation. (2011). *Load Forecasting Survey And Recommendations*, http://www.nerc.com/docs/docs/pubs/NERC_Load_Forecasting_Survey_LFWG_Report_111907.pdf, accessed September 17, 2011.

[5] SaskPower. SaskPower. (2010). *Load Forecast*, http://www.saskpower.com/, accessed July, 21, 2011.

[6] Ward, N. (2011). *Saskatchewan- The Canadian Encyclopedia*, http://www.thecanadianencyclopedia.com/articles/saskatchewan, accessed October 27, 2011.

[7] Fan, S. (2008, May 4 - May 8, 2008). Multi-Area Load Forecasting for System with Large Geographical Area. Clearwater Beach, Florida. *Industrial and Commercial Power Systems Technical Conference, IEEE.*

[8] Feinberg, E. (2005). *Applied Mathematics for Restructured Electric Power Systems,* New York, Springer Publishing.

[9] Fan, S. (September 30 - October 2, 2007, 2007). Short-term Multi-Region Load Forecasting Based on Weather and Load Diversity Analysis. Las Cruces, New Mexico. *In: 39th North American Power Symposium, IEEE.*

[10] Witten, I. (2005). *DATA MINING Practical Machine Learning Tools and Technique,* San Fransisco, Morgan Kaufmann.

[11] Nau, R. (2011). What's the bottom line? *How to compare models,* http://www.duke.edu/~rnau/compare.htm, accessed November, 10, 2011.